Praise for *In the*

"All Indian Nations should take heed of this book! It is devoted to the proposition that Native American rights are inherent and inalienable human rights. *In the Light of Justice* explains how the UNDRIP can strengthen Native American rights in a human rights framework. Let us answer the call and work to uplift the laws and policies of the United States so that they comport with the human rights standards of the UNDRIP."

—Wallace Coffey, Chairman, Comanche Nation

"*In the Light of Justice* is a timely and truly remarkable book. Walter brings a wonderfully creative mind and decades of fighting in the trenches for indigenous rights to the task of placing the UN Declaration on the Rights of Indigenous Peoples into proper historical perspective, showing that it is a document of millennial importance. As the book points out, the Declaration stands as a sharp rebuke to the colonialism of the past and provides a roadmap for future action—a roadmap for the world to move forward in a good way through cooperation with indigenous peoples, in whose lifeways and ethic may lie the answer to many of the world's most intransigent problems. Walter shows how the Declaration can and must be used constructively and creatively to this end. It is an important book, not just for indigenous peoples, but for the world."

—John Echohawk, Executive Director, Native American Rights Fund

"Walter Echo-Hawk's skillful analysis of the UN Declaration on the Rights of Indigenous Peoples offers a brilliant and impassioned justification for a new era of federal Indian law. Echo-Hawk demonstrates that the current doctrine defines Native peoples through the 'lens of conquest, colonialism, and race,' thus cementing injustice into law. He then develops the roadmap of justice by illuminating the human rights principles that must become part of domestic law, as well as the elements of the social campaign that will be necessary to shift the hearts and minds of Americans about what 'justice' entails for the Native Nations of these lands. Echo-Hawk is a seasoned attorney and an insightful scholar, but he is also a masterful storyteller, weaving an Indigenous cultural narrative throughout this work that is profound, moving, and quite powerful. This book is a must-read for students and scholars of Federal Indian law, as well as the leaders and advocates that serve Indian Country."

—Rebecca Tsosie, Regent's Professor of Law, Arizona State University

"This is the book I have been waiting for: a truly probing study of justice that comes down elegantly on the side of restorative and reparative actions that heal body and soul, individual and community. Walter Echo-Hawk's book is a plea for the transformation of our current system by, as native people say, 'making things right.' His compassionate scholarship proves that acts of reparation and atonement, alongside the implementation of the United Nations Declaration on the Rights of Indigenous Peoples, will be a catharsis and a new beginning for all peoples."

—Phil Cousineau, author of *Beyond Forgiveness: Reflections on Atonement* and *The Art of Pilgrimage*

"Walter Echo-Hawk's new book clearly demonstrates the potential of the UN Declaration on the Rights of Indigenous Peoples to positively impact United States Indian law and, most importantly, sets out a strategy and a process for implementing the Declaration into American law. Everyone who is interested in indigenous issues in the United States, or in international law and indigenous peoples, needs to read this book."

—Robert J. Miller, professor and author of *Native America, Discovered and Conquered: Thomas Jefferson, Lewis & Clark and Manifest Destiny* (2006)

"Walter Echo-Hawk has done it again. In his masterful work *In the Courts of the Conqueror: The Ten Worst Indian Law Cases Ever Decided*, Professor Echo-Hawk held the mythology created by the black robes of American law up to the light of truth, reason, and simple justice. In doing so, he exposed the myths for what they are: a dark side of American jurisprudence that is continuing reliance upon long held notions of racial and cultural superiority used to dispossess Indian peoples of their lands, property, and human rights. Now his voice calls for reconsideration of these notions in light of the principals of human rights recognized by the United States and the family of nations in the United Nations' recent Declaration on the Rights of Indigenous Peoples. His long years as a litigator and scholar clearly inform his balanced approach to measuring federal Indian policy against the standards of the Declaration, giving credit where due yet clearly identifying areas where changes are warranted. Echo-Hawk calls for the healing of Native America, and in the process for all of America, and has presented a blueprint for restorative justice within the context of the best of the American system, which is worthy of serious consideration by every jurist, politician, and patriotic American."

—G. William Rice, Professor and Co-Director, Native American Law Center, University of Tulsa College of Law

IN THE LIGHT OF JUSTICE

The Rise of Human Rights in Native America and the UN Declaration on the Rights of Indigenous Peoples

Walter R. Echo-Hawk

FULCRUM
GOLDEN, COLORADO

Library of Congress Cataloging-in-Publication Data
Echo-Hawk, Walter R.
In the light of justice : the rise of human rights in Native America and the United Nations Declaration on the Rights of Indigenous Peoples / Walter R. Echo-Hawk.
p cm
ISBN 978-1-55591-663-3
1. Indians of North America--Legal status, laws, etc. 2. Human rights--United States. 3. United Nations. General Assembly. Declaration on the Rights of Indigenous Peoples. I. Title.
KF8205.E24 2013
342.7308'72--dc23
2013006705

Printed in the United States of America
0 9 8 7 6 5 4 3 2

Design by Jack Lenzo

Fulcrum Publishing
4690 Table Mountain Dr., Ste. 100
Golden, CO 80403
800-992-2908 • 303-277-1623
www.fulcrumbooks.com

TABLE OF CONTENTS

FOREWORD

The United States of America is the greatest nation on earth, or so it is often said. This expression reflects homage to the visionary founders and the democratic innovation they implanted, a fundamental faith in the country's political and economic system, and celebration of a common ethos of liberty and equality that is understood to mark American identity. Yet it is simply a matter of fact, with which Americans must contend, that the claim to exceptional greatness is wed to historical processes that defy it, if indeed the greatness of a country is dependent upon an elevated commitment to what is right and just, rather than merely being a function of power.

Embedded in the story of the country is the glorification of settlement and westward expansion over what is usually portrayed as previously untamed and uncivilized lands, glorification that is animated by a national myth of Manifest Destiny. The underbelly of this story includes the costs to the country's indigenous, or native, peoples, who suffered material loss and social and cultural upheaval on a massive scale. Other parts of the underbelly include slavery, a diminished legal status for women, and legally sanctioned discrimination against immigrants of non-European origin, among other phenomena of oppression. A full appreciation of this underbelly leads to a less glorified telling of the American story, and to understanding America's greatness as a *projection*—a historically and still not fully realized one—from the most enlightened components of the country's institutions and practices.

The Constitution memorializes the country's commitment to a path toward "a more perfect Union" with conditions of justice and liberty. But the path toward fulfilling this commitment largely bypassed the indigenous peoples of the continent, as the country proceeded to build and its economy expanded, in significant part at their expense. The pattern of injustices inflicted upon Native Americans is well documented and little controverted in any serious way. This part of American history is often overlooked in the dominant historical narrative, however. Or, if remembered, it is kept as merely something of the past best forgotten.

Building on his previous book, *In the Courts of the Conqueror: The 10 Worst Indian Law Cases Ever Decided*, Walter Echo-Hawk explains how the harm historically inflicted on the indigenous peoples still commands attention because of the ongoing effects of the past on conditions today. In this book Echo-Hawk helps us understand why justice requires confronting the combined injustices of the past and present, and he points to tools for achieving reconciliation with indigenous peoples, focusing on the United Nations Declaration on the Rights of Indigenous Peoples as such a tool.

A number of years had gone by since I had last seen Echo-Hawk when I met him at a gathering of indigenous leaders and experts at the University of Tulsa in May 2012. The gathering was a part of the twelve-day tour of the country that I undertook to examine the conditions of Native Americans and to discuss the significance of the *Declaration*, all as part of my work as the United Nation's Special Rapporteur on the Rights of Indigenous Peoples. At that and similar gatherings across the country, I was impressed by the continuing vibrancy of indigenous peoples and their communities and their resolve to maintain the defining characteristics of their diverse indigenous identities, under equitable conditions, within the larger American society that has grown up around them. I was equally impressed by the multiple manifestations of the deep, still open wounds that have been left by the underbelly of the American story.

What Echo-Hawk accomplishes in this book is to shed much needed light on the character of these wounds, which still fester in the absence of reconciliation, and to point an enlightened path forward. While most acutely felt by the indigenous peoples of the country, these wounds are also afflictions on the country as a whole. They damage its moral standing and its claim to greatness. And, as the world has come to realize, the wounds will not go away by attempts to relegate their origins to historical curiosity or contemporary irrelevance.

Responding to the similar conditions of indigenous peoples worldwide, the United Nations General Assembly adopted the *Declaration on the Rights of Indigenous Peoples* in 2007. The *Declaration* represents an acknowledgment of the ongoing human rights problems faced by indigenous peoples today across the globe and a recognition that the roots of these problems lie in widespread wrongs, derived from similar patters of domination set in motion by colonization. It provides important impetus and guidance for measures to address the human rights concerns of indigenous peoples that are rooted in historical and continuing systemic failure and to move toward reconciliation. An authoritative instrument with broad support, the *Declaration* marks a path toward remedying the injustices and inequitable conditions faced by indigenous peoples, calling on determined action to secure their rights within a model of respect for their self-determination and distinctive cultural identities.

As Echo-Hawk explains, the *Declaration* is grounded in a global consensus among governments and indigenous peoples worldwide that is joined by the US government as well as the indigenous peoples in the country. It was adopted by the General Assembly with the affirmative votes of an overwhelming majority of UN Member States amid expressions of celebration by indigenous peoples from around the world who had long been advocating for the *Declaration*. At the urging of indigenous leaders from throughout the country, President Obama announced the United States' support for the *Declaration* on December 16, 2010, reversing the United States' earlier position, and he did so before a gathering at the White House of leaders of indigenous nations and tribes.

The president's announcement of support for the *Declaration* was accompanied by a widely circulated written statement, which, despite including what some see as qualifications to the US support, affirmed that, in its essential terms, the *Declaration* has been formally accepted as part of US policy. Difficulty remains, however, in seeing this acceptance fully implemented into action. Echo-Hawk shows how aspects of US law remain infused with colonial era legal doctrine and are at odds with the terms of the *Declaration* and the human rights values that undergird it.

In the report I completed on the conditions of Native Americans in my capacity as UN Special Rapporteur,* I found that significant federal legislation and programs have been developed over the last few decades that are favorable to indigenous peoples and fall generally in line with the *Declaration*, in contrast to earlier exercises of federal power. Especially to be commended are the many new initiatives taken by the Federal Executive to advance the rights of indigenous peoples in the last few years. At the same time, however, I found that existing federal programs need to be

* *The Situation of Indigenous Peoples in the United States of America*, U.N. Doc. A/HRC/21 /54 (2012).

improved upon and their execution made more effective. Moreover, new measures are needed to advance toward reconciliation with indigenous peoples and address persistent deep-seeded problems related to historical wrongs, failed policies of the past, and continuing systemic barriers to the full realization of their rights as affirmed in the *Declaration*.

By its very nature, the *Declaration on the Rights of Indigenous Peoples* is not itself legally binding, but it is nonetheless an extension of the commitment assumed by UN Member States, including the United States, to promote and respect human rights under the United Nations Charter, customary international law, and various multilateral human rights treaties, including treaties to which the United States is a party. Echo-Hawk provides lucid explanation of the connection between the *Declaration* and the United States' obligations under international human rights law.

Whatever its precise legal significance, the *Declaration* embodies a common understanding about the rights of indigenous peoples on a global scale, upon a foundation of fundamental human rights, including rights of equality, self-determination, property, and cultural integrity. It is a product of more than two decades of deliberations in which the experiences and aspirations of indigenous peoples worldwide, along with the relevant laws and policies of countries across the globe, were closely examined with a view toward promoting human rights.

With these characteristics, the *Declaration* should now serve as a beacon for executive, legislative, and judicial authorities to guide all their decision making on issues concerning the indigenous peoples of the country. Echo-Hawk explains how the *Declaration* can and should have a role in overcoming the rights-diminishing strains of legal doctrines with colonial origins, in favor of rights-affirming strains that are consistent with contemporary human rights values. Moreover, as Echo-Hawk reiterates as his central theme, the *Declaration* is an instrument that should motivate and guide steps toward still needed reconciliation with the country's indigenous peoples, on just terms. From his eloquent narrative we see how the *Declaration* is a complement to the tools of reconciliation that are found in the traditions to which *we* are heirs, *we* being understood in a broad, inclusive sense.

Echo-Hawk shows us the seeds of change in the *Declaration*. With the *Declaration*, he tells us in the book's beginning, we are in a rare moment of potential transformation, of a tectonic shift toward a new era of human relations that extends the promise of justice beyond the boundaries set by the past. It is a moment to move farther along the American path of greatness. This book inspires and moves us to seize that moment.

—S. James Anaya

Regents' and James J. Lenoir Professor
of Human Rights Law and Policy
The University of Arizona; and
United Nations Special Rapporteur
on the Rights of Indigenous Peoples

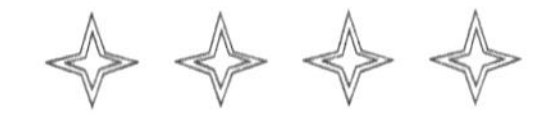

PREFACE AND ACKNOWLEDGMENTS

This book was written in rural Oklahoma, on my dusty patch of ground in the Pawnee Nation. The land in my area is composed of numerous Pawnee Indian allotments, but many residents rarely go to town and are seldom seen. My family and I live just five miles from the home place of Jim Thorpe, the great American Indian athlete, and that is our claim to fame in the Twin Mounds area. Though I live in a grassroots indigenous area, it is possible to think global thoughts. This book follows on my earlier study of the law, *In the Courts of the Conqueror* (2010). I want to further develop a theme in that volume: the implications of the *United Nations Declaration on the Rights of Indigenous Peoples* (2007). Though I was not involved in making the landmark international instrument, I followed the progress with great interest from afar during my days as a Native American Rights Fund staff attorney. My book saw it as an important development—an authoritative barometer for measuring Native American rights and even a vehicle for strengthening them. However, *In the Courts of the Conqueror* was published before the United States endorsed the *Declaration* on December 16, 2010. Since then, Native America has begun studying its contents and implications at various gatherings around the country. To contribute to that self-education process, this essay provides baseline information about the *Declaration* and analyzes some of its ramifications. In many respects, this book is about who we are as the American people and who we might become.

The *Declaration* invites us to view federal Indian law in a new way. It is possible to go beyond that amoral body of law to conceive of Native American rights as "human rights." Indeed, we can pole vault over the Indian Self-Determination Policy to situate federal Indian law and policy in a human rights framework, and the *Declaration* shows how to realign some of our outmoded legal doctrines with principles of justice heretofore absent in Native American law. When viewed through a human rights lens, we can at once see values that are higher than the state. This vista sees fundamental freedoms that transcend our shores to inure to the benefit of every person worldwide. At first blush, it is hard to fathom these possibilities, or elevate our engrained thinking about American Indians in the American setting, especially when our nation has never engaged in a serious national conversation about the nature and contents of human rights for Native Americans. However, the language of human rights in the *Declaration* is familiar to every American because it birthed the republic, and, at every major juncture of American history, human rights precepts were upon the lips of the people to propel the rise and growth of our democracy. Indeed, the *actual* use of human rights precepts throughout American history is extensive, though not generally appreciated. *That stands to reason in the Land of the Free.* Consequently, even though the *Declaration* borrows human rights from modern international law and applies them to the unique circumstances of indigenous peoples, the precepts it uses are decidedly home-grown, and those principles insist on a national discourse in the United States on the nature of indigenous justice and rights at this juncture in American history.

While the United States endorsed the *Declaration* in 2010, it stopped short of implementing it. The instrument requires the United States to take measures to implement its provisions in cooperation and consultation with Native Americans, but the government has not met with Native Americans to discuss how we might go about that task. For its part, Indian Country has been occupied with reading the document and has not organized to develop a plan of action. It is timely to contribute information and analysis as we approach the implementation phase. That is the purpose of the current volume, *In The Light of Justice*.

This book could not have been written without the support and encouragement of many. I am indebted, first and foremost, to S. James Anaya, United Nations Special Rapporteur on the Rights of Indigenous Peoples, for his gracious assistance in writing the introductory foreword. I have known this brilliant indigenous lawyer for many years and greatly admire his important, pioneering contributions to the field of international indigenous human rights law over the past decades. I must also thank my brother, Lance G. Echo-Hawk, a practicing behavioral health specialist, for his invaluable professional contributions, insights, and perceptions regarding the nature of human suffering, societal trauma in Native American communities, and the need to heal the wounds of the past. *Iriway torahe, Irari!* Similarly, I hasten to thank my long-time friend, author Phil Cousineau, for putting together his wonderful book, *Beyond Forgiveness: Reflections on Atonement* (2011), which puts forward principles that heavily influenced my thinking. I am grateful to three other friends for their contributions. First, to Law Professor G. William Rice (United Keetoowah Band), University of Tulsa College of Law, and one of the few elite American Indian attorneys to argue and win a case before the United States Supreme Court, for his advice, encouragement, and support. Second, to Ms. Faye Hadley, also from the College of Law, who spent many hours assisting the research that went into the book. And last, to my law partner, D. Michael McBride, III, who contributed invaluable thoughts and editorial assistance.

Recognition is also in order for the University of Tulsa College of Law, including Dean Janet Levit and Vice-Dean Gary Allison, for the technical and logistical support rendered to me in the making of this book. Finally, I am indebted to several people for their inspiration: Tim Coulter (Citizen Potawatomi Nation), Executive Director at the Indian Law Resource Center, for his leadership and representation during the making of the *Declaration* and for his passionate work to implement it in the United States; Law Professor Lindsay Robertson, University of Oklahoma School of Law, for his work on the *Declaration* and interest in implementing it; Chairman John "Rocky" Barrett (Citizen Potawatomi Nation) for his early tribal support during the making of the *Declaration* and his travel to Geneva during that historic time; and to Chairman Marshall McKay (Yocha Dehe Wintun Nation) for his vision to see the *Declaration* implemented in the United States. Chairmen Barrett and McKay are two of the truly great tribal leaders for the 21st century, and I thank them for their leadership.

The list is not complete without thanking my family members—Pauline, Anthony, Amy, Bunky, Anaya, Alexie, Feather, and Jeanine—for their patience, love, and unflagging support during the making of this book, and for the excellent original artwork that Bunky contributed to the book. Last, but not least, this book is respectfully dedicated to all of the indigenous peoples who were involved in the making of the *Declaration* and their families: *Nowah-iri! Riwe Rasuta, Torahe!* Thank you! You did something good!

—Walter R. Echo-Hawk

by Bunky Echo-Hawk (Yakama-Pawnee artist)

"In Reverence of Justice"

PART ONE
Understanding the Declaration

You see, there is only one color of mankind that is not allowed to participate in the international community, and that color is red. The black, the white, the brown, and the yellow—all participate in one form or another.

—Russell Means (Oglala Sioux), September 20, 1977

CHAPTER ONE
The Seeds of Change

Once in a great while, a signal event comes along to change the course of history. Prominent examples abound in world history. One catalyst for change that sparked the growth of liberty was the Magna Carta (1215). Though it took only a baby-step toward freedom, it ranks today among the greatest constitutional documents of all time. Another history-changing event was the "discovery" of America. Columbus's voyage of discovery has been described as the "greatest event since the creation of the world."[1] Indeed, humanity changed dramatically after 1492, when Europe rushed to colonize the globe over the next five hundred years. During that period, indigenous peoples were engulfed in every colonized land. Life around the world was fundamentally restructured while indigenous rights were swept away. Another seminal event in the history of democracy is the American experiment, birthed by the human rights principles written into the Declaration of Independence and the US Constitution. These documents symbolized our nation's radical departure from Old World traditions of oppression and intolerance to provide the fullest measure of liberty ever enjoyed by any Western civilization. In a similar vein, *Brown v. Board of Education* (1954) was a watershed legal event in the 20th century.[2] It fundamentally altered America by declaring engrained racial segregation unconstitutional, and set the nation upon a brand new path that, two generations later, allowed an African American to be elected President of the United States. These and other rare, earth-shaking events planted the seeds for change. They set into motion forces that shaped the lives of millions and determined the fate of nations.

This book is about planting the seeds of change. It focuses on a landmark event that promises to shape humanity in the post-colonial age. On September 13, 2007, the UN General Assembly adopted the *United Nations Declaration on the Rights of Indigenous Peoples*.[3] Drawing directly from contemporary international human rights law, the *Declaration* comprehensively covers the full range of property, civil, political, economic, social, cultural, religious, and environmental rights of indigenous peoples. It compiles human rights from the corpus of international law and formulates them into minimum standards for protecting the survival, dignity, and well-being of indigenous peoples. In so doing, the *Declaration* makes international law accountable to indigenous peoples. It tells us how recognized human rights should be interpreted and applied in the indigenous context, and by defining the content of emerging norms, it speeds their crystallization into norms. Further, its broad scope addresses the full range of Native American concerns in the United States. At its core lies the inherent right to "self-determination," the centerpiece of federal Indian policy in the United States since 1970.

Importantly, the rights enshrined in the *Declaration* reflect the authentic aspirations of the world's indigenous peoples.* After all, they participated in the development of the landmark document. During three decades, indigenous advocates did pioneering work conducted in transparent processes to move the draft through the established UN human rights channels, step-by-step, toward adoption by the General Assembly. This amazing feat denotes the first time that indigenous peoples accessed the United Nations to play a pivotal role in drafting, developing, and negotiating an important standard-setting document. Final adoption was the crowning success of that groundbreaking effort to make indigenous voices heard by member nations in UN hallways and assembly rooms. The product of that work may mark a turning point for millions of Native peoples around the world.

For the most part, the rights in the *Declaration* are drawn from existing international human rights law—treaties that are legally binding on signatory nations and norms found in customary international law.[4] James Anaya, the UN Special Rapporteur on the Rights of Indigenous Peoples, explained in recent Senate testimony:

> Although the Declaration is not itself a treaty, it is a strongly authoritative statement that builds upon the provisions of multilateral human rights treaties to which the United States is bound as a party, within the broader obligation of the United States to advance human rights under the United Nations Charter.[5]

---

* "Indigenous peoples" are defined for purposes of this book as non-European peoples living in lands colonized by Europeans before the settlers, administrators, and militaries arrived. The indigenous peoples of the United States are the "Native Americans," which include American Indians, Alaska Natives, and Native Hawaiians.

Rights created by treaty and international conventions carry high normative value. In many respects, the *Declaration* merely codifies important rights that indigenous peoples *already* possess under international law, but that were beyond reach by vulnerable minorities captive to hostile or indifferent domestic forums in their own nations. The *Declaration* now points the way for bringing to the world's indigenous peoples, at long last, the same human rights protections universally enjoyed by the rest of humanity. This harbinger of change asks every nation to restore the human rights of Native peoples that fell by the wayside during the colonial era. If that call is answered, the *Declaration* will someday be seen as the Magna Carta for the world's indigenous peoples. If implemented, those measures will change the world and fundamentally alter the way that humanity currently views some 350 million indigenous peoples who reside in over 70 nations.

The seeds of change must be planted in the United States. To become operational and enforceable in our own land, the provisions of the *Declaration* cannot be realized until they are fully incorporated into our domestic legal system. This requires steps be taken to implement the instrument. While many provisions of the *Declaration* might be indirectly enforceable in US courts to the extent that they reflect existing treaty obligations or customary international human rights law, it must be stressed that the *Declaration* does not itself carry the automatic force of binding law.[6] This is so even though the instrument incorporates recognized human rights drawn from other sources of existing international law. *Cohen's Handbook of Federal Indian Law* teaches that treaties or covenants are legally binding upon signatory nations, whereas declarations are generally considered non-binding, "aspirational" statements that are not directly enforceable in US courts—even if accepted by the United States.[7] Thus, critics dismiss the *Declaration* as a mere General Assembly resolution with no legally binding character, and they argue that it is just a policy tool for states.[8] However, the debate over the legal character of the *Declaration* need not distract implementation of the UN standards. Fine distinctions between hard and soft international law are not determinative factors in securing US compliance with the *Declaration*. To the contrary, the legal status of specific human rights norms is "far from a determinative factor in promoting compliance with these norms."[9] When the Supreme Court of Belize recently applied the *Declaration* to protect indigenous land rights, that Court observed:

> General Assembly resolutions are not ordinarily binding on member states. But where these resolutions or Declarations contain principles of general international law, states are not expected to disregard them.[10]

As such, the *Declaration* can provide guidance and persuasive authority to spark social, cultural, and political transformations, which often run deeper into the fabric of a nation than superficial legal change. Furthermore, as will be discussed in Chapter Four, some standards might be indirectly enforceable. Courts can enforce the standards to the extent that they constitute existing treaty obligations or customary international law. In addition, other rights affirmed in the *Declaration* can become enforceable customary international law after they have evolved into "international norms" through widespread acceptance and practice by affected nations.[11] Many provisions in the *Declaration* possess high normative value derived from existing human rights established in UN treaties and conventions. The growing acceptance of these standards of conduct by affected nations can be seen in the worldwide judicial trend since 2007 and in surveys of state usages and practices.[12]

The enforceability of these provisions will no doubt be tested in the courts along the way. For present purposes, it is sufficient to note that every domestic and international court that has thus far considered the *Declaration* has adopted and applied its provisions to resolve indigenous issues.[13] US courts should follow that trend, in appropriate cases, now that the United States has endorsed the *Declaration*. After all, when indigenous justice issues are at stake in modern courts, contemporary international law routinely exerts "a legitimate and important influence on the development of common law, especially when international law declares the existence of universal human rights."[14] US courts hardily endorsed settled principles of international law to define indigenous rights in the early republic, and there is no reason to eschew that body of law in the 21st century.

Importantly, the *Declaration* envisions a more direct and collaborative route to effectuate its provisions and fully realize indigenous human rights. It calls upon states to work in consultation with indigenous peoples to develop appropriate measures to affirmatively implement the standards into the domestic law and policy of individual nations. This process requires public education, action by all sectors of government, proactive advocacy, litigation, legislation, and changes in government policy. Where entrenched social problems are concerned, sweeping social change is often required, similar to those reforms brought about by the great American social movements, such as the Civil Rights Movement, Women's Movement, Environmental Movement, and the American Indian Sovereignty Movement. Likewise, a social movement must demand progress before substantial changes are made to embrace the UN standards. Since many standards reflect existing international law, difficulties encountered along the way might be surmounted or eased by pointing to that source of binding law. However, the focused attention of a generation is needed before the seeds of change bear fruit in the United States.

The Need for Human Rights Discourse

The United States has long been baffled about the "Indian problem," ever since it set the colonization process into motion. Over the years, the indigenous legal framework developed in the absence of human rights, and it is possible to see several features with an anti-indigenous function. The *Declaration* invites us to view Native American rights for the first time as "human rights"—that is, as the rights and fundamental freedoms that all human beings enjoy as a matter of right.[15] The language of human rights is familiar. However, Americans have not engaged in serious discourse about the human rights of American Indians. Nor is there a systematic program for correcting wrongs suffered by them. This is puzzling, because we Americans are a just people. Most Americans are committed to remedial justice and are well aware of the abuses inflicted on Native Americans by the government. Though the *Declaration* obviously grants reparation, it is dismissed by many who are unwilling to discuss its purposes and contents because of two paralyzing psychological barriers. First, at the outset, we are baffled by an alien document that speaks of "international human rights." To some, this is strange language. *Can't we simply resort to the Bill of Rights?* Second, we are overcome by anxiety and discomfort at the thought of making amends for collective wrongs committed against Indians, because that is how our nation was built. Thus, reparation calls our legitimacy into question, and that heartburn causes us to run swiftly from our inner demons. We must confront and overcome these two barriers in order to discuss the fundamental rights and freedoms of Native Americans.

1. The Language of "Human Rights" Is as American as Apple Pie

Discourse about the nature of human rights is familiar ground in the United States, although we do not often use the words "human rights." It must be remembered that our nation sprang from the human rights principle, which is quite literally our foundational creed. During the birth of the nation, the proposition that each human being is endowed by "the sacred rights of mankind" that "can never be erased or obscured by mortal power" gripped the Founding Fathers as a fundamental organizing principle for the new republic.[16] Variously described as the "rights of man," "natural rights," or the "rights of mankind," the idea of human rights was understood by the first-generation as a body of natural, inalienable rights of all persons that derived from a larger authority and higher source—human rights that no government could deny and that all free and democratic governments were formed to protect.[17] In fact, the denial of these inalienable rights led to the American Revolution. The Declaration of Independence memorialized the ideals that animated the United States:

> We hold these truths to be self-evident, that all men are created equal, that they are endowed by their Creator with certain inalienable rights, that among these are life, liberty, and the pursuit of happiness. That to pursue these rights, governments are instituted among men, deriving their just powers from the consent of the governed.

Our revolution was based on human rights. Those precepts forged a nation unlike any other that had gone before it, and they guided a great "experiment upon the theory of human rights," in the words of President John Quincy Adams.[18] Resonant human rights precepts were upon our lips at every important juncture in American history. They were used to inspire the rise and growth of the democracy, profoundly affecting the writing of the Bill of Rights and the fulfillment of human rights in the

Abolitionist Movement, the Slavery Debates, the Civil War, the Women's Movement, and the Civil Rights Movement of the 20th century.[19] The actual use of those precepts is extensive. That is why we are the "Land of the Free."

Under the American Creed set forth in the Declaration of Independence and our organic documents, our rich history reveals a nation dedicated to protecting human rights at home and abroad. This defining characteristic led to unprecedented freedom and an extraordinary legacy.[20] It is no wonder that when Americans look into the mirror we can admire what we see. Nonetheless, our nation has not always lived up to its ideals. Our path sometimes took torturous detours, paved with injustice and rank human rights violations that often plague nations. To be sure, our commitment to human rights was sorely compromised by slavery; our core values were abandoned in the eugenics movement; and our highest principles were contradicted by systematic racial discrimination of oppressed groups. However, in each of these dark times, a resort to the human rights principle impelled Americans to self-correct these shortcomings, though sometimes at great cost, and to redeem our core values, which insist upon the dignity of every human being. To meet those challenges, every generation has had to resort to, and sometimes relearn, the self-evident truths expressed in our human rights charter, the Declaration of Independence; and in every instance, the language of human rights was at the core of the discourse leading to self-correction. Resort to the human rights framework has thus proven invaluable. It provides a larger perspective, grounded in universal values to evaluate perplexing social ills and a sound framework for weighing competing interests to find a path that best comports with core values. For example, in the contentious repatriation debate of the late 1980s over the proper disposition of Native American human remains, the Native American, museum, and science communities became bogged down—stymied by self-interest—until they agreed to be guided by the human rights principle. That principle allowed them to structure competing interests in a just framework designed to avoid trammeling human rights. Agreement was soon reached on major sticking points, and that created a positive framework for the historic passage of a new human rights law, the Native American Graves Protection and Repatriation Act.[21]

In addition, the language of human rights is familiar to the courts. Given the pervasive human rights dimension in US history, it is not surprising to find extensive use of human rights precepts by the courts throughout judicial history.[22] Chief Justice John Marshall was the first Supreme Court justice to use the phrase "human rights." In *Fletcher v. Peck* (1810), he recognized that courts "are established to decide on human rights."[23] After surveying the use of human rights by the federal courts, Professor Jordan J. Paust concluded:

> Although few in the legal profession may be sufficiently aware, the actual use of human rights precepts in U.S. history has been substantial and concern for human rights has been associated with most major politico-legal developments in the United States over the last two-and-one-half centuries. Not surprisingly then, one can also discover a rich, often splendid history of use of human rights and equivalent phrases by U.S. courts over the last two hundred years.[24]

This book has an international focus, because the *Declaration* is an international instrument connected to modern international law. However, it speaks a home-grown language readily understood by Americans.

2. We can make amends to Native America, and Discourse is the First Step.

In the law, the remedial concept of *reparation* is defined as "the act of making amends" for a wrong that has been committed.[25] It includes any "measure aimed at restoring a person and/or a community of a loss, harm or damage suffered consequent to an action or omission."[26] It is an act of atonement that repairs damage, heals an injury, and allows both the victim and the wrongdoer to go forward in good faith once justice has been restored and all of the injurious consequences of the wrong have been wiped clean. The principle function of a legal system is to ensure adequate reparation to victims of individual or collective wrongs. As eloquently stated by Justice Guha Roy, High Court of Calcutta:

> That a wrong done to an individual must be redressed by the offender himself or by someone else against whom the sanction of the

> community may be directed is one of those timeless axioms of justice without which social life is unthinkable.[27]

At its essence, the goal of every legal system is reparation. Indeed, the moment when adequate reparations are actually granted to an injured party is the very moment when justice crystallizes; and in that moment, justice is realized.[28] As such, the law ensures that every right is protected by a remedy to insure its effectiveness. This is certainly the case in human rights law.[29]

The discourse of reparations for indigenous peoples for historical and lasting wrongs committed by governments during the colonization and nation-building processes entails the responsibility of states to repair damage done to aboriginal inhabitants, and it involves fundamental notions of remedial justice. In the indigenous context, law professor and UNESCO consultant, Federico Lenzerini, describes reparations as:

> measures aimed at restoring justice through wiping out all the consequences of the harm suffered by the individuals and/or people concerned as the result of a wrong, and at re-establishing the situation which would have existed if the wrong had not been produced.[30]

International human rights treaties, conventions, and declarations envision restorative justice as transformative social action intended to restructure relationships that gave rise to indigenous grievances and address root problems that led to the systematic abuse of their rights through remedies that become part of the healing process.[31] In this vein, the *Declaration* has a remedial purpose. It is aimed at restoring the human rights of indigenous peoples that fell by the wayside during the colonization of their homelands. Indeed, the instrument itself is a form of reparation because it makes international human rights law accountable to indigenous peoples. It defines human rights and fundamental freedoms in the unique indigenous context, and it prescribes the duties of the state necessary to fully realize these human rights. The standards of the *Declaration* explain how human rights, articulated in existing treaties, and norms should be interpreted and applied in the indigenous context so that indigenous peoples can enjoy the same human rights as the rest of humanity. To provide reparations and restorative justice for indigenous peoples, the *Declaration* prescribes a broad range of state duties. They are designed to repair lasting harm and continuing damage inflicted upon indigenous peoples and restore their human rights. These measures bring indigenous peoples into the body politic in a just manner with their rights as indigenous peoples intact. Finally, the *Declaration* asks states to effectuate these rights and duties in consultation and cooperation with indigenous peoples.

We cannot contemplate this far-reaching program of reparation without a serious national discourse on the nature and content of Native American human rights and a conversation about the steps that must be taken to operationalize the provisions of the *Declaration*. America has never undertaken a thorough effort at reparations for Native Americans. Nor has it engaged in a human rights dialogue about the fundamental freedoms of the First Americans. This inattention stands in marked contrast to the ways in which Americans have addressed themselves to all of the other growing pains of democracy in our history, which have been tremendous and many. We fought the Revolutionary War to restore human rights for British settlers, the Civil War to end slavery, and many other wars against tyrants throughout the 20th and 21st centuries to defend human rights. We struggled mightily to protect the human rights of oppressed groups at home and remedy, through national soul-searching, collective wrongs inflicted upon blacks, Japanese-Americans, women, inhabitants of American territories abroad, and oppressed immigrant groups at home—in essence everyone impacted by the American experiment, except Native Americans. The nation has not seriously addressed the by-products of Manifest Destiny in the same way that it came to terms with the institution of slavery and engrained discrimination against black citizens. In 1987, Historian Patricia Nelson Limerick observed:

> To most twentieth century Americans, the legacy of slavery was serious business, the legacy of conquest was not. . . . The subject of slavery was the domain of serious scholars and the occasion of sober national reflection; the subject of conquest was the domain of mass entertainment and the occasion of light-hearted national escapism. An element of regret for "what we did to the Indians" had entered the picture, but the dominant

feature of conquest remained "adventure." Children happily played "cowboys and Indians" but stopped short of "masters and slaves."[32]

Federal courts contribute to the inattention. While they are conversant with human rights, federal Indian law is bereft of those precepts. It is a strangely amoral body of law that stands in stark contrast to the profound commitment to remedial justice found elsewhere in American legal culture. When wrongs to Indians and Indian rights are concerned, the federal courts don the robes of the "courts of the conqueror," in the words of John Marshall in *Johnson v. M'Intosh* (1823), and they cannot resort to "principles of abstract justice" when defining Indian rights.[33] After freeing itself from the constrains of justice, the *Johnson* Court held: "Conquest gives a title [to Indian land] which the Courts of the conqueror cannot deny," and "however extravagant the pretension of converting the discovery of an inhabited continent into conquest may appear it becomes the law of the land and cannot be questioned."[34]

For the rest of the century, the Supreme Court insisted that justice has no place in formulating the foundational doctrines of federal Indian law. In *Cherokee Nation v. Georgia* (1831), Justice Johnson voted to deny the Cherokee Nation access to the courts to protect itself against the aggression of Georgia. He eschewed morality, stating: "With the morality of the case I have no concern; I am called upon to consider it as a legal question."[35] Thus freed from moral strictures, he rejected the full right of self-determination to Indian nations for that right could not be accorded to a lowly "race of hunters," because they are a "restless, warlike, and signally cruel" race with "inveterate habits and deep seated enmity," who could only "receive the territory allotted to them as a boon from a master or conqueror."[36] *Lone Wolf v. Hitchcock* (1903) reiterated that Indian property rights do not derive from inalienable rights; rather, they rest upon "good faith" and "such considerations of justice as would control a Christian people in the treatment of an ignorant and dependent race."[37] Under the doctrine of confiscation announced in *Tee-Hit-Ton Indians v. United States* (1955), Indian occupancy of ancient tribal homelands developed into simple "permission from the whites to occupy" the land—a bare entitlement that depends entirely upon the "compassion" and "grace" of the American people:

> No case in this Court has ever held that taking of Indian title or use by Congress requires compensation. The American people have compassion for the descendants of those Indians who were deprived of their homes and hunting grounds by the drive of civilization. They seek to have Indians share the benefits of our society as citizens of this Nation. Generous provision has been made willingly to allow tribes to recover for wrongs, *as a matter of grace, not because of legal liability.*[38]

Justice Reed explained that in a conquered land, the Indians' right to land is a "gratuity," and nothing more:

> Every American schoolboy knows that the savage tribes of this continent were deprived of their ancestral ranges by force and that, even when the Indians ceded millions of acres by treaty for blankets, food and trinkets, it was not a sale but the conqueror's will that deprived them of their land. Our conclusion does not uphold harshness as against tenderness toward the Indians, but it leaves with Congress, where it belongs, the policy of Indian gratuities for the termination of Indian occupancy of Government-owned land rather than making compensation for its value a rigid constitutional principle.[39]

The amoral approach to defining fundamental freedoms in Indian cases was taken in *Employment Division v. Smith* (1990). The *Smith* Court dramatically departed from established religious freedom jurisprudence. It narrowly construed the First Amendment to deny constitutional protection for the oldest, most continually practiced indigenous religion in the Western Hemisphere, the Indian peyote religion.[40] The unpopular decision provoked a firestorm of criticism from legal scholars and church and civil libertarian groups, and the decision was ultimately overturned by Congress a few years later through the passage of several laws that restored American religious liberty.[41] But what struck Professor John Delaney was the *tone* in which the *Smith* majority opinion repudiated the Indians' religion. In the opinion, "there are no pages, no paragraphs, not even a sentence, that respectfully detail [*sic.*] Smith's and Black's religious interest in the annual sacramental rite of their Native American Church."[42] Even when the right to worship is at stake, the court could not utter a single word of respect for the Indians' interest. The cold analysis is devoid of the human rights dimension:

> [T]he *Smith* majority opinion is replete with angry words rejecting the Native American claim followed by an emphatic repudiation of any judicial role in considering such a claim. The contrast with the respect for the claims of the Seventh-Day Adventists in *Sherbert* and *Hobbie,* the Jehovah's Witnesses in *Thomas*, the unaffiliated Christian in *Frazee,* the Amish parents in *Yoder,* and the Native American in *Roy,* is especially vivid. In these cases, the diverse claims remained at the center of the Court's formulation and analysis. In *Smith,* the Court's formulation and analysis cause Alfred Smith, Galen Black, and the central religious rite of their faith, to fade away to the periphery. In our legal culture, informed by belief in the dignity and worth of all people, such reasoning should be suspect. It is especially unfortunate that, after "many years of religious persecution and intolerance" of Native American religions by majoritarian institutions, the Court, which speaks for all of us, spoke so badly.[43]

In short, it is hard to find *any* human rights discourse in Indian cases, even though the courts freely and extensively use human rights precepts in non-Indian cases. The "courts of the conqueror" apply doctrines devoid of human rights in an amoral body of law where justice has no place. This paradigm is in marked contrast to the human rights framework of the *Declaration*, which defines Indian rights to self-determination, self-government, culture, property, territory, and religion as fundamental human rights. This concept has eluded our courts for over two hundred years. The *Declaration* allows us to re-conceptualize our notions about Indian rights; and it permits us to see them as human rights derived from the same notions of justice, equality, and non-discrimination that are found in the Declaration of Independence, which make a far superior, more just foundation for Indian rights than the nefarious 18th and 19th century notions of conquest, discovery, and race that underpin Indian rights as defined by federal Indian law. However, this sea-change in judicial thought by the self-described "courts of the conqueror" cannot be accomplished without judicial discourse and re-evaluation. Until then, the higher values expressed in modern international human rights law and the *Declaration*, which lead to reparative justice, are beyond reach.

It is strange that there has never been a focused national discourse on the status, nature, and content of the human rights of Native Americans. That dialogue is long overdue. Endorsement of the *Declaration* by the United States in 2010 provides the occasion for discourse. It is true that periodic studies were conducted in the 20th century to assess the state of Federal Indian Affairs, evaluate federal Indian policies, and examine the conditions of the Indians. Some were sea-changing examinations that became catalysts for change, like the *Meriam Report* (1928) and the *American Indian Policy Review Commission Final Report* (1977).[44] But this generation has not initiated a coherent and comprehensive review of Indian policy, judicial trends, or the situation of Native Americans. We are simply coasting under the Indian Self-Determination Policy initiated by President Nixon in 1970 and have not evaluated indigenous conditions, problems, or rights in over thirty-five years.

Civil society has fallen asleep at the wheel, along with the political branches of government. This inattention has opened a pathway for the Supreme Court to quietly trim back Native American rights, a trend that began with the Rehnquist Court in 1985 and continues today in the Roberts Court. In recent decades, the Supreme Court has assumed plenary judicial power over Indian tribes and taken the lead, over the political branches, in defining the sovereignty, treaty, political, property, cultural, and human rights of Native Americans—a role that the Supreme Court eschewed over the past hundred and fifty years in deference to the political branches. Content to focus on other beltway business, the political branches have largely abdicated the duty of protecting Indian tribes to nine black-robed figures, who now decide the fate of Indian tribes and define their rights, relationship to the United States, and place in society, all done from behind closed chamber doors. This is an unsatisfactory and potentially noxious situation. Without checks and balances, judicial hegemony over Indian tribes can slide toward judicial tyranny, because the legacy of conquest is deeply embedded in Supreme Court doctrines, leaving no room for human rights.

For example, instead of recognizing the Indian right of self-determination as a human right, as done by Articles 3 and 4 of the *Declaration*, the Supreme Court views tribal sovereignty solely in the context of conquest under its new "implicit divesture rule" of *Oliphant v. Suquamish Indian Tribe* (1978) and its progeny.[45] Before *Oliphant,* federal Indian law recognized that Indian tribes retained all of their inherent sovereign powers not voluntarily given up in treaties or expressly taken away by Congress. By contrast, the new doctrine grants broad discretion to the courts to impose additional and far-reaching limitations on tribal sovereignty: tribal government powers can be stripped by the courts *by implication as a necessary result of their dependent status* whenever a judge deems them inconsistent with the interests of the United States. Under this subjective test, self-determination can be assaulted by the *Supreme Court, because it is not considered an inalienable human right* (as required by the *Declaration,* numerous treaties, and settled norms in customary international law), but rather the right of self-determination is defined by judicial fiat. We have seen how this works: tribal sovereignty is steadily being divested on an *ad hoc* basis, quite literally, at judicial whim. The legacy of conquest lies at the heart of the "implicit divestiture rule." Tribal self-government can be eroded, because it is not viewed as an inalienable human right.

Despite the global trend in recent years favoring indigenous rights discourse and reparations for indigenous peoples, there is a deep-seated psychological barrier in the United States that prevents remedial justice for collective wrongs inflicted upon Native Americans, and even discourse about their human rights. The barrier stems from two sources. First, the legacy of conquest sorely impugns our self-image, core values, and origin myth; and we cannot face these inner demons without being overcome by paralyzing guilt. Second, our legal system of remedial justice is adept at righting wrongs against victims who present individual claims, but it stops short at reparative justice for collective wrongs committed against groups, especially when the wrongdoer is the American nation. Judicial recognition of national wrongs might bring the legitimacy of the nation or its policies into question. An example of that torment is seen in *State v. Foreman* (1835), when the Tennessee Supreme Court applied harsh and unjust legal doctrines against the Cherokee Nation. The Court worried aloud:

> To abandon the principle now is to assert that [our English forebears] were unjust usurpers, and that we, succeeding to their usurped

> authority and void claims to possess and govern the country, should in all [honesty] abandon it, return to Europe, and let the subdued parts again become a wilderness and hunting ground.[46]

As agents of the sovereign, judges cannot question the legitimacy of the United States, nor assault evil, but constitutional policies; and this gives a perverse meaning to the adage "justice is blind." In the case of Indians or Indian Tribes, that concept is turned on its head: jurists go as far as to avert their eyes from justice rather than call the legitimacy of the state or its policies into question.

This book argues that we need not be paralyzed by psychological factors, such as guilt or an over-inflated self-image. There is good cause for a grand self-image. After all, our nation did spring from universal human rights principles, and we have fought wars as a democratic people to protect those ideals at great sacrifice. Whenever we fell short of our ideals, we have always tried to self-correct by resorting to our core values.

But this legacy has created an inflated self-image, called "American Exceptionalism," that sees the American people as the most exceptional people on earth.[47] That high self-esteem is impossible to maintain when the injustices against Native Americans have not been addressed or repaired. That unfinished business also mars the great American origin story, which imagines a nation created through the "consent of the governed." That notion is contradicted by the presence of subjugated tribal peoples who were conquered and colonized. Do we rule Indian tribes under extra-constitutional doctrines of conquest? Our origin story will not ring true until that contradiction is cleared up by restorative justice of the type called for by the *Declaration*. We must enter into the realm of remedial reparations, not so much as to render monetary damages or compensation, but to undertake acts to repair damage and make things right.

Until then, we shall always have an ugly stain upon our origin story that is almost impossible to explain away, even by our greatest leaders and finest legal minds. For example, Teddy Roosevelt's attempt to gloss over this stain is unpersuasive. He stated: "The settler and pioneer have at bottom had justice on their side; this great continent could not have been kept as nothing but a game preserve for squalid savages."[48] When seen through modern eyes, that explanation makes us look like a racist nation.

When we look into the mirror, we see a glorified frontier past. But that image cannot be reconciled with the many ignoble acts of dispossession, violence, forcible removal, systematic discrimination, destruction of culture and habitat, and enforced assimilation. Under modern standards, those acts are descriptive of a genocidal pattern. Even learned jurists are overtaxed when called upon to rationalize that pattern. During the zenith of the Indian Removal Movement in the 1830s, Chief Justice Catron of the Supreme Court of Tennessee attempted to explain and justify the mistreatment of Indians by the South in *State v. Tennessee* (1835). His explanation is a not one of glory:

> Our claim is based on the right to coerce obedience. The claim may be denounced by the moralist. We answer, it is the law of the land. Without its assertion and vigorous execution, this continent never could have been inhabited by our ancestors. To abandon the [doctrine of discovery] now is to assert that they were unjust usurpers, and that we, succeeding to their usurped authority and void claims to possess and govern the country, should in all honesty abandon it, return to Europe, and let the subdued parts again become a wilderness and hunting ground.[49]

We are committed to the equality principle expressed in the organic documents of our democracy. But we cannot reconcile the double-standard in our shoddy treatment of Native Americans with equality principles that obtain for everyone else.

Our self-image demands "moral purity," according to an insightful article written by law professor David C. Williams.[50] However, what we did to the Indians shows that we are not pure as the driven snow, nor are we the most exceptional people on earth. Instead, we are heirs to a more humble, down-to-earth legacy—one with inherited problems familiar in settler states created by conquest and colonization. But our grandiose self-image does not let us confront that legacy in serious national discourse, because that dialogue forces us to admit that moral purity and American Exceptionalism are beyond reach. Against that psychological barrier, it is easier to ignore the problems created by that legacy, or simply cover it over with distorted policies, unjust legal fictions, and nefarious legal doctrines, and to live with the unsatisfactory explanations of the sort offered by Teddy Roosevelt and Justice Catron. The Indians are like the skunk at the picnic. They threaten our self-image, undermine our origin story, and show that we have not lived up to our ideals. Yet we cannot bring ourselves to address the root problems that have created this situation.

To compound our paralysis, the legacy of conquest creates a psychological barrier for the courts that inhibits judicial discourse about Native American human rights and makes reparations for collective historical wrongs inflicted on them unthinkable. Since 1823, the "courts of the conqueror" have defined tribal rights primarily in the framework of conquest. That creates a dilemma for federal judges. According to Professor Williams, if America created a sovereign through appalling misconduct, then it might seem that America really does not have a right to exist.[51] That fear animated Chief Justice Catron's remarks. As agents of the sovereign, judges cannot question the legitimacy of their own power, or intimate that the sovereign is illegitimate. The impulse to perfection makes reparations by the sovereign unthinkable to many Americans, as well.[52] Thus, America can easily make amends to other minority groups without calling its sovereignty or legitimacy into question, but that is not the case with Native Americans, who assert unique collective claims for the unjust taking of their sovereignty, territory, religious freedom, cultures, and ways of life. Against those claims, we cannot admit that we have feet of clay. Instead, we must avoid discourse, go to great lengths to fashion unjust legal fictions and nefarious doctrines to deny any hint of illegitimacy, and, at all costs, avoid reparations for the wrongs inflicted upon Native Americans at the hands of the government during the conquest, subjugation, and colonization of North America.

Professor Williams asserts that we must puncture these barriers. He insists that we do have feet of clay, just like every other nation; but nevertheless, that humbling realization does not prevent reparations:

> If no country is morally pure, then it cannot be that America's own dubious roots require it to foreswear any and all sovereignty over North America. The United States can keep its sovereignty even if acquired under shady circumstances; judges can go on deciding cases, and the legislature can go on making statutes.[53]

It is entirely possible to confront our inner demons and normalize our self-esteem. *Shucks, it's not so bad being just like ordinary human beings.* These steps allow us to (1) enter into a dialogue aimed at repairing wrongs committed against Native Americans, (2) heal a painful past through acts of atonement, and (3) move forward as a stronger nation. In that process, we can even harness "guilt" and "shame" and redirect these sentiments as a constructive remedial force:

> [T]he right sort of guilt can be good, especially for those who dread guilt so much that it deforms their social policy. For one thing, it acts as a goad to change: even though we cannot make all right, we are nonetheless not off the hook. We must do what we reasonably can by way of reparation and accept that there will always be a moral remainder. Admittedly, like Calvin's responsibility without free will, such an attitude carries only limited psychological incentives: you do the right thing, make amends, and you still feel bad. But this sort of guilt also frees us: if we live in dread of guilt, we must construct a temple of illusions, banishing all thought that the tribes might be legitimate claimants for far-reaching remediation. But if we accept that guilt is an inevitable feature of human life, that moral purity is not possible for us, then we can explore the possibility of reparations. We tasted guilt, and it did not poison us. It merely opened our eyes.[54]

We have courageously made amends for historical wrongs committed against slaves, blacks, and other immigrant groups. There is no reason to run swiftly from appropriate acts of atonement for the legacy of conquest. We can confront the fact that our core values were seriously degraded by the exploitation of Native Americans. Through discourse, we can see that our established patterns for coping with that legacy have cultivated a lack of equity that is so deeply embedded that we have become blinded to the inequities under our feet, and that illuminates the need to rebuild equitable relations with the First Americans. Discourse allows us to approach the *Declaration* and come to terms with its mandates in the spirit described by Professor Nicholas A. Robinson:

> The U.N. Declaration on the Rights of Indigenous Peoples is a unique

and precious legal instrument, one that draws us all into the river purposely. By struggling to come to terms with the Declaration's mandates, contemporary magistrates of government are obliged to redesign their settled but unjust practices and seek to do equity. In doing equity, they shall build the just relations with Indigenous Peoples and by extension with all of life.[55]

It is true that most people do nothing to make amends for historical wrongs until awakened by some event or other big consequence that grabs their attention and brings them "kicking and screaming" into the process. The *Declaration* opens the door, and we have sleeping giants in our midst that can bring the body politic into dialogue about the legacy of conquest. The first giant is that there is a new locus of power. It is found in the growing number of Americans who descend from, strongly identify with, or proudly appreciate the Native American heritage of our nation. They are more numerous than we think, because they are us. Mainstream society no longer abhors the Native peoples of the United States. It rejected that attitude long ago and has even moved beyond tolerance. Today it wants to preserve the indigenous legacy and see it flourish. As a result, many among us are ready to face lingering inequities from the legacy of conquest and see what can be done about them. The second sleeping giant is our accumulated wisdom traditions. Though dormant until summoned, they can heal historical wrongs. Gleaned from the human experience over millennia, principles of atonement provide a powerful healing framework for addressing the legacy of conquest. When invoked, the highest values and virtues known to the human race exhort us to initiate a time-tested healing process, one that sees actualization of the *Declaration* as an act of atonement. We shall examine these sleeping giants and see if we can awaken them. Equitable discourse *with* America's indigenous peoples can open our eyes to the need to heal a painful past and allow the American people to move forward and truly become the champions of freedom that our self-image impels us to be.

Political Ramifications of the *Declaration*

Beyond the human rights sphere, the UN guidepost furnishes nations with much-needed answers to perplexing political problems. The *sine qua non* of legitimacy for the exercise of government power over people in every democracy is the *consent of the governed*. As stated in the Declaration of Independence, governments derive "their just powers from the consent of the governed." That consent is lacking in conquered and colonized lands, including the democracies that conquered, dispossessed, subjugated, and forcibly assimilated their indigenous peoples. This legacy leaves nations to suffer a stigma of illegitimacy in the governance of aboriginal populations. Every modern nation that sprang from a European colony falls into this predicament, because they were built upon a history of dispossession and subjugation of their Native peoples. That injustice paralyzes many folks with guilt about "what we did to the Indians," but those regrets rarely lead to concrete steps to remedy lingering injustice. Consequently, many modern democracies remain frozen in an unjust past, stymied by guilt, and unable to heal the past. Their unfinished nation-building work is to rectify injustices committed against indigenous peoples during the nation-building process. That cannot be accomplished until the vestiges and mindset of colonialism are discarded and a better path is found for consensually bringing indigenous peoples into the body politic on a more just basis. After all, until a just and consensual relationship is established, settler societies remain mired in injustice and cannot stride toward the culture that modern values demand.

The *Declaration* answers these thorny political questions that plague nations with indigenous peoples. It helps them complete the nation-building process by providing internationally approved guidelines for striking a just balance between indigenous and non-indigenous rights, relationships, and responsibilities. By embracing those standards of conduct as the framework for addressing indigenous issues, nations can move away from the legacy of colonialism and evolve into more just cultures. This pathway brings indigenous peoples into the body politic on a *consensual basis* with their political, human, property, and cultural rights intact. The *Declaration* thus addresses a pressing universal question: *How should modern nations comport themselves toward their Native peoples in a post-colonial age?*

Will the UN Standards Plant the Seeds of Change in the US?

Landmark events are often unheralded. Their significance sometimes eludes the public, taking years to be seen, much less achieved. After all, no one could have predicted how the birth of Jesus would enrich the lives of millions over the centuries, nor at all fathom how Elvis would rock the music world in the span of a single lifetime. Even Columbus died in obscurity just as the immense treasures of his remarkable discovery were unfolding, and it took decades of social turmoil before the fruits of the *Brown* decision were seen in American society. Similarly, approval of the *Declaration* was scarcely noticed in 2007. Many tribal leaders were unaware of that event, even though the making of the *Declaration* took over twenty years and was strongly supported by several Indian tribes and many leading Native rights organizations and individuals. Even fewer know that the United States provisionally endorsed the *Declaration* in 2010. (The United States was the last nation on earth to endorse the *Declaration*, and did so only with many State Department qualifications.) Like a whisper, from such humble and obscure beginnings, the seeds of change can take root and sprout into powerful forces that shape history, though sometimes this involves a long and difficult path.

The UN *Declaration* raises many questions. Tribal leaders, advocates, and activists wonder how to implement these standards in the United States. Here skeptics concerned only with local issues and existing law give much pause. The naysayers ask, "Why should hard-pressed Indian Nations undertake the time and expense of mounting a national campaign to implement UN standards? Will Native life, rights, and well-being be strengthened in the process?" Government officials wonder about impacts on existing laws, administrative structures, practices, and policies. And hunched over their hand-held devices, some self-absorbed neighbors, who are completely preoccupied with their daily needs and personal pursuits in our self-indulgent society, impatiently ask, "Why should I care?"

For legal practitioners, the paramount question is: How will the *Declaration* impact the future of federal Indian law? This body of law furnishes the legal framework for protecting the rights of Indian tribes and Alaska Natives. Since 1970, Indian Nations achieved many impressive nation-building advances within that framework during the modern era of federal Indian law. However, there is a troubling "dark side" embedded in that body of law, as mentioned above, which renders hard-won tribal rights vulnerable. Many agree that federal Indian law is in deep trouble today.[56] It desperately needs a lifeline after an incredible battering by an often insensitive Supreme Court, which has created a legal crisis in Indian Country by steadily eroding Native rights since 1985, when the court ruled against Indian nations in over 80 percent of their cases.[57] Does US endorsement of the *Declaration* usher in a new era for federal Indian law?

Since this book is about the *Declaration*, it is by necessity concerned with inalienable human rights and the reaffirmation of a government grounded in the essential nature of mankind. It is an ethical study about how to implement the *Declaration* to produce equitable relations between indigenous and non-indigenous peoples, and it explores notions of reparative justice that allow peoples to heal historic injuries and move forward as a stronger whole.

In ten chapters, I provide baseline information for understanding and implementing the *Declaration*. I argue that the UN standards must be incorporated into American law and social policy. For background, Chapter Two examines how the *Declaration* was made. Chapter Three scrutinizes the purposes, nature, and contents of the *Declaration*. Chapter Four addresses the legal status of the *Declaration*. Chapter Five explains why the UN standards are needed in the United States. Chapter Six looks at the environmental reasons for embracing the *Declaration*. Chapter Seven considers the impact of the *Declaration* upon the future of federal Indian law, and Chapter Eight compares the UN standards with federal law and policy to identify the weaknesses, shortcomings, and loopholes that need fixing before the goals of the *Declaration* can be achieved. Chapter Nine offers practical thoughts, theoretical considerations, and organizational ideas for implementing the *Declaration*, including a stirring case study of the socio-legal movement that led to the landmark decision in *Brown v. Board of Education* (1954). Finally, after we are armed with baseline information, why should we act? If our nation answers the call, it must embark upon a cause to restore neglected human rights and rebuild Native American cultures. What set of principles should motivate, guide, and anchor that reform? Chapter Ten draws upon time-tested principles of reparative justice and atonement to provide a foundation for making Native America whole.

As we lift our eyes up to the task set before us by the *Declaration*, each person is presented with a rare opportunity, for only once in a great while does the chance to correct injustice come along in the course of one's life. When it arrives, let each act to do the right thing. At this juncture in American history, it has fallen to our generation the task of restoring that which was taken away many years ago. This is a social imperative. It can be aptly described as a new and much more positive "White Man's Burden," to place an old euphemism into a novel context. It is one shared by Native America. The "Red Man's Burden" that is placed upon Indian Country by the *Declaration* is to reject the remaining vestiges of colonialism that continue to harm Native life and culture. It calls upon modern-day warriors to reform the "dark side" of federal Indian law so that tribal rights can be protected by a more just body of law, and it seeks to consolidate nation-building gains made in the past three decades by our tribal nations. As a catalyst for change, the *Declaration* is an important tool to help achieve goals that were beyond reach by prior generations. The fight for those goals has only just begun. As we array ourselves for battle, we can call upon the Ancestors of the American people *of every race*, confidently resort once again to the human rights principles of the Declaration of Independence, and gird ourselves for what might be the final stage and the last and best page of the American Revolution.

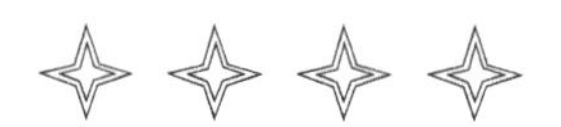

CHAPTER TWO
The Making of the Declaration

> In 1975, my cousin, the late Ed Burnstick, said to me, "Willie, get packing because we are going to Wounded Knee." I was in the middle of my law exams and was unable to attend. However, the seeds of the Declaration were sown there, at Wounded Knee, where Indigenous peoples began drafting their first statement of principles which was the forerunner to the Declaration.
>
> —Chief Wilton Littlechild (2010)[1]

The rise of indigenous peoples in international law is a stirring tale that took place during my lifetime. The development and approval of the *Declaration* was a remarkable achievement by a global indigenous movement. How was the *Declaration* made? When asked about the seamy-side of lawmaking in the dark corners of Congress, lobbyists warn, "You do not want to know how sausages or laws are made." Pork-barrel politics often shock the conscience, and the "Good Ole Boy" network can produce unjust laws. I experienced one example as a Native American Rights Fund attorney. After the Supreme Court halted construction of the Tennessee Valley Authority's infamous Tellico Dam under the Endangered Species Act in 1978, a senator crept into the Senate Chamber late at night to add a non-germane amendment to an appropriations bill. The rider exempted construction of the dam from the Endangered Species Act and "any other law."[2] Thus, while the public slept, the tip-toe maneuver sidestepped the Supreme Court ruling, and all other laws, to complete the pork-barrel project without any legislative hearing whatsoever—regardless of harm to endangered fish or to Cherokee holy places that would be inundated by the dam. When the stunned Cherokees sought to prevent TVA flooding of their holy places, federal courts upheld the completion of the dam under the nefarious amendment without batting an eye. No matter how it was made, the courts obeyed Congress' command, stating: "No law is to stand in the way of completion and operation of the dam."[3] By contrast, the *Declaration* was developed and approved in the light of day, without any pork-barrel politics, cronyism, short-cuts, or big-spending lobbyists. Rather, the General Assembly vote on September 13, 2007, came after more than twenty years of development in open, transparent, and established processes. Those lengthy deliberations provide legitimacy, since all of the procedures were observed and every member nation had a full and fair opportunity to develop, review, and vote on the instrument in the established channels. That legislative history is memorialized by the UN officials, diplomats, and indigenous advocates who participated in the process.[4] Their stirring tale goes beyond the scope of this book and is only summarized here.

To place the making of the *Declaration* into historical context, it must be remembered that international law contained no legal protections for indigenous peoples during the Colonial Era (c. 1492–1960).[5] To the contrary, early international law had an anti-indigenous function: It legalized colonialism. It supplied rules at the dawn of the Colonial Era to govern relations among the nations of Europe while they expanded across the globe, guide dealings with the non-Christian world, and facilitate colonization. Various legal principles, doctrines, and fictions were conceived to legalize the settlement and appropriation of native land and to subjugate indigenous peoples.[6] Under doctrines of dispossession (such as discovery, *terra nullius*, conquest, and guardianship), theories that allowed the use of war to seize the New World, and legal fictions postulating racial, religious, and cultural superiority, the early law of nations saw Indians as infidels with inferior cultures.[7] Nearly every colony treated natives as barbarous savages with diminutive political, property, and human rights. Their situation went unprotected, because the law of nations only addressed the external international relationships among European nations and left all of their internal affairs to the exclusive domain of domestic law. This bifurcation granted them unilateral authority to deal with colonized indigenous peoples within the territories subject to their colonial claims as an internal matter. The categorical exclusion of the rights of indigenous peoples from the protections of international law consigned the fate of colonized millions to the domestic law of their colonizers. As might be expected, aborigines fared poorly under that regime. Unbridled by outside restraints, colonizers and their offspring freely trammeled aboriginal rights in a scramble for land and resources. Their domestic law fostered dispossession, subjugation, oppression, and the forcible assimilation of indigenous peoples—and

sometimes even resulted in genocide. Indigenous rights fell by the wayside as tribal peoples, and their ways of life, were pushed to the margin in their homelands, and sometimes to the brink of extinction.

In short, early international law was not accountable to tribal peoples. It regarded them as objects subject to the exclusive domestic jurisdiction of the settler states that invaded and subjugated them, and it did not concern itself with protecting their rights. According to one UN expert, it "developed historically to support the forces of colonialism and empire that have trampled the capacity of indigenous peoples to determine their own course under conditions of equality."[8] That state of affairs was in full force as late as 1970, when the modern era of federal Indian law began to take root in the United States, but during the second half of the 20th century, the days of this inequitable loophole became numbered due to four related forces: (1) the creation of the United Nations in 1945, (2) the decolonization movement, (3) the growth of the UN human rights system and evolution of modern international human rights law, and (4) the international indigenous rights movement that took hold in last three decades of the 20th century. As will be seen, these factors domesticated international law over the past six decades and made it accountable to indigenous peoples.

After five hundred years, colonialism fell into disrepute in the 20th century, when most remaining European colonies were dismantled. In 1960, the UN officially repudiated colonialism.[9] The UN decolonization resolution stated "the peoples of the world ardently desire the end of colonialism in all its manifestations," because colonialism "impedes the social, cultural, and economic development of dependent peoples." It declared that "all peoples have the right of self-determination" (i.e., the right to "freely determine their political status and freely pursue their economic, social, and cultural development"); and it asked the colonial regimes to "transfer all powers to the peoples of those territories."[10] That historic step toward a paradigm shift initially benefitted colonists and settlers by facilitating their drive to independence, but the lot of colonized indigenous peoples remained unchanged in the emergent nations. They remained relegated to the margins of society with diminutive rights, living on a diminished land base, incapable of sustaining their way of life. As noted by Siegfried Wiessner:

> The problem with the UN's decolonization process was this: the choice as to the political future of colonized peoples was not given to the individual peoples conquered, but to the inhabitants of territories colonized by European conquerors, within the boundaries of the lines of demarcation drawn by the colonizers. Thus the colonizers, by constituting the new country's "people" under the new sovereign's control, continued to rule the colonized from their graves. Orderly as the decolonization process was, it did not account for the peoples who were not yet back on the agenda of the state-centered international decision makers.[11]

The plight of indigenous peoples could not materially improve until the UN human rights system, and emerging body of modern international human rights law, took the unique circumstances of indigenous peoples into account.

That did not happen overnight. It took decades to bring indigenous issues into focus at the United Nations. Before 1971, the problems and needs of the world's indigenous peoples were not on the agenda.[12] In 1971, UN attention turned to indigenous peoples as part of the general fight against racism. In that year, the Commission on Human Rights authorized a study on discrimination against indigenous peoples. Special Rapporteur Martinez Cobo completed the study in 1984. It called UN attention to the shocking predicament of indigenous peoples, who had slumped into dire circumstances as the world's most disadvantaged and downtrodden peoples.[13] Cobo's work prompted the formation of the UN Working Group on Indigenous Populations (WGIP) in 1982. The WGIP was tasked with developing international standards on indigenous rights. In carrying out its mission over the next few years, this organ opened the doors of the UN human rights system to indigenous peoples, and that access helped make the UN much more accountable to indigenous peoples today. One of the early indigenous advocates was Wilton Littlechild, a Cree Indian lawyer from Canada who served in the Canadian Parliament's House of Commons from 1988 to 1993. Littlechild was part of the first indigenous delegation to UN in 1977. He recalls that early period:

> It was the vision of elders, who were fighting for our treaty rights. They realized that all the laws were written by our colonizers, all the judges

> were appointed by their governments, and that we would never get justice under their rules. So we went to the United Nations seeking an independent forum where our concerns would be treated fairly.[14]

In a similar vein, before 1982, the emerging body of international human rights law also took little notice of the specific needs and circumstances of indigenous peoples, as UN human rights treaties, conventions, protocols, and the larger body of customary international law were being developed for the rest of humanity.[15] In the 1980s, that larger body of law began taking notice of indigenous rights, and a common understanding of the nature and content of those rights began to emerge. Those developments contributed to the making of the *Declaration*. For example, the ILO's Indigenous and Tribal Peoples *Convention No. 169* (1989) was adopted to replace an earlier version that would assimilate tribal people into settler societies. The *Convention* called attention to the situation and conditions of tribal and indigenous peoples in the post-colonial world, updated international thought about their rights in the post-colonial era, and adopted "new international standards on the subject with a view to removing the assimilationist orientation of the earlier standards."[16] The draft *Declaration* built on those standards, as well as the work of other UN organs in the late 1980s and early 1990s. That work, in which the United States actively participated, applied general UN treaties and conventions to indigenous peoples, such as the Human Rights Committee work under the *International Covenant on Civil and Political Rights* (ICCPR), the work of the Committee on the Elimination of Racial Discrimination under the *Convention on the Elimination of All Forms of Racial Discrimination*, and the work of the Committee on Economic, Social and Cultural Rights under the *International Covenant on Economic, Social and Cultural Rights*.[17] That trend helped crystallize a broad understanding of indigenous human rights on the basis of general human rights norms and a wide array of international treaties and conventions. The practices and standards developed by these organs for evaluating state conduct continue to be mainstreamed into UN programs and policies today. That trend facilitated WGIP work to develop what was destined to become the most definitive statement of indigenous rights ever made in the modern era of international law, as the WGIP applied conventions, treaties, and customary international human rights law to the situation of indigenous peoples when developing the draft *Declaration.*

Starting in 1985, the WGIP began drafting the *United Nations Declaration on the Rights of Indigenous Peoples.* Eight years later, in 1993, the first draft was produced. At the next level, it was endorsed in 1994 by the Sub-Commission on the Prevention of Discrimination and Protection of Minorities, and it advanced to the Commission on Human Rights. In that body, the text underwent further review, refinement, and development by state actors, diplomats, and indigenous representatives. Over the next twelve years, they performed intensive work during face-to-face negotiations in eleven annual sessions. In defending the text during this time, Andrea Carmen (Yaqui), Executive Director of the International Indian Treaty Council, recounts that indigenous advocates had "a tough time" and were being told by states who wanted to weaken the text that they were living in a dream world.[18] The protracted negotiations produced a compromise text that the Commission endorsed in 2006, and the draft was forwarded to the General Assembly for final consideration. There, each member nation would get to resolve any final concerns about the text and vote on the measure. At that stage, additional changes were made to accommodate demands made by African states.

The General Assembly vote came on September 13, 2007. In a landslide, an overwhelming majority of 144 nations voted favor of the *Declaration*, with four votes against (the United States, Canada, Australia, and New Zealand), and eleven abstentions. By the end of 2010, all four nations that voted against the *Declaration* reversed their position, and two of the abstaining nations have also endorsed the instrument. The measure thus enjoys universal endorsement by all of the voting nations. That widespread approval of 150 nations lends further legitimacy to the instrument, as it takes its place in the UN human rights system.

All along the way, tribal people from around the world coalesced into an international movement, as they participated with diplomats and UN officials in developing, drafting, and negotiating the *Declaration.* It is hard to imagine tribal people in ceremonial garb working alongside straight-laced Western diplomats, but that is precisely what happened! Native American interest in exploring international relief can be traced to the occupation of Wounded Knee in 1973, the 71-day occupation that called attention to neglected problems in Native America.[19] Wounded Knee sparked the decision to go to Geneva, where the arrival of "Red Indians" caused a stir. Over the decades the Native American cadre grew. Native American attorneys, tribes, and NGO organizations played an important role. These advocates included the Six Nations, Navajo Nation, Lummi Nation, Citizen Potawatomi Nation, United Keetoowah Band of Cherokees, Sac and Fox Nation, Cherokee Nation of Oklahoma, Muscogee (Creek) Nation, Inuit Circumpolar Conference, National Congress of American Indians, International Indian Treaty Council, Indian Law Resource Center, Native American Rights Fund, and many others. These pioneers entered the international realm, where no Indian tribe had gone for almost two hundred years.

While most Native American advocates in the United States focused on the domestic body of federal Indian law as the legal framework for the tribal sovereignty movement, a few far-sighted lawyers left the pack to explore international avenues for protecting indigenous rights. One pioneer was Robert Coulter (Citizen Potawatomi Nation), the founder and executive director of the Indian Law Resource Center. He began drafting the prototype declaration with tribal leaders in the United States, Canada, and Central and South America in 1976. Looking back over thirty years later, he recounted the motives and goals for that early work:

> We knew of the terrible inadequacy of legal regimes and the gross violations of indigenous peoples' human rights in most countries. We turned to international law primarily because of the need to overcome and improve national laws and practices and because of the desire to regain a place for indigenous peoples in the international community.[20]

Prompted by the inadequacies of federal Indian law and the failure of federal courts to protect indigenous rights in modern times, Coulter and his Native American colleagues turned to the UN and international law, hoping to call attention to "the injustices of domestic law and using human rights law to improve federal law, policies, and practices."[21]

S. James Anaya (Apache-Purepecha) is another pioneer. I first met this brilliant lawyer, author, and scholar in the 1980s, when he was general counsel for the National Indian Youth Council. In those days, he was already versed in litigating native rights in international institutions and in Latin-American courts. His groundbreaking treatise, *Indigenous Peoples in International Law*, remains the classic legal text on the rights of indigenous peoples in international law.[22] Professor Anaya has chronicled the early conferences between tribal and UN spokespersons, which led to the formation of the WGIP, the organ that became "the largest UN forum dealing with human rights issues, with participation in annual meetings growing from some thirty people in its first sessions in 1982 to over eight hundred in 2001."[23] Those meetings produced an international identity that spurred the indigenous movement at the UN. Today Professor Anaya is the UN Special Rapporteur on the Rights of Indigenous Peoples. He is a leading expert charged with interpreting and implementing the *Declaration*. His UN reports trace the emerging understanding of indigenous rights in the modern era of international human rights law over the last three decades and explain how important norms expressed in the *Declaration* can be found in the larger body of customary international law and in the instruments of the UN human rights system.[24]

As the *Declaration* took shape in the UN, American legal scholars at home, including the noted Arizona law professor, Robert A. Williams, Jr. (Lumbee), produced research that scrutinized the nefarious doctrines embedded in federal Indian law and traced their medieval roots in early international law.[25] Those scholars laid a foundation for law reform in the United States.

A debt of gratitude is owed to the makers of this monumental instrument. It is the only standard-setting human rights instrument created with the participation of the rights holders themselves. It creates a new climate for considering indigenous law and policy. Through the standards developed by these pioneers, 350 million indigenous peoples can rise—like the mythical phoenix—from the ashes of colonization and take their place in modern nations with their human rights as Native peoples intact. Their work has reverberated around the world, as seen in these remarks:[26]

> [T]oday I can announce that the United States is lending its support to this declaration. The aspirations it affirms—including the respect for the institutions and rich cultures of Native peoples—are one[s] we must always seek to fulfill. What matters far more than words—what

matters far more than any resolution or declaration—are actions to match those words.

—Barack Obama, President of the United States of America, endorsing the *Declaration* (Dec. 16, 2010)

That the government endorse the United Nations Declaration on the Rights of Indigenous Peoples as adopted by the United Nations General Assembly on 13 Sept. 2007 and that Parliament and Government of Canada fully implement the standards contained therein.

—House of Commons, Canada Parliament (April 8, 2008)

The Government of Bolivia granted legal status to the United Nations Declaration on the Rights of Indigenous Peoples by the adoption of Act No. 3760 of 7 Nov. 2007. Bolivia has therefore taken the lead in the field of indigenous rights, since it is the first country in the world to have taken this measure.

—Bolivia (Feb. 11, 2008)

The need for legal protection of indigenous peoples' rights is at the top of the international agenda. The recent adoption of the United Nations Declaration on the Rights of Indigenous Peoples after 20 long years of delay provides confirmation of this fact, the Declaration is an instrument for legal, administrative, and policy reform for the nations of the world.

—Peru (Feb. 12, 2008)

The Declaration has been endorsed by both Government and Parliament of Greenland and it has raised expectations of citizens and interest groups. We need to take a closer look at our own compliance with this important (human) rights instrument.

—Greenland, Delegation of Denmark (Aug. 11, 2009)

The Declaration constitutes one of the most significant achievements in this field of human rights, and we are confident that it will advance the rights and ensure the continued development of indigenous peoples around the world. The EU was encouraged by the wide support to the Declaration from Indigenous peoples' representatives, as well as the large number of States. The challenge before us now is to make sure that the indigenous peoples will in fact enjoy the rights recognized in the Declaration.

—Portugal, on behalf of the European Union (Sept. 26, 2007)

The Declaration is a visionary step towards addressing the human rights of indigenous peoples. It sets forth a framework on which States can build or rebuild their relationships with indigenous peoples. [I]t provides a momentous opportunity for States and indigenous peoples to strengthen their relationships, promote reconciliation and ensure that the past is not repeated.

—UN Secretary-General Ban Ki-moon (Aug. 9, 2008)

[T]he Committee recommends that the declaration be used as a guide to interpret the State party's obligations under the Convention relating to indigenous peoples.

—UN Committee on the Elimination of Racial Discrimination (May 9, 2008)

The Inter-American Committee on Human Rights (IACHR) Rapporteurship hopes that the recently approved UN Declaration will facilitate the prompt approval of the OAS Declaration so that the rights of indigenous peoples of the Americas can be recognized and protected.

—Inter-American Commission on Human Rights (Set. 18, 2007)

The recent adoption by the General Assembly by an overwhelming majority of the UN Declaration on the Rights of Indigenous Peoples will provide a new and comprehensive framework for the Special Rapporteur in pursuing the realization of the rights of indigenous peoples, numbering over 315 million around the world, constituting one of the world's most vulnerable groups. Indeed, the adoption of the Declaration requires the continuation of the mandate of the Special Rapporteur, with a view to promote its implementation.

—Egypt, on behalf of the African Group

Today, Australia joins the international community to affirm the aspirations of all Indigenous peoples. The decades of work culminated in a landmark document that reflects and pays homage to the unique place of Indigenous peoples and their entitlement to all human rights as recognized in international law. Today, Australia gives our support to the Declaration.

—Government of Australia (April 3, 2009)

Today, New Zealand changes its position: we are pleased to express our support for the Declaration.

—Simon Power, New Zealand Minister of Justice (April 20, 2010)

The African Commission is confident that the Declaration will become a very valuable tool and a point of reference for the African Commission's efforts to ensure the promotion and protection of indigenous peoples' rights on the African continent.

—Communique on the UNDRIP, Brazzaville,
Republic of the Congo (Nov. 28, 2007)

The Inuit Circumpolar Council and the Saami Council welcome this momentous occasion. For the first time, the world community has proclaimed a universally applicable human rights instrument in order to end centuries of marginalization and discrimination, and to affirm that Indigenous peoples are peoples, equal in dignity and rights with all other peoples.

—Statement of the Arctic Region (Sept. 13, Sept. 2007)

With the passage of the Declaration we herald the dawning of a new era for relations between pacific Indigenous Peoples and States, as well as UN agencies and bodies.

—Pacific Regional Caucus (Sept. 13, 2007)

[The UN Declaration] will be an instrument and tool which we will use to raise the awareness of the society at large on our rights and to make governments address the situation of indigenous peoples who have long suffered from injustice, discrimination, and marginalization.

—Asia Indigenous Peoples Caucus (Sept. 13, 2007)

The Declaration recognizes our collective histories, traditions, cultures, languages, and spirituality. It is an important international instrument that supports the activities and efforts of Indigenous peoples to have their rights fully recognized and implemented by state governments.

—Phil Fontaine, AFN National Chief (Sept. 13, 2007).

CHAPTER THREE
Mounting the Big Horse:
Examining the Purpose, Nature, and Contents of the Declaration

Over two hundred years ago, my Otoe relatives were camped in a horseshoe bend, alongside a river. Suddenly, they were attacked by alien warriors in overwhelming numbers! In the pony herd stood a very large horse that belonged to my great-great-great grandfather. To save his people, my grandfather tied a long buffalo-hair rope to the big horse and rode it across the river. Together, they pulled the people across the water to safety. For rescuing his people, my grandfather was given the name Big Horse. That name is still carried by my *Shunatona* ("Big Horse") relatives to this day.[1] The *Declaration* is like that Big Horse. It can help people in need, by pulling them from the grip of injustice and bringing human rights enjoyed by the rest of humanity. This chapter describes the nature and contents of the *Declaration*.

Purpose and Nature of the UN Declaration

The *Declaration* comprehensively addresses indigenous issues, including Native American concerns in the United States. It is reproduced in its entirety in the appendix. The preamble and forty-six articles reflect the needs and authentic aspirations of indigenous peoples in a human rights framework. The text not only lists the human rights that constitute "minimum standards" for the "survival, dignity and well-being of indigenous peoples of the world," but it also defines the obligations of nations toward their indigenous peoples and provides guidelines for implementing and interpreting the rights and obligations contained in the instrument. Before we examine the content of the forty-six articles, a few preliminary observations about the purpose and nature of the *Declaration* are in order.

The standards in the *Declaration* do not create new or special rights for indigenous peoples. Rather, they arise from norms and obligations that are generally applicable to the rest of the human race under principles of modern international human rights law.[2] The standards elaborate upon that larger body of law—including the core treaties, conventions, and protocols of the UN human rights system—to clarify how it *should be applied* to the "specific cultural, historical, social and economic circumstances" of indigenous peoples.[3] Thus, one purpose of the *Declaration* is to connect the human rights of indigenous peoples to the larger body of international human rights law and make that body of law more accountable to the needs and circumstances of indigenous peoples. That connection serves to close a loophole in international law. As such, the preamble sees the standards as a major step forward in recognizing and promoting the rights and freedoms of indigenous peoples and in the development of the UN human rights field. Declarations in the UN human rights field play an important role in the development of international law because they "represent the dynamic development of international legal norms and reflect the commitment of states to move in certain directions, abiding by certain principles."[4] Indeed, many leading legal experts believe that numerous provisions of the *Declaration* constitute customary international law (See Table 2, Chapter Four). That view is strengthened by every court that has considered the *Declaration*—they have uniformly adopted and applied the standards, making it clear that nations are not free to disregard the standards and are expected to abide by them.[5]

The *Declaration* has a distinct remedial purpose. It is driven by the persistent denial of basic human rights of indigenous peoples by the entrenched forces of colonialism, dispossession, discrimination, and assimilation practices that are justified by nefarious legal doctrines from a bygone era. These powerful forces have long prevented the full application of modern international law, and associated human rights, to indigenous peoples.[6] The preamble describes the problem seen by the General Assembly: it was concerned that "indigenous peoples have suffered historic injustices" from the "colonization and dispossession of their lands, territories, and resources" and this condition prevents them from exercising "their right to development in accordance with their own needs and interests."[7] The preamble recognizes an "urgent need" to respect and promote (1) "the inherent rights of indigenous peoples which derive from their political, economic and social structures and from their cultures, spiritual traditions, histories and philosophies, especially their rights to their lands, territories, and resources"; and (2) the treaties and other agreements with indigenous peoples.[8]

To create conditions for surmounting these problems in a human rights framework, the preamble focuses on principles of equality, diversity, and justice. It proclaims that indigenous peoples are "equal to all other peoples," yet retain a right to be different and be respected as such.[9] In a stride toward rich human diversity, it acknowledges that indigenous peoples "contribute to the diversity and richness of civilizations and cultures, which constitute the common heritage of humankind," and, finally, the preamble declares that indigenous peoples "should be *free from discrimination* of any kind" in the exercise of their rights.[10] The equality principle sternly condemns all forms of discrimination, once and for all, against tribal peoples (including discriminatory doctrines of domestic law regimes):

> [A]ll doctrines, policies and practices based on or advocating superiority of peoples or individuals on the basis of national origin or racial, religious, ethnic or cultural differences are racist, scientifically false, legally invalid, morally condemnable and socially unjust.[11]

This grounding in modern values creates a more just foundation for indigenous rights in the 21st century, and a better climate for promoting them, than the medieval notions of colonialism, conquest, religious intolerance, ethnocentricity, and racial discrimination that underpin early international law and the domestic law regimes that adopted those outmoded values to define tribal rights. That new foundation is sorely needed in many former colonies and settler states before the conditions of indigenous peoples can materially improve.

For example, Indian rights in the United States rest on a foundation fashioned in the 19th century. Much of that foundation remains sound today and should be retained, especially the "inherent tribal sovereignty" doctrine of *Worcester v. Georgia* (1832) and its protectorate framework for protecting Indian nations that exist in the United States as "domestic dependent nations."[12] However, other foundational principles in federal Indian law are embarrassingly outmoded and make Indian rights vulnerable. Those include doctrines of discovery, conquest, and of unlimited Congressional power in Indian affairs, as well as several engrained legal fictions that deem Indians racially and culturally inferior. Rights that spring from that dark well are forever vulnerable and invariably discriminatory. A stronger, more just foundation for Indian rights in the United States is needed—one grounded in a modern world that rejected the doctrines of dispossession long ago—so the Supreme Court can justify decisions based upon values other than conquest, colonization, or racial superiority. The pivotal question becomes: What should the new foundation be? That new foundation can be provided by the precepts of the *Declaration.* The core principles, such as, equality, justice, inherent human rights, and self-determination, which lie at the heart of the *Declaration,* allow jurists and lawmakers to re-conceptualize the foundation for Native American rights in the United States. These precepts can supplement the *Worcester* foundation for Indian rights, if incorporated into federal Indian law, and replace the unjust principles that have long weakened Indian rights. A sounder foundation springs from the values found in contemporary international human rights law.

Another goal of the *Declaration* is nation-building. The paramount challenge of every settler state is to replace the legacy and mindset of colonialism with laws, policies, and legal principles that create a just balance for protecting the rights and relationships of its Native peoples, so they can enter the body politic on a consensual basis, with their rights as indigenous peoples intact. This unfinished business has long confounded and eluded many modern democracies. The *Declaration* provides the pathway for belated nation-building. The standards foster nation-building by creating conditions for justice and help nations mature in several important respects. First, recognition of indigenous rights will "enhance harmonious and cooperative relations between the State and indigenous peoples, based on principles of justice, democracy, respect for human rights, non-discrimination, and good faith."[13] Second, respect for tribal knowledge, cultures and traditional practices will "contribute to sustainable and equitable development and proper management of the environment."[14] Indeed, our nation has not been able to develop a sound land ethic. That cannot be achieved until Native American values, traditional knowledge, and spiritual ties to the land are recognized, respected, and incorporated into the way that America looks at the land.[15] Third, the application of international law and treaty obligations to indigenous peoples creates a "strengthened partnership" between them and the state.[16]

These benefits are brought about by restoring indigenous rights. These are crucial nation-building steps because they serve to heal an inherited legacy of injustice through acts of atonement and reconciliation that allow civil society to move forward with a more just culture.

Overview of UN Standards and Guidelines for Interpreting Them

The UN standards are linked to ten core themes that run throughout the *Declaration*. They are: (1) self-determination and indigenous institutions; (2) equality; (3) life, integrity, and security; (4) cultural rights; (5) education and public media; (6) participation in decision-making and free, prior, and informed consent; (7) economic and social rights; (8) land, territories, and resources; (9) treaties and agreements; and (10) implementation and interpretation.

1. The Self-Determination Principle

Self-determination is a fundamental principle of the highest order fixed in international law. It adheres to every sovereign nation and is also a core human right for all peoples of humanity.[17] As a human right, it means that all peoples are entitled to be in control of their own destinies and live within governing bodies that are devised accordingly.[18] This universal right is accorded to the human family by the *UN Charter* and international human rights law.[19] Article 3 of the *Declaration* extends the same right in the same language to indigenous peoples without qualification:

> Indigenous peoples have the right to self-determination. By virtue of that right they freely determine their political status and freely pursue their economic, social and cultural development.

The framework for indigenous rights is founded on self-determination since no other right in the *Declaration* can be realized without it.[20] Indeed, all other articles are linked to self-determination. They further define its content or provide the tools for realizing that principle.

Self-determination is exercised through self-government and indigenous institutions. Thus, Article 4 affirms a right to self-government in internal and local affairs, as well as the ways and means for financing that autonomous function. Self-government rights include (1) the power to determine the identity, structures and membership of the nation in accordance with indigenous customs, traditions, and procedures, and to determine the responsibilities of its members (Art. 33, 35); and (2) a right to promote, develop, and maintain distinctive indigenous structures, customs, spirituality, traditions, procedures, practices, and juridical systems in accordance with international human rights law (Art. 34). Furthermore, the right to belong to an indigenous community or nation in accordance with the group's customs and traditions must be free from any form of discrimination (Art. 9). Finally, Article 5 affirms the right to maintain and strengthen indigenous peoples' "political, legal, economic, social and cultural institutions, while retaining their right to participate fully, if they choose, in the political, economic, social and cultural life of the State."

Self-determination in the indigenous context does not include a right to succeed from states that recognize human rights, because the *Declaration* disclaims intent to dismember the territorial integrity or political unity of states.[21] Rather, indigenous self-determination runs parallel to state sovereignty and takes place within the body of the state.[22] As explained by Federico Lenzerini:

> [T]he spread of contemporary practice favorable to the recognition of indigenous autonomy seems to demonstrate that, to a certain extent, the idea of indigenous sovereignty, as parallel to State sovereignty (that is to say that the territorial State, pursuant to international law, can to a certain extent regulate, but not preclude, its exercise), has emerged in the context of the international legal order, giving rise to a provision of customary law binding on States to grant a reasonable degree of sovereignty to indigenous peoples. Although such sovereignty is to be exercised within the realm of the supreme sovereignty of the territorial State, it actually produces the result of shifting some aspects of State sovereignty, providing indigenous peoples with some significant sovereign prerogatives that previously belonged to the State and that, at least in principle, may be opposed to the State itself under general international law. This outcome certainly represents an excellent step forward in the context of the evolution of international law towards a just, fair, and "pluralistic" legal system.[23]

Self-determination allows indigenous peoples to (1) determine their relationship with the state, (2) be involved in setting up the structure under which they live, and (3) maintain their own political system and institutions. These rights are inextricably linked to other cultural, economic, land, and political rights in the *Declaration*.[24] As Vine Deloria, Jr. has stated, indigenous sovereignty "consist[s] more of a continued cultural integrity than of political powers and to the degree that a nation loses its sense of cultural identity, to that degree it suffers a loss of sovereignty."[25] Since indigenous self-determination with these attributes is seen as an inalienable human right, it follows that the power of the state to diminish, curtail, abolish, or terminate the right is no longer unfettered.

2. Equality and Non-Discrimination

Many citizens take conditions of equality for granted. Great strides were made in the 20th century to promote equality for the human race. The challenge posed by the *Declaration* is to extend those principles to indigenous peoples. This is done by the preamble and Articles 1, 2, and 15. They condemn discrimination against indigenous peoples and affirm to them the same human rights enjoyed by the rest of humanity.

Article 1 connects and extends the human rights and fundamental freedoms of the *UN Charter*, Declaration of Human Rights, and international human rights law to indigenous peoples. Article 2 proclaims them "equal to all other peoples" with "the right to be free from any kind of discrimination." As mentioned earlier, the preamble condemns all forms of racial, religious, and cultural discrimination as "racist, scientifically false, legally invalid, and socially unjust." Article 15 prohibits discrimination in public media and education.

This framework fosters the social conditions necessary for implementing the *Declaration*, because indigenous rights cannot be fully realized in settler states until the universal values of equality are extended to indigenous peoples. Discrimination has always been a tremendous problem for indigenous peoples.[26] There are long histories of virulent forms of racial, cultural, and religious discrimination in colonized lands. Prejudice pervaded colonialism. The peculiar forms of racism have many faces, but all stem from the same premise: *tribal people are inferior*. That mindset accompanied the dispossession processes and became engrained in most doctrines, laws, policies, and programs affecting tribal people. During colonization, all things "native" were inferior and dangerous in Eurocentric minds. By disparaging tribal people, and holding their ways of life in contempt, settlers could justify distasteful acts of colonization. As tribal people were engulfed, settler states pronounced them "primitive," with savage ways of life and barbarous or childlike customs. Far from fostering conditions of equality, this attitude sees aboriginal people as subhuman, animal-like creatures. In many places they were vilified as "vermin," "monkeys," "savage beasts," "wolves," "pigs," "baboons," "vipers," "curs," "cockroaches," or "insects." That climate breeds exploitation, injustice, violence, and, at its worst, incubates conditions for genocide.

In short, the mindset of discrimination against tribal people is anathema to human rights. Where it persists, their rights are scarcely recognized, if at all. It is hard to eradicate a long heritage of discrimination from the modern institutions, customs, social mores, policies, and laws of settler nations with such histories, especially when it permeates the domestic order. In particular, courts and legal systems became entrenched with that heritage. They eagerly embraced and applied doctrines of discrimination during the early nation-building process. Today they are often among the last to discard those doctrines, long after the rest of society has repudiated nefarious ideas about tribal people. Against this background, the principles of equality, non-discrimination, and enjoyment of human rights are the starting point for recognizing rights in the *Declaration* and a precondition for promoting them.

3. Survival Rights: Life, Integrity, and Security

Survival is a paramount concern of tribal peoples. Many groups went extinct in the 20th century. Others are endangered today, as they cling to primal religions and hunting, fishing, and gathering ways of life in aboriginal habitats. Many small tribes live in remote places under the threats of violence, removal, habitat destruction, and assimilation; some are stalked by poor conditions, war, and genocide. As such, they are the most vulnerable people in the world. The cultural holocaust confronting the world's remaining tribal cultures concerns everyone, because they store a treasure trove of ancient wisdom and knowledge, including the earliest modes of human existence, with spiritual ties to the natural world and rich cosmologies long forgotten by modern society in the industrialized age. When these cultures die, "vast archives of knowledge and expertise are spilling into oblivion, leaving humanity in danger of losing its past."[27] This dire situation presents a universal question: How should the modern world comport itself toward the last remaining tribal peoples and their ways of life? The *Declaration* creates conditions for their survival as culturally distinct peoples. Its remedies seek to halt the alarming slide toward extinction and homogenization seen in the 20th century, without creating the "living museums" seen in some settler societies.

Articles 7–9 prohibit the destruction of indigenous peoples. Article 7 affirms an individual right to life, physical integrity, liberty, and security *and* a group right to live as distinct peoples in freedom, peace, and security, free from genocide, violence, and the forcible removal of children.[28] Article 8 prohibits forced assimilation and the destruction of indigenous culture. It requires effective state mechanisms to prevent harm to group integrity, cultural values, and ethnic identity by acts of dispossession, forced removal, forced assimilation, and discriminatory propaganda. Article 9 confirms a right to live within the state as an autonomous self-determining group, free from discrimination:

> Indigenous peoples and individuals have the right to belong to an indigenous community or nation, in accordance with the traditions and customs of the community or nation concerned. No discrimination of any kind may arise from the exercise of such right.

These are ingredients for bare survival. They allow tribal groups to survive, live, and prosper, just like any other group of human beings. We can only regret the loss to the human family caused by the disappearance and decline of the world's tribal peoples in the past, but that trend can be reversed under the UN standards.

4. Cultural Rights

The protection of culture is a major theme in the *Declaration*. Most provisions are directly or indirectly linked to cultural preservation, and with good reason: culture gives meaning to human existence. It allows us to become fully human. As such, in the larger body of international law, the right to culture is widely recognized by international treaties, jurisprudence, and practice as an integral part of human rights.[29] And cultural diversity is considered by UNESCO "as necessary for humankind as biodiversity is for nature."[30] The *Declaration* extends the right to culture to indigenous peoples, with the same respect and protection enjoyed by all other cultures.

Scant protection exists for tribal culture in too many places. The lack of protection contributed to the disappearance of many cultures in the 20th century. They succumbed to a multifaceted assault on culture described by the International Law Association:

> Throughout history, patterns of cultural violence against indigenous peoples have included seizure of their traditional lands, expropriation and commercial exploitation of their cultural objects without their consent, misinterpretation of indigenous histories, mythologies and cultures, suppressing of their languages and religions and even their forcible removal from their families and denial of their identity. Recent years have witnessed the development of new practices of violating indigenous cultures; in particular, with the emergence of "modernisation", States and international corporations have started expanding their activities into regions previously considered remote and inaccessible, including many indigenous territories. While on the one hand indigenous activism brought publicity about the occurring violations, on the other hand it renewed the interest for acquiring indigenous arts, cultures and sciences, eventually resulting in the commercialization of indigenous cultures. A new wave of tourism has also disrupted indigenous historical and archaeological sites. Moreover, biotechnology and demand for new medicines have intensified the interest in traditional botanology and medicine, resulting in misappropriation of indigenous traditional knowledge and biopiracy.[31]

To counteract the assault on culture, the *Declaration* affirms many sweeping human rights. Together, they comprise a "Magna Carta" for protecting cultural survival and actualizing cultural self-determination for indigenous peoples.

Articles 7 and 8 prohibit acts that destroy indigenous culture, as discussed earlier, while Articles 11 through 13 protect the exercise of indigenous culture. Article 11 affirms the right to practice and revitalize cultural traditions and customs. It also safeguards the physical manifestations of culture (such as archeological and historical sites, artifacts, designs, ceremonies, literature, and the arts) and mandates redress for the taking of cultural, intellectual, religious, and spiritual property without the free, prior, and informed consent of indigenous peoples or in violation of their laws, traditions, and customs. Article 12 focuses on religious liberty. It accords rights (1) to exercise spiritual and religious customs, traditions, and ceremonies; (2) to private access to religious and cultural sites; (3) to the use and control ceremonial objects; and (4) to repatriate human remains. (The repatriation rights of (3) and (4) must be afforded in fair and efficient mechanisms.) Article 13 protects the trappings of culture. It affirms to indigenous peoples a cultural right to revitalize, use, develop, and transmit to future generations their languages, histories, oral traditions, philosophies, writing systems, and literature, and to designate and retain their own names for their communities, places, and persons; and states are obligated to take effective measures to protect this right. Articles 24 and 31 protect cultural rights to traditional medicines, knowledge, expressions, cultural heritage, and all forms of indigenous intellectual property rights; and states are obliged to help realize these rights in cooperation with indigenous peoples.

The cultural rights affirmed by these articles correspond to well-established standards of customary international law.[32] Recent surveys of international and state practices find that the goal of assimilation of indigenous cultures "has largely been abandoned in favor of preservation and reinvigoration of indigenous cultures, languages and religions."[33]

5. Education and Public Media

The *Declaration* is aimed at correcting injustices in education and public media. The International Law Association explains the need for remedial standards:

> Throughout history, education of indigenous peoples has been used by many countries as a tool of forced assimilation and cultural destruction; also, stereotypic and even racist portrayals of indigenous peoples have been perpetrated throughout non-indigenous societies in the media

> and elsewhere, often backed by or tacitly approved by governments themselves. Thus, the articles take on a special meaning and purpose in terms of redressing wrongs (such as forced assimilation or discrimination in education, media, and public life), as well as repairing, restoring, and strengthening indigenous communities and cultures.[34]

Article 14 makes education accountable to indigenous peoples. It affirms to each person the right to an education without discrimination. Furthermore, education may not be used to assimilate children or strip away their culture. On the contrary, it should respect and promote indigenous culture, and states must provide a bicultural education for indigenous peoples "in their own culture and in their own language." In addition, indigenous peoples have the right to establish their own school systems in their own languages with culturally appropriate teaching methods.

Public media is a *double-edged* sword. Whether on TV, in the movies, or in school books, public media is a powerful tool that permeates society. It can promote good or evil, tolerance or intolerance, equality or racism, peace or genocide. Dominated by non-indigenous voices, public media can distort information, create inaccurate or injurious myths affecting indigenous peoples, or ignore them altogether as invisible peoples without relevance or importance in the states where they live. To combat prejudice, eliminate discrimination, and promote a culture of tolerance, as well as understanding and good relations between indigenous peoples and all segments of society, Article 15 makes public media and information accountable to cultural pluralism and the conditions for equality. It states: "Indigenous peoples have the right to the dignity and diversity of their cultures, traditions, histories, and aspirations which shall be appropriately reflected in education and public information." Article 16 integrates the media in two ways. First, it affirms the right of indigenous peoples to establish their own media in their own languages, and, second, it recognizes the right of access to all forms of non-indigenous media without discrimination. The state's duty to make public media accountable to indigenous peoples under Articles 15 and 16 is linked to its duties to protect the culture, foster self-determination, and permit the exercise of indigenous rights free from any form of discrimination.

Articles 14 through 16 continue a trend seen in laws, constitutions, rules, programs, and practices in nations around the world.[35]

6. Participation in Decision-Making; Free, Prior and Informed Consent

States frequently make decisions affecting vital indigenous interests with little or no input from indigenous peoples, even in democratic forms of government. When the decision-making power over indigenous peoples is absolute and unbridled, state edits can trample human rights without accountability, whether such edits arise from executive, legislative, or judicial action. The *Declaration* seeks to curb this inequity by affirming the right of participation by indigenous peoples in government decisions that affect their lives. Without effective input, intolerable conditions emerge and governance becomes rough-shod; aboriginal interests invariably fall unaddressed by the wayside, and harmonious and cooperative relations are stymied—simply because decision-makers ignore marginalized people who live under the feet of the government. To remedy this situation, Articles 3–5, 10–12, 14, 15, 17–19, 22, 23, 26–28, 30–32, 36, 38, 40, and 41 create an extensive right to participate in decision-making in issues affecting indigenous rights and interests. The nature of the right is described in Article 19:

> States shall consult and cooperate in good faith with the indigenous peoples concerned through their own representative institutions in order to obtain their free, prior and informed consent before adopting and implementing legislative or administrative measures that may affect them.

The "free, prior and informed consent" standard runs throughout the *Declaration*. Under this standard, consent must be *free* (i.e., without coercion, manipulation, pressure, or intimidation), *prior* (to approval, with time to gather and evaluate facts), *informed* (by all relevant information available to make a decision), and reached with involvement by authorized indigenous leaders, representatives, or decision-making institutions pursuant to their own procedures.[36] These elements apply to every proposal affecting indigenous interests—including legislative, administrative, project, or policy proposals—including government undertakings that affect:

- Indigenous cultures, property, land, and religious places;
- Treaties and agreements with indigenous peoples;
- Large developments and tourism in tribal territory;
- Use of natural resources, genetic material, and intellectual property;
- Laws and policies pertaining to indigenous peoples; and
- Socio-economic, health, and educational programs.

In implementing this framework for decision-making, states and indigenous peoples will confront difficult issues. Do the consent provisions mean that indigenous peoples must always give their consent prior to the application of any laws or administrative decisions to them? In UN debates about Article 19, some states believed that the consent provisions amount to a "veto power" with far-reaching consequences and a disruptive effect upon democratic political systems. To address and temper that concern, revisions were made in the final text of Article 19. The phrase "shall obtain consent" was changed to "shall consult and cooperate in good faith" to obtain consent.[37] That change in emphasis might open working space to incorporate effective provisions into domestic systems during the implementation process.[38] At minimum, the consent provisions clearly replace paternalism and unbridled power with true accountability whenever indigenous interests may be affected, and it is clear that government edicts that neglect, disregard, or fail to consider indigenous concerns do not pass muster.

In addition, Article 5 reaffirms a right to participate fully in the political, economic, social, and cultural life of the state. This is done by individuals, or through tribal governments and institutions, which act in the self-determination framework as a nexus between indigenous peoples and the state to facilitate increased and effective participation in the public life of the state. When read against all of the other rights in the *Declaration*, the participatory rights of indigenous peoples are intended to bring them into the body politic under conditions of respect, equality, and justice, with their human rights as indigenous peoples intact.

7. Economic and Social Rights

The very purpose of colonialism was to occupy the land and extract wealth for the benefit of settlers and elites in Europe. With the spread of colonialism, a massive one-way transfer of property and wealth from indigenous to non-indigenous hands occurred, and that phenomena became the central economic feature in colonized areas. As the natives were systematically stripped of their land, natural resources, traditional means of subsistence, and cultural wealth, they saw their habitats destroyed by development, and they swiftly became the poorest, most disadvantaged people in the world, according to every socio-economic indicator. The International Law Association describes the deplorable economic and social problems confronting indigenous peoples today:

> For many of the world's indigenous peoples the impact of colonialism and the consequent loss of autonomy and independence has resulted in their economic exploitation and marginalisation. The loss of control over their resources, the exploitation of those natural resources in ecologically unsustainable fashion, the often brutal and forced use of indigenous labor including systematic abuse of child labor, and similar forms of discriminatory and demeaning behaviors by settlers, authorities and companies have led to economic impoverishment and social harm. The situation is captured in many countries by indicators that measure the gap between economic and social outcomes for indigenous peoples as against the majority of the population. Such gaps cannot only be explained in terms of differing aspirations and a lesser emphasis on material outcomes. They are indicators of real poverty and social distress. In particular, significantly lower life expectancy, low educational attainment, high rates of criminalization, and significant problems such as alcohol and substance abuse and domestic violence are indicators of harm and dysfunction.[39]

Articles 17, 20–24, 26, and 44 are designed to reverse these conditions and improve the lot of indigenous peoples. Taken together, they constitute a modern-day "Marshall Plan" to rebuild the social and economic conditions of the world's indigenous peoples through a human rights framework.

As a first step, Article 17 addresses labor. Under the equality principle, it reaffirms to indigenous peoples all rights secured by international and domestic labor law and requires states to take specific measure to protect indigenous children. Second, Article 20 restores traditional economies. Subsection 1 affirms the right to maintain indigenous political, economic, and social systems, and it also protects indigenous "means of subsistence and development" as well as the right to "engage freely in all their traditional and other economic activities." Subsection 2 requires redress whenever that means of subsistence is deprived. Similarly, Article 26.2 provides a right for indigenous peoples to develop "the lands, territories and resources that they possess." Article 21 recognizes a right to *improvement* of economic and social conditions and requires effective measures by the state to improve those conditions. Subsection 2 (as well as Article 22) requires that special attention be paid by the state to the needs of indigenous elders, woman, children, and the disabled. They must be protected from violence and discrimination (Article 22) and women are granted all rights in the *Declaration* equally with men (Article 44). Article 23 states that indigenous peoples have the right to determine, develop, and prioritize strategies for exercising their right to development, with active involvement in socio-economic programs affecting them (including administering those programs through their own institutions). Article 24 addresses health. It secures the right to traditional medicines and health practices, including the conservation of medicinal plants, animals, and minerals, and it reaffirms the right of access to all social and health services without discrimination. It proclaims "an equal right to the enjoyment of the highest attainable standard of physical and mental health" and requires states to take necessary steps to fully realize this right.

8. Land, Territories, and Resources

Unrelenting greed drove the spread of colonialism to the far corners of the earth. The imperative of every settler colony was to occupy the land. Wholesale displacement was necessary to wrest the land from aboriginal owners. The largest land grab ever witnessed was accomplished by every means known to humankind (See Table 1, Chapter Three). A partial list includes everything from invasion and warfare to individual acts of violence, massacre, threats, coercion, theft, trickery, bribery, alcohol, trinkets, lies, treaty cessations, confiscation, acts of genocide (in all its known forms), and outright removal—not to mention the widespread use of law to make everything perfectly legal. Even the Pope was involved. After five hundred years, many indigenous peoples' resources were picked clean, except for isolated pockets of land—and those vulnerable remnants were up for grabs whenever wanted by states, corporations, or power elites.

TABLE 1

How colonies/settler states acquired indigenous land.

(In Alphabetical Order: The ABC's of Colonialism)

A–acts of Congress, armed force, adverse possession, allotments, alcohol

B–bloodshed, bribery, broken promises, bullets

C–canons, cavalry, chicanery, colonial charters, conquest, confiscation, condamnation, courts, coup d'état

D–deeds of sale, discriminatory land rights, discovery doctrine, driving game away, disease, duress

E–easements, ecocide, executive orders, executive acts

F–forced allotment, fraud, falsification of documents

G–guardianship, genocide, germs, guns, gunboats

H–homestead laws, harassing, haranguing, hunting down natives

I–Indian wars, invasion, intimidation, international conventions, inequitable laws, illegal violence

J–jingoistic legal opinions, just wars, judicial acts

K–kangaroo courts, killing

L–land grabs, land rushes, laws, lies, lotteries, legal fictions, leases, legislative acts

M–massacre, military expeditions, militarizing Indian land, money, murder, miscarriages of justice

N–naval operations, non-recognition of indigenous property rights

O–occupation, offers to purchase, operation of law, overthrow, onslaughts of development

P–papal bulls, plenary power, poison, presidential proclamations, purchase

Q–quelling rebellion, quests for gold

R–removal, relocation, royal edits, resource exploitation

S–soldiers, sailors, speculation, swords, Supreme Court opinions, survey errors

T–taxes, termination laws, theft, treaties, trickery, trinkets, trade, transfer of Indian land to missionaries, trusteeship

U–unfettered power, unmitigated greed, unchecked avarice

V–violence, vehement denial of indigenous land and human rights

W–war

X–xenophobic laws and policies

Y–yoking tribes and indigenous yeomen to unjust laws

Z–zoning, zealous drive for land and resources by colonial powers

To halt and reverse the trend toward dispossession, Articles 10, 25–30, and 32 recognize broad rights to land, territories, and resources. These rights are among the most important rights in the *Declaration* because land is the wellspring for indigenous society and cultural identity. These societies sprang from soil and maintain strong ties to the homeland habitats that birthed their religions, ways of life, cosmologies, histories, economies, and identities. Because the human rights that flow from indigenous land are many, the loss of land is intolerable. Under the *Declaration*, indigenous peoples have a right to:

1. Maintain and strengthen their spiritual relationship with traditionally owned or otherwise occupied and used lands, territories, waters, and coastal seas (Art. 25);
2. Own, use, develop, and control those areas and resources (Art. 26);
3. Determine the development strategies and priorities (Art. 32); and
4. Forcible removal is prohibited without their free, prior, and informed consent (Art. 10).

As duty-bearers, states must: (1) recognize and protect these areas and resources with due respect for indigenous customs, traditions, and land tenure (Art. 26); (2) establish impartial processes in consultation with indigenous peoples to recognize and adjudicate their rights; (3) provide redress for property taken without free, prior, and informed consent (Art. 27, 28); (4) consult to obtain such consent before approving projects affecting those areas or resources; and create mechanisms and measures for redress and mitigation (Art. 32); (5) conduct conservation programs to protect the environment and productive capacity of those lands and resources (Art. 29); and (6) refrain from military activity on the land unless justified by public necessity and agreed to by affected indigenous peoples (Art. 30).

9. Treaties and Agreements

Some nations, like the United States, have a long treaty-making history with indigenous peoples. The agreements affected interests vital to the signatories. They acquired and opened indigenous land to settlement, fixed boundaries, made peace, fixed political relationships, and often reserved important rights to the indigenous signatories in exchange for their land and other concessions. During the first one hundred years of its existence, the United States concluded hundreds of treaties, as the primary means used by the republic to deal with tribal nations and implement Indian policy. After the United States unilaterally ended the treaty making era, the United States continued to make important agreements with Indian tribes well into the 20th century. Many treaty provisions and agreements were violated by states or never fulfilled. The preamble notes an "urgent need" to respect and promote indigenous treaty rights and agreements with states.[40] Article 37 requires states to recognize, observe, and enforce them, and it emphasizes that a "strengthened partnership" will emerge when treaty relationships are honored.[41] Indeed, new treaties can constitute one acceptable method for implementing the UN standards, including the one that requires free, prior, and informed consent before the state takes actions affecting indigenous peoples.

10. Implementation and Interpretation

The *Declaration* is not a self-executing instrument. It presents a map of action, with standards "to be pursued in a spirit of partnership and mutual respect."[42] Implementation requires affirmative action by indigenous peoples, state institutions, and civil society. Guidelines are provided for interpreting and implementing the *Declaration*.

Implementation through a respectful and collaborative approach is widely endorsed. After all, the "process" followed in any great venture is often as important as the goal. War calls for warlike methods; whereas pursuit of justice requires good faith and widespread collaboration among all sectors of society. Consequently, consultation, partnership, and cooperation are the touchstones for achieving the strengthened partnership and "harmonious and cooperative relations between the State and indigenous peoples, based on principles of justice, democracy, respect for human rights, and good faith," which the *Declaration* seeks.

States are key partners in the implementation process. They have important obligations as duty-bearers. The *Declaration* tasks them with providing effective measures, mechanisms, technical assistance, and funding to fully realize the rights affirmed in the *Declaration*. Article 38 describes the state obligation:

> States, in consultation and cooperation with indigenous peoples, shall take the appropriate measures, including legislative measures, to achieve the ends of this Declaration.

The *Declaration* requires many specific measures, taken in good faith, to effectively protect and fully realize specific rights. Most of them must be developed, implemented, and administered *bilaterally* by the state—that is, in consultation and cooperation with indigenous peoples as active participants, and with due respect given to their customs and laws. Importantly, courts are not considered sacrosanct. Article 40 requires a juridical system that is: (1) fair, (2) independent, and (3) transparent—with access to (4) prompt and effective mechanisms to resolve disputes, adjudicate indigenous rights, and remedy infringements in decisions that "give due consideration to the customs, traditions, rules and legal systems of the indigenous peoples concerned and international human rights."

To meet their duties under the *Declaration*, states must, at minimum, do the following:

- Provide: (1) financial and technical assistance (Art. 39); (2) culturally appropriate education (Art. 14); (3) equal access to health and social services (Art. 24); (4) assistance to ensure that state-owned and public information and media is accountable to indigenous peoples and free from any form of discrimination (Art. 15–16); (5) conservation programs for indigenous lands, territories, and resources (Art. 29); (6) fair and independent adjudicatory mechanisms to resolve disputes by decisions that give due recognition to indigenous customs, traditions, law, and land tenure (Art. 40); (7) improved social and economic conditions (Art. 21); (8) legal recognition and protection for indigenous lands, territories, and resources (Art. 26).

- Prevent: (1) any acts that deprive or destroy cultural integrity, identity, or culture (Art. 8); (2) militarization of indigenous land without public necessity and indigenous consent (Art. 30); (3) discrimination against indigenous peoples when exercising their right to belong to an indigenous community or nation in accordance with the customs and traditions of the group (Art. 9); and (4) storage of hazardous waste on indigenous lands or territories without their consent (Art. 29);

- Redress: (1) unauthorized takings of cultural property and human remains (Art. 11–12); (2) harm to subsistence rights, lands, territories, and resources (Art. 20, 28, 32); (3) removal of indigenous peoples without their consent (Art. 10); (4) dispossession of lands, territories, and resources (Art. 8); (5) any form of forced assimilation or integration (Art. 8); (6) any form of propaganda designed to promote or incite racial or ethnic discrimination against indigenous peoples (Art. 8); (7) infringements upon human rights (Art. 40);

- Protect: (1) rights to land, territories, resources, language, history, names, and cultural heritage and expressions, including intellectual property rights (Art. 13, 26–27, 31); (2) women and children from exploitation and violence (Art. 17, 22); traditional medicine practices, including medicinal plants and animals (Art. 24); (3) border crossing rights of indigenous peoples divided by international borders (Art. 36); (4) indigenous peoples from prejudice and discrimination (Art. 15);

- Consult/Cooperate: (1) before approving any laws, administrative measures, projects, or socio-economic or health programs affecting indigenous peoples, lands, territories, or resources (Art. 19, 23, 29, 32, 38); (2) in devising mechanisms to protect indigenous peoples from discrimination in public information and media (Art. 15, 16), as well as economic exploitation, violence, and discrimination (Art. 17, 22); (3) in developing and administering fair and effective adjudicatory mechanisms to protect indigenous rights (Art. 27); (4) in protecting cultural rights (Art. 31) and border crossing rights (Art. 36); (5) and in taking measures to achieve the ends of the *Declaration* (Art. 38); and

- IMPROVE: (1) education and socio-economic conditions (Art. 14, 21).

These are wide-ranging obligations. They implicate every branch of government and require an ambitious nation-building program conducted systematically by the government and indigenous peoples in a spirit of cooperation.[43] Article 38 suggests that governments and indigenous peoples should develop a national plan for identifying appropriate measures to achieve the ends of the *Declaration*. Some nations, like Bolivia, simply enacted a law that adopts the provisions of the *Declaration* in wholecloth.[44] However, indigenous organizations recommend that the parties undertake a comprehensive review of existing laws, policies, programs, and problems as the starting place for developing a national plan of action, with clear timelines and priorities.[45] It goes without saying that implementation of the *Declaration* is the key to realizing indigenous human rights. According to Professor Anaya:

> In the end, the Declaration on the Rights of Indigenous Peoples will have little practical meaning in the lives of those it is intended to benefit unless its standards are implemented at the local level and adhered to by state authorities. [T]he Declaration explicitly addresses states and calls upon them to take the measures necessary to make the articulated rights reality. This feature of the Declaration corresponds with the duty states generally have to safeguard human rights and provide remedies when they are violated, a duty that relates to the international

> law on state responsibility in regard to unlawful acts and omissions. In order for the Declaration to be implemented in any given country, the rights affirmed must come to be—in one way or the other—respected and promoted in the state's administrative practices, incorporated into its legal system, and enforced by courts or other authorities with power to mandate or take corrective action.[46]

Guidelines for interpreting the *Declaration* are important. They help us understand the content of indigenous rights and duties of the state. At the outset it is important to bear in mind that the articles cannot be considered in isolation. They are closely linked to one another and to the larger body of international human rights law. To fully grasp the meaning of an article, one must read it against the *Declaration* in its entirety and in relation to applicable international law.

Five rules guide the interpretation of the *Declaration*:

1. The recognized rights constitute "minimum standards for the survival, dignity and well-being of the indigenous peoples of the world." (Art. 43)
2. The rights are interpreted in accordance with "principles of justice, democracy, respect for human rights, equality, non-discrimination, good governance and good faith." (Art. 46)
3. The rights are also understood against the backdrop of international human rights law and standards (17, 19, 22–23, Art. 34); and courts must give "due consideration" to international human rights when deciding indigenous issues (Art. 40).
4. Acceptable limits are placed upon the rights and duties. Article 46 does not authorize any action that would be contrary to the UN Charter, dismember the territorial integrity or political unity of states, or impair the rights and freedom of others.
5. To satisfy their obligations, governments bear a rigorous standard of achievement: the full application of each provision, with effective measures to fully realize rights affirmed in the *Declaration*. (See, e.g., Art. 42)

In summary, the purpose, nature, and contents of the *Declaration* confirm that this remarkable instrument is very much like the "Big Horse" in my grandfather's story. In its comprehensive provisions, we can see the coming of a New Age.

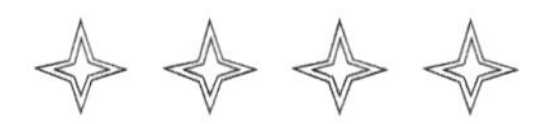

CHAPTER FOUR
Legal Status of the Declaration

> When the United States declared their independence, they were bound to receive the law of nations, in its modern state of purity and refinement.
> —United States Supreme Court, *Ware v. Hylton,* 1 L. Ed. 569 (1796).

From the very beginning, international law strongly shaped indigenous rights in North America. This body of law guided European expansion into the New World, as the Old World kingdoms forged treaty relationships with tribal nations. It provided rules for colonizing North America to minimize violence among colonial powers competing for hegemony over the continent. After independence, Chief Justice John Marshall drew heavily from the law of nations to make indigenous law for the new republic.[1] In *Johnson v. M'Intosh* (1823), the Supreme Court incorporated the international law doctrines of discovery and conquest into domestic law.[2] They were adopted in whole cloth to define tribal land rights. A decade later, the Marshall Court used the law of nations to define tribal sovereignty in our political system and fix the Indian nations' relationship with the United States.[3] In *Worcester v. Georgia* (1832), the Court looked to settled international law and the international practices of nations of the day to fashion the foundational principles of federal Indian law.[4] In short, the international legal realm was a primary source for defining tribal rights in the United States. Its central place in our legal framework is described in *Cohen's*:

> In establishing the fundamental rules governing the relationship between Indian tribes and the United States, early United States Supreme Court cases relied extensively on international law. The discovery doctrine, the existence and scope of Indian title to property, and even the concept of inherent tribal sovereignty, all originated in international norms, which the Supreme Court adapted to the American setting.[5]

Given this dynamic interaction, our domestic law should logically keep pace with international norms on indigenous issues. Indeed, courts usually interpret international law as it has evolved and exists today, not as it was hundreds of years ago,[6] and modern international law exerts a strong influence on the development of common law when it "declares the existence of universal human rights."[7] This should be especially true in the United States, where customary international law forms a part of the federal common law and where the United States has long held a leadership role in the protection of human rights.[8]

The need to keep abreast of modern international law is the challenge examined in this book. That goal cannot be assured without taking systematic steps to implement the *Declaration*. It is not a self-implementing instrument; nor can we safely assume that federal courts will enforce every provision without the aid of an act of Congress. To understand the legal character of the *Declaration* and the need to implement its provisions into American law and social policy, this chapter tours the international legal realm to explore several questions. What is the nature of international law (sometimes referred to as "the law of nations")? How are rules made in international law? We shall focus on the role and purpose of declarations in the UN human rights system and explore how evolving international norms and the practices of nations can sometimes crystallize or ripen into binding and enforceable domestic law. Guidelines will emerge for identifying which parts of the *Declaration* are currently enforceable in the courts and those needing legislation before they become enforceable.

At the outset, three general observations can be made about the legal character of the *Declaration*. First, the *Declaration* as a whole is not itself a legally binding instrument that is directly enforceable in federal courts as binding law of its own accord. At most, specific provisions can be enforced by courts to the extent they reflect customary international law or existing treaty obligations.[9] The bulk of this chapter examines relevant treaty obligations and customary law norms that might relate to provisions of the *Declaration*. Otherwise, the *Declaration* is not a self-executing treaty or convention, and its provisions must be effectuated and carried into law by acts of the legislative, executive, and judicial branches of government before enforceable legal rights and duties can be recognized by US courts.

This rule comports with language in the *Declaration*, and it reflects prevailing expert opinion.[10] After all, Article 38 asks states to take appropriate measures to achieve the ends of the *Declaration* in cooperation and consultation with indigenous peoples. At the same time, a comparison of the *Declaration* with existing UN human rights treaties shows "significant synergy between general state human rights obligations and the rights affirmed in the Declaration."[11] In addition, many experts believe that key rights in the *Declaration* arise from, are connected to, and constitute settled rules of customary international human rights law, such as:

1. A right to self-determination that secures to indigenous peoples the right to decide their future within the state where they live;[12]
2. A right to autonomy or self-government in states where indigenous peoples live, together with a right of consultation and participation in government decisions affecting them;
3. A right to culture, including the right not to be subjected to genocide and ethnocide;
4. A right to traditional lands and natural resources, including the right of not being removed without the consent of indigenous peoples;
5. A right to reparation and redress for wrongs suffered for breach of rights recognized by customary international law; and
6. A right to expect that treaties will be honored and enforced.[13]

For the most part, these key rights are familiar in American courts where they are often recognized and protected under federal Indian law, constitutional law, statutory law, or federal common law. The enforceability of these rights as customary international law or as US treaty obligations can be tested during the implementation of the *Declaration* in the coming years. As the noted international law scholar Siegfried Wiessner points out, we can safely assume that "the U.S. Supreme Court will enforce self-executing treaties and customary international law."[14]

Second, consistent with the above rule, the *Declaration* sets out the path for achieving its ends. After the president's endorsement in 2010, the provisions of the *Declaration* must be incorporated by the US government, in consultation and cooperation with indigenous peoples, into our law and policy. The implementation process is accomplished through positive measures taken by the legislative, executive, or judicial branches—by acts that are designed to operationalize and fully realize the rights and duties affirmed in the *Declaration*. This is the process envisioned by the General Assembly, as seen in the language of the *Declaration*, and it is the avenue emphasized in this book.[15] The call for positive or special measures to implement the *Declaration* is well-described in UN Special Rapporteur Anaya's Report to the UN Human Rights Council (2008):

- 45. The Declaration requires that "States, in consultation and cooperation with indigenous peoples, shall take the appropriate measures, including legislative measures, to achieve the ends of this Declaration" (art. 38). This general mandate is further elaborated on in other provisions, with specific affirmative measures required from States in connection with almost all the rights affirmed in the Declaration.

- 46. The kind of State action required to operationalize the rights affirmed in the Declaration thus entails an ambitious programme of legal and policy reform, institutional action and reparations for past wrongs, involving a myriad of State actors within their respective spheres of competence. The former chair of the Working Group on Indigenous Populations, Ms. Erica-Irene Daes, described this process as "belated State-building," a process "through which indigenous peoples are able to join with all other peoples that make up the State on mutually agreed upon and just terms, after many years of isolation and exclusion. This spirit of cooperation and mutual understanding between States and indigenous peoples is a theme throughout the Declaration, including in the provision which underlines the value of historical and modern treaties or compacts as mechanisms to advance relations of cooperation between indigenous peoples and States (art. 37).[16]

The UN report details implementation work that can be done in all sectors of government by key actors, such as the domestic courts, legislative bodies, and administrative agencies to mainstream the *Declaration* into domestic law and policy, including awareness-raising work among civil society (i.e., the body politic of the state) and indigenous peoples themselves.[17] Broad-based state action is needed to systematically implement and fully realize the rights and duties affirmed in the *Declaration*:

> The Special Rapporteur fully acknowledges the serious technical difficulties, as well as the economic, social, and political obstacles, that States encounter in undertaking the kind of systemic action and reforms required to fully and effectively respect the rights of indigenous peoples and to reverse the long-standing patterns of abuse and discrimination that they face. In the light of such difficulties, the United Nations system has considered that the situation of indigenous peoples is a matter of global concern and of urgent priority, and is deemed to play an important role in supporting State action towards the implementation of the Declaration.[18]

Third, regardless of its enforceability as binding law, the *Declaration* is an "authoritative statement" of indigenous rights in the United States, with standards that build on UN treaties within the broader obligation of the United States to advance human rights under the *UN Charter*.[19] In that regard, the *Declaration* carries immediate power in several important respects: (1) it can be used by tribal litigants to influence courts in pending lawsuits as a persuasive authority when interpreting or reinterpreting federal Indian law doctrines and judicially made law; (2) it can guide and influence lawmakers and policymakers when making new Indian laws and policies; (3) the widely approved international standards are a barometer for measuring state conduct, laws, and practices and for judging that conduct in the court of world opinion; (4) the UN standards can guide Indian Country in setting the agenda for social and legal reform for the 21st century; and (5) as mentioned above, courts can enforce provisions of the *Declaration* that constitute customary international law or existing treaty obligations of the United States. At the end of the day, compliance with international standards hinges more on their moral power and growing acceptance in the usages and practice of affected nations than upon their binding character in international law. Just as modern nations have renounced torture, genocide, piracy, slavery, and cruel and unusual punishment in the world today, the human rights of indigenous peoples will be restored by nations primarily because it is the *right thing to do* in the post-colonial age.

Overview of International Law in the Modern Era

A full treatment of the complex body of comprehensive international law and its many doctrines is outside the scope of this book. For present purposes, an overview of pertinent aspects of international law provides a context for placing the *Declaration* into the proper perspective for implementing the provisions of this international instrument into the law and policy of the United States. Accordingly, this section will define modern "international law" and briefly explore how it makes rules of conduct—particularly those international rules related to the *Declaration* that might be considered binding upon the United States and enforceable as federal law in American courts.

Historically, early international law regulated only the relations among nations and was concerned with the concomitant obligations that those relations impose upon nations; it did not address the domestic internal affairs of independent sovereign nations, which were traditionally left to the exclusive domain of domestic law. Thus, Vattel's *Law of Nations* described international law as "the science which teaches the rights subsisting between nations or states, and the obligations correspondent to those rights."[20] The early law of nations imposed obligations upon nations but did not necessarily give rise to private rights that could be enforced by individual persons in domestic courts, except for a rather small body of individual rights admitting of a domestic judicial remedy, such as the immunities and privileges of diplomats or the rights in maritime law that emerged from settled international customary usages and practices.[21] As late as 1963, the prevailing definition of traditional "international law" was "the body of rules and principles of action that are binding upon civilized states in their relations with one another."[22] In short, states alone were subjects of international law—only they were able to hold legal rights and duties derived from the law of nations, and the individual rights of people existed only as domestic rights of the state. That arrangement placed the human rights of individuals *vis-à-vis* their own governments beyond the pale of international law. However, bodies of law continually grow and expand as the needs of society grow and expand, including the focus of international law.

The scope and focus of international law dramatically expanded over the past fifty years. This growth was spurred by several factors, including the creation of the United Nations, the decolonization movement, and the growing field of international human rights law, with its recent emphasis on indigenous issues.[23] As a result, international law is no longer concerned only with relations among nations. It also embraces other entities, such as international organizations—and *individuals* when their human rights are concerned. *Black's Law Dictionary* defines "international law" in the 21st century as:

> The legal system governing the relationship between nations; more modernly, the law of international relations, embracing not only nations but also such participants as international organizations and individuals (such as those who invoke their human rights or commit war crimes).[24]

Modern international law most definitely confers fundamental rights upon people vis-à-vis their own governments, and this is done through treaties and customary international law, the two major sources of international law.[25]

Prior to World War II, human rights were not considered part of international law; rather they attached to the relation between the state and individuals within the purview of domestic jurisdiction, beyond the reach of international law. However, in the modern age, a state's treatment of its own citizens is clearly a matter of international concern.[26] Blatant human rights violations in nations like Rwanda, Bosnia, and South Africa no longer go unchecked by the international order. To be sure, the doctrine of state sovereignty still reigns supreme in the international arena. However, after World War II, the all-powerful states can no longer commit atrocity behind the shield of sovereignty. This dramatic transformation in the nature of international law is described by Professor Wiessner:

> Hitler's blatant abuse of the shield of sovereignty to commit the horror of the Holocaust and his unprovoked attacks on other countries yielded a qualitative change in international law. Its focus shifted to creating individual rights on the international plane via a commitment to human rights, establishing group rights through the right to

> self-determination of peoples, of prohibiting aggression, and delegating powers to the UN and its Security Council to make binding decisions regarding the maintenance of international peace and security. The United Nations and its Charter provided the key mechanisms for this transformation. Thus, international law moved slowly from an exclusively consent-based system to a values-based international legal order.[27]

After the Nuremberg Trials, international law came to regulate the relationship between a nation and its own citizens, particularly in the area of human rights, and it is no longer considered antithetical in the modern era for individuals to assert international legal rights against their own governments.[28] As one recent federal court decision explains, "[t]he singular achievement of international law since the Second World War has come in the area of human rights," and the duties and rights that devolve from the law of nations "now include not merely *states* but also *individuals*."[29]

International Law: How It Is Made, Ascertained, and Enforced

Any discussion about the *Declaration* invariably raises questions about its legal status in international and domestic law, including its enforceability in US courts. Few wade into these murky waters, and most are perplexed by the perceived complexities, uncertainties, and ambiguities of the law of nations. International law has its own institutions of enforcement—such as committee monitoring pursuant to treaties, adjudication in various international tribunals, and collective humanitarian intervention—but the primary means of enforcement has always been domestic legal systems.[30] We shall focus on domestic enforcement because federal courts have routinely ascertained and applied international law since the early days of the republic. Their longstanding role as domestic enforcement mechanisms is described by Professor Wiessner:

> Beyond international law's own structures of enforcement, domestic legal systems should be looked at as the main engines of enforcing international law. In most domestic legal systems, the authoritative and controlling prescriptions of international law have been incorporated as standards of domestic legal systems, invited into the normative

> system of internal law through, usually, prescriptions of the highest rank, such as a constitutive document. In the United States, treaties, at least those of the "self-executing" kind, form part of the "supreme Law of the Land" as defined by the United States Constitution. Customary international law is seen as a standard of federal common law to be used by the courts either on the same level of normative strength as acts of Congress, or on a level just below. Courts in the United States, as well as in other domestic systems, therefore, remain important battlegrounds for the enforcement of international indigenous rights.[31]

This section examines the legal status of the *Declaration* in international law and US law. If the *Declaration* contains legal rights or duties recognized in international law, how are they enforced and protected? Do international rules of conduct become enforceable by US courts as federal law?

As a preliminary matter, it is necessary to consider the nature of "rules" in legal systems. Rules of conduct created by any legal system, whether domestic or international, are grounded in state consent. That is, they emanate from the free will of nations, because the restraints or obligations are self-imposed—they are set in place by nations *themselves* through the operation of domestic or international law.[32] Rules of conduct are made in international law from two principal sources: (1) treaties or conventions, and (2) customary international law derived from the usages and practices of nations.[33] According to *Cohen's*, international law is applied by US courts in three principle ways: "as part of a treaty ratified by the United States, as part of customary international law applied as federal common law, and as an interpretive aid in the construction of United States constitutional or statutory law."[34]

Though sometimes complex, the written and unwritten law of nations produces rules of conduct, and courts have the means of discerning the existence, content, and nature of international standards. The Supreme Court has applied the law of nations and instructed lower courts how to approach the task of discovering the nature and content of international law.[35] To ascertain the nature and content of these rules, courts examine the language of international instruments, and they consult the works of learned scholars or jurists, the general usage and practice of nations, or judicial decisions that recognize and enforce international law—especially when customary international law is concerned.[36] Judges must navigate these waters because international law "is a part of the laws of the United States which federal courts are bound to ascertain and administer in an appropriate case."[37] Those waters tell us how international law can sometimes become "federal law" that US courts must enforce.

1. Role of Treaties and Declarations in International Law

Two kinds of international instruments set standards of behavior agreed to by signatory nations: (1) treaties and conventions possess the force of law in ratifying nations, and (2) declarations and resolutions carry non-binding moral power as statements of principle.[38] Both set standards of behavior.

A US treaty agreement becomes the "supreme Law of the Land" once it is ratified by the Senate.[39] As the law of our land, treaty violations can be directly enforced in US courts in appropriate cases. However, treaties that place binding obligations on the US government do not always create a basis for private lawsuits or automatically constitute binding federal law that is enforceable in federal courts.[40] Rather, the enforceability of treaties turns on a judicial distinction between "self-executing" and "non-self-executing" treaties.[41] John Marshall introduced this distinction in *Foster and Elam v. Neilson* (1829).[42] A self-executing treaty has a distinctive legislative character and upon ratification is automatically *enforceable* as federal law by courts, without the need for an act of Congress.[43] Courts consider several factors to determine whether a treaty is "self-executing."[44] A treaty is self-executing when it (1) involves the rights and duties of individuals, (2) does not cover a subject for which legislation is required under the Constitution, and (3) does not leave discretion to the parties in applying the particular provision.[45] By contrast, the courts enforce "non-self-executing" treaties only after they are implemented, or carried into effect, by appropriate legislation.[46] This is so because they merely contain a commitment by signatory nations to take future action through their political branches. This long-standing rule was recently applied in *Medellin v. Texas* (2008), where the Supreme Court reiterated that a non-self-executing treaty, such as the *UN Charter*, "is not binding domestic law unless Congress has enacted statutes implementing it," emphasizing that US obligations arising from non-self-executing treaties are not binding domestic law in the absence of implementing legislation.[47] Moreover, the *Medellin* Court stressed that the president does not have the power to unilaterally convert a non-self-executing treaty into a self-executing treaty, stating: "The responsibility for transforming an international obligation arising from a non-self-executing treaty into domestic law falls to Congress."[48] Though non-self-executing treaties are incapable of being invoked in US courts without enabling or implementing legislation, they can still play an important role in litigation without such legislation. According to *Cohen's*, they can be raised as a defense to a lawsuit, used to interpret statutes, and rights created by them can arguably be raised in administrative proceedings.[49] They also serve, along with declarations, as evidence to the existence of rights recognized by customary international law, which is another source of enforceable federal law in US courts.

In contrast to treaties, a "declaration" is not a legally binding international instrument. According to *Cohen's*, a declaration is generally considered an "aspirational statement that is not legally binding and not directly enforceable in US courts even if accepted by the United States."[50] Declarations serve several purposes in international law. According to the United Nations, declarations "represent the dynamic development of international legal norms and reflect the commitment of states to move in certain directions, abiding by certain principles."[51] Indeed, when determining whether international law can be enforced as federal law, courts can look to the standards in declarations, as well as treaty obligations, as evidence of customary international law.[52]

The *United Nations Declaration on the Rights of Indigenous Peoples* falls into this category.[53] Rather than contemplating automatic enforceability, language in the *Declaration* calls upon nations to take certain action. The instrument states that it is "a standard of achievement to be pursued in a spirit of partnership and respect," and it is "a further step forward" in recognizing indigenous rights by the UN human rights field.[54] Consequently, in the absence of measures taken to implement the *Declaration,* none of its provisions are directly enforceable in US courts. However, as discussed below, some provisions of the *Declaration* might be *indirectly enforceable* under certain circumstances when they relate to existing US treaty obligations.[55] Those provisions might be indirectly enforceable as treaty obligations, and other provisions that evince customary international law might be enforceable as customary international law.[56]

2. UN Human Rights Treaty System

The *Declaration* is an integral part of the United Nations human rights system. The text refers to the *UN Charter* and to the treaties, covenants, declarations, programs, and activities that comprise the UN human rights field, such as: the *Universal Declaration of Human Rights*, *International Covenant on Economic and Social Rights* (ICESR), *International Covenant on Civil and Political Rights* (ICCPR), the *Vienna Declaration and Programme of Action*, and general international human rights law obligations of the world community.[57] This connection requires us to read the *Declaration* against that framework to understand its place in international law.

The *Universal Declaration of Human Rights* (1948) is the foundational instrument for the UN human rights treaty system.[58] It is a comprehensive declaration ratified by the United States. In thirty articles, it creates a vision of human rights for all of humanity in the modern age, and those rights are elaborated in subsequent treaties that codify the *Universal Declaration*.

Core treaties that codify the *Universal Declaration* and comprise the UN human rights system include the: (1) *International Convention on the Elimination of All Forms of Racial Discrimination* (CERD) (1965), signed by 175 nations, with US ratification in 1994;[59] (2) ICESCR (1966)—the United States has not signed; (3) ICCPR (1966), signed by 167 nations, with US ratification in 1992;[60] (4) *Convention on the Elimination of All Forms of Discrimination against Women* (CEDAW) (1979), signed by 187 nations, not including the United States; (5) *Convention against Torture and Other Cruel, Inhuman or Degrading Treatment or Punishment* (CAT) (1984), signed by 149 nations, with US ratification in 1994; (6) *Convention on the Rights of the Child* (CRC) (1989), signed by 193 nations, not including the United States; (7) *International Convention on the Protection of the Rights of all Migrant Workers and Members of their Families* (CRMW) (1990), signed by 45 nations, not including the United States; (8) *Convention on the Rights of Persons with Disabilities* (CRPD) (2006), signed by 106 nations, not including the United States; and (9) numerous protocol agreements that implement these treaties in more detail.[61]

These multilateral treaties are legally binding on the signatory nations. They prescribe a broad range of human rights and fundamental freedoms, including prohibitions against all forms of discrimination, genocide, and torture; and they guarantee self-determination, equality, religious freedom, and the cultural integrity of minorities. As discussed below, these rights are linked to rights in the *Declaration*, though not specifically tailored to indigenous peoples. That is the task of the *Declaration*. It clarifies how the larger body of treaties should be interpreted and applied in the indigenous context.

When a country signs a UN treaty, this expresses its intent to become a party to the treaty and be obligated to refrain from acts that would defeat the treaty and take actions required by the treaty. Upon ratification, the signatory nation becomes bound by the treaty. Additional countries may ratify treaties that they did not sign. Importantly, during ratification of UN treaties, a country can add reservations that limit the application of a treaty within the ratifying nation. This is a standard practice by the United States. When the Senate ratified CERD, CCPR, and CAT, it attached a reservation to each, declaring that it is not a self-executing treaty. Hence, they are not enforceable by courts without the aid of implementing legislation.[62] The Senate reservations are animated by a desire not to change domestic law or create private causes of action unless this is done through the normal legislative process.[63] Thus, "the political branches have not generally authorized the application of the norms embedded in the treaties as domestic federal law."[64] Appropriate legislation is needed before those international human rights are enforceable in US courts.[65] Nonetheless, these treaties are the law of the land under the Constitution, and they become enforceable once domesticated. Furthermore, treaties are "proper evidence of customary international law because, and insofar as, they create *legal obligations* akin to contractual obligations on the State parties to them," especially when an overwhelming majority of nations have ratified them and consistently act in accordance with their principles.[66]

3. How UN Treaties Reinforce Rights in the Declaration

Several UN treaties, covenants, and declarations ratified by the United States prescribe rights and duties that correspond to those in the *Declaration*. The *Declaration* must therefore be read against this larger body of international law, and these international instruments create a powerful framework for implementing the *Declaration* into the law and policy of the United Sates.

The synergy begins with the *UN Charter*. This multilateral treaty sets forth the right of self-determination for all peoples, including indigenous peoples, and it requires member nations to respect and promote human rights. These obligations connect the *Charter* to the *Declaration*. According to the courts, the *Charter* is not self-executing, but it places a clear obligation upon the United States to observe its prescriptions and promote its goals.[67] That obligation provides a framework for implementing the *Declaration* by the United States.

In thirty articles, the *Universal Declaration of Human Rights* lists numerous human rights for all of peoples of the world. Many directly correspond to provisions in the *Declaration*. Though not legally binding, the *Universal Declaration* has exerted a profound influence on the conduct of nations since 1948. As the venerable foundation for the UN treaty system, the *Universal Declaration* enjoys "considerable indirect legal effect"—earned through widespread acceptance by nations around the world—to such a degree that its prescriptions amount in all likelihood to customary international law.[68] While binding treaties carry heavier weight than aspirational declarations in creating norms of customary international law and in evidencing the binding practices of nations, several prescriptions in the *Universal Declaration* are indistinguishable from norms currently recognized by customary international law, such as the prohibitions against slavery, torture, cruel and usual punishment, prolonged and arbitrary detention, and systematic racial discrimination.[69]

The *Universal Declaration* is codified by the CCPR, a multilateral treaty—ratified by the United States—with the force of law that prohibits torture, enslavement, forced labor, and arbitrary detention, and it also protects numerous fundamental freedoms. Article 1 of the CCPR recognizes the right of self-determination for all peoples (just like the *Declaration*), and this is a legal basis, grounded in international law, for protecting tribal sovereignty and self-determination in the United States.[70] Similarly, Article 27 protects minority religious and cultural rights, as well as other fundamental freedoms that plainly mirror rights in the *Declaration*, and the protection of these cultural rights has been relied upon by several international tribunals to protect indigenous land rights.[71] Though the CCPR is not a self-executing treaty, its rights and prescriptions might be indirectly enforceable as customary international law to the extent that they reflect settled usages and practices of nations.[72]

The CERD is a multilateral human rights treaty ratified by the United States in 1994. It seeks to eliminate all forms of racial discrimination in signatory nations. This prohibition, which corresponds to the equality and non-discrimination provisions of the *Declaration*, seemingly applies to discriminatory legal doctrines that affect American Indians in the United States.[73] Moreover, the United Nations has recognized the unique forms of racism faced by indigenous peoples from a long history of conquest and colonization, and the non-discrimination mandate of CERD applies to indigenous cultural integrity.[74] The application of the treaty to indigenous peoples is seen in the *CERD General Recommendation on Indigenous Peoples* (1997), which calls upon states to respect indigenous culture, history, language, and ways of life, and to ensure their social and economic development and safeguard their effective participation in public life.[75] While the Senate declared that CERD is not a self-executing treaty during ratification, its provisions can still be raised as a defense in judicial proceedings, possibly form the basis for an administrative action, and serve as a guide when interpreting federal legislation.[76] Further, the non-discrimination obligation embraced by 175 nations suggests that this principle is a norm in customary international law. Someone should perhaps mail a copy of CERD to the United States Supreme Court because the court still relies upon judicial precedent heavily tainted with racism and colonialism, long after the United States ratified the treaty. CERD condemns that practice. Preambular Paragraph 3 requires courts in signatory nations to discard racism ("all human beings are equal before the law and are entitled to equal protection of the law against any discrimination and against any incitement to discrimination"); Preambular Paragraph 4 requires courts to discard the law of colonialism ("the United Nations has condemned colonialism and all practices of segregation and discrimination associated therewith, in whatever form and wherever they exist").

While the UN treaties are not self-executing, they have spawned a large body of customary international law, which will be discussed next.[77] Since that body of law is part of federal common law, many unfulfilled treaty obligations can piggyback into our courts as customary international law.

4. Customary International Law Is part of US Law

Customary international law is a major source of international law. It carries the same binding force, and equal authority, as treaties.[78] This source of law emanates from the collective international community.[79] *Cohen's* defines it as:

> [R]ules of behavior that originate in international custom not necessarily found in any specific document. Customary law is "the oldest and original source of international law," and consists of rules nations follow because they consider themselves to be legally obligated to do so. A customary law norm binds a nation even if it has not formally recognized the norm, although open dissent exempts a nation from its requirements. While the content of international customary law is generally determined by evaluating the general practices of the community of nations, not every common act of various nations constitutes a custom for purposes of international law. Only those rules that nations believe themselves obliged to perform become binding customary law.[80]

These rules codify the customs and practices of nations that have become so widespread over time that they have ripened or crystallized into "norms." This happens when a preponderance of nations develop a common understanding of the norm's content and expect future behavior to conform to the norm.[81] Once the existence of a norm and its content are established, it becomes a binding rule in customary international law, and "preemptory norms" are so important that they are binding on states regardless of their consent.[82]

Methodologies exist for determining when an emerging norm has ripened into a settled rule of customary international law. They are laid out by scholars, treatises, and courts.[83] Though defining norms is "no simple task," they are discernible from treaties ratified by an overwhelming majority of nations, from declarations that espouse principles of conduct for the behavior of nations, from widespread state practices, and from other "myriad decisions made in numerous and varied international and domestic arenas."[84] To define norms, courts and experts examine all sorts of evidence on the customs and usages of nations, including the works of expert jurists and commentators.[85] They also survey state and international practices, policies, and laws to determine how widespread and representative a rule is in the practices of nations and whether it commands their general assent.[86] The need for widespread consensus is important;[87] and the Supreme Court requires norms to be "specific, universal and obligatory."[88]

In the United States, proven customary international law forms a part of the federal common law.[89] The Supreme Court has frequently applied the law of nations and explained how it is ascertained and applied as federal common law.[90] When no other source of domestic law governs, customary international law is decisive, as the Supreme Court explained in 1900:

> International law is part of our law, and must be ascertained and administered by the courts. For this purpose, where there is no treaty, and no controlling executive or legislative act or judicial decision, resort must be had to customs and usages of civilized nations; and as evidence of these, to works of jurists and commentators, who by years of labor, research and experience, have made themselves well acquainted with the subjects which they treat. Such works are resorted to by judicial tribunals, not for the speculation of their authors concerning what the law ought to be, but for trustworthy evidence of what the law really is.[91]

Enforcement of customary international law *cum* federal common law does not depend upon the "self-executing" versus "non-self-executing" distinction that is applicable to treaties.[92] Instead, norms are *automatically* enforceable by courts in appropriate cases as "a standard of federal common law to be used by the courts."[93] An exhaustive review of case law and authoritative treatises leaves no doubt—our courts are "bound to identify, clarify and apply customary international law."[94] For example, when the Court of Appeals in *Filartiga v. Pena-Irala* (1980) held that torture violates a customary international law norm, it recognized that "the law of nations has always been part of the federal common law."[95]

In recent years, the courts have been increasingly called upon to ascertain and apply customary international law. In so doing, however, the Supreme Court urges "great caution" in adapting the law of nations to private rights. As mentioned above, it requires claims based on the law of nations to rest on solid norms defined with a high degree of specificity.[96] Not just any practice will do. To qualify as a "norm" and become customary international law, a practice must command the "general assent" of nations—such as the widespread renunciation of piracy, torture, and genocide by nations. This is a high bar. It is not met by idiosyncratic rules that are open to sharp conflict among nations.[97] It is set by wary courts to minimize eruptions in foreign relations and to avoid interference with the management of foreign affairs by the political branches.

The formation of new rules of customary international law is a continual and on-going process. In modern times, it can be accelerated, especially when human rights are concerned. This stems from modern communications, which reveal state practices quickly, and discrete events that evince customary international law—such as rulings by international bodies or acts that promulgate treaties.[98] This rapid development has produced a growing body of law, with an open-ended list of recognized human rights. One commentator notes:

> There is widespread agreement that [customary international law] now protects the rights to be free from genocide, slavery, summary execution or murder, "disappearance," "cruel inhuman or degrading treatment," "prolonged arbitrary detention," and "systematic racial discrimination." An intergovernmental human rights committee recently asserted that [customary international law] also protects "freedom of thought, conscience and religion," a presumption of innocence, a right of pregnant women and children not to be executed, and a right to be free from expressions of "national, racial, or religious hatred." A prominent human rights organization's list of "potential candidates for rights recognized under customary international law" includes "the

> right to free choice of employment; the right to form and join trade unions; and the right to free primary education, subject to a state's available resources." The list continues to grow. As a leading authority on international human rights has observed, "[g]iven the rapid continued development of international human rights, the list as now constituted should be regarded as essentially open-ended. . . . Many other rights will be added in the course of time."[99]

Because today's developing norms are tomorrow's settled rules of international law, courts must keep abreast of developments that transform emerging norms into norms when ascertaining and applying customary international law. Once an indigenous right becomes a norm, the domestic legal status of customary international law in the United States becomes significant: those norms are then enforceable as federal common law. As such, when rights in the *Declaration* constitute customary international law, they are enforceable by the courts.[100]

5. Emergent Indigenous Human Rights Norms

According to leading authorities, some indigenous rights affirmed in the *Declaration* have ripened into norms of customary international law. That transformation stands to reason, given the growing recognition of indigenous rights in international law and the practices of nations since 1970. The pace of crystallization accelerated in the 21st century. UN approval of the standard-setting *Declaration* in 2007 was a giant step. This was followed by the endorsement of an overwhelming majority of nations—nearly 150—by 2012. That widespread approval sparked world-wide activity that propelled the crystallization of emerging norms. This torrent of activity is "like a flooding river under an unstoppable rain," in the words of the International Law Association.[101] It brought intense focus on indigenous human rights that is evident in: (1) the jurisprudence and pronouncements of international bodies that rely on the *Declaration* to protect indigenous rights and to interpret how treaties should be applied to indigenous peoples, and (2) the progressive incorporation of the *Declaration* into the UN human rights system, regional international human rights systems, and domestic legal systems with jurisdiction over millions of indigenous peoples.[102]

Numerous surveys have monitored the crystallization of indigenous rights since 1992.[103] They measure the birth of norms—from the progressive march of incipient rights over time, to their evolution into emerging norms, and finally their crystalization into new rules of customary international law—by surveying state and international practices, policies, and laws to assess patterns of consensus, recognition, and assent. The surveys cover two periods, the pre-*Declaration* era (1992–2007) and post-*Declaration* era (2007–2012).

Evolution of the self-determination right of indigenous peoples in customary international law is important. This right is considered vital by indigenous peoples. Supported by the pillars of self-government and autonomy, indigenous institutions, and cultural integrity, the indigenous right of self-determination provides the framework and foundation for every other right in the *Declaration*. In 1992, Curtis G. Berkey evaluated the status of this human right in customary international law.[104] Based upon the widespread acceptance of self-determination as defined by the *UN Charter*, human rights resolutions, treaties, and studies, he concluded that self-determination is a norm applicable to all peoples as a rule of customary international law.[105] However, Berkey concluded that the norm did not apply to indigenous peoples, because the extent of its application to them, as well as its content and meaning in the indigenous context, were not sufficiently defined.[106] Indeed, in 1992 the parameters of indigenous self-determination were being clarified at the UN in the standard-setting discussions, debates, and negotiations surrounding the draft *Declaration*. Because the right was still evolving, Berkey concluded that self-determination was an emerging norm "gradually becoming part of customary international law."[107] This pre-*Declaration* analysis predicted "the time may soon come when the terms and boundaries of the rights of self-determination will crystallize into a justiciable form and the international community will accept it for indigenous peoples."[108]

Four years later, an in-depth analysis was done by Professor Anaya in his groundbreaking treatise, *Indigenous Peoples in International Law* (1996). Among other things, this major work defined the content of indigenous self-determination.[109] It agreed that self-determination for all peoples is "widely acknowledged to be a principle of customary international law and even *jus cogens*, a preemptory norm," and traced the evolution of the indigenous right at the UN. Significantly, it found that several crucial elements of the indigenous right that undergird self-determination and define its content had coalesced into norms.[110] These included norms supporting indigenous self-government and autonomy, non-discrimination, cultural integrity, and land rights. Under the "non-discrimination norm," Anaya determined "it is no longer acceptable for the states to incorporate institutions or tolerate practices that perpetuate an inferior status or condition for indigenous individuals, or their cultural attributes."[111] As to the "self-government norm," Anaya found a "sui generis self-government norm," comprised of two parts: (1) governmental and administrative autonomy for indigenous communities, and (2) effective participation in all decisions affecting them by the larger institutions of government.[112] Though indigenous self-government can take many diverse forms under the norm:

> The underlying objective of the self-government norm, however, is that of allowing indigenous peoples to achieve meaningful self-government though political institutions that reflect their specific cultural patterns and that permit them to be generally associated with all decisions affecting them on a continuous basis.[113]

As to the cultural component of self-determination, by 1996, a "cultural integrity norm" arose from international and domestic standards and practices to protect "the survival and flourishing of indigenous cultures through mechanisms devised in accordance with the preferences of the indigenous peoples concerned."[114] As to the land component of self-determination, the treatise determined:

> It is evident that certain minimum standards concerning indigenous land rights, rooted in otherwise accepted precepts of property, cultural integrity, and self-determination, have made their way not just into conventional law but also into customary law.[115]

Finally, the treatise found growing consensus about the social welfare and development rights of indigenous peoples in 1996: "Although there is controversy about the outer bonds of state obligations to promote indigenous social welfare, a core consensus exists that states are in some measure obligated in this regard."[116] The crystallization of these norms gave form and content for the indigenous right of self-determination by 1996, as aspects of this emerging norm were being developed and defined in the United Nations standard-setting work on the *Declaration* throughout the decade.

In 1999, Professor Siegfried Wiessner conducted a comprehensive survey of international and domestic laws, policies, and practices to identify indigenous human rights norms and emerging norms.[117] He noted the outstanding controversies in the UN debates surrounding the indigenous right of self-determination at the end of the decade (i.e., whether "indigenous peoples" should be defined, whether they are "peoples" for purposes of international law, and whether self-determination in the indigenous context includes a right to succeed from a state, and so on).[118] As the 20th century closed, the survey determined that several other indigenous human rights have "matured and crystallized into customary international law," stating:

> While the specific ramifications of these prescriptions are still evolving and remain somewhat ambiguous, there is widespread agreement and concordant practice, in both international and domestic law, that (a) indigenous peoples are vulnerable groups worthy of the law's heightened concern; (b) that indigenous peoples are entitled to practice their traditions, to celebrate their culture and spirituality, to protect their language, and to maintain their sacred places and artifacts; (c) that they are, in principle, entitled to demarcation, ownership, development, control, and use of the lands which they have traditionally owned or otherwise occupied and used; (d) that they have, or should be, given, powers of self-government, including the administration of their own system of justice; and (e) that governments are to honor and faithfully observe their treaty commitments to indigenous nations.[119]

Widespread consensus over these key principles was evident in UN discussions over the draft *Declaration*—no government opposed them—and Wiessner found that "a consensus has emerged, and has been translated, with whatever imperfections, into widespread, virtually uniform state practice."[120]

Two more surveys were conducted in the pre-*Declaration* era by important treatises, *Indigenous Rights in International Law* (2004 ed.) and *Cohen's Handbook of Federal Indian Law* (2005 ed.). In the first treatise, Professor Anaya updated his 1996 survey with new data and case law that reconfirmed the self-government, cultural integrity, non-discrimination, and land rights norms found in 1996.[121] He found that norm-building activity placed key indigenous rights somewhere between emerging norms and norms—that is, he found that widely accepted "core precepts" of indigenous human rights "are indicative of customary international law."[122] He saw norms taking shape through the common understanding of the nations he observed in 2005 over the core elements of those rights, even though their outer contours were still emerging, with sufficient crystallization to mark their parameters in the international arena:

> As customary international norms take shape around a certain consensus of what counts as legitimate in relation to indigenous peoples, the specific contours of these norms are still evolving and remain somewhat ambiguous. Yet a lack of perfect uniformity in the relevant practice and opinion does not negate the norms' existence in some form. Despite imprecision in the outer contours of a new general of internationally operative norms; their core elements increasingly are confirmed and reflected in the extensive multilateral dialogue and processes of decision focused on indigenous peoples and their rights. Even though imprecise and still evolving, common understandings about the rights of indigenous peoples—understandings that can be characterized as customary international law—are sufficiently crystallized to mark the parameters of any discussion or decision in the international arena in response to the demands of indigenous peoples.[123]

The second treatise, *Cohen's*, examined the emerging norms of self-determination and land rights.[124] Because the right of self-government is embedded in the *UN charter* and human rights treaties, *Cohen's* found that self-determination is indisputably a fundamental right under international law and a settled norm for all peoples and nations; however, it found that application of this right to indigenous peoples was still emerging: "There is far from universal agreement about its exact scope or content and even less about its application to indigenous peoples."[125] That said, *Cohen's* saw progress in addressing and clarifying these issues in the international documents being developed by the OAS, ILO, and UN (including the draft *Declaration*). That norm-building activity foretold that "some recognition of the right of self-determination for indigenous peoples may become part of legally binding international law at some time in the future."[126] Thus, two years before the *Declaration* was approved, *Cohen's* concluded:

> [W]hile self-determination has achieved the status of an undisputed legal right in current international law, the extent and manner in which the right of self-determination currently applies to indigenous peoples living within a nation-state are still unclear. The efforts of the ILO, U.N., and OAS to specify the rights of indigenous peoples provide evidence of an emerging consensus that indigenous peoples are entitled to many, if not all, benefits of the right of self-determination.[127]

Cohen's also evaluated the indigenous right to land and territory and found that it is an emerging norm. On the international level, it found growing consensus on four key elements of the right: (1) greater protection for sacred sites; (2) protections against removal from indigenous land without free, prior, and informed consent, together with a right to redress for violations of this right; (3) a right to control development on indigenous land; and (4) restitution or restoration of lands traditionally owned or otherwise used that have been confiscated, occupied, used, or damaged.[128] On the domestic level, *Cohen's* found a "worldwide trend toward increased recognition of unique property rights for indigenous peoples" in recent decisions and laws of countries.[129]

A giant step in defining the contours of the emerging norms was taken on September 13, 2007, when the General Assembly approved the *Declaration*. This was a defining moment: overwhelming approval reflected widespread consensus over rights specified in the text. This major development, which was hailed by indigenous peoples, UN officials, voting nations, and by regional international bodies around the world alike, undoubtedly spurred the crystallization of specified rights, including the indigenous right of self-determination. Indeed, the text of Article 3 applies the universal right of self-determination to indigenous peoples in the same language as the *UN Charter* and human rights treaties. It states:

> Indigenous peoples have the right to self-determination. By virtue of that right they freely determine their political status and freely pursue their economic, social, and cultural development.

By 2012, three more surveys were conducted in the post-*Declaration* era by (1) Anaya's *International Human Rights and Indigenous Peoples* (2009), (2) a comprehensive report on indigenous land rights prepared by the Inter-American Commission on Human Rights (2009), and (3) the International Law Association (2010).

The assessment in *International Human Rights and Indigenous Peoples* (2009) reaffirmed findings on indigenous human rights norms made by earlier surveys and cited 21st century cases that rely upon international law, including Article 26 of the *Declaration*, to protect indigenous land rights.[130] Reinforced by the specific recognition of indigenous rights in the *Declaration*, Anaya formulated four norms from the prior surveys: (1) a cultural right to indigenous cultural identity, spirituality, language, and traditional ways of life; (2) a self-determination right with contours that have been significantly cleared through widespread agreement over the self-government, political, autonomy, cultural, spiritual, social, and economic elements of this right; (3) a right to own, use, control, and develop indigenous lands traditionally owned or otherwise occupied and used; (4) and a right to the observance of treaties.[131]

The Inter-American Commission on Human Rights (2009) survey considered the *Declaration* to be part of the *corpus juris* that defines the content of indigenous land rights in the Americas (i.e., in the thirty-five independent nations that belong to the OAS) where all tribal peoples of the Western Hemisphere reside.[132] It surveyed recognized indigenous rights to lands, territories, and natural resources, together with the indigenous right to participate in decisions affecting this property and the states' obligation to protect these recognized indigenous land rights.

Finally, the International Law Association (2010) undertook to examine the rights and norms expressed in the *Declaration* to ascertain whether they have reached the status of customary international law.[133] Applying the evidence and standards for ascertaining the existence of norms, the Association concluded that some "key provisions" in the *Declaration* "can reasonably be regarded as corresponding to established principles of general international law" in the areas of "self-determination, autonomy or self-government, cultural rights and identity, land rights, as well as reparation, redress and remedies."[134] In short, by 2010, it found widespread state and international practices and policies that confirm the recognition and protection of indigenous "cultural rights, land rights, and autonomy and participation in the decisions affecting [indigenous peoples]," as well as the right to reparation and redress for land loss and wrongs suffered.[135] (These practices were observed around the world in Argentina, Australia, Bangladesh, Belize, Botswana, Brazil, Cambodia, Canada, Chile, Colombia, Costa Rica, Ecuador, the European Union, India, Japan, Laos, Malaysia, Mexico, New Zealand, Nicaragua, Norway, Paraguay, Peru, Philippines, South Africa, Taiwan, United States, and Venezuela.)[136] The Association determined that the adoption of the *Declaration,* after more than twenty years of negotiation, confirms that the international community has come to a consensus on the existence of six customary rules of binding force in international law, stating: "[I]t is today indisputable that 'customary norms concerning indigenous peoples and their pull toward compliance' are actually a reality"; and it formulated these rules as follows, each of which ought to be enforceable federal common law per our earlier discussion. I respectfully quote the Association at length:

- indigenous peoples have the right to self-determination that secures to indigenous peoples the right to decide, within the territory of the State in which they live, what their future will be;

- indigenous peoples have the right to autonomy or self-government. It translates into a number of prerogatives, including: the right to be represented in the national government; the right to participate in national decision-making with respect to any project that may affect their rights or their ways of life; the right to be consulted with respect to any project that may affect them as well as the related right that projects suitable to significantly impact their rights and ways of life are not carried out without their prior, free and informed consent; the right to regulate autonomously their internal affairs according to their customary law and to establish, maintain, and develop their own legal and political institutions, in a way that is consistent with the rules on fundamental human rights. States have the obligation to recognize and ensure respect for the laws, traditions and customs of indigenous peoples;

- indigenous peoples have the right to recognition and protection of their cultural integrity. This includes not only the right to not be subject to genocide (which amounts to a rule of *jus cogens*), but also the right to be free from ethnocide. The latter right presupposes that all the prerogatives that are essential to preserve the cultural identity of indigenous peoples *according to their own perspective* must be preserved, including, *e.g.*, the right to use ancestral lands and natural resources according to their own tradition, the right to profess and manifest their religion in community with other members of the group, the right to pursue their traditional medicines and burial traditions, etc.;

- indigenous peoples have the right to their traditional lands and natural resources. This right is not only confined to that of not being removed from the lands that they possess at present, but extends to restitution of the ancestral territories from which they have been removed in the past (except when restitution is *absolutely* impossible; in this event, equivalent effective reparation is to be granted in favour of the community concerned), provided that their cultural link with those lands continues to exist. Land rights also imply that the peoples concerned must be allowed to manage their lands autonomously and according to their customary rules; this prerogative is strictly connected with the rights to self-determination and autonomy or self-government;

- indigenous peoples have the rights to reparation and redress for the wrongs suffered. This right amounts to a rule of customary international law to the extent that it is aimed at redressing a wrong resulting from a breach of a right that is itself part of customary international law. In fact, redress is an essential element for the effectiveness of human rights; therefore, any human rights-related obligation brings in itself the *inherent* requirement that any breach of the relevant right is effectively and adequately repaired. This implies, *a fortiori*, that, with respect to any human right protected by customary international law, a corresponding obligation exists—*also pursuant to customary international law*—according to which whatever violation of the right concerned presupposes that the victim(s) of such a violation must be granted access to effective and adequate remedies. Therefore, this logical legal reasoning eventually leads to the conclusion that, to the extent that certain rights of indigenous peoples are protected by customary international law—as it is actually the case—parallel obligations exist also in the realm of general international law binding States to grant effective and adequate reparation in favour of indigenous peoples for any breach of the said rights. Although in principle States may decide what kind of reparatory measures are to be granted in each concrete situation, reparation must be in any case *adequate and effective, i.e.,* capable to remove—to the maximum extent possible—the effects of the wrong *as they are perceived by the communities concerned.* This means, in practice, that in some cases States may not be really free to choose the kind of redress to be granted; in particular, when an indigenous community has been deprived of its traditional lands, in principle the form of reparation to be accorded is restitution, whether and to the extent that is actually feasible. The rule in point includes the requirement that effective mechanisms for redress are available and accessible in favour of indigenous peoples;

- indigenous peoples have the right to expect that all treaties, and other agreements to which they are a direct party with a State, that were fairly negotiated, shall be honoured and fully implemented in a manner respecting the spirit and intent of the understanding of the Indigenous negotiators as well as the living nature of the solemn undertaking made by all parties. The enforcement of this right is inextricably linked to the various provisions of the UNDRIP that guarantee access to "effective mechanisms" for redress, "just and fair redress" and "just and fair procedures for the resolution of conflicts and disputes.[137]

Conclusions about the Legal Status of the *Declaration*

For the above reasons, the *Declaration* carries much heavier weight as a matter of international and domestic law than do most international declarations. Key provisions of the *Declaration* are linked to treaties ratified by the United States and are therefore the supreme law of the land, even though the treaties are not self-executing. Moreover, those and other provisions, in all likelihood, constitute customary international law that US courts are bound to ascertain and apply in appropriate cases as federal common law. The synergy between the *Declaration* and international human rights law is depicted in **Table 2**:

TABLE 2

Comparing the Declaration with Selected Treaties, International Instruments, and Indigenous Rights Norms in Customary International Law (As interpreted by Treaty Monitoring Bodies).

UN DECLARATION on The Rights of Indigenous Peoples	TREATY or other INTERNATIONAL INSTRUMENT	INDIGENOUS RIGHT in Customary International Law
Non–Discrimination & Equality: Arts. 1–2, 9, 15; 4–6, 8	1. CERD, Arts. 2, 5, 6, and General Recommendation No. 23 (1993); 2. CCPR, Art. 26–27; 3. CESCR, Art. 1; 4. UN Charter, Art. 1(2) 5. ILO Art. 2–4(3), 19; 6. CRC, Arts. 29 (d). 7. ACHR (OAS Treaty, 1969), Art. 24. 8. Univ. Dec. Hum. Rts, Arts. 1–2, 7 (UDHR)	Norm: Anaya (2004, 1996); Restatement (3rd), §702 (1987) (general non-discrimination and equality norm)

UN DECLARATION on The Rights of Indigenous Peoples	**TREATY or other INTERNATIONAL INSTRUMENT**	**INDIGENOUS RIGHT in Customary International Law**
Self-Determination (includes self-government, autonomy, & indigenous institutions): Arts.3–4; 7, 17	1. CCPR, Art. 1; 2. CESCR, Art. 1; 3. ILO 169, Arts. 7–9; 4. UN Charter, Art. 1(2) 5. UN Decolonization Res. (1960), Art. 1	Norm: ILA (2010); IACHR (2009); Anaya (2009, 2004, 1996) (elements are norms); Wiessner (1999). Emerging Norm: Cohen's (2005); Anaya (2004, 1996); Wiessner (1999); Berkey (1992)
Cultural Rights: Arts. 5, 7–8, 11–13, 24, 31, 34	1. CESCR, Art. 15; 2. CCPR, Art. 12, 13, 18, 27; HRC Gen. Com. #23; 3. UNESCO Convention on Cultural Diversity ; 4. ILO 169, Arts. 2, 4 (1), 5, 8 5. CERD (Gen. Rec.); 6. UDHR, Art. 18 (religious freedom), 27	Norm: ILA (2010); Anaya (2009, 1996); Wiessner (1999). See also, Bradley & Goldsmith (1997) at 841 n. 169–170 (general religious freedom norm)
Life/Integrity/Security: Arts. 7–9	1 Genocide Convention; 2. CCPR, Arts. 6–27; 3. CAT; 4. CRC, Art. 30; 5. ILO 169 Art. 3, 11, 18; 6. UDHR, Arts. 3–6	Norm: Restatement (3rd), §703 (genocide norm)
Education/Media: Arts. 14–16	1. CESCR, Art. 13; 2. CERD, Art. 4, 6; 3. ILO 169, Arts. 21–30; 4. UDHR, Arts. 26	Trend: ILA (2010, 1994). See, Bradley & Goldsmith (1997) (education norm)
Participation: decisions & free/prior/informed consent: Arts. 5, 19, et al.	1. CCPR, Art. 25; 2. CERD (Recom.); 3. ILO, in passim	Norm: IACHR (2009); Anaya (2006, 1996)

UN DECLARATION on The Rights of Indigenous Peoples	TREATY or other INTERNATIONAL INSTRUMENT	INDIGENOUS RIGHT in Customary International Law
Economic/Social Rights: Arts. 17, 20–24, 44	1. ILO, Art 2(2), 7, 20–31 2. UN Charter, Art. 55–6 3. CESCR, Arts. 2, 9–13; 4. UN Dec. Rt. to Develop., Arts. 1–8, 10; 5. UDHR, Art. 21	Consensus on Core Elements: Anaya (1996); Wiessner (1999)
Land/Territory/Resources: Arts. 10, 25–30, 32	1. ILO 169, Art. 5, 7(4), 13–17 2. CCRP, Art. 27; 2. UDHR, Art. 17	Norm: IACHR (2009); Anaya (2004, 1996); Wiessner (1999). Emerging Norm: Cohen's (2005)
Treaties/Agreements: Art. 37; 8, 15		Norm: ILA (2010); Anaya (2009); Wiessner (1999)
Justice/Remedies/Reparation. Art. 28, 6	1. CCPR, Arts. 2–5, 9; 2. CERT, Art. 6; 3. ILO 169, Arts. 12, 16, 18; 4. UDHR, Arts. 8, 10, 28; See also, "Basic Principles & Guidelines: Rt. to Remedy & Reparation for Violation of Int'l. Hum. Rts. Law," U.N.G.A. Res. 60/147 (2005); "Study: Restitution for Hum Rts. Violations," UN doc. E/ C N.4/ Sub.2/1993/8 (1993)	Norm: ILA (2010)

Two conclusions can be safely drawn from the legal status of the *Declaration*. First, US courts, lawmakers, agencies, lawyers, and Indian tribes should pay serious heed to the provisions of the *Declaration* and give them appropriate weight in litigation, lawmaking, and policymaking. When possible, our laws, legal doctrines, and constitutional law should be interpreted in a manner that is consistent with, and not in violation of, the *Declaration,* related treaties, and applicable international human rights law. On that rule of construction, our jurisprudence is clear: the Supreme Court requires that federal law be construed to comport with international law, whenever that is possible.[138] Second, when we see that the *Declaration* is fixed firmly to the UN human rights treaty system and customary international human rights law, a powerful legal framework for implementing its provisions and principles emerges: by aligning our treatment of Native Americans with the UN standards, we are simply taking steps to domesticate existing treaty obligations, including the fulfillment of the United States' pledge to promote and advance human rights under the *UN Charter*. Thus, implementation is authorized by treaties, and any measures taken to domesticate those international obligations become the supreme law of the land.

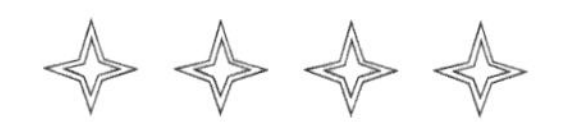

by Bunky Echo-Hawk (Yakama-Pawnee artist)

"Down and Out"

PART TWO
The Need for the Declaration

They gave us meat, but they took away our liberty.

— Sitting Bull (Hunkpapa Sioux) (c. 1882).

CHAPTER FIVE
The Legacy of Conquest

This chapter explores the need for embracing the *Declaration* in the United States. First, it examines the impacts of conquest through the lens of large-scale social trauma. This vantage point enables us to see how injustice was embedded into the law and our institutions, and it reveals unhealed injuries in American life. As we confront this legacy, the question becomes: Can the *Declaration* heal those wounds? Secondly, we shall identify political problems associated with the growth and development of the American democracy that can be solved by the *Declaration*—namely, belated nation-building necessary to incorporate Native peoples into the national community on a just basis, with their rights as indigenous peoples intact.

Correcting these long-standing problems through a human rights approach is needed, even in the world's leading democracy. Our historical commitment to human rights is unparalleled. But we have not always lived up to our ideals, and our treatment of American Indians is one case in point. The *Declaration* invites us to confront our legacy of conquest, see where we have fallen short in our treatment of the First Americans, and at long last apply our core values to their unique circumstances. This chapter argues for a national plan of action to implement the *Declaration*.

The central purpose of the *Declaration* is restorative justice—to repair the persistent denial of indigenous rights by entrenched forces implanted by the legacy of colonialism.[1] Consequently, the *Declaration* has direct application to every nation with a history of conquest and dispossession, including the United States. At first blush, it may seem that the *Declaration* has little application, because our laws probably come closer than most nations in meeting the standards of the *Declaration*. That is to be expected, given the core values expressed in our organic documents. Unlike most nations with large indigenous populations, we have a comprehensive body of law concerned with the rights, relationships, and responsibilities among Indian tribes, the states, and the federal government based upon treaties, statutes, court decisions, and policies. That body of law is called federal Indian law, and it defines the place of indigenous peoples in our society and establishes their political, property, cultural, and human rights. By contrast, the law in many settler states has inadequate or no legal protections for indigenous peoples at all. In those nations, the legal system is unaccountable to indigenous peoples, or, worse yet, the law is used to prey upon and exploit the aboriginal peoples. Nonetheless, there is ample room for improvement in our body of law and social policies to better assure the human rights of Native Americans and reaffirm our historical commitment to the core values that have animated the republic since its inception.

We Can See the Legacy of Conquest through a "Social Trauma Lens"

What is the legacy of conquest? Much has been written about the "Winning of the West." We tend to glorify American history in school books and mass media. However, there is no escaping the dark side of Manifest Destiny: it took a terrible toll on American Indian tribes, Alaska Natives, and Native Hawaiians. In 1492, at least five million American Indians inhabited the land now comprising the United States. By 1900, only 250,000 were left alive. That four-hundred year period witnessed an astounding population collapse of about 1.5 million persons per century, one of the largest ever seen in world history.[2] The human race has experienced staggering "die-offs" due to calamity and genocide. During the Middle Ages, Europe experienced mass death due to war, disease, and famine, when more than 40 percent of its population was decimated.[3] Rwanda suffered a sudden death toll in 1994 due to genocide, when 11 percent of the population was killed and only 29 percent of the Tutsi population survived the horrors of a one-hundred day nightmare.[4] In Europe, only 37 percent of the Jewish population survived the Holocaust.

As terrifying as these numbers are, only about 5 percent of the American Indians survived by 1900.[5] The staggering mass death rate brought the American Indian race in the United States to the brink of extinction. The depopulation of my own Pawnee people is a case in point. In the 1700s, the estimated population of the four confederated Bands of the Pawnee Nation was 22,000. By 1900, only 635 Pawnees remained—the sole survivors of a traumatic encounter with Manifest Destiny, with a 2.3 percent survival rate. After recounting the tumultuous history of our people, my uncle, the late Francis ("Witty") Echo Hawk, told me, "It is a miracle that any of us are left alive; only the strongest survived." Acute human suffering of this nature and magnitude has a name. Social science researchers describe the chronic aftereffects of severe trauma observed in human survivor populations—such as Holocaust survivors, Rwanda genocide survivors, Cambodian refugees, Bosnian ethnic cleansing survivors, Vietnam War veterans, prisoners of war, and survivors of other traumatic events, like torture, war, disaster, or the sudden unexpected deaths of loved ones—as *Posttraumatic Stress Disorder* (PTSD).[6] In the American Indian population, PTSD is classified by mental health and social science researchers into a distinct subcategory variously denominated as *Postcolonial Stress Disorder* (PCSD), *Historical Trauma*, or *Historical Unresolved Grief*.[7] The trauma that pervades the cataclysmic histories experienced by American Indian populations, such as the Lakota and Klamath Indians, is deposited by intergenerational transfer of unresolved grief into the survivors' offspring. The impact of that traumatic history upon their social pathology is seen in the appalling life and mental health statistics that mark tribal communities today. Sadly, those communities exhibit the same profile as survivors of massive trauma, complete with the inherited suffering and unresolved grief found in survivor groups. It is deeply troubling that the studies find a heart-breaking resemblance between Native Americans and survivors of massive war trauma and that tribal communities resemble the scene of a terrible crime, where residents reel from inherited suffering and scars of depression, prolonged unresolved grief, substance abuse, and suicide. And what is the crime? It is the legacy of conquest.

Why was the conquest and colonization of Native America so virulent? Scholars have identified the causes for the alarming American Indian population decline. They identify six major causes: (1) extended warfare and killing over a one-hundred year period that included the illegal use of force; (2) the spread of disease among tribal people by settlers during the course of colonial expansion; (3) the forcible separation of Indian children from their parents and tribes by the government during the nineteenth and twentieth centuries and placement into non-Indian settings and institutions where the children could be brainwashed of their cultures for assimilation into the settler society; (4) the forcible removal of Indian nations from their lands and territories, resettlement, and widespread dispossession of Indian land; (5) the destruction of tribal habitats, ecosystems, and subsistence resource bases, which contributed to the tribal demographic collapse; and (6) the forcible assimilation and the intentional destruction of tribal cultures, languages, and religions by the government.[8]

What animated the settlers' aggression? It can be argued that trauma breeds trauma. The immigrants were a traumatized group fleeing tough conditions in Europe. During the 14th century, disease, starvation, and war produced a high mass death rate that decimated Europe. Immigrants to America were the survivors, and they sought to escape truncated and impoverished life under oppressive conditions. Driven by these traumatic events, they fled to America to escape dire circumstances, leaving everything behind. The refugees fought over the new land and resources with all of their might, as if their lives depended on it, because in every sense of the word, it did. To them, colonization was a life or death struggle. They were animated by survival and the massive social trauma in their own history, which had fueled their spread into Indian Territory. This was not a pleasure cruise. The settlers meant to occupy the land, no matter what the cost. As the Tennessee Supreme Court explained in 1835, settlers "were obliged to conquer and to govern, or to perish," and Indian tribes must "accept a master, or perish."[9]

Dr. William Glasser, a prominent American psychiatrist, once wrote, "Whatever happened in the past that was painful has a great deal to do with what we are today."[10] The concept of *historical* or *societal trauma* helps explain many of the forces at work in American history, especially when we view Manifest Destiny through the lens of large-scale social trauma.[11] For purposes of this discussion, *social trauma* is defined as:

> [T]he traumatic consequences of events or situations that are potentially traumatogenic (natural calamities, wars, accidents, kidnapping, mourning, exposure to risks and danger, etc.), which involve a community or one's own definable social group (family, peer groups, etc.).[12]

On a broader scale, *societal trauma* applies to human suffering created by traumatic events and is shared throughout an entire social group, including historical trauma and all forms of traumatization.[13] Examples include war, terrorism, disease, famine, pestilence, racism, poverty, oppression in the absence of justice, genocide, a history of mass death, culture loss, identity loss, marginalization, discrimination, and successive social traumas that go unhealed (such as slavery followed by racial discrimination, famine followed by plagues, genocidal aggression followed by oppression, and so on).[14] Societal trauma scars the victim and aggressor communities, and the trauma encountered by one generation can be passed down through the generations when it is left unhealed.

It is possible to list some of the characteristics seen in traumatized populations and individuals and their responses to trauma. On the one hand, victims can suffer a wide variety of trauma responses, such as:

1. A shared sense of shame, humiliation, dehumanization, and guilt;
2. A shared transmission of transgenerational trauma;
3. Health and wellness statics are often disproportionally negative;
4. The collective psyche is adversely affected;
5. Unhealthy and self-destructive norms, attitudes, and behaviors appear;
6. Violence is directed at and within the group;
7. Shame-based traits appear in the culture and individual personalities; and
8. Victims are unable to forgive the perpetrator society.[15]

On the other hand, a dominant social group that victimizes another is usually a homogenous society that operates in survival mode, in which its own survival needs are thought to trump healing needs or acts of justice. Unrecognized fear often motivates social action in an aggressor society built upon a legacy of injustice that must maintain itself upon a foundation of oppression, and it is predisposed to use aggression to solve national problems. Aggressor societies can exhibit these characteristics and tendencies:

1. National narratives are grounded in historical distortions and the denial of any national wrong-doing;
2. It has a Conquest/Conqueror identity;
3. It is a guilt-based group;
4. It demonizes and demeans the victimized group to justify national

behavior and harbors uninspected racism, prejudice, discrimination;
5. Solidarity is based on commonly held fears and hatreds directed at the victim;
6. It marginalizes grief and suffering in the victimized group; and has a high tolerance for social injustice for that group; and
7. It exhibits a repeating cycle of abuse and national aggression.[16]

The societal trauma in Native American history is brought on by the successive march of war, disease, mass population loss, conquest, colonization, dispossession, subjugation, and marginalization. Left unhealed, that trauma is deposited by intergenerational means into the cultural and socio-economic indicators that characterize Native American communities today. Native Americans live under the plenary power of Congress and legal doctrines saturated by racism. Their dispossessed communities are marked by the socio-economic indicators of historical and societal trauma, characterized by: (1) the highest rate of violent crime in the nation (American Indians are twice as likely to be victimized by violent crime as any other ethnic group, 34 percent of Native American women will be raped in their lifetime, and 39 percent will be subject to domestic violence, mostly at the hands of non-Indians, according to Justice Department data); (2) the surviving remnants of Native American cultures, languages, tribal religions, holy places, and intellectual property rights to their heritage and identity are under assault by the dominant society on many fronts; (3) the highest high school drop-out rate in the nation (36 percent) and low academic achievement in public schools that perpetuate culturally destructive curricula and educational policies proven to deny American Indian children equal education opportunity; (4) public media that is unaccountable to Native Americans, filled with racial stereotypes, but devoid of any real depictions of American Indians or any journalistic coverage of their issues, which contributes to the lack of public information about Native Americans and their place in society; (5) the highest poverty rate in the nation, where one in three Indians living on the reservation live below the poverty line; (6) the lowest life expectancy rate in a nation where the average American secures 60 percent more healthcare annually than Native Americans, and where the rate of alcoholism among Native is 627 percent greater than all other races, tuberculosis is 533 percent greater, diabetes is 249 percent greater, accidents are 204 percent greater, suicide is 72 percent greater, pneumonia and influenza are 71 percent greater, and homicide is 63 percent greater; (6) by 1955 land held by American Indian tribes had shrunk to just 2.3 percent of its original size. These are socio-economic indicators of large-scale historical societal trauma. The provisions of the *Declaration* address each of these open wounds and hold the promise of healing them through a fair and balanced human rights approach.

To round-out the tragic picture painted by the above social ills, when viewed through the lens of large-scale societal trauma, the larger society itself carries many self-destructive traits of the aggressor society model: indifference is the order of the day. History books tell a distorted story that denies national wrong-doing. Indians are blamed for the socio-economic problems that stalk them, and we are long-accustomed to ruling them under notions of conquest and nefarious legal doctrines, in a distinctly amoral body of law, with a high tolerance for injustice. At the same time, white guilt prevents discourse about this situation. So does Native American rage. How can we rectify the legacy of conquest? The *Declaration* not only provides an opportunity for discourse, but it also supplies the ingredients for restorative justice that will allow everyone concerned to heal the wounds of the past. Indeed, mental health and social science researchers advocate both decolonization and the restoration of culture as part of the intervention and treatment of PTSD, PCSD, historical trauma, and unresolved grief observed in traumatized Native American communities. The *Declaration* is a prescription for those ills: It asks the United States to address those root problems with a broad range of social, economic, educational, and cultural measures. They become acts of atonement that when properly done can heal the wounds of a painful and unjust past.[17]

The Legacy of Conquest Impels Scrutiny of Federal Indian Law

The legacy of conquest and colonialism has been implanted into the American mindset, institutions, and legal regime so deeply that we are blinded to its presence. But its imprint is clearly visible in the legal culture. The task of justifying the unjustifiable fell to the courts. As may be expected, the jurists were hard-pressed. They had to depart from high principles that normally animate the republic. They created a body of law with three discernable, and sometimes overlapping, lines of judicial thought: (1) conquest, (2) colonization, and (3) the tribal sovereignty and protectorate principles. When considered in light of the *Declaration*, we see doctrines that are compatible with modern standards and those that fall short. If we adopt the *Declaration* as our framework, the incompatible doctrines will be laid to rest, because they have outlived their time.

1. The Doctrine of Conquest

"Conquest" has a dark and menacing connotation. It bespeaks naked aggression, brute force, and raw power—all exerted in the invasion and appropriation of territory, and in the subjugation and governance of the inhabitants of a conquered land. The history of conquest is as old as the human race; and it has produced iconic figures like Hitler, Genghis Khan, Napoleon, Pizzaro, the Romans, and Vikings, as well as many would-be conquerors or petty tyrants, such as Castro, Saddam Hussein, and Idi Amin. *Webster's* defines "conquest" as the act of conquering, especially territory "appropriated in war" or acquired "by force of arms."[18]

Conquest is not normally considered a legitimate source of governmental power in a free and democratic society, for to do so would suggest that force, not the consent of the governed, is the moral justification for government. Instead, democracies rely on constitutional law to govern their citizenry and guide relationships with political subdivisions. Unlike any other segment in US society, Native America is subject to the law of conquest, which has an anti-indigenous function: doctrines of conquest allow the government to divest Indian land title, extinguish aboriginal title, confiscate aboriginal land, and exercise dominion over Indian peoples and their property without their consent or the normal constitutional limitations that protect the rights of others. Only Indian Nations live under that supposed basis for governmental power.

Chief Justice John Marshall began the judicial discourse on conquest when he fashioned the doctrine of discovery. In *Johnson v. M'Intosh* (1823), he wrote that "title by conquest is acquired and maintained by force" and the "conqueror prescribes its limits."[19] This rule flew in the face of international law, since bare conquest has never been considered sufficient to convey good title under the law of nations (i.e., we do not "own" Iraq or Afghanistan simply because we invaded those nations). Thus, Marshall had to craft an exception to the hard and fast rule that conquerors must respect property rights in the lands they invade. He wrote that the normal rule is "incapable of application," because the United States was confronted by "fierce savages, whose occupation was war." He therefore considered it impossible to mingle with Indians, incorporate them into a colonial social structure, or govern Indian nations as distinct peoples, because the savages "were ready to repel by force of arms every attempt on their independence." Thus, the nation had to "resort to some new and different rule, better adapted to the actual state of things." The new rule fashioned in *Johnson* was a legal fiction that converted the mere "discovery of an inhabited country into conquest."[20] *Johnson* also ruled that the act of discovery operates to transfer legal title to Indian land to the United States, and the government may extinguish any remaining Indian interest in the land by purchase or conquest "by the sword."[21] Marshall justified injustice by announcing the infamous doctrine of conquest:

> Conquest gives a title which the Courts of the conqueror cannot deny, whatever the private and speculative opinions of individuals may be respecting the original justice of the claim which has been successfully asserted. It is not for the Courts of this country to question the validity of this title, or to sustain one which is incompatible with it.[22]

By conflating the doctrines of discovery and conquest, the Marshall Court gave the United States "all the powers of a conqueror," in the words of the late David H. Getches, Dean of Colorado University's college of law.[23]

Indian law opinions quickly began to fill with metaphors of war.[24] The early opinions were written during the Indian Wars (1790–1890) with an unmistakable military mindset, sometimes by judges who were themselves veterans of military conflicts with Indian tribes. During the Indian Removal Movement, Justice Thomas Johnson reiterated in *Cherokee Nation v. Georgia* (1831) that "discovery gave the right of dominion over the country discovered," including "the absolute appropriation of territory [and] the annexation of it to the domain of the discoverer."[25] His opinion reflects the mindset of a nation poised for the removal of the

Indian race from the South and for war. He viewed Indian land rights through the eyes of a conqueror, stating that Indians merely "receive the territory allotted to them as a boon from a master or conqueror." He also characterized Georgia's claims of land ownership and dominion over the Cherokee nation as a "war in disguise" that cannot be resolved by "any arbiter but the sword."[26] The Supreme Court thus declared, in no uncertain terms, that Indian nations are proper subjects for conquest, and courts should not interfere.

In short order, the southern judiciary donned the mantle of the conqueror and wrote jingoistic opinions dripping with hostility and racial animosity that spurred the Removal Movement.[27] That jurisprudence places Indians along the side of slaves, as racially inferior beings without any treaty, political, property, or human rights, subject to the "guardianship" of the South. In wrenching away their humanity, the Supreme Courts of the South made much of the fact that the United States has fought many wars against Indian nations.[28] After discussing the jurisprudence of conquest, the Alabama Supreme Court concluded:

> Have we not in all these cases, clear proof, that, in the understanding of all the civilized world, a discovered Indian country was a conquered country: that the new sovereign always so considered it, and exercised the rights of a conqueror over his new subjects? And is the judiciary to overturn the political course of the country, and by an investigation, not of law and precedent, but of abstract right, to determine that this course of policy has been wrong, and not only wrong, but illegal? It is not for the Courts, no matter what may be their opinion on abstract right, to interfere.[29]

When it applied the doctrine to sanction state power over the Creek Nation, the Alabama Supreme Court did not mince words about the fate of Creek Indians under state rule. It ominously stated that Alabama "has always looked forward with confidence to the time when the whole state would be freed from its Indian population."[30] The Southern judiciary intended that "conquest" be real in every deadly sense of the word. Placing aside considerations of justice, the Tennessee Supreme Court wrote that conquest is "the destiny of man"; settlers "were obliged to conquer and to govern, or to perish"; and Indian tribes are compelled "to accept a master or perish."[31]

By 1955, evolution of the myth of conquest in the law was so prevalent that the Supreme Court assumed every American Indian and Alaska Native tribe had been conquered, even though few as a matter of fact actually lost their land or sovereignty by force of American arms. Justice Stanley Reed wrote an opinion in *Tee-Hit-Ton v. United States* (1955) that applied the doctrine of conquest to uphold the confiscation of aboriginal tribal land in Alaska by Congress without compensation:

> Every American schoolboy knows that the savage tribes of this continent were deprived of their ancestral ranges by force and that, even when the Indians ceded millions of acres by treaty in return for blankets, food, and trinkets, it was not a sale but the conqueror's will that deprived them of their land. In the language of Chief Justice Marshall, "however extravagant the pretension of converting the discovery of an inhabited country into conquest may appear; if the principle has been asserted in the first instance, and afterwards sustained; if a country has been acquired and held under it; if the property of the great mass of the community originates under it, it becomes the law of the land and cannot be questioned. [32]

There are several obvious problems with this line of judicial thought that place the continued use of the doctrine of conquest by 21st century courts into question. First of all, the factual and legal basis for the doctrine of conquest rests on dubious ground. As a matter of fact, nearly every Indian acre on the continent was *purchased* by the United States through treaties or statutes and not acquired by force of military arms.[33] As a legal matter, *Worcester v. Georgia* (1832) rejected the notion that conquest can be equated with discovery as factually incorrect and an absurd legal fiction. Furthermore, it held that the "domestic dependent nation" status of Indian nations is not considered conquest under federal or international law.[34] It is time to retire foolish legal fictions from the law. There is a far more legitimate source of government power in Indian affairs: the United States Constitution. As such, the doctrine is unnecessary and superfluous. The primary purpose served by the doctrine today is two-fold and nefarious. First, it allows the Supreme Court to define Native American rights through the framework of conquest. In this respect, it furnishes a convenient base for fashioning new doctrines of judicial dispossession, such as the "doctrine of implicit divestiture" used by the Rehnquist and Roberts Courts in recent years to trim tribal sovereignty whenever the justices think the exercise of tribal government is against the interests of the United States.[35] Second, since the doctrine has never been repudiated by the Supreme Court, it lies about like a loaded weapon, ready for use, and it is certainly available to influence judges in handing down decisions in Indian cases.

Furthermore, the clothes of a conqueror simply do not fit a free and democratic nation. It is repugnant to our core values to define indigenous rights in the framework of conquest, especially when the Bill of Rights and the Declaration of Independence provide the framework for the human rights and fundamental freedoms of everyone else.

Nor does the framework of conquest have any place in the principles espoused in the *Declaration.* The notion of conquest is anathema to human rights. The aim of conquest is to strip the conquered of their rights, whereas the goal of human rights law generally, and the *Declaration* in particular, is to restore those rights. The *Declaration* recognizes that indigenous rights within the states in which indigenous peoples find themselves should be "based on principles of justice, democracy, respect for human rights, non-discrimination and good faith," not principles of conquest.[36] Article 46(3) requires provisions in the *Declaration* to be "interpreted in accordance with principles of justice, democracy, respect for human rights, equality, non-discrimination, good governance, and good faith," and not based on might alone, raw power, or the whim of a conquering tyrant. By contrast, the judicial saber-rattling in Indian jurisprudence is animated by hostility and deep-seated racial animosity, as expressed in the opinions discussed above. The *Declaration* can help rid conquest from the legal system and supplant that dark framework for defining Native American human rights with higher principles more compatible with core American values and better suited to guide relations with Native Americans.

Prevailing international standards insist that nations scrap the doctrine of conquest and judicial mindset that goes along with it. We need not rule Indian tribes and peoples as conquered subjects, nor is it appropriate view the "Land of the Free" through the eyes of a conqueror; in the 21st century we have no need for the self-described "courts of the conqueror." The values that underpin notions of conquest are dark, and they contradict the core values expressed in the Declaration of Independence that are supposed to guide our nation. However, it is painfully difficult to confront the legacy of conquest and realign federal Indian law, because it exposes the inner demons from our history that impugn our inflated self-image as a nation deeply committed to human rights. This psychological barrier prevents the discourse necessary to free Native Americans from the bondage placed upon them by the notions of conquest in our legal culture.

2. The Law of Colonialism

Colonialism is another train of thought in federal Indian law. Chief Justice John Marshall imported the law and mindset of colonialism from early international law.[37] In *Johnson*, he adopted the Doctrine of Discovery in whole cloth and expanded it to fit the American setting. It has an anti-indigenous function and suffers from similar problems that make it an unsatisfactory framework for defining Native American rights.

In Marshall's enlarged doctrine, the act of discovery operates to grant legal title to Indian land to the United States. Marshall went on to wed the act of discovery to conquest, thereby creating another legal fiction to support his version of discovery: a discovered country is automatically a conquered country. The *Johnson* doctrine is used in other British colonies, such as Canada, Australia, and New Zealand.[38] Professor Robert J. Miller defines the doctrine as follows:

> The Doctrine of Discovery is an international law principle under which European countries, colonists and settlers made legal claims against the lands, assets, and human rights of indigenous peoples all over the world in the fifteenth through twentieth centuries. In essence, the Doctrine provided that newly-arrived Europeans automatically acquired property rights in land and sovereign, political, and commercial powers over indigenous peoples without their knowledge or consent. When Europeans planted their flags and religious symbols in "newly discovered" lands, they were using the well-recognized legal

> procedures and rituals of the Doctrine of Discovery to demonstrate their country's legal claim to indigenous lands and peoples. The doctrine was created and justified by feudal, religious, racial, and ethnocentric ideas, all premised on the belief of European and Christian superiority over other cultures, religions, and races of the world.[39]

The law of colonialism developed further with the addition of the guardianship principle taken from early international law. *Cherokee Nation* incorporated that principle from Victoria's law of nations, which granted enormous powers of intrusion. Victoria assumed that Indians had no laws or civilization and were incapable of self-government:

> It might, therefore, be maintained that in their own interests the sovereigns of Spain might undertake the administration of their country, providing them with prefects and governors for their towns, and might even give them new lords, so long as this was clearly for their benefit.[40]

Cherokee Nation asserted that "[Indians] are in a state of pupilage. Their relation to the United States resembles that of a ward to his guardian."[41] The guardianship role of the government was utilized to expand federal hegemony over the internal affairs of Indian nations and displace their governments in *United States v. Kagama* (1886), which ruled that "[t]he power of the general government over these remnants of a race once powerful, now weak and diminished in numbers, is necessary to their protection."[42] The White Man's Burden was manifested in the civilization, Christianization, and tutelage programs and policies between the 1880s and 1934, when the government's guardianship powers over American Indians were at their zenith. It guided efforts to stamp out tribal culture, religion, and languages in order to forcibly assimilate the wards of the government and prepare them for citizenship.[43] In this period, when overzealous bureaucrats subjected Indians to what Felix S. Cohen described as "the greatest concentration of administrative absolutism in our government structure," the absolute power of the government over the lives of American Indians was upheld by the courts in the name of guardianship; the jurists in those cases described Indians as a barbaric, primitive, and inferior race of people, with contemptible governments, cultures, religions, and ways of life.[44] The duty of the government under the White Man's Burden was to stamp out these savage vestiges of Native life and replace them with the trappings of Western Civilization. Because it is premised on the presumed racial, religious, and cultural supremacy of Europeans, the law of colonialism is heavily tainted with racism *for all concerned*. On the one hand, white Americans are stereotyped as colonial masters,[45] who embrace outmoded policies.[46] On the other, Indians are branded as a racially, morally, and intellectually inferior race of people.[47] The institution of guardianship was used extensively by colonizing nations to manage indigenous peoples and control their property, as James Anaya observed in *Indigenous Peoples in International Law*:

> As colonizing states and their offspring consolidated power over indigenous lands, many such states adopted trusteeship notions akin to those proposed earlier by Vitoria as grounds and parameters for the nonconsensual exercise of authority over indigenous peoples. Pursuant to this philosophy, associated with the now infamous school identified as "scientific racism," the objective of trusteeship was to wean native peoples from their "backward" ways and to "civilize" them.[48]

In the United States, the guardianship principle gave rise to the "plenary power" doctrine, which grants Congress absolute power over American Indian tribes, peoples, and their property. This extraordinary power does not derive from the Constitution, as explained in *Lone Wolf v. Hitchcock* (1903):

> Congress possessed a paramount power over the property of the Indians, by reason of its exercise of guardianship over their interests, and such authority might be implied, even though opposed to the strict letter of a treaty with the Indians.[49]

Lone Wolf summoned *absolute* legislative power—that is, the unfettered exercise of power, unrestrained by any constitutional limitations and not subject to judicial review.[50] This troubling anomaly harkens us back to the greatest threat to liberty in our form of government—Alexis de Tocqueville's "tyranny of the majority."

Colonialism is not an appropriate framework for defining the human rights of Native Americans. Five reasons for rejecting this framework spring to mind.

First, it suffers from pronounced invidious racism that is no longer acceptable or appropriate in the 21st century.

Second, the brand of colonialism that emerges from the dark side of federal Indian law in the above cases does not envision a benign protectorate. Some American colonies on foreign soil might be described as benign regimes, where US governance was guided by the welfare of the Native peoples and where it administered property for their benefit. That was the situation described in *Carino v. Insular Government of the Philippine Islands* (1908), where the United States respected tribal land rights in the Philippines, because the purpose of that colony was to "administer the property and rights 'for the benefit of the inhabitants thereof.'"[51] In the Philippines, "our first object in the internal administration of the islands [was] to do justice to the natives, not to exploit their country for private gain."[52] *Carino* distinguished our Philippine governance from the harsher colonial rule of Indian tribes at home under *Lone Wolf* principles by noting that "the dominant purpose of whites in America was to occupy the land."[53] Thus, we protect indigenous rights in the Philippines, but confiscate aboriginal land at home. Likewise, *Tee-Hit-Ton* reconciled that different treatment of colonized natives on the same basis: we acquired the Philippines to benefit the natives, whereas "the settlement of the white race in the United States" guides colonization of Indian land at home, because "the dominant purpose of the whites in America was to occupy the land.'"[54] When we gaze upon colonized land through the eyes of *Lone Wolf* and *Tee-Hit-Ton*, we see resources that lay available for the taking, economic exploitation is the guiding star, and all institutions are designed to set in motion a one-way transfer of property from indigenous to non-indigenous hands. It is hard for settlers with this mindset to adapt to the land, as the indigenous peoples have done.[55] A legal culture that perpetrates that mindset becomes a barrier to shedding the legacy of colonialism, coming to grips with the legitimate needs of indigenous peoples, and maturing into a more just culture that has adapted to the land we call home, thereby becoming more native to place, like the indigenous peoples have done. In addition, unfettered colonialism creates an intrusive regime run by a paternalistic federal government. Armed by plenary power, it can trump tribal self-government or replace it with trusteeship or guardianship. That regime is a far-cry from the rights to self-determination, self-government, and indigenous institutions specified in the *Declaration*.[56]

Third, instead of fostering the maturation and growth of democracy in settler states, the domestic law of colonialism fosters numerous legal fictions pertaining to Native peoples. It is amazing to see the lengths that jurists go in fashioning legal fictions and doctrines to support the taking of other peoples' land and the governance of Native peoples as colonized subjects. Some legal fictions in the law of colonialism were examined in *In the Courts of the Conqueror: The 10 Worst Indian Law Cases Ever Decided* (2010), such as: (1) aboriginal land is vacant land; (2) the Pope of the Catholic Church can give the Western Hemisphere to Spain; (3) royal charters empower colonists to settle Native territory as if they were the first human beings in the area; (4) the discovery of North America by European explorers transfers legal title to Indian land to the United States; (5) the discovery of North America by Europeans can be equated with the conquest of that continent; (6) the normal rules of international law requiring conquerors to respect property rights in the lands they invade do not apply in America because the Indians are hostile; (7) native land is "wasteland" or a "savage wilderness" that one owns, uses, or wants and is available for the taking by colonists—therefore any aboriginal interests in the land are extinguished upon the arrival of the British; (8) Native peoples have no concept of "property," do not claim any property rights, or are incapable of owning land; (9) Christians have a right to take land from non-Christians because Heathens lack property rights; (10) Native lands are "surplus" lands; (11) native peoples are incapable of governing themselves—they need us to govern them; (12) native people are racially inferior; and (13) Europeans can engage in "just war" against Native people if they do not submit to colonization.[57]

These legal fictions demonstrate that the law of colonialism is built upon an unjust house of cards. Courts normally develop and apply legal fictions (i.e., assumptions of fact used by a court to decide a case) to reach just results, such as the creation of a "constructive trust" in the case of fraud.[58] They are "understood by lawyers and judges to be false," but "are rarely questioned as anything other than a tool the law uses to ensure a fair or consistent conclusion."[59] By contrast, legal fictions are used to achieve unjust results in Indian cases. When these fictions are shattered as unjust falsehoods and stricken from the law in cases like *Mabo and Others v. Queensland* (1992), the law of colonialism at once shrivels in the light of justice.[60] Without that mythological clothing, settler states stand naked upon dubious moral ground as "unjust usurpers."[61] That discomfort explains why it is so hard to give up devices that hide misdeeds beneath a legal facade; nevertheless, modern courts should not resort to unjust legal fictions to support unfettered colonialism in federal Indian law or to define the human rights of Native Americans in the post-colonial age.

Fourth, colonialism has been rejected by the world community. The United Nations *Declaration on the Granting of Independence to Colonial Countries and Peoples* (1960) condemns colonialism as a repugnant and oppressive institution that prevents colonized peoples from fully realizing their rights to development, to self-determination, and to the full enjoyment of human rights. Colonialism is hard on the land, the natural world, and the indigenous peoples who inhabit the natural world.

Fifth and finally, the *Declaration* flatly rejects the framework of colonialism for defining indigenous rights. It subscribes to principles of justice, equality, democracy, good faith, and good government as the framework for defining and interpreting the human rights of Native Americans. In the post-colonial age, it is time for the Supreme Court to find principles other than conquest and colonialism to decide Native American cases. The *Declaration* points to the human rights principle, and it leaves no room for the law of colonialism.

3. The Tribal Sovereignty and Protectorate Principles

The third line of thought is the tribal sovereignty principle, and its related protectorate principle. The tribal sovereignty principle begins with the premise that the self-government powers of Indian tribes are inherent powers of a limited sovereignty that have never been extinguished.[62] This premise is supported by numerous Supreme Court decisions, beginning with *Worcester v. Georgia* (1832).[63] Under that line of cases, tribal self-government powers are not delegated to the tribes by Congress. Instead, they are *inherent powers* arising from the preexisting sovereignty of Indian tribes as independent nations long before contact with European nations. After contact, the inclusion of Indian nations into the territorial boundaries of the republic under the protection of the United States necessarily limited some aspects of their preexisting sovereignty, but did not extinguish it. Furthermore, the retained governmental powers cannot be divested by any authority except a treaty or act of Congress—and, in more recent times, by judicial limitations imposed by the Supreme Court under federal common law pursuant to the much-criticized "implicit divestiture theory."[64]

Cohen's describes the origins and nature of the tribal sovereignty principle:

> Most Indian tribes were independent, self-governing societies long before their contact with European nations. The history of tribal self-government forms the basis for the exercise of modern powers. Indian tribes have consistently been recognized, first by the European nations, and later by the United States, as "distinct, independent political communities" [citing *Worcester*], qualified to exercise powers of self-government, not by virtue of any delegation of powers, but rather by reason of their original tribal sovereignty. The right of tribes to govern their members and territories flows from a preexisting sovereignty limited, but not abolished, by their inclusion within the territorial bounds of the United States. Tribal powers of self-government are recognized by the Constitution, treaties, judicial decisions, and administrative practice. They necessarily are observed and protected by the federal government in accordance with a relationship designed to ensure continued validity of Indian self-government insofar as governing powers have not been limited or extinguished by lawful federal authority. Once recognized as a political body by the United States, a tribe retains its sovereignty until Congress acts to divest that sovereignty.
>
> Perhaps the most basic principle of all Indian law, supported by a host of decisions, is that those powers lawfully vested in an Indian nation are not, in general, delegated powers granted by express acts of Congress, but rather "inherent powers of a limited sovereignty which has never been extinguished." [citing *United States v. Wheeler*, 435 U.S.

> 313, 322–323 (1978)] The Supreme Court has observed that "Indian tribes still possess those aspects of sovereignty not withdrawn by treaty or statute, or by implication as a necessary result of their dependant status." [citing *Wheeler* at 323]. This principle guides determinations of the scope of tribal authority. The tribes began their relationship with the federal government with the sovereign powers of independent nations. They came under the authority of the United States through treaties and agreements between tribes and the federal government and through the assertion of authority by the United States. Federal treaties and congressional enactments have imposed certain limitations on tribal governments, especially on their external political relations, and the Supreme Court has issued some common law rulings that introduce further limitations as a matter of federal common law. But from the beginning the United States permitted, then protected, continued internal tribal government. In so doing, the United States applied a general principle of international law to the particular situation of the Indians.[65]

The tribal sovereignty doctrine mitigates hardships imposed on Native America by notions of colonialism and conquest. It was formulated in *Worcester* during the twilight of Chief Justice Marshall's distinguished career, at a time when his thinking about the place of American Indians in society and law had fully matured. By 1832, he had seen—to his surprise and dismay—how his prior rulings in *Johnson* and *Cherokee Nation* had been used to harm American Indian tribes. He was now prepared to address indigenous circumstance head-on and set a path for correctly understanding the rightful place of Indian tribes in the American setting.

Worcester rejected the South's dark version of Indian law founded on conquest and abject racism, which closely resembles the law of slavery, which the South embraced. Instead, *Worcester* dispensed with notions of conquest and ruled that the incorporation of Indian nations into the republic is not conquest at all. It also rejected the notion that discovery grants land title and dominion as far-fetched. Interestingly, *Worcester* did not employ racism at all to define indigenous rights, but simply described Indians in a straight-forward manner. Furthermore, the landmark decision made it clear that Indian nations and the United States have a protectorate relationship that requires the United States to protect, not destroy or prey upon the Indian nations through unfettered colonialism. The protectorate relationship among nations was commonly found in international relations of the day, and it did not have anything to do with the institutions of colonialism or conquest. Finally, the *Worcester* Court abandoned the use of nefarious legal fictions, sticking instead to the "actual state of things" throughout the opinion. Thus freed from the "dark side" of federal Indian law, the Supreme Court ruled that Georgia had no right to tread on the sovereignty of the Cherokee Nation in one of the best cases ever decided. (*See,* discussion of *Worcester* in Chapter Seven.) It is important to remember that in 1832 the rest of the nation was lined-up to commit a gross miscarriage of justice: the forcible removal of the Indian race from the South. In this dark period, it was only the Supreme Court that declared the state framework for removal illegal. That single ray of light illustrates the defining role of the courts to act as a bulwark of justice when vulnerable groups are faced with oppression by the tyranny of the majority.

It is significant that *Worcester* did not use prejudicial racial stereotypes in defining the rights and status of Indian tribes. Abandoning derogatory racial stereotypes for the very first time, the Supreme Court described American Indians as "a distinct people, divided into separate nations, independent of each other and of the rest of the world, having institutions of their own, and governing themselves by their own laws."[66] *Worcester* established the principle that the borders of Indian reservations form an inviolate barrier to intrusion by state laws: "The treaties and laws of the United States contemplate the Indian territory as completely separated from that of the states; and provide that all intercourse with them shall be carried out exclusively by the government of the union."[67] Thus, Georgia's laws asserting dominion over the Cherokee Nation were declared a nullity, because the "Indian nations had always been considered as distinct, independent political communities, retaining their original natural rights, as the undisputed possessors of the soil, from time immemorial" and treaties made with Indian nations are "the supreme law of the land."[68] The court concluded:

> The Cherokee Nation, then, is a distinct community occupying its own territory, with boundaries accurately described, in which the laws of Georgia can have no force, and which the citizens of Georgia have no right to enter, but with the assent of the Cherokee themselves, or in conformity with treaties, and acts of congress.[69]

Worcester's doctrine of tribal sovereignty thus establishes four bedrock principles in federal Indian law: (1) the Indian tribes enjoy a sovereign right of self-government that is not divested by their inclusion in the United States and is free from interference by the states, (2) Indian treaties must be honored as the supreme law of the land, (3) the doctrine of discovery and edicts from Europe do not divest Indian land or sovereignty, and (4) reservation borders are protective barriers against hostile states and land-hungry settlers. These principles form a protective shield for the rights of Indian tribes recognized by federal Indian law that endures to this day, despite the battering by the Rehnquist and Roberts Courts in recent years.

Worcester also explained the political charter of Indian tribes in the American setting. After articulating the legal status of Indian tribes as "domestic dependent nations" with inherent sovereignty that exist as separate political communities within the United States, the Marshall Court had to devise an appropriate political relationship between the tribes and United States, best suited for maintaining that legal status. During that early period in the American Republic, the states voluntarily entered the Union by processes defined in the Constitution. As the contours of the political system were taking shape, the Indian tribes also began entering the Union. They came through treaties with the United States made under the Treaty Clause. Marshall saw Indian nations entering into the republic by treaties, in which self-governing, domestic dependent nations exist free from unwarranted state intrusions in a protectorate safeguarded by a stronger nation.

Worcester explains the protectorate nature of the political charter and makes it clear that conquest is not the means by which the tribes entered the Union. Treaty stipulations placing signatory Indian nations under the protection of the United States do not operate to "conquer" them, nor deprive them of their sovereignty. Rather, they create a "protectorate relationship" between two nations of the type commonly found in the international realm. The Court stated:

> This relation was that of a nation claiming and receiving the protection of one more powerful; not that of individuals abandoning their national character, and submitting as subjects to the law of a master.[70]

Worcester borrowed the protectorate system directly from the international law and relations of his day. Indeed, *Worcester's* definition is similar to *Black's Law Dictionary* (2009) definition of a *protectorate* as:

> the relationship between a weaker nation and a stronger one when the weaker nation has transferred the management of its more important international affairs to the stronger nation.[71]

The protectorate system can be found in international relations since the rise of nation-states. It permits a stronger nation to protect a more vulnerable one from power politics in the international sphere by acquiring control over its external affairs, while the weaker nation retains sovereignty over its internal affairs. There are many political reasons to form a protectorate relationship, because it can foster trade, peace, security, protection, and otherwise advance the self-interests of nation-states. Once established, a protectorate nation enjoys increased security from predation by third-parties in the exercise of its internal sovereignty under the protection of the stronger nation.

The protectorate relationship between Indian nations and the United States is well-described in *Worcester.* Indian nations are the "weaker nations" in the arrangement, but they are not described as "colonies" or "conquered subjects." The central feature of the relation, then and now, is the duty assumed by the stronger nation to protect the sovereignty, well-being, and integrity of the weaker nation. That duty does not permit the stronger nation to trample, prey upon, or oppress the protected nation. Marshall stressed: "Protection does not imply destruction of the protected."[72] In addition, Indian nations do not surrender their right to self-government by entering into the relation:

> [T]he settled doctrine of the law of nations is, that a weaker power does not surrender its independence—its right to self government, by associating with a stronger, and taking its protection. A weak state, in order to provide for its safety, may place itself under the protection of one more powerful, without stripping itself of the right of government, and ceasing to be a state. Examples of this kind are not wanting in Europe. "Tributary and feudatory states," says Vattel, "do not thereby cease to be sovereign and independent states, so long as self government and sovereign and independent authority are left in the administration of the state." At the present day, more than one state may be considered as holding its right of self government under the guarantees and protection of one or more allies.[73]

Protected Indian nations retain political hegemony over internal affairs, but their international relations are managed by the United States. In all other respects, they *continue* to exist as separate, self-governing communities within the American political system as "domestic dependent nations" under the protection of the United States.

Under the *Worcester* protectorate system, the United States gains an ally, but it *does not acquire the right to exploit or subjugate protected Indian nations.* This rule parts company from conquest and colonialism. It insists upon a more benign political relationship that creates "no claim to lands, no dominion over [Indian] persons" on the part of the United States.[74] Instead, domestic dependent Indian nations are bound to the United States "as a dependent ally, claiming the protection of a powerful friend and neighbor, and receiving the advantages of that protection, without involving a surrender of their national character."[75]

Three bedrock features characterize the *Worcester* protectorate relation. First, Indian tribes are described as "nations," and are not considered "colonies" or "conquered states" divested of sovereignty, except for external international affairs. Second, as the stronger power, the United States is both *obliged and empowered* to protect Indian nations. *Protection* is the central purpose of the political relationship. It guides and circumscribes the power exercised by the United States. As the stronger nation, it is obliged to exercise that power when necessary to protect and maintain the tribes' status as protectorate nations. Third, the protectorate relation does not give the United States license to harm Indian nations, or divest their political, property, cultural, or human rights. The commandments from *Worcester* that prohibit harm and require protection are at the core of the protectorate relation.

Followed to its logical conclusion, the protectorate principle significantly affects other doctrines in federal Indian law. Once we lay aside the incompatible doctrine of conquest and law of colonialism, the protectorate framework fundamentally reshapes the plenary power, guardianship, and trusteeship doctrines, and places them into their proper role as tools to protect Indian nations. Once we give the protectorate principle proper effect, the "dark side" of plenary power, guardianship, and trusteeship is trimmed away: we can see that the so-called "plenary power" of Congress is a misnomer that is more accurately described as "protectorate power," aimed only to protect, and not destroy or oppress; and the guardianship and trusteeship powers become derivative powers available to protect, and not divest, tribal sovereignty, property, cultural integrity, religious freedom, and traditional ways of life. Indian nations should flourish under the *Worcester* framework, because the Supreme Court brought no "dark side" to the protector-protectorate relationship. Nothing in *Worcester* suggests a nefarious purpose. We cannot properly impute intent to exploit, oppress, or undermine Indian nations that voluntarily entered into the Union, any more than the United States intended to oppress states that joined the Union. Under *Worcester*, there is no legal basis to rule by conquest, no room to manufacture unjust legal doctrines, and tribal sovereignty is not subject to divestiture at the whim of any branch of the federal government (indeed, in the protectorate setting, it is hard to imagine how any exercise of tribal self-government offends US interests, except succession or treaties with foreign nations entered into without United States consultation). The protectorate system creates a benevolent regime that opposes the anti-indigenous goals of conquest, discovery, and colonialism, which are antithetical to a political system protective of indigenous rights.

During the modern era, Indian tribes mounted a Tribal Sovereignty Movement to reclaim their dignity and assert their self-government powers. Through litigation, legislation, and social change that gave effect to the *Worcester* framework, Indian nations defined, refined, and activated their inherent powers of self-government.[76] Today, the American political system contains more than five-hundred full-service tribal governments that maintain a government-to-government relationship with the federal government. In recent years, tribal sovereignty has been under assault by the Rehnquist and Roberts Courts. They have lost sight of John Marshall's inherent tribal sovereignty principle and the political charter of Indian nations in the protectorate framework. Nonetheless, the Marshall Court got it right. *Worcester* provides the best framework for defining self-determination in the American setting. It is not only compatible with the *Declaration*, but the UN standards can supplement the inherent tribal sovereignty doctrine by adding more details about how the distinct political communities recognized by *Worcester* can be preserved and protected in the American setting. The convergence of *Worcester* and the *Declaration* produces a powerful and legally sound framework for recognizing and defining Native American rights.

There is a tension between these three lines of judicial thought. It represents the internal struggle between the good side of the law, which is protective of indigenous rights in the setting of a benign protectorate, and the "dark side," which strives to undermine that regime. On the one hand, inherent tribal sovereignty in a protectorate setting represents the best that any western legal system has to offer, but on the other hand, over the past one hundred and fifty years, that line of thought has forced Native Americans to struggle in order to free themselves from the yoke placed upon them by the doctrines of conquest and colonialism. That long-standing tension in the law must be resolved. The *Declaration* weighs in on the side of protecting Native America, and it tips the scale toward a more protective body of law. The need for the *Declaration* to resolve this tension in our legal culture and place our outmoded nefarious legal doctrines to rest is at once compelling and manifest. Colonialism and rule by conquest have been repudiated by the international community since World War II as anathema to human rights.

When examining the major lines of judicial thought in federal Indian law, the *Declaration* provides an important interpretative guidepost that courts can follow to (1) select the most compatible lines of thought for defining Native American rights, (2) interpret or re-interpret Indian law doctrines in the post-colonial age, and (3) prune outmoded trains of thought that are no longer appropriate.[77] Above all, the *Declaration* adds strength to tribal sovereignty. It urges courts to treat self-government as an inalienable human right. When courts interpret the right of self-government through a human rights lens, tribal sovereignty must be understood as inviolate and not subject to defeasance.

The *Declaration* Helps America Complete Its Nation-Building Process

Pressing political problems can be solved by implementing the *Declaration* into our social fabric and political order. The formation of nations involves the steps taken by groups to form societies and create governing institutions that define the political order. During the rise of free and democratic nations, indigenous peoples in colonized lands were frequently left out of the nation-building process. As colonized people living under the thumb of their masters, they were relegated to the margin during the formation and growth of the nation, as the colonies gained independence, built nascent institutions, and grew into the modern democracies seen today. As such, indigenous needs were often overlooked in the development of modern laws and institutions, which focused only on confining indigenous peoples to the original structures created by colonialism. Excluded from the nation-building process, marginalized and subjugated indigenous peoples find themselves living subject to a modern political system they did not make, had no role in developing or administering, and to which they did not consent. After maturing states emerged from a colonizing culture, the dilemma now faced by them is: *What to do about the indigenous people?*

The issue of incorporation is a critical ingredient for democracies founded upon the consent of the governed. Their legitimacy depends upon consensus and non-coercion in every sector of society. From that foundation, modern democracies strive toward positive trends and institutions—those that create conditions of justice and equality so citizens can live in an open society, with mutual understanding, respect, and diversity. Those desirable goals are ideally achieved through consensual processes followed by citizens and immigrants, not coercion. However, these elements are missing when indigenous peoples are concerned, and that poses a legitimacy problem in the treatment and governance of indigenous peoples by the nation-state. On the one hand, all agree that indigenous peoples cannot remain relegated to the margin in the midst of free and democratic nations, living under laws and institutions that perpetuate oppressive colonial conditions from a bygone era, long after the descendants of settlers have abandoned settlerism, with its anti-indigenous outlook. However, what is the best approach for bringing indigenous peoples into the national community? This is a vexing question, because their situation falls outside of the general pattern for the formation and growth of nations.

The normal mode for incorporating immigrants into the national community aims for inclusion in a multicultural society, based upon a consensual foundation, usually one individual at a time. However, indigenous peoples already inhabit the nation. They predate it, with their own pre-existing governments, and they wish to preserve their lands, territories, and cultures. Furthermore, like the rest of humanity, they also aspire toward self-determination through self-government and their own indigenous institutions. Against these widely held indigenous aspirations, nationalism often insists on assimilation. Forcible assimilation demands that indigenous peoples discard their group rights, collective aspirations, and cultural heritage to integrate into the body politic. However, indigenous peoples are unwilling pay that price. It is difficult for them to follow the usual path of integration and assimilation chosen by most immigrants. Immigrants willingly come to a new land, seeking to become members of mainstream society in the adopted nation of their choice. That is a vastly different situation from indigenous peoples, who are aboriginal inhabitants engulfed by a settler population.

The usual path followed by immigrants is voluntary assimilation: they move to a new land, learn the language, customs, culture, and history of their adopted homeland, and shed their own, which is often seen as necessary in order to "fit in." They embrace the laws and institutions of their new home as their own. They work hard to assimilate, applying for citizenship and taking the oath of allegiance, and they then strive to integrate into a multicultural society, seeking only an equal opportunity. For them, the strong drive of nationalism toward assimilation is not a problem, because that is their goal. After a generation or two of hard work toward that end, immigrant populations become successfully integrated. They assimilate socially, politically, culturally, and economically into their new homeland; and they identify so completely with it that only little vestiges of their former cultures, languages, and heritages from their native land remain. Indeed, many descendants of immigrant families, in subsequent generations, no longer know where their ancestors came from. They have become Americans.

That model for incorporation does not work well for indigenous peoples, due to their different circumstances and aspirations. To accommodate their situation, host nations must go beyond the normal modes of incorporation and foster a multicultural society with a "multinational" dimension capable of bringing indigenous peoples into a national culture on a consensual basis where their political, cultural, and human rights as indigenous peoples are recognized and respected.[78] A *multinational society* refers to a free, democratic, and multicultural society that recognizes the indigenous nations that exist in its midst—that is, a social order akin to modern American society, where five hundred tribal governments comprise an integral part of the domestic political system. In an insightful article, sociologist Duane Champagne maintains that a multinational model helps democratic nations become consensually based political orders by including indigenous peoples in a society built upon justice, mutual understanding, respect, non-coercion, and diversity.[79] To be sure, these are the best ingredients for legitimacy in democratic societies emerging from a colonizing culture that seek to go beyond the legacy of conquest.

To complete the nation-building process, the challenges in each settler state are to find the best way to incorporate tribal people on consensual basis and foster the conditions for justice, mutual understanding and respect, non-coercion, and diversity so that their human rights as indigenous peoples can be recognized and respected. Responses to this perplexing problem may differ among modern nations. But the need to bring indigenous peoples into the body politic is described by Professor Erica-Irene Daes, former chair of the UN Working Group on Indigenous Populations, as *belated nation-building*.[80] It entails the development of measures to secure a future in which self-determination for indigenous inhabitants is assured. According to Professor Daes, belated nation-building is marked by peaceful negotiations and meaningful participation by indigenous peoples in a consensual process:

> ...through which indigenous peoples are able to join with all other parties that make up the State on mutually-agreed upon and just terms, after many years of isolation and exclusion. This process does not require the assimilation of individuals, as citizens like all others, but the recognition and incorporation of distinct peoples in the fabric of the State, on agreed terms.[81]

Until belated nation-building is completed, host nations remain mired in injustice, frozen in an age of conquest and colonialism, and the core values and ideals enjoyed by everyone else are beyond the reach of indigenous peoples. Yet, some modern states resist building a multinational society. Weak nations with unstable foundations see indigenous rights as a threat to the political order and refuse to acknowledge them altogether. This pattern is seen in Mexico and several nations in Latin America. Even in strong nations the recognition of indigenous rights can be difficult. Those strongly unified nations that drive toward a socially and culturally homogenous civil society sometimes become so highly regimented that divergent indigenous rights are not tolerated. For example, it is hard to imagine the existence of indigenous rights in a highly regimented nation like the Third Reich, which marched toward an Aryan society. In totalitarianism, any deviation from the established norm is seen as a threat to the nation, and unwilling participants are coerced into the social order. In the democracies with strong tendencies toward assimilation and homogeneity, the underlying political assumption is that all people are in agreement with living life in such a regimented national order and participating in a monolithic political structure. However, that assumption does not apply to indigenous peoples, as Professor Champagne notes:

> For a relatively homogenous national community or a community of immigrants who are seeking religious or political freedoms, the idea of national consensus on the unified institutions of the nation-state is generally reasonable. The consensus underlying both the unified nation-state and the multicultural nation-state does not apply to indigenous peoples who have had governments, institutions, culture, and land that predate the formation of the nation-state. Indigenous

> peoples are either not parties to the formation of the nation-state or are unwilling participants forced into citizenship. In both cases, the indigenous people are coerced into participation in the nation-state that, in many cases, does not recognize most issues of importance for the indigenous peoples.[82]

In the above circumstances, Champagne predicts conflict and instability even in strong nations, like the United States, with solidified foundations:

- The nation-state is inherently unstable because it cannot achieve the consensus that is required to support the national community and state structure. Groups such as indigenous peoples, whose values, institutions, traditions, and land claims are not incorporated as part of the original act of nation-state creation and consensus, are left with relatively coerced cultural, institutional, and political participation in the national community and state structure. Coercive measures for participation and incorporation of native peoples do not create voluntary participation but only compliance and the informal pursuit of native rights within national and international arenas. The nation-state model will pit indigenous peoples, submerged nations, and some minority and gender groups against the cultural and legal hegemony of the nation-state, and will not lead to full participation or recognition of rights and citizenship. Granting of full citizenship merely abstracts and legally absolves the rights and values of indigenous peoples, and forces indigenous peoples to pursue alternative, non-nation-state avenues of securing their rights and values.

- The fundamental flaw of the unified or multicultural nation-state is that it assumes all peoples are in agreement with the consensual principles of nation-state organization and participation. If a group (such as indigenous peoples) is not in agreement with the fundamental organization and rules of participation of the nation-state, then it is encouraged and forced to participate under alien rules. Such forced and nonconsensual participation breaks the basic principles of consensual participation in the nation-state and leads to cultural, political, legal, and territorial hegemony by the national community

> and nation-state, and the conscious subordination of rights, values, institutions, self-government, and territorial claims. The continued non-recognition of indigenous rights will lead to inherent social, political, and legal conflicts that may not be solvable under the unified or multicultural nation-state models.[83]

Champagne wisely counsels that multiculturalism must extend its scope to include "not only religion, ethnicity, and race but also nationality, lifestyle and indigenous rights" in order to become a multinational society; and until the state recognizes their rights, indigenous peoples will not consensually participate. [84] In the absence of indigenous justice, he predicts that "[s]table nation-states will not be achieved through paths of coercion and domination, since such regimes engender resistance and subtle forms of nonparticipation, which disrupt political, social, cultural, and economic relations."[85]

In the United States, many conflicting approaches have been taken by the government to incorporate Native Americans into the national community. The zigzagging methods range from the *Worcester* protectorate system to the Indian Removal Movement that segregated the Indian nations from the rest of society; from exterminating the Indian race altogether during the peak of the Indian Wars, to peaceful policies of civilizing reservation Indian wards of the government for assimilation (circa 1886–1934); from rebuilding tribal governments under the Indian Reorganization Act, to dismantling them by the Indian termination and assimilation policies of the 1950s; and, finally, back to the restoration of self-government and Indian control over their own destiny under the Indian Self-Determination Policy from 1970 to the present. The *Declaration* reaffirms the Indian Self-Determination Policy, but asks us to go one step beyond into the human rights realm.

During my career as a native rights advocate, I have seen people and policymakers debate the best approach for incorporating Native Americans into the body politic. Many assert the political charter described in the *Worcester* framework; others, such as Professor Champagne, advance the analogous multicultural society model, with a multinational dimension. Racists take the "spear-an-Indian, save-a-fish" approach; whereas, the conservative backlash wants to terminate the United States' political relationship with Indian tribes, abrogate treaties, and forcibly assimilate Native Americans into Hometown America, as long as they live across the tracks. Some paternalistic liberals support self-determination, so long as they are in charge. Many uniformed, but well-meaning folks take the simplistic "Bill of Rights" approach. They ask, *Why not just provide Indians with equality before the law, and nothing more—just like anyone else?* The need for human rights tailored to indigenous circumstances eludes the armchair constitutionalists. They see indigenous rights as "special rights," and that raises a specter of discrimination, since ordinary whites do not hold such rights (even though they do not need indigenous rights because their human rights are already fully recognized and protected). This view is held, even though neither the Supreme Court nor the *Declaration* sees indigenous rights as "special rights."[86]

We can "sort the wheat from the chaff" through a focused national discourse on the nature and content of Native American human rights. Such a dialogue has never been conducted in our nation. However, the *Declaration* calls for that long-overdue conversation. It weighs in on the side of recognizing indigenous rights and protecting them under familiar principles of justice, equality, non-discrimination, and good faith. In addition, the *Declaration* validates the Indian Self-Determination Policy as the right approach toward the incorporation of Native America into the national community. It also reaffirms the *Worcester* framework as the most consistent, multinational political model for achieving self-determination for indigenous peoples in the American setting. Because of its compatibility in these important respects, the belated nation-building in the United States called for by the *Declaration* does not entail major political surgery, nor does it require the importation of disruptive alien concepts. When viewed from that perspective, and especially in comparison to the task faced by many other nations, the United States need only take a few remaining baby-steps to (1) reaffirm the *Worcester* framework, (2) stay the course set by the Indian Self-Determination Policy, and (3) uplift those laws and policies that fail to meet the UN standards in consultation and cooperation with Native Americans. These steps to implement the *Declaration* are nation-building steps.

We can go "down the yellow-brick road" using the *Declaration* as our step-by-step guide, confident that the nation-building measures provided by that instrument are consistent with our core values, knowing that the road ahead is paved by universal standards approved by the world community. After all, the *Declaration* is aimed at strengthening nations. It asserts that recognition of indigenous rights "will enhance harmonious and cooperative relations between the State and indigenous peoples, based on principles of justice, democracy, respect for human rights, non-discrimination and good faith."[87] By taking the belated nation-building steps outlined in the *Declaration* and strengthening compatible lines of judicial thought, we can heal historical trauma, overcome the legacy of conquest, and make it a thing of the past. The devil, of course, lies in the details, as in all important junctures of American history when the nation took steps to restore justice for oppressed segments of the American population.

CHAPTER SIX
Toward an American Land Ethic

There are envrionmental reasons for implementing the *Declaration* that cannot be ignored. The *Declaration* not only serves to protect and preserve indigenous habitat, as well as related land and use rights of indigenous peoples and their cultural survival in our industrialized society, but those provisions also create a healthy byproduct—the conditions needed to forge an American land ethic, which is a vital step toward an environmentally sound civilization. This chapter examines the disparate ways that the human family has traditionally looked at the land, explores the forces that stymie a land ethic in the United States, and explains the congruency between protecting indigenous rights and developing a land ethic for the American setting.[1]

A clear "land ethic" is sorely needed. Without it, our modern society cannot summon the political will to address the environmental problems that threaten our existence. A land ethic helps humanity lead a sustainable existence, as every civilization must. It is also a key ingredient to social change, for without a land ethic, the American people cannot fully mature from a nation of immigrants and settlers recovering from a rapacious frontier history of Manifest Destiny and stride toward a more just culture that has adapted to the land and incorporates valuable indigenous knowledge and values of its native peoples into the social fabric. This social evolution is a natural healing and adaptation process followed by immigrant populations in colonized lands. In the post-colonial era, they shed the trappings of conquerors and mindset of colonists found in "settler states" and resolve to become more "native" to place.

A land ethic has been hard to achieve in the United States. In 1948, Aldo Leopold, the influential ecologist, forester, and father of public wildlife management, lamented: "There is as yet no ethic dealing with man's relation to land and to the animals and plants which grow upon it."[2] Planting the seeds for that ethic, Leopold urged society to decolonize the way we look at the land and evolve a land ethic as the social product of a mature society. He predicted that such an ethic would fundamentally change our role from "conquerors" of the land, and the animals and plants that grow on it, to members of a biotic land-community that co-exists on the same land:

> In human history, we have learned (I hope) that the conqueror role is eventually self-defeating. Why? Because it is implicit in such a role that the conqueror knows, *ex cathedra*, just what makes the [land] tick, and just what and who is valuable, and what and who is worthless. It always turns out that he knows neither, and this is why his conquests eventually defeat themselves.

Unfortunately, Leopold's land ethic did not take root in the twentieth century. To be sure, encouraging progress was made with the passage of watershed public land laws, conservation statutes, and environmental legislation. This body of law reflects changing social values toward the end of the century. However, old habits die hard.

There are several reasons why a land ethic has not taken root, which shall be examined later in this chapter. As noted by Leopold, for most of American history, the United States has looked upon the land as a conqueror. It fought Indian nations, then vigorously colonized their land from 1776 well into the twentieth century. That legacy is firmly embedded in our minds, legal institutions, economy, and notions of race. We have the minds, hearts, ears, and eyes of settlers; and we romanticize the American past through movies, dime novels, school books, and song. While slavery and discrimination against blacks are not romanticized, kids play "cowboys and Indians," while grown-ups disparage Indians for entertainment on television and at sporting events, as if Americans still view themselves as cowboys, conquerors, and colonizers. That attitude also informs the way we look at the land. Governor Sarah Palin fervently chanted the mantras of the conqueror, "Drill, baby, drill" and "mine, baby, mine" in 2008, hoping that it would carry her to the White House.[3] Even many professional foresters who followed in Leopold's footsteps lost sight of his ideals in their stewardship of the public lands when they fell under the sway of agency big-wigs in recent administrations. This is painfully visible in the Forest Service's shoddy treatment of Native American holy places, which continues to this very day.[4] To many agency politicos, the natural world must be quantified only for its resource value to the "conquerors" (to use Leopold's term). By contrast, the Native experience on the land stands in opposition to that mindset. It teaches that some places are holy ground, we have important relatives in the animal and plant kingdoms, and humans must cooperate with the natural world to survive. These ideals are certainly not Native American "quirks." They are universal values engrained into early human biology long ago, as humans spread across the planet, so that the hunters, fishers, and gatherers who depended upon indigenous habitat could flourish and survive. Unfortunately, the values of indigenous peoples cannot be taken seriously in a colonized land by people and institutions that still see themselves as conquerors; then there is always the race factor (*we do not want to live like Indians, these savages are racially inferior and lead a barbarous lifestyle*). That mindset makes us hostage to an unjust past, and it prevents us from looking at the land like the Native American cultures do. Leopold's call to decolonize the way we look at the land simply cannot be heard until that mindset is seen, understood, and discarded. The forces that underpin that mindset should be searchingly examined, and this chapter will begin that inquiry. As will be seen, decolonizing the way that we look at the land goes hand-in-hand with decolonizing the way we look at Native Americans, and the restoration of their rights opens a door to a new way of looking at the land.

How does America view the land in the twenty-first century? What is the role of federal land managing agencies in shaping our land ethics? Do they help or hinder the search for Leopold's land ethic? This chapter is concerned with the barriers faced by our nation in finding Leopold's land ethic. We must understand the forces at work that hinder agencies from assuming leadership, as the stewards of public lands, in developing an American land ethic that discards the role of the conqueror and allows our nation to adapt, mature, and become a more just society. As will be seen, none of the barriers should be "news" to anyone, but it is useful to list them in one place.

The challenges of adapting to the land are especially hard in former colonies that perpetuate a "settler state" outlook. That mentality looks at the land primarily in economic terms, as a "resource" to be exploited. Once the fuel that sparked that outlook has run dry, many nations have matured, and folks now wish to become more "native" to place and shed the harsh frontier trappings that characterized Manifest Destiny. One of the challenges is to build a sound land ethic, one that adapts closely to the habitat and cooperates with the natural world. Otherwise, modern states run the age-old risks faced by every non-sustainable civilization that failed to adapt to the land: overuse, despoliation, and, ultimately, extinction. Consequently, it is important to understand the mentality that prevents adaptation.

Sadly, the land-managing agencies have not developed a national land ethic, even though they are "stewards" of public lands. There is a strong environmental case for requiring agency leaders to embrace the *Declaration* in managing public lands, because it encourages them to raise their eyes to a greater vision of stewardship—one that forges a sustainable land ethic. In the United States, the federal government is the largest landowner, followed somewhere near the top by the many indigenous American Indian and Alaska Native nations who own almost one-hundred million acres.[5] Indian lands often border federal enclaves; neighboring tribal communities can have sacred sites or cultural resources under federal management, and they can hold treaty or subsistence rights to the use of public lands and waters for hunting, fishing, or gathering purposes. As landowners and stewards, Indian tribes and federal land managing agencies demonstrate their "land ethic" to the rest of the nation through their land use practices, actions, and policies. In that capacity, they necessarily play important roles in shaping how the American public views the land and how we, as a modern, industrialized nation, should comport ourselves with the humans, fish, birds, animals, and plants that inhabit the natural world, and the natural world itself.

The need for land managers to know about indigenous cultural resources on their lands and adjacent Indian lands in their management of public lands arises from the mandates imposed on agencies by modern public land laws, such as the American Indian Religious Freedom Act of 1978 ("AIRFA"), the National Environmental Policy Act ("NEPA"), the National Historic Preservation Act ("NHPA"), the Native American Graves Protection and Repatriation Act ("NAGPRA"), the Alaska National Interest Lands Conservation Act of 1980 ("ANILCA"), the Endangered Species Act ("ESA"), and others, including the wilderness laws. In addition, Executive Order 13007 (1996) requires federal agencies to protect Native American sacred sites.[6] The agency ethnology programs attempt to meet that need by working with traditional communities on contemporary cultural issues to investigate links between cultural values and the cultural and natural resources located on public lands, as necessary to comply with the above laws, though they've only achieved a checkered record of success. On the one hand, the National Park Service is a world leader in preserving the natural world and its cultural treasures. Agency pioneers who developed the NPS ethnography programs to comply with the above laws, such as Jerry Rogers and Muriel Crespi, led land managers into the modern era, as society began to change the way that it looked at public lands. They laid groundwork for opening the eyes of the agencies to an indigenous way of looking at the land. Rogers writes:

> Barely in time, before some traditional knowledge is lost altogether, the National Park Service has begun to recognize that benefits of working with tribes flow to the Service from the tribes as well as the other way around. As the Service works to help visitors comprehend their own interdependence with other species, traditional tribal reverence for the earth and her systems is becoming a persuasive addition to the findings of science and scholarship. Today's coldly utilitarian views must be moderated if the dominant cultures are not to overtax the earth's ability to sustain a large human population. This change will happen more readily if the lessons of science are presented in tandem with the older, deeper, and more spiritual lessons from generations of indigenous cultures. It is not unusual for National Park visitors to liken an opening among giant redwoods to a cathedral, or to describe their experiences in nature as sacred. Such metaphor is important to what National Parks stand for, and to the willingness of the public to use and support parks. The willingness can benefit greatly by learning from cultures for which the concept is more than metaphorical.[7]

Today, parks and protected areas around the world are paying closer attention to the values and needs of indigenous peoples.[8] Western-style conservation philosophy need not crush primal cultures. That philosophy can and should be consistent with indigenous cultures to the great benefit of both park managers and the people who depend upon indigenous habitat in the park for their way of life and cultural integrity. These are steps in the right direction, to be sure.

The *Declaration* calls upon federal agencies to fulfill a larger goal than merely complying with federal land laws. As stewards of our public lands, federal land agencies are charged with possessing a higher degree of knowledge about the nature of the land and its cultural significance to the American public. It is incumbent upon them to help lead our nation toward a land ethic for the twenty-first century. That task can only be done by managing public lands in accordance with principles described in the *Declaration*, which allow agencies to recognize, respect, and incorporate indigenous values when managing places important to indigenous peoples. By incorporating indigenous wisdom in the management of public land, important ingredients for a land ethic emerge.

This challenge requires much more than a bare bones ethnography program run by a room full of cultural anthropologists telling agencies about the cultural significance of their lands. Instead, to synthesize our "cultural resources" into an American Way of looking at the land, and teach that ethic to the general public and succeeding generations, this task requires a comprehensive interdisciplinary approach, guided by comparative religion experts, Indian studies scholars, historians, ecologists, ethnobotanists, wildlife and fishery biologists, traditional tribal religious leaders, and tribal hunters, fishers, and gatherers. This task cannot be accomplished by cultural anthropologists alone, for obvious reasons. They lack the broad expertise listed above, and, sometimes, anthropologists are hampered by professional conflicts of interest, as the repatriation movement and processes have shown. In addition, it is unfortunate that agency anthropologists usually report only to mid-level managers and their professional studies frequently lie buried on dusty shelves to never become part of the public discourse. Accordingly, this book recommends that agency ethnography programs continue, but only in a *larger interdisciplinary infrastructure* designed for a bigger societal task in synthesizing a land ethic: we need a "Land Ethic Program" to achieve Leopold's vision.

It is appropriate and timely to rise and stride toward Leopold's vision as we implement the *Declaration*. This historic measure calls upon the United States to implement minimum standards, in consultation with Native Americans, to protect their dignity, survival, and well-being. It sets forth numerous principles designed to "decolonize" the way that we treat Native peoples, and the lands traditionally used by them, through increased state protection of their lands, traditional subsistence, ways of life, and habitats. Implementation of those standards holds the promise of changing the way that America looks at the land. Federal land agencies can foster that social change, or resist it and therefore be among the last to look upon the land through the eyes of a bygone era.

The Way Societies View the Land Reveals Their Innermost Character

The way that societies view the land tells much about them—revealing the character, values, history, and aspirations of a people. As we chart the course toward a land ethic, there are many models in our diverse human family. Our task is to select the best model, or synthesize the best from among them, when fashioning the most appropriate model for our nation in the post-colonial era. Here is a summary of the leading models followed by the human family.

The "primal" cosmology of hunters, fishers, gatherers, and traditional tribal farmers sanctifies the human presence in the natural world. (The word "primal" is used because this is man's first worldview.) Their cosmology shows humans how to comport themselves with animals and plants. It allows humans to cooperate with natural processes and to thrive in the natural world by following the earliest mode of human existence. In primal cosmology, only a thin line exists between humans and the animals and plants that live in tribal habitats—and everything, including the land itself, has a spirit. Dr. Gregory Cajete, an Indian cultural studies scholar, provides an excellent description of the complex underpinnings of this cosmology in Native North America.[9]

By contrast, farmers with the westernized worldview must combat nature to survive. Their way of life depends upon strict human control of the biology and behavior of animals and plants, remaking the land, and restructuring the hydrologic system in order to survive by making the land, water supply, plants, and animals more productive for humans.[10] In the end, nature is conquered, and the wild animals, plants, and insects are eradicated as pests. The agriculturalist worldview that arose from the Middle Eastern civilizations informs the way most modern societies look at the land. As will be explained, it sanctifies the conquest of nature, exalts humans over all other life on earth, and rationalizes our subjugation of animals, plants, and natural processes.[11] And it is a vastly different outlook from that of the traditional agriculturalists with indigenous traditions who share the traditional worldview of the hunters, fishers, and gatherers in all important respects pertinent to this discussion.

These two cosmologies present viable ways of life. Both are venerated human worldviews. But they are fundamentally different and frequently come into conflict. In fact, this conflict accounts for much of the human misery and atrocity between indigenous and non-indigenous peoples around the world since 1492. The hunting, fishing, and gathering model is nearly extinct today. The age-old struggle between the two competing cosmologies began after the rise of agriculture, beginning some ten thousand years ago. It seems farmers and hunter-fishers from these two disparate traditions just can't get along, nor can those who follow their worldviews. In any event, after the conquest of nature and the industrial revolution in the past five hundred years, only a few small pockets of hunting, fishing, and gathering cultures survive in tribal habitats around the world. Nevertheless, this earliest mode of human existence remains a viable model for a land ethic needed by a modern nation that has forgotten how to comport itself with the natural world.

Importantly, data about those lifestyles has been preserved by ethnographers before they went extinct and much more can be gleaned from the surviving tribal communities around the world. The United States contains one of the largest concentrations of those cultures left in the world—the American Indian and Alaska Native nations, who still reside in their indigenous habitats, practice traditional religions, and hunt, fish, or gather as part of their traditional subsistence. The ancient cosmology is seen in their languages, songs, stories, ceremonies, ideals, and values, as well as their art, artifacts, and architecture. The way that they comport themselves with their habitat, and the animals, birds, fish, and plants of their world, tells us much about primal cosmology; and their worldview provides an attractive model for key ingredients in an American land ethic, because it is the cosmology that arose from our soil long ago.

There are additional ways of looking at the land. Conquerors view land in military terms, as "territory" to be seized. Rape, booty, and subjugation color their eyes as they gaze upon a conquered land. War and conquest rank among our oldest human traditions, and many lands have been scarred by the ravages of war, as they fell as "prizes" into the hands of conquerors. However, Leopold eschewed the role of conqueror as the foundation for looking at American soil.

Colonialism offers yet another model, one followed by Europeans for over five hundred years. In the Colonial Era (c. 1492–1960), the nations of Europe competed to colonize the rest of the world. During this lengthy period, settlers view colonized land in economic terms, as a "resource" to be exploited. This model has many drawbacks, in large part because they settled lands belonging to *other people*, usually located thousands of miles away from their homeland, in order to appropriate natural resources to enrich themselves and their homeland kingdoms. Thus, European settlers immigrated to distant lands to Christianize natives, subjugate them, and steal their resources. A land ethic based on those notions cannot easily be developed for colonized land, because, in nearly every colony, the colonists did not adapt to the land as the indigenous peoples had done. Instead, the settlers retained the language, religion, values, and identity of their homeland while distancing or alienating themselves from the native population through discrimination, marginalization, and suppression, which worked to stamp out the indigenous cultures in the colony. In that sense, settlers were, from a cultural standpoint, very much strangers or aliens to the land they colonized, although the immigrants obtained stewardship of the land. This happened in America, as described by Standing Bear, a Dakota chief, in 1933:

> The white man does not understand the Indian for the reason he does not understand America. He is too far removed from its formative processes. The roots of his tree of life have not yet grasped the rock and soil. The man from Europe is still a foreigner and an alien. But in the Indian, the spirit of the land is still vested; and it will be until other men are able to divine and meet its rhythm. Men must be born, and reborn to belong. Their bodies must be formed of the dust of their forefathers' bones.[12]

This estrangement from the land is evident in the way that nineteenth and twentieth century American settlers treated indigenous plants on the Great Plains. They raced through the landscape without understanding even the plants beneath their feet. An early ethnobotanist, Melvin

R. Gilmore, studied those plants and their uses by the Indians on the Nebraska prairie, which deeply shaped the cultures of the Plains Indians. After investigating the vast body of Native plant knowledge about the extant indigenous plant community, Gilmore lamented in 1914 that the native plants and their uses as food, medicine, and material were largely overlooked by the incoming settlers who displaced the Indians:

> The people of the European race in coming into the New World have not really sought to make friends with the native population, or to make adequate use of the plants or the animals indigenous to this continent, but rather to exterminate everything found here and to supplant it with the plants and animals to which they were accustomed at home. It is quite natural that aliens should have a longing for the familiar things at home, but the surest road to contentment would be by way of granting friendly acquaintance with the new environment. We shall make the best and most economical use of all our land when our population shall have become adjusted to the natural conditions. The country cannot be wholly made over and adjusted to a people of foreign habits and tastes. There are large tracts of land in America whose bounty is wasted because the plants which can be grown on them are unacceptable to our people. This is not because these plants not are in themselves useful and desirable, but because their valuable qualities are unknown.[13]

By contrast, Native Americans were heavily influenced by indigenous vegetation that shaped their cultures. They forged deep relationships with plants and maintained them on a metaphysical level. Newcomers overlooked the plants, as seen today in the Klamath River basin of Southern Oregon. There, Indian gatherers enjoy the bounty provided by the rich indigenous plant communities that grow naturally along the rivers and streams without having to plant, irrigate, fumigate, and fertilize them. On the other hand, their neighbors struggle to fight nature, eradicate native plants as weeds, reorder the hydrology, and irrigate crops. This is done only at great cost and with massive help from myriad federal power, irrigation, and price subsidies. Unfortunately, that enormous effort to reorder the natural world has polluted the streams, drained wetlands, watered the desert, lowered lake levels, degraded the landscape, brought about massive fish kills, and placed many fish and animals upon the endangered species list. When viewed against the Klamath way of life, the farmers maintain a destructive lifestyle that heavily burdens our coffers, simply because they are unaware of the bounty that the Great Spirit has provided to the land beneath their feet. This has been the case in Southern Oregon since pioneer days, when early settlers starved while living in nature's grocery store, among abundant edible plants, medicines, and materials that they could not see.

Colonialism does not afford an attractive model today. It is not a sustainable system, and this highly oppressive institution was rejected as repugnant by the international community following World War II, after many of the world's last remaining colonies achieved their independence. As that era was coming to a close, Leopold wisely urged America to decolonize the way it looks at the land. The *Declaration* strongly supports that view. As we decolonize America, the standards in the *Declaration* can point the way to an appropriate model for developing a land ethic in a post-colonial world.

Four Powerful Forces Stymie a Land Ethic in the United States

American society has been alienated from the land and the natural world by several powerful forces. Each must be confronted, understood, and discarded before an American land ethic can be fully developed and implemented. They are listed here.

1. The Cosmological Problem

The first root problem that bars formation of a land ethic is a cosmological problem. It is found in the cosmology of Westernized agriculturalists, as described earlier, which informs the way that Westerners look at animals and plants in the natural world. It has vilified and suppressed to the point of extinction the equally viable primal cosmology of hunting, fishing, and gathering cultures, as well as the traditional agriculturalists among the indigenous peoples of the world who share the primal worldview. The former worldview is described by Jim Mason, an American authority on human-animal relations, in *An Unnatural Order* (2005) as "dominionism," that is, the ten-thousand-year-old Western belief system that exalts human subjugation over all life on earth.[14] Since the rise of agriculture over time, this aggressive cosmology has overtaken the competing worldview found in our primal hunting, fishing, and gathering cultures. The latter is humanity's older, primal cosmology. It exalts life on earth, forges a spiritual bond between humans and the creatures found in their habitats, and this way of life depends upon cooperation with the natural world.[15] For those societies embedded in the primal world, the sanctity of nature is taken seriously, and it forms a cornerstone of primal religion. The balance between these venerated worldviews has been sorely breeched in the modern world, which has relegated the primal belief system to a few surviving pockets in tribal communities around the world.

The balance between these worldviews needs to be restored before an American land ethic can emerge, because unchecked "dominionism" works to alienate humans from animals and plants. Animal-human relations in this mindset were summed-up by Sigmund Freud in 1917:

> In the course of his development towards culture man acquired a dominating position over his fellow-creatures in the animal kingdom. Not content with this supremacy, however, he began to place a gulf between his nature and theirs. He denied the possession of reason to them, and to himself he attributed an immortal soul, and made claims of divine descent which permitted him to annihilate the bonds of community between him and the animal kingdom.[16]

Freud described our supposed supremacy as "human megalomania."[17] This cosmology is a powerful, ten-thousand-year-old force that alienates modern man from the land. The restoration of measured balance and respect between these worldviews will be difficult, because "dominionism" is deeply embedded in the modern mindset. It is sanctified by Western religion, strengthened by science, bolstered by secularism, and cemented into our lives by technological revolutions. Nonetheless, that outlook must be curbed and reconciled with the primal hunting, fishing, and gathering cosmology, ideals, values, and beliefs that are still maintained, almost exclusively, by traditional indigenous peoples. If we can justly mediate the cosmological conflict and find the best in both worldviews, perhaps a land ethic will emerge for the twenty-first century. If we cannot, the world's surviving hunting, fishing, and gathering cultures will pass into extinction, along with the habitats and knowledge that supported man's earliest mode of existence in non-industrial societies.

2. The Religious Question

The second barrier to forging a sound land ethic has to do with religion, including our history of religion in the United States and the diminishing role of the sacred in modern American life. As will be explained, these factors hinder creation of a land ethic because they work to (1) blind us from seeing the spiritual side of Mother Earth, (2) rob animals and plants of their kinship with humans as living things with a spirit of their own, and (3) hinder society's ability to incorporate indigenous values, wisdom, and needs into America's land ethics. The predominant religious faith in the United States, Christianity, simply does not impart a spiritual side to American land, nor to the animals, birds, fish, and plants in North America. It teaches that holy ground lies only in a few faraway spots located in the Middle East, within the lands of another culture. Furthermore, in the origin story of this religion, which was founded by early agriculturalists, God placed all living creatures, and the earth herself, into the service of humans, as lowly mindless beings without feelings or souls. In turn, Genesis places a gulf between humans and animals as the natural order of things:

> And the fear of you and the dread of you shall be upon every beast of the earth, and upon every fowl of the air, upon all that moveth upon the earth, and upon all the fishes of the sea.[18]

These are excellent beliefs for farmers and others, but they present obvious drawbacks for building a sound land ethic in this part of the world.

The religious belief that "nothing is sacred" in the natural world was implanted on American shores by European newcomers. They believed that the Native Americans had no religion and their sacred ties to the land, animals, and plants were "savage superstitions" that must be stamped out as inferior, barbarous heresy and the work of their "devil." In a classic case of religious discrimination, the tragic history of religion that followed amounted to a wholesale government policy to stamp out indigenous primal religions. That shameful history of religious genocide was finally repudiated by Congress in the 1978 with the passage of the AIRFA policy to protect and preserve remaining pockets of traditional Native American religion.[19] A land ethic founded upon a religious heritage, which teaches that "nothing is sacred" in the natural world, is wrong-headed, because it is at odds with the long human experience on this planet. It decouples us from a broader human legacy that teaches otherwise. It unleashes "dominionism" into our relationship with the land, because it frees humans from any moral restraint in their treatment of animals and plants.

We must break the bonds of religious discrimination to see the land beneath our feet more clearly. Once freed from the shackles of religious intolerance, an America emerges as a land filled with indigenous holy places, a wondrous land where everything has a spirit, including the earth, water, every living thing, and even the mystical powers of the universe. At once, even our American skies are holy, because they contain the heavens, teeming with higher celestial powers and primal forces. Just ask the Native peoples, or see the land through their eyes. They are heirs to indigenous religions that arose from the land. Their traditions can provide valuable lessons for living on the land, and they can contribute critical ingredients for an American land ethic.

One valuable lesson is to see that the land contains holy ground. In our own land, Native Americans have walked upon sacred ground to places where the world was created, or made medicine in holy places since time immemorial. However, larger society cannot see the sacred land beneath its feet. In ancient times, all of humanity revered the sacred found in the natural world. Today, many have forgotten how to listen to the spiritual power that springs from the land, even though the Bible reminds us that sacred places exist. Indeed, worship at sacred sites is done all over the world, as a basic attribute of religion.[20] In short, the modern world is filled with holy places. Can it be that the United States is the only land without holy ground?

Sadly, we are blinded to Native American religious traditions by our own intolerance. Senator Daniel K. Inouye noted how early religious prejudice became the foundation for relations with Native people:

> In the minds of Europeans, tribal religions of the New World were inferior. Thus, it is not surprising—especially given Europe's own heritage of religious discrimination among unpopular Christian denominations and against the non-Christian world religions—that intolerance became a basic feature in the Pilgrim's and other colonists' relationship with the Indians. Indeed, although early settlers came to America to escape religious persecution, Old World prejudices were transplanted in the Colonies, [in] which discrimination became commonplace.[21]

This mindset overlooks what Huston Smith classifies as one of the "primal religions" of the world in his classic text, *The World's Religions.*[22] He sees tribal religions as "primal" because they came first and are the oldest religious traditions of the human race. According to Smith, these religions represent "human religiousness in its earliest mode," and they allow tribal people to "retain insights and virtues that urbanized, industrialized civilizations have allowed to fall by the wayside."[23] He explains that tribal religions cannot be considered in a vacuum, but must be understood within the context of the primal world, for tribes in their aboriginal places are embedded in their indigenous habitats so solidly that the line between nature and the tribe is not easy to establish. In the primal world, no sharp division exists in the lines that divide humans from animals and plants, as all are thought to possess the same spirit. As Black Elk (Lakota) put it:

> All things are the works of the Great Spirit. He is within all things; the trees, the grasses, the rivers, the mountains, and the four-legged animals, and the winged peoples. He is also above all these things and people.[24]

Animals are like people who talk, plants have spirits just like us, and humans can exchange forms with their opposites in the natural world. As a result of these traditions, humans are kin to animals and plants, closely connected by physical, social, and spiritual ties. These traditions also teach that we are relatives, not masters. Furthermore, in the primal mind, the landscape, forces of nature, and the animals and plants that inhabit the natural world have a spiritual side that escapes modern man.[25] Rather than demonize and degrade this worldview, Smith ranks primal religions alongside of the major historical religions and found that no one religion is superior.[26] Based upon that finding, he advises us to discard religious discrimination and view indigenous religious traditions as part of a single mosaic in of world religions.[27]

Bare-footed religious intolerance and the rise of secularism make it hard to follow Smith's advice. We cannot recapture the "sacred" found in the natural world when the place of the sacred has greatly diminished in modern society over the past one hundred years due to the elevation of science over religion. The rise of secularism was traced by the late Vine Deloria, Jr., in a series of insightful articles.[28] He observed that Medieval Europe once followed two traditions of thought, which regarded faith and reason as "equally viable paths to truth."[29] In that part of the world, organized religion was gradually overtaken, for a variety of reasons, by secular science in demonstrating truth. This trend has continued in the United States. Deloria observed in 1992 that a "major phenomenon of this century has been the erosion of the power and influence of organized religion in American society."[30] This demise gave birth to what he termed the secular "civil religion," in which churches took a backseat to the melding of scientific, secular, and bureaucratic thinking by administrators and institutions across the land, which hold purely secularized views and see the world through the eyes of the hard sciences. Taken to its logical extreme, that attitude morphs into base "scientism" (to borrow Huston Smith's term) when it rejects all other sources of knowledge, such as religion, philosophy, and the humanities.[31] *Scientism* asserts that science is the only, or best, path to knowledge, capable of describing all of reality, with authority over all other interpretations provided by religion, philosophy, or mystical, metaphysical, or humanistic explanations.[32] The "civil religion" and "scientism" view birds, plants, and animals in the natural world, and human beings predominately as phenomena that can be explained only by scientific investigation. God is taken out of nature. In fact, "God is dead" in the eyes of scientism. As Julian Huxley pronounced during the middle of the twentieth century, "it will soon be impossible for an intelligent or educated man or woman to believe in god as it is now to believe that the earth is flat."[33] By the end of that century, the sacred was largely banished from public life.

As a result of these forces, religion exists only on the margins of modern society in the twenty-first century. Many urbanites and agencies mistakenly see western science as the only pathway to truth and knowledge about reality. Not to be confused with science, this attitude is bare scientism described by Huston Smith. That worldview is fraught with limitations when it comes to fashioning a land ethic. Scientism cannot see the Great Spirit, quantify the Great Mystery, nor peer into the Spirit World. That spiritual realm lies beyond the pale of science and eludes pointy-headed scientism.

Christianity, religious intolerance, secularism, and scientism are powerful forces. They work to sever ties to the land, because they cannot see the spiritual side of Mother Earth. They deny that holy ground exists on American soil. They assert that the land, animals, and plants possess no sacred quality. A scientific land ethic that excludes the sacred excludes indigenous wisdom, because it sees science as the only path to understanding the natural world. Indigenous values that teach otherwise have no place in that ethic. In short, these forces prevent us from finding that which is "sacred" on the land and in the natural world. They effectively close our eyes to the sacred in our world and act to take God out of nature, even though that is where the Great Spirit abides. This is troubling, because a land ethic for our industrialized nation cannot be founded upon science and technology alone, for they *caused* much of the environmental trouble and lack the tools, knowledge, wisdom, and moral willpower to solve that crisis.

This unfortunate predicament was cemented into the law of the land by the United States Supreme Court in the Indian religion cases of the twentieth century. In *Employment Division v. Smith* (1990) and *Lyng v. Northwest Indian Cemetery Protective Association* (1990), the court went to great lengths to deny extant constitutional protections for Native American religious practices. In so doing, the court seriously weakened the First Amendment, restricted American religious freedom, and, most importantly, placed the protection of that liberty into the hands of Congress where it must find protection through secular political processes. That completes the secularization process by firmly placing the sacred under the control of the secular. It opens the door for unchecked scientism and fosters a land ethic that eschews the sacred. To fashion a workable land ethic, balance must be restored between the sacred and the secular. Our survival and well-being depend on recapturing the sacred in American life as we look upon the land.

3. The Legacy and Mindset of Colonialism

The third force that stymies our search for Leopold's vision is the legacy of colonialism, mentioned earlier and discussed in Chapter Five, which has persisted in this nation centuries after Americans achieved their independence from England. The early settlers simply replaced England's colonial policy for dealing with Indian tribes with their own colonial system. These forces continue to color the way we view the land. As mentioned earlier, this mindset estranges settlers from the land, preventing adherents from adapting because of the continual drive to exploit colonized land as an economic resource. That mentality opposes a land ethic built upon any other values or principles. We must confront and discard that legacy, once and for all, because it leads to environmental destruction. After all, colonization of Native lands is *invariably* accompanied by destroying the habitat that supports the tribal way of life. Colonies displace the Natives, extract natural resources from the land, and remake the natural world for agriculturalists and manufacturers. Thus, conquest of nature often accompanies the settlement of Native territory.

In *The Conquest of Paradise* (1990), historian Kirkpatrick Sale examined the astounding level of environmental degradation that accompanied European colonization of the New World.[34] In 1823, Chief Justice John Marshall described the familiar ebb and flow of colonization in the United States:

> As the white population advanced, that of the Indian necessarily receded. The country in the immediate neighborhood of agriculturalists became unfit for them. The game fled into thicker and more unbroken forests, and the Indians followed. The soil, to which the crown originally claimed title, being no longer occupied by its ancient inhabitants, was parceled out according to the will of the sovereign.[35]

In just a few short decades, for example, the colonizing Europeans virtually destroyed the plains habitat of my own hunting and traditional farming tribe—the Pawnee Nation—while they slaughtered countless millions of buffalo and wolves and pulled steel plows through native plant communities. When the Native people resisted, the law and military invariably supported the destruction of indigenous habitat, often with harsh life-altering consequences. The depopulation of the American Indians and destruction of their cultures following European contact has been attributed, in part, to the accompanying destruction of indigenous habitats.[36] Simply put, deforestation, dewatering, and destruction of the wild animals and plants that sustained Indian tribes led to their collapse. Many went extinct following the conquest of nature in North and South America.

The land ethic of colonists is hard on indigenous people, wild animals, and native plants. No land ethic based upon abject colonialism should be allowed to stand, ever. Although the Colonial Era has come to an end, that mindset lingers in America. It opposes a land ethic that follows the vision of Leopold.

4. The Problem of Leadership

Who shall lead the way to an American land ethic? The fourth barrier to achieving Leopold's dream arises from structural problems that plague federal land agencies. One would think that they should lead. However, certain weaknesses hamper their leadership or, worse yet, have sometimes actually caused agencies to work against a land ethic during the modern era of public land law over the past thirty years. We must open our eyes to these problems to see what can be done to address them.

First, the Supreme Court in *Lyng* and *Smith* allows federal land agencies to run roughshod over tribal holy places on federal land. So does Congress. That deplorable conduct continues unabated to this very day, despite Executive Order 13007 (1996), which directs agencies to comport themselves differently. This outright loophole in the legal system works against the formation of a land ethic. Agencies cannot develop a land ethic on the one hand while destroying holy places with the other. Destroyers forfeit the moral authority to lead and cannot inspire public confidence, especially among the Native peoples who possess ingredients for a land ethic.

Second, when it comes to land ethics, internal conflicts of interest frequently hamstring agencies, which then fall prone to political cronyism by agency big-wigs or become the hapless hostage of special interest groups. Such is the nature of agencies that answer to many masters. During these unfortunate periods when professional land management takes a backseat, pork barrel projects rule the day and relationships with tribal communities are undercut. The public insists upon a more even keeled approach. The nasty lapses in stewardship are a serious barrier to agency leadership. If unchecked, the credibility problems will continue to relegate agency leadership to the margins, leaving the task of developing a land ethic to others. We need an independent "Land Ethics Program" that is immune to these lapses, a societal program that strides toward Leopold's vision as the direct by-product of the American people working together, in collaboration with Native Americans, to implement the *Declaration.*

Toward a Land Ethic that Incorporates Native American Wisdom Traditions

I cannot close without presenting a Native American perspective on a land ethic for comporting ourselves with animals and plants in North America. As Dr. Cajete explains, Native American cultures spring from the land itself. They derive from a traditional hunting, fishing, gathering, and planting existence. That way of life produced an astounding primal cosmology that revels in Mother Earth's remarkable ability to support life. It proclaims Mother Earth as the foundation for human culture—that is, our ethics, morals, religion, art, politics, and economics derive from the cycles of nature, the behavior of animals, the growth of plants, and from inextricable human interdependence with all living things that are endowed with a spirit of their own. In the cosmology of Native American gatherers, plants hold an esteemed place of honor as the foundation for human and animal life. The Native American perception of animals mirrors hunting cultures around the world, and it is an ancient way of life in Native North America. This tradition evolved songs, dances, ceremonies, art forms, and a spiritual reverence for animals, producing an elaborate worldview that explains how humans should comport themselves with animals. These indigenous wisdom traditions derive from the very cultures and ways of life that the *Declaration* seeks to protect and preserve through a human rights framework. The wisdom traditions are nothing short of national treasures that offer an environmental framework for creating an American land ethic.

Perhaps historians, Indian studies scholars, and world religion experts can put flesh on these observations, with help from traditional Indian religious leaders and tribal hunter-fisher-gatherers. These accumulated wisdom traditions can inform a sound American land ethic. In crafting a land ethic best-suited for our soil, ecologists, biologists, ethnobotanists, and cultural anthropologists can add their expertise about cultural and natural resources to traditional indigenous knowledge; together society can synthesize what amounts to a uniquely American land ethic. Until that time comes, the land speaks to those who listen. Here are some Native voices from the land.

> In the beginning of all things, wisdom and knowledge were with the animals, for *Tirawa*, the One Above, did not speak directly to people. He spoke to people through his works, the stars, the sun and moon, the beasts, and the plants. For all things tell of *Tirawa*. When people sought to know how they should live, they went into solitude and prayed until in a vision some animal brought wisdom to them. It was *Tirawa* who sent his message through the animal. He never spoke to people himself, but gave his command to beast or bird, which came to some chosen person and taught him holy things. So it was in the beginning.
>
> —Eagle Chief (Pawnee), 1907.[37]

> A long time ago the Creator came to Turtle Island and said to the Red People: "You will be the keepers of Mother Earth. Among you I will give the wisdom about Nature, about the interconnectedness of all things, about balance and living in harmony. You Red People will see the secrets of Nature. The day will come when you will need to share the secrets with other people of the Earth because they will stray from their Spiritual ways. The time to start sharing is today.
>
> —Mohican Prophecy.[38]

> All people have a liking for some special animal, tree, plant or spot of earth. If they would pay attention to these preferences and seek what is best to make themselves worthy of that to which they are attracted, they might have dreams that would purify their lives.
>
> —Brave Buffalo (Lakota), 1918.[39]

> The Indian tried to fit in with nature and to understand, not conquer or rule. Life was a glorious thing, for great contentment comes with the feeling of friendship with the living things around you.
>
> —Luther Standing Bear (Lakota), 1931.[40]

> All animals have power, because the Great Spirit dwells in all of them, even a tiny ant, a butterfly, a tree, a flower, a rock.
>
> —Pete Catches (Lakota Medicine Man), 1973.[41]

> One should pay attention to even the smallest crawling creature for these may have a valuable lesson to teach us, even the smallest ant may wish to communicate to a man.
>
> —Black Elk (Lakota Medicine Man), 1932.[42]

> A tree is like a human being, for it has life and grows; so we pray to it and put our offerings on it that God may help us.
>
> —Lakota (1894).[43]

> When you look at all the other parts of creation, all the other living creatures—the Creator endowed them with gifts that are far better than ours. Compared to the strength of the grizzly bear, the sharp sightedness of the eagle, the fleetness of the deer, and the acute hearing of the otter, we're pitiful human beings. We don't have any of those physical attributes that the Creator put into everything else. For that reason, we have to be compassionate with one another and help one another—to hold each other up.
>
> —Rueben Snake (Ho Chunk), 1993.[44]

The stories told by the land are about its peoples—their origins, struggles, values, and beliefs. The songs and histories that it whispers are often profound, ancient, or can take on sacred meaning. Sometimes, the tragic stories are not pretty, in haunting places such as Sand Creek, the Washita River, and other massacre sites or places where injustice took place. The land also tells the sacred stories of the birds, animals, plants, and the natural phenomena that comprise human habitats. The lessons learned from the land are what give us our identity and make us fully human. Mother Earth will continue to shape society and nurture the human spirit until modern man finally exits the natural world altogether and retreats into man-made environments. Many have already retreated to the "Brave New World" made by urban dwellers living in secular industrialized landscapes during the scientific age. Shielded from the natural world, their worldview contrasts sharply with the cosmology of Native peoples who reside in indigenous habitats embedded in the natural world. They have no room for indigenous values when looking at the land. Nevertheless, the worldviews of the world's surviving hunting, fishing, gathering, and traditional planting cultures have much to offer to nations searching for a land ethic in the twenty-first century, but those wisdom traditions have been largely forgotten, dismissed as "primitive," disparaged as "inferior," or demonized by the modern world. The *Declaration* asks us to replace that mindset with respect for indigenous values and incorporate those values alongside of our own. When we do, we see that America has a primal legacy. Despite a secular mindset, our nation is well-endowed with indigenous wisdom traditions that transcend modernity. Everyone is an heir to the hunters', fishers', gatherers', and traditional farmers' legacy. They left indelible tracks in each person because our ancestors became fully human in the natural world. That cosmology is alive and well. It lies on the land beneath our feet. The *Declaration* allows us to recapture the best in that worldview and fashion a land ethic for the twenty-first century, because it insists that we preserve indigenous cultures and protect the habitats that gave rise to them; and it calls upon the United States to ensure an effective right of Native Americans to transmit their ways of life to future generations.

CHAPTER SEVEN
How Does the *Declaration* Affect the Future of Indian Law?

This chapter provides an overview of domestic law pertaining to Native Americans. It will explore possible impacts of the *Declaration* on the "good" and "bad" sides of federal Indian law. By positioning the UN standards next to those sides of the law, we can see how the *Declaration* can shape the law in the 21st century.

A brief overview of federal Indian law is helpful. Historically, this legal framework for indigenous rights in the United States has been used in two ways: firstly, as a "shield" to protect indigenous rights and, secondly, as a "sword" to strip away those rights. As a man-made construct, the law is necessarily imperfect, with "good" and "bad" sides. We will examine both sides, beginning with the "good" side—to measure how the "10 best Indian cases ever decided" stack-up against the UN standards. Then, we will peer into the "dark side" of the law to round-out our overview. We will see how the "10 worst Indian law cases ever decided" would have turned out if the *Declaration* was the controlling law of the land at the time they were decided and if the courts had had to apply its standards to resolve those cases. These analyses help us consider a burning question: How does the *Declaration* affect the future of federal Indian law?

The 10 Best Indian Law Cases Ever Decided

During the modern era, great strides were made by the Tribal Sovereignty Movement within the framework of federal Indian law. At its best, and in its finest hour, federal Indian law is a vibrant shield for protecting the political, property, cultural, and human rights of Native Americans; and it probably comes closest to meeting the minimum standards of the *Declaration* as any body of law on earth. An examination of the 10 best cases illustrates the point. Though the holdings of these cases have been modified over time, they represent a high water mark in our legal culture that fulfills in its finest hour the human rights, fundamental freedoms, and principles expressed in the *Declaration*.

1. *Worcester v. Georgia (1832)*[1]

Worcester heads the list. As indicated in Chapter Five, the inherent tribal sovereignty and protectorate principles laid down by the Marshall Court created the foundational principles of federal Indian law: (1) Indian tribes are distinct political communities, with an inherent sovereign right of self-government free from interference by the states; (2) US treaties with Indian nations must be honored as the supreme law of the land; (3) the doctrine of discovery and edicts from Europe do not divest Indian land or sovereignty; and (4) reservation borders are protective barriers against hostile states and land-hungry settlers. Under *Worcester,* indigenous rights must be protected by the United States as the protector nation in a protectorate relationship with Indian nations, and the doctrine of conquest has no place in defining Native American rights. Applying these principles in a modern-day context, the Supreme Court began the modern era of federal Indian law in *Williams v. Lee* (1959) by holding that states have no power over Indian tribes, Indians, or Indian affairs on Indian reservations.[2]

Unfortunately, justices with other agendas lost sight of the *Worcester* principles over the years.[3] For example, following Marshall's death, Andrew Jackson's Supreme Court restored the discovery doctrine, and it remains the law of the land to this very day.[4] In *United States v. Kagama* (1886), the Supreme Court sustained federal criminal jurisdiction over Indian country. That holding greatly expanded federal hegemony over Indian nations, and it ushered in a federal trend to supplant tribal governments.[5] *Lone Wolf* upheld the power of Congress to break treaties and take tribal land against the will of the Indians under the plenary power doctrine. For more than one-hundred and fifty years, the general rule was that only Congress could trim the inherent sovereignty retained by Indian tribes.[6] The Supreme Court departed from that long-standing rule a few decades ago, and it started placing additional, judge-made limitations upon the inherent sovereign powers of Indian tribes. This federal common law approach to defining tribal sovereignty is done under the "implicit divestiture theory," which is anchored solely in the Court's own subjective policy views concerning the proper scope of tribal governmental authority.[7] After constant judicial nibbling under that nebulous theory, the tribal sovereignty principle of *Worcester* lay sorely wounded by 2001. In *Nevada v. Hicks* (2001), Justice Scalia painted a pint-sized picture of tribal sovereignty—one that is no longer inherent, but something that seemingly exists only at the sufferance of the Supreme Court:

> State sovereignty does not end at a reservation's borders. Though tribes are often referred to as "sovereign" entities, it was "long ago" that "the Court departed from Chief Justice Marshall's view that 'the law of [a State] can have no force' within reservation boundaries."[8]

Our task is to steer the Supreme Court back to *Worcester,* one of the greatest cases ever decided. *Worcester's* principles are far more compatible with the self-determination framework of the *Declaration* than any other line of judicial thought found in federal Indian law. Both see self-government as an *inherent* right. By its nature, an inherent right is *not subject to defeasance* at the whim of the Great White Father. John Marshall got it right, and he did not envision the pint-sized picture painted by Justice Scalia.

2. *United States ex rel. Standing Bear v. Crook (1879)*[9]

This case is about liberty, human rights, equality, and access to the courts. In 1877, the government removed the peaceful Ponca tribe from its Nebraska homeland and relocated every man, woman, and child six hundred miles to the south, to a new reservation in Oklahoma Indian Territory. After one-fourth of the tribe died in Oklahoma, Chief Standing Bear resolved to leave the reservation and return to Nebraska in order to save himself, his remnant band, and to bury his son in aboriginal soil. Severing tribal relations, Standing Bear and twenty-five followers left the reservation. They walked to Nebraska in the frigid winter snow. Soon after arrival, the Ponca were arrested by General George Crook and placed under military arrest, pending their return to Oklahoma. Standing Bear sued for his freedom and that of his people in a *habeas corpus* action. His case was brought under a federal law that allows any "person" in custody to challenge the legality of his confinement. Standing Bear asserted that the government had no lawful authority to arrest and hold his people for the purpose of returning them to Oklahoma. The United States vigorously opposed the writ. It argued: (1) the court had no jurisdiction to hear a case brought by an Indian, taking a position supported by the *Dred Scott* rationale, which prevented slaves from using federal courts, the government asserted that none but free American citizens are entitled to sue in federal courts; and (2) relying on the government's power to do as it pleases with Indians, under the cloak of guardianship, the United States contended that the government's actions are lawful, because the Indians left their reservation without permission—they therefore were arrested by the military at the request of the Secretary of the Interior and placed into custody for the purpose of being returned to their reservation.

Judge Elmer Scipio Dundy allowed the suit. He held that "an Indian is a person within the meaning of the laws of the United States"; and Standing Bear could therefore bring a *habeas corpus* action under the act. Rejecting the government's contention that Indians cannot bring suit in federal courts since they are not citizens, the court observed that "it would be a sad commentary on the justice and impartiality of our laws to hold that Indians, though natives of our own country, cannot legally test the validity of an alleged illegal imprisonment in this manner, as well as a subject of a foreign government who may happen to be sojourning in this country, but owing it no sort of allegiance." He then examined the legal basis for incarcerating the Indians and could find none. Judge Dundy asked: If Indians could be forcibly removed to a reservation by the government without any apparent legal authority, why not place them in prison? Despite the government's assertion of guardianship authority, the arbitrary use of unfettered power was reprehensible to the federal judge:

> I can see no good reason why they might not be taken and kept by force in the penitentiary in Lincoln, or Leavenworth, or Jefferson City, or any other place which the commander of the forces might, in his judgment, see proper to designate. I cannot think that any such arbitrary authority exists in this country.[10]

In the absence of any discernible authority for arresting the Ponca, Judge Dundy set the Indians free. His order is landmark because it recognized inherent human rights in these words: "Indians possess the inherent right of expatriation, as well as the more fortunate white race, and have the inalienable right to 'life, liberty, and the pursuit of happiness,' so long as they obey the laws and do not trespass on forbidden ground." This outcome was remarkable in 1879, for in that same year, the military had arrested, confined, and ultimately massacred Dull Knife's band of Northern Cheyenne Indians, with impunity, based upon a similar set of facts: they had peaceably left their Oklahoma reservation to return to their northern homeland.[11] During this period, the government assumed it had the power to place Indians under arrest and confine them on reservations, without any apparent legal authority at all.[12]

Standing Bear rang the bell of freedom, equality, and human rights for American Indians in the 19th century. It was decided by a courageous judge in a dark time, when the nation was at war with Indian tribes and tribal peoples had no reliable access to the courts. Judge Dundy's focus on human rights came in an era when the Supreme Court described American Indians as an inferior race of people, without the same rights as whites under the law, who are subject to the absolute power of the government. *Standing Bear* deconstructed those unjust legal doctrines and granted freedom to oppressed people in the same way that *Brown v. Board of Education* deconstructed the law of segregation and brought justice to African-Americans.[13] Because *Standing Bear* insisted on justice in an unjust time, it is the American Indians' *Brown v. Board of Education*, even though *Standing Bear* does not enjoy the same fame as *Brown.* Unfortunately, Judge Dundy was ahead of his time. His solitary decision freed the Ponca, and they are able to reside in their Nebraska homeland today as a result of their court victory. However, the principles that animated the decision went unheeded by a nation hell-bent for Manifest Destiny. Consequently, the *Standing Bear* decision soon drifted away, overlooked, into a turbulent sea, and it was ultimately obscured by the tides of judicial history. Though *Standing Bear* rowed against the tide in 1879, its core values are reaffirmed today by the *Declaration*. Judge Dundy would be pleased. He opened the courthouse doors to Native Americans and provided them with hope that our tribunals are places of justice. That is precisely what Article 40 of the *Declaration* is all about:

> Indigenous peoples have the right to access to and prompt decision through just and fair procedures for the resolution of conflicts and disputes with States or other parties, as well as to effective remedies for

> all infringements of their individual and collective rights. Such a decision shall give due consideration to the customs, traditions, rules and legal systems of the indigenous peoples concerned and international human rights.

3. *Ex Parte Crow Dog (1883)*[14]

The government ignored tribal law when it prosecuted Crow Dog. He was convicted of murder by a federal court for killing Spotted Tail on the two Indians' reservation. Crow Dog was awaiting execution when the Supreme Court overturned the conviction in 1883. Due to the exclusive power of Indian tribes over their members and territory, the Court said Crow Dog could not be prosecuted in federal courts in the absence of a specific congressional law granting criminal jurisdiction over reservation Indians. The decision lets tribes govern their internal affairs in their own territory. *Ex Parte Crow Dog* reiterated that the United States has a duty to protect the "self-government" rights of Indian tribes, including the regulation of "domestic affairs" and "maintenance of order and peace among their own members by the administration of their own laws and customs."[15] *Crow Dog* thus effectuates *Worcester's* sovereignty principle. The deference paid by this line of cases to self-government mirrors the universal human right of self-determination enjoyed by the human family in modern times, as a preemptory norm and foundational principle of the *Declaration*.

Unfortunately, Congress reacted swiftly to the decision. It enacted a law to specifically authorize federal courts to exercise criminal jurisdiction over major crimes committed by Indians in Indian country. The act "opened the way for a new level of interference in the internal affairs of Indian tribes."[16] But the salient fact remains: in its finest hour, self-government and exclusive tribal control over the internal affairs of Indian tribes are part of the American legal tradition. *Crow Dog* gave effect to the *Declaration*, way back in 1883. Too bad it was short-lived.

4. *Winters v. United States (1908)*[17]

The *Declaration* recognizes broad rights of indigenous peoples to their lands, territories, and natural resources, including water. As will be discussed *infra*, federal Indian law also recognizes a broad, and sometimes unique, range of tribal property in which Indian tribes have a legally enforceable interest, including land, natural resources, and water.[18] Tribal water rights were recognized in *Winters,* when the Supreme Court announced the "Winters Doctrine." The Court relied on fairness and justice notions to hold that Indian water rights are impliedly reserved whenever the United States sets aside land for Indian uses—even though the treaty, executive order, or act creating the reservation might be silent as to water. That rule of construction was considered necessary to fulfill the purposes of the reservation, because land is useless without water and life impossible. Under the Winters Doctrine and other principles in Indian water law, tribes enjoy well-established rights to large, but sometimes unquantified, amounts of water.[19]

5. *Washington v. Washington State Commercial Passenger Fishing Vessel Ass'n (1979)*[20]

In the modern era, the Supreme Court began recognizing and enforcing United States treaties with Indian nations. In 1974, the famous *Boldt* decision surprised the nation. The district court upheld the treaty-protected off-reservation fishing rights of the Puget Sound tribes at "usual and accustomed" fishing sites, free from state interference, and it apportioned fifty percent of the harvestable salmon runs to the tribes to effectuate their treaty rights. On appeal, the Supreme Court recognized the vital importance of the salmon to the religions, cultures, subsistence, and traditional economies of the signatory tribes, and affirmed Judge Boldt's ruling, despite stringent opposition and widespread defiance by the State of Washington and commercial fishermen. The Supreme Court stressed: "A treaty, including one between the United States and an Indian tribe, is essentially a contract between sovereigns."[21] To halt widespread defiance of the district court's orders, the Supreme Court sternly stated it has the power to enforce its order and "to enlist the aid of the appropriate federal law enforcement agents in carrying out those steps."[22] *Fishing Vessel,* and its progeny, is another example of American justice at its very best. It shows that domestic law can promote and respect indigenous treaty rights as envisioned by the *Declaration*. However, lurking closely beneath the surface, the plenary power doctrine allows congressional abrogation of Indian treaties with impunity. The *Declaration* would place a bridle upon that power. Article 37 recognizes an inherent right to treaty recognition and enforcement, and that inherent right is an indefeasible right.

6. *California v. Cabazon Band of Mission Indians (1987)*[23]

In *Cabazon*, a state sought to regulate gaming by an Indian tribe on its reservation. Against the backdrop of tribal sovereignty and the rule that states have no power over Indian tribes unless authorized by Congress, the Supreme Court formulated a preemption test. Under the test, the *Cabazon* Court determined that important federal and tribal interests in the self-determination and economic development of Indian tribes preempted any state regulatory interest, and the Court therefore allowed tribal gaming on the reservation free from state regulation.[24] The Court stated: "Self-determination and economic development are not within reach if the Tribes cannot generate revenues and provide employment for the members."[25] *Cabazon* comports well with the right to self-determination and the right to development in the *Declaration*. Today, gaming is a multi-billion dollar industry conducted by Indian nations on their lands pursuant to the self-determination and sovereignty principles of federal Indian law, as recognized in pertinent federal legislation. Furthermore, the rule that states have no civil jurisdiction over Indian tribes unless allowed by Congress operates to allow tribal governments to levy taxes, regulate land use in tribal areas, issue license tags, regulate businesses in Indian country, and enjoy sovereign immunity from suit, just like any other government—free from unwarranted interference by the states. These powers are exercised by tribal governments over "Indian country," which is broadly defined in *Oklahoma Tax Commission v. Sac and Fox Nation* (1993) as "all lands set aside by whatever means for the residence of tribal Indians under federal protection, together with trust and restricted Indian allotments";[26] and this territory can sometimes include non-Indian activity on fee land located within the boundaries of Indian reservations.[27]

7. *People v. Woody (1964)*[28]

The full measure of religious freedom for indigenous peoples is protected in Articles 11, 12, 24, and 25 of the *Declaration*. They are accorded broad human rights to practice and revitalize their cultural traditions and customs. This includes rights to practice ceremonies and spiritual and religious traditions; to protect religious places and maintain a spiritual relationship to the land; to control ceremonial objects; to maintain traditional medicine (including conservation of vital plants, animals, and minerals); and to repatriate human remains. Furthermore, religious rights are protected through fair and transparent mechanisms, developed in conjunction with the indigenous peoples concerned, that provide effective remedies, including restitution for religious property taken without their free, prior, and informed consent.

By contrast, it is almost impossible to find *any case* that protects Native American religious liberty in the United States.[29] Despite the importance of the spiritual side of life to Native America, the courts almost uniformly deny protection for the free exercise of religion. *People v. Woody* (1964) is a notable exception. In *Woody* three Navajo were arrested during a peyote ceremony and charged with the illegal use of peyote. California claimed that peyote use was harmful to Indians and that a religious exemption for them would adversely impact the enforcement of state drug laws. The California Supreme Court ruled that the free exercise clause of the First Amendment protects their right to use peyote for religious purposes, despite a state law that outlawed the use of peyote. In a straightforward application of existing constitutional law, the *Woody* Court found that the state's case rested upon "untested assertions" and the Indians' worship did not harm any compelling government interest:

> We have weighed the competing values represented in this case on the symbolic scale of constitutionality. On the one side, we have placed the weight of freedom of religion as protected by the First Amendment; on the other, the weight of the state's "compelling interest." Since the use of peyote incorporates the essence of the religious expression, the first weight is heavy. Yet the use of peyote presents only a slight danger to the state and to the enforcement of its laws; the second weight is relatively light. The constitutional scale tips in favor of the constitutional protection.[30]

Consequently, the Navajos were freed. In granting a religious exemption to the California drug laws to protect their religious freedom, the *Woody* Court described the larger interests at stake:

> We know some will urge that it is more important to subserve the rigorous enforcement of the narcotic laws that to carve out of them an exception for a few believers in a strange faith. They will say that the exception may produce problems of enforcement and that the dictate of the state must overcome the beliefs of a minority of Indians. But the problems of enforcement here do not inherently differ from those of other situations which call for the detection of fraud. On the other hand, the right to free exercise of religious expression embodies a precious heritage of our history. In a mass society, which presses at every point toward conformity, the protection of a self-expression, however unique, of the individual and the group becomes ever more important. The varying currents of the subcultures that flow into the mainstream of our national life give it depth and beauty. We preserve a greater value than an ancient tradition when we protect the rights of the Indians who honestly practiced an old religion in using peyote one night at a meeting in a desert hogan near Needles, California.[31]

Woody is a classic example of American justice at its best. The landmark decision was solidly grounded in the First Amendment doctrines of the day, and it was followed by state courts in Oklahoma and Arizona. Unfortunately, the *Woody* line of cases was short-lived. In *Employment Division v. Smith* (1990), the Supreme Court ruled that the First Amendment does not protect the religious use of peyote by Indians.[32] *Smith* opened the door to criminal prosecution for practicing the oldest, most continuously observed indigenous faith in the hemisphere. Congress overturned *Smith*.[33] Federal courts should study the religion provisions of the *Declaration:* nearly 150 nations endorse indigenous religious freedom, a proposition that completely eludes our caretakers of the First Amendment.

8. *Kandra v. United States (2001)*[34]

The *Declaration* protects indigenous habitat.[35] As used here, *indigenous habitat* means: a functioning, healthy, and productive ecosystem comprised of the traditional lands, waters, and natural resources (including animals, plants, and fish) in ancestral homelands currently or traditionally owned, occupied, or used by indigenous peoples to carry on their cultures and traditional ways of life. Indigenous habitat gave rise to aboriginal cultures and cosmologies, and without it aboriginal cultures and ways of life cannot survive. Conservation of indigenous habitat, and protecting traditional uses, are difficult legal challenges in the United States because that habitat is usually located off the reservation, outside of tribal control; for the most part, federal law does not protect aboriginal interests in indigenous habitat located outside of tribal ownership or control.[36] General protection of sensitive natural areas and wildlife are few, because the law still views the land primarily through the eyes of a colonist and sees nothing as sacred in the natural world. Federal Indian law falls short of providing dependable legal protections for vital aboriginal interests in indigenous habitat—interests crucial to the survival of tribal hunting, fishing, and gathering cultures in North America—especially when indigenous habitat is located off the reservation and outside of tribal control. In those instances, tribes must look to other sources of law, such as environmental or historical protection statutes, and cobble together legal theories that might serve to protect tribal interests.

Nonetheless, the law is slowly becoming more accountable to the natural world. In the past few decades, this development has stemmed from two major influences: the passage of modern conservation laws and litigation to protect tribal interests in indigenous habitat. For example, the Endangered Species Act (ESA) is "the most comprehensive legislation for the preservation of endangered species ever enacted by any nation," and it provides "a means whereby the ecosystems upon which endangered and threatened species depend may be conserved."[37] ESA litigation requires courts to develop for the very first time a body of law that identifies, articulates, and protects the crucial habitat needs of animals, plants, and fish. They must become versed in protecting the natural world when endangered species are concerned. In a similar vein, Indian litigation forces courts to consider aboriginal interests in the natural world and to hear evidence, time after time, that Native Americans view land, water, plants, and animals as sacred, even though they rarely protect tribal interests.[38] These influences are slowly "indigenizing" our legal culture—that is, making the law more accountable to American habitats. Baby-steps are taken when judges announce "truths" about the natural world, such as these profound insights: (1) animals and plants have intrinsic value;[39] (2) we cannot measure a species' worth by dollars;[40] (3) nor is a species' importance measured by its "scientific value" to man alone;[41] (4) endangered species are *more important* than projects that jeopardize their existence or destroy critical habitats;[42] and (5) fish need water and habitat.[43] *Shucks, Native Americans could have told them that!* These judicial insights are self-evident axioms in tribal cosmology, but indigenous knowledge is not taken seriously until it is confirmed by scientists in environmental litigation.

When federal Indian law and environmental law *converge* in the same case, a powerful legal theory can sometimes emerge in rare cases to protect indigenous habitat. *Kandra v. United States* (2001) furnishes an important example. In *Kandra*, a district court relied upon the government's Indian trust obligations and ESA obligations to protect indigenous habitat in the manner envisioned by the *Declaration*. *Kandra* illustrates that domestic law can meet the land and natural resource standards of the *Declaration*, even if only upon rare and fleeting occasions.

Kandra arose during a severe water drought in the Klamath River basin of southern Oregon and California in 2001. The drought affected the water supply for the Bureau of Reclamation's Klamath Irrigation Project. The massive project stores water in Upper Klamath Lake to irrigate 200,000 acres of arid, high desert land. Since the early 1900s, project operations impacted water levels for the lake and the Klamath River. Project water diversions, dams, canals, drainage systems, dikes, and agricultural irrigation altered the hydrology and habitat of the river basin's ecosystem. For nearly one hundred years, the project diverted massive amounts of water for irrigation, with no regard for the impact upon fisheries or tribal rights. By 2001, three fish species and eagles in affected habitat tottered on the brink of extinction. They were listed as "endangered" or "threatened" under the ESA. The fish were also natural resources subject to the Klamath Tribes' treaty fishing and water rights. The water shortage meant that Reclamation did not have enough water required to meet all of the competing water needs to irrigate project farmland, provide water for fish and wildlife refuges, and provide necessary water levels in Upper Klamath Lake and the Klamath River for the critical habitat of endangered and threatened species, as required by the agency's ESA and Indian trust obligations. To meet its ESA and tribal trust obligations, the agency allocated water to protect critical habitat of endangered and threatened species. That left no water for farming, for the first time in nearly one hundred years. The farmers promptly sued Reclamation. They claimed the agency violated their contract rights to water and sought to enjoin its water allocation plan.

Judge Aiken recognized that "Reclamation must balance diverse, and often competing, demands for Project water" among the project irrigators, wildlife refuges, critical habitat for endangered species, and its "obligation to protect tribal trust resources such as the sucker fish and salmon."[44] After weighing the competing needs against the agency's legal obligations, the court denied the farmers' request for an injunction. The farmers' "severe economic hardship" did not "tip sharply in their favor" when balanced against (1) the threatened extinction of multiple species and (2) harm to the Tribes due to the loss of fish. Judge Aiken wrote:

> Threats to the continued existence of endangered and threatened species constitute ultimate harm. "Congress has spoken in the plainest of words, making it abundantly clear that the balance has been struck in favor of affording endangered species the highest of priorities" [citing *TVA v. Hill,* 437 U.S. at 194]. The Klamath and Yurok Tribes rely on the fish as a vital component of the Tribes' cultures, traditions, and economic vitality. Many customs revolve around the fish harvest, which is now reduced, or in the case of the suckers, non-existent. Loss of fish results in a loss of food, income, employment, and sense of community.[45]

Accordingly, the court held that the farmers' rights are "subservient" to the ESA requirement that federal agency actions not jeopardize the critical habitat of endangered species and to Reclamation's obligation to protect tribal rights:

> Reclamation "has responsibilities under the ESA as a federal agency. These responsibilities include taking control of the project when necessary to meet the requirements of the ESA, requirements that override the water rights of the irrigators" [*Patterson,* 204 F.3d at 1213]. Similarly, the United States, as a trustee for the Tribes, is obligated to protect the Tribes' rights and resources. [citations omitted] Water rights for the Klamath Basin Tribes "carry a priority date of time immemorial" [*Adair,* 723 F.2d at 1414]. These rights "take precedence over any

> alleged rights of the Irrigators" [*Patterson,* 204 F.3d at 1214]. Reclamation, therefore, has a responsibility to divert the water and resources needed to fulfill the Tribes' rights.[46]

Indigenous habitat was protected in *Kandra* during the "Water War of 2001." Even though the habitat was located outside of Klamath tribal land, the fish migrated into their treaty fishing area, and they needed the off-reservation habitat to survive.

Unfortunately, the victory was fleeting. In the very next year, Reclamation returned to "business-as-usual," by diverting most of the water supply for agriculture and leaving too little water for salmon. As a result, the horrified nation witnessed the largest fish kill ever seen in the Klamath River. One commentator described the disaster as follows:

> In late September 2002, an unprecedented disaster occurred in the Klamath River. Commercial fishermen, local tribe members, biologists, government officials, and members of the general public looked on in horror as thousands of dead and dying fish floated and flopped by, swept along by the Klamath's current. Hundreds more lined the banks, their bloated and rotting carcasses emitting an overwhelming stench. Sea birds gorged themselves, leaving the banks strewn with half-eaten bodies and forming a morbid canvas of silver scales, red blood, and bright orange flesh. During those first few days of the crisis, scientists removed about 1,500 dead salmon from the waters of the Klamath River. A week later, the estimated number of dead fish had climbed to 10,000. By the end of the month, estimates ranged from 12,000 to 30,000 dead fish—the worst die-off in recorded or spoken history. The fish died from a gill disease, probably the result of reduced water flows into the Klamath River. Flows into the river were diverted during the summer of 2002, as part of an irrigation system designed to bring water to a naturally arid landscape.[47]

Three problems make it hard for existing law to protect indigenous habitat in a reliable manner, as envisioned by the *Declaration.* First, ESA protection is often too little and too late. The ESA is limited to preventing extinction and does not require the preservation of harvestable populations needed to satisfy tribal rights. In addition, ESA protection is not triggered until a species declines to the brink of extinction, and then the act operates to put the species on life-support, only for so long as it is listed as threatened or endangered. Earlier and higher levels of habitat protection are needed to protect tribal interests in indigenous habitat, so that animals, plants, and birds do not become endangered and to preserve *harvestable* populations to sustain tribal ways of life. Second, courts often assume that ESA and tribal concerns are congruent and enforcement of ESA protections automatically satisfies the government's trust obligation to protect Indian trust resources.[48] Thus, while courts may recognize a trust duty, the protection of trust resources is not extended beyond the minimal standards required by the ESA. Finally, unlike a private trustee, the government does not always owe Indian beneficiaries the duty of undivided loyalty when there is a conflict of interest between Indian and other interests that the agency is required by law to protect.[49] When conflicts arise, the government can represent both interests at the same time—that is, the Indian interests *and* the very interests that oppose them! This untenable situation was allowed in *Nevada v. United States* (1983), where the Supreme Court explained "the government cannot follow the fastidious standards of a private fiduciary, who would breach his duties to his single beneficiary solely by representing conflicting interests without the beneficiary's consent."[50] (No wonder Indians do not sleep well at night, wondering what their trustee is doing behind their backs.) In *Kandra*, the government acted as a trustee to protect tribal trust resources in the face of conflicting obligations to provide irrigators with water, but only because its obligation toward to the Indians was coupled with ESA obligations to protect the fish that were subject to tribal fishing and water rights; and the relief provided by *Kandra* was fleeting, for in the very next year, Reclamation went back to "business as usual" to the detriment of the salmon fishery. The *Declaration* might require protection of indigenous habitat as an integral part of Reclamation's mission, because of the state duties to protect indigenous lands, resources, and traditional means of subsistence.

9. *Comanche Nation v. United States (2008)*

The *Declaration* goes to great lengths to ensure that the cultural rights of indigenous peoples are protected; and it utilizes the "free, prior, and informed consent" standard as the tool for protecting indigenous rights and ensuring effective participation by indigenous peoples in any government decision that affects their interests. By contrast, there is no federal law with "teeth" to protect cultural property; and free, prior, and informed consent is not required before the government can impact tribal interests. At most, federal law provides procedural, but not substantive, protections for cultural property; and only bare consultation—not free, prior, and informed consent—is required before the government impacts cultural property. Despite these inadequacies, when the courts are at their best, the UN standards can be satisfied. This is seen in *Comanche Nation v. United States* (2008), one of the best Indian cases ever decided.[51]

The Medicine Bluffs are located in the Wichita Mountains in southwest Oklahoma, upon military land at Fort Sill, which was established in 1869. The Medicine Bluffs is a Comanche holy place. From time immemorial, the Comanche have gathered at their traditional site for prayer, to gather medicinal and religious plants and engage in intensely private spiritual experiences tied to natural setting. The southern slope is the pilgrimage route used by traditional religious practitioners to approach the bluffs. Camps were made on the southern approach to support those who ascend the bluffs for religious purposes; and sweat lodges were built along the slope, where plants were gathered among the native grasses, plants, and trees for religious and healing purposes, as well. An unobstructed view of the Bluffs from the southern approach is central to the spiritual experience of the Bluffs. For these reasons, Medicine Bluffs was listed on the National Register of Historic Places in 1974. The military planned to build a 43,000 square foot training facility in an open field at the base of the southern approach to Medicine Bluffs, which would obstruct the viewscape needed by the Comanche religious practitioners.

Section 106 of the National Historic Preservation Act of 1966, 16 U.S.C. §470 *et seq.* (NHPA), required the military to consult with the Comanche before any federal undertaking that would impact properties listed on the National Register of Historic Places for the purpose of determining and mitigating any adverse impacts. The military mailed the Comanche Nation information about the proposed facility but did not describe its location vís-a-vís Medicine Bluffs. The material promised consultation before any construction activities began. A letter from the

Chairman of the Comanche Nation objecting to the project was treated by the military as only a concern about unmarked graves and was for the most part dismissed, despite internal emails by military staff warning that the proposed location would interfere with Comanche religious practices at Medicine Bluffs. No consultations took place between the tribe and the military, and the final environmental impact statement made no mention of the obstruction of the viewscape of the Bluffs by the project. The military's official letter to the Comanche Nation requesting consultation under Section 106 made no mention of Medicine Bluffs or viewscapes of the Bluffs, nor did it provide the precise location of the proposed facility. Further, it incorrectly represented that "the area of the undertaking has been determined to be clear of any cultural structures" and there is "no effect on the Traditional, Cultural, and Religious land and or historic resources." Moreover, the letter was silent regarding related construction in the southern approach to the Bluffs, and there was no evidence that the military discussed the cumulative impacts of the project with the Comanche Nation. The failure of the military to inform the Comanche Nation about impacts on the southern slope were based in part upon the military's mistaken belief that only the northern face of the Bluffs held religious and cultural significance to the tribe.

Based upon the above facts, the Comanche Nation sued the military to enjoin construction. The Comanche relied upon two grounds: (1) the project would "substantially interfere" with the exercise of Comanche religious practices in violation of the Religious Freedom Restoration Act, 42 U.S.C. §2000bb *et seq.* (RFRA), and (2) the military violated Section 106 of the NHPRA, because it failed to make a reasonable and good faith effort to consult with the Comanche Nation to identify and resolve any adverse effects on Medicine Bluffs resulting from the proposed construction project as required by Section 106 and applicable regulations. Following a five-day evidentiary trial and a site visit to Medicine Bluffs by United States District Court Judge Timothy D. DeGiusti, the court entered an order agreeing with the Comanche Nation on both counts and entering a preliminary injunction in one of the best Indian cases ever decided.

The District Court ruled in favor of the Comanche Nation on both counts. First, it held that the Comanche Nation established its RFRA claim, because the evidence clearly established three dispositive facts: (1) the Bluffs are a sacred site of the Comanche people; (2) construction of the facility would substantially burden tribal religious practices in the southern approach to the Bluffs, because it would disrupt the natural environment, interfere with the central line of sight to the Bluffs, and increase traffic disruptive of religious practices; and (3) while the facility was essential to the training mission of Fort Sill, the military failed to prove that construction at that particular location was the least restrictive means of furthering that government interest, as required by RFRA. Second, the court held that the Comanche Nation successfully established its NHPA claim, because the Section 106 process was flawed. It found that the military failed to make a "reasonable and good faith effort" to identify historic properties that might be affected by the project and to consult with the Comanche Nation about that property, because army officials (1) "virtually ignored the concerns regarding the viewscape up to the Bluffs from the southern approach," (2) failed to consult with the tribe on that issue, and (3) sent inadequate information to the Comanche Nation about the project, which made it impossible for the tribe to assess project impacts on tribal interests. Accordingly, the court issued a preliminary injunction to halt the project.

Comanche Nation is one of the most remarkable Indian cases ever decided, because it protects the free exercise of religion at a tribal holy place located on federal land. Unfortunately, this lone decision is an anomaly in American jurisprudence. All other federal courts have denied protection for sacred sites. Finally, the Supreme Court held in *Lyng v. Northwest Indian Cemetery Protective Association* (1988) that there is no principle under the First Amendment to protect tribal worship at holy places located on federal land, and the *Lyng* doctrine was recently applied by the Ninth Circuit Court of Appeals to deny a tribal RFRA claim to protect a holy place from desecration by the Forest Service in *Navajo Nation v. US Forest Service* (2008).[52] *Comanche Nation* was able to navigate around *Lyng* and its progeny by following Tenth Circuit case law interpretation of the "substantial burden" provisions of RFRA—demonstrating that, where there is a will, there is always a way. *Comanche Nation* also found that the government failed to meet Section 106 consultation requirements, which are less rigorous than the "free, prior, and informed consent" standard of the *Declaration*. If the military consulted with the Comanche Nation with the goal of obtaining its free, prior, and informed consent, extensive litigation could have been avoided.

10. *Santa Clara Pueblo v. Martinez (1978)*[53]

During the modern era of federal Indian law, courts acted to restore tribal control over the internal affairs and social relations of Indian tribes, in line with *Worcester* and *Crow Dog* of the 19th century and the modern Indian Self-Determination Policy. The Supreme Court decision in *Santa Clara* also embodies this trend, because it protected a Pueblo's right to self-government and its power to determine tribal membership in accordance with its unique cultural and religious traditions. The case involved a legal challenge to tribal membership laws, which were said to violate the due process and equal protection provisions of the Indian Civil Rights Act. In rejecting the challenge, the Supreme Court found that the act did not require tribes to follow Anglo-American concepts of equal protection and due process in determining their membership, because they have the power to establish their own forms of government best suited to their cultures as "distinct, independent political communities" retaining their right to self-government with "the power of regulating their internal and social relations" and "to make their own substantive law in internal matters" and "enforce that law in their own forums."[54] This historic decision meets the *Declaration's* standards for protecting indigenous rights to self-determination, self-government, indigenous institutions, and culture in several important respects.

The Supreme Court eschewed unwarranted federal intrusions upon traditional values important to the Pueblo's cultural survival. It held that an Indian nation is free to maintain or establish its own form of government, and as a distinct political community, each tribe can determine its own membership.[55] That deference restores *Worcester's* principle that Indian tribes are distinct political communities with self-government power to regulate their internal and social relations. The Court applied the congressional policy of furthering Indian self-determination and tribal self-government in a decision that strengthens tribal courts and extends sovereign immunity from suit to the Pueblo.[56] In affirming the rights to self-government and indigenous institutions, including the Pueblo's ability to make its own laws, the Court strengthened the ability of Indian tribes to maintain themselves as culturally and politically distinct entities, as the *Declaration* also envisions. And the court reversed the trend of the federal government to supplant tribal governments, which was set in motion in the 19th century by *Kagama*, by limiting federal intrusions upon tribal sovereignty unless and until Congress expresses a clear intent to do so.[57]

At its best, our legal culture subscribes to the self-government principle of the *Declaration* as it relates to the internal affairs of Indian tribes. The fundamental problem is that federal Indian law does not see tribal self-government as an *inherent human right*, and as such indefeasible. Instead, *Santa Clara* ominously declared that "Congress has plenary authority to limit, modify or eliminate the powers of self-government which the Tribes otherwise possess."[58] Human rights should not rest upon such fragile ground and depend upon the good will of Congress for their existence. That kind of political vulnerability is not tolerated by international human rights law, and the *Declaration* standards operate to curb the plenary power of Congress to eliminate human rights of indigenous peoples, including their self-government rights.

The Ten Worst Indian Law Cases Ever Decided

The above survey of federal Indian law at its best suggests that our legal culture is fundamentally compatible with the UN standards, even though the cases cited are sometimes fleeting victories and many rulings have been modified or eroded over time. To round-out our overview of domestic law, we shall briefly examine the "dark side" of federal Indian law. The need to incorporate the UN standards into our law and social policy in order to provide dependable legal protections is readily apparent when we peer into the "dark side" of federal Indian law, as done in my survey, *In The Courts of the Conqueror: The 10 Worst Indian Law Cases Ever Decided* (2010). That book studied unjust cases found in federal Indian law that turned on nefarious legal doctrines heavily tainted by notions of race, colonialism, and unjust legal fictions—cases that have never been overturned and are still used by the Supreme Court to decide Indian cases. Here, we shall perform a brief exercise to see how the UN standards would affect the outcome of those cases. What would the outcome be if the UN standards were controlling law at the time those cases were decided, and the Supreme Court had to apply them to resolve the cases? As will be seen, the holdings would be much different, and there would be no resulting "dark side" to the law in the ten cases studied below.

1. *Johnson v. M'Intosh (1823)*

In *Johnson*, the Supreme Court transferred legal title of land owned by Indian nations to the United States under the doctrines of discovery and conquest in an unjust decision that converted Indian tribe landowners into mere tenants of the federal government.[59] The Court justified its doctrines of dispossession by describing Indian "heathens" as a vile race of people with inferior character, habits, and religion.[60] By contrast, the *Declaration* flatly rejects the use of any doctrine based on racial superiority as "racist, scientifically false, legally invalid, morally condemnable, and socially unjust."[61] Article 8.2(b) prohibits any act that has the aim or effect of dispossessing indigenous peoples of "their lands, territories, or resources." Article 26 recognizes tribal land rights and requires nations to give legal recognition and protection of those lands. And Article 27 requires nations to adjudicate indigenous land rights in "fair, independent, impartial, open and transparent" processes, which were sorely lacking in the *Johnson* proceeding.[62] Had these provisions been the law in 1823, the outcome of *Johnson* would have been much different. Tribal land ownership rights would have been fully recognized in accordance with the non-discrimination principle of the *Declaration*, and the notions of racism, discovery, conquest, and land dispossession would not be embedded in federal Indian law.

2. *Cherokee Nation v. Georgia (1831)*

The legal framework for the removal of the Indian race from the South arises from the Indian Removal Act, *Cherokee Nation v. Georgia* (1831), and the cases extending state hegemony over Indian tribes and their lands in Georgia, Alabama, and Tennessee.[63] By contrast, Article 10 of the *Declaration* prohibits forcible removal of indigenous peoples from their lands and territories without their free, prior, and informed consent. Articles 26–28 protect their land rights, and Articles 3–4 protect the self-determination and self-government rights of indigenous peoples. These provisions would have stopped the Indian Removal Movement dead in its tracks had the *Declaration* been the law of the land at the time that the legal framework for removal was being developed.

3. *Connors v. United States and Cheyenne Indians (1898)*

The legality of the Indian wars and use of military force to keep Indians on their reservations as a part of the War Department's Indian policies of the 1870s were implicated in *Connors v. United States and Cheyenne Indians* (1898).[64] That case, involving Indian depredation claims and the massacre of the Northern Cheyenne who escaped from Fort Robinson, would never have been brought had Article 7 been in force on the Great Plains in the 19th century. It guarantees to indigenous peoples their inherent rights to life, liberty, and physical and mental integrity, and it safeguards their right to live in peace and freedom without being subject to any acts of violence. The United States would have had to pursue its policies peacefully, and the lives of over 50,000 American Indians slain in the forty wars fought between the United States and Indian tribes would have been spared. The *Connors* case, with its heartbreaking facts concerning the massacre of Cheyenne men, women, and children, would have never been brought in a nation at peace with its Native peoples.

4. *Lone Wolf v. Hitchcock (1903)*

The *Lone Wolf* decision is fundamentally at odds with the *Declaration.* Instead of breaking treaties, taking tribal land against the will of the Indians, and ruling Indian people by the absolute power that Congress wielded without judicial review, as sanctioned in *Lone Wolf,* Article 37 requires nations to recognize and enforce treaties, and Article 8 prevents acts that dispossess Indian land, while Articles 18–19 curb the plenary power of Congress by guaranteeing Indian tribes the right to participate in any legislative or administrative action that affects them. Other articles in the *Declaration* require the government to obtain the prior, free, and informed consent of indigenous peoples before taking action that affects their rights. The noxious Lone Wolf doctrines are a dead letter under the *Declaration.*

5. Sandoval Trilogy and the "Dark Side" of Guardianship

In the Courts of the Conqueror examined the "dark side" of guardianship when the federal government abused its guardianship powers over the lives, property, and internal affairs of Indian tribes during 1886–1934.[65] In this oppressive period, the government banned the practice of tribal religion and dictated all aspects of highly regimented Native life as part of the government's enforced assimilation, tutelage, civilization, and Christianization policies. Courts that allowed that abuse of power, including the infamous Code of Indian Offenses, would have been forestalled by the right to self-determination of Articles 3–4 and by Article 8(1), which prohibits forced assimilation. Furthermore, the *Declaration* strongly protects the indigenous right to culture in Articles 11–13. If these protections were the law in 1886–1934, the stride toward citizenship would not have been marked by human rights infringements caused by these government excesses, which caused, in large part, the historic trauma still seen in tribal communities today.

6–7. Taking the Kids and the Dead

The widespread practices of taking Indian children from their families and also the dead from Indian graves in American legal history were studied by *In the Courts of the Conqueror.*[66] These noxious practices would not have been allowed if the Declaration's protections were in place. The thousands of pre-Indian Child Welfare Act (ICWA) cases that removed one in four Indian children from their families prior to 1978, for placement in non-Indian foster families and institutions, would have come out differently if Article 7 were the law of the land.[67] It prohibits the forcible removal of Indian children; and states may not deprive indigenous persons of their cultural values and ethnic identity under Article 8. Lastly, had Article 12 been controlling law and social policy, the untold thousands of dead bodies, millions of funerary and sacred objects, and objects of cultural patrimony could not have been improperly taken from tribal graveyards and communities during the pre-NAGPRA era before 1990, because Article 12 provides a right of repatriation.[68]

8–9. Indian Religion Cases Decided by the Rehnquist Court

The adverse Indian religion cases of the Supreme Court in *Lyng v. Northwest Indian Cemetery Protective Association* (1988) and *Employment Division v. Smith* (1990), which stripped traditional tribal religious practices of constitutional protection, would have come out differently if the Rehnquist Court had to apply Articles 11–12, because they affirmatively protect indigenous religious liberty and tribal holy places as a human rights matter.[69]

10. *Tee-Hit-Ton Indians v. United States (1955)*

The novel Supreme Court doctrine of confiscation of aboriginal land under the doctrines of discovery and conquest in *Tee-Hit-Ton*, which saw Indians as nothing more than "savage tribes," would not have been possible under Articles 26–29 of the *Declaration*, because they protect aboriginal lands, territories, natural resources, and uses; and they require nations to help tribes conserve and protect aboriginal habitat. Furthermore, the doctrines of race and dispossession relied upon in *Tee-Hit-Ton* would be foreclosed by the *Declaration*, as indicated above.

In short, there would be no dark side to federal Indian law if the *Declaration* controlled the outcome of the above cases. Equally important, the *Declaration's* principles allow us to re-conceptualize the foundation for Native American rights in the United States under a vastly different set of values than the outmoded values of the 19th century, which underpin the dark side of federal Indian law, when the Supreme Court drew heavily from principles of discovery, conquest, and the supposed racial inferiority of American Indians to fashion the legal framework for indigenous rights. Rights that arise from that dark well are forever vulnerable in the self-described "courts of the conqueror" of *Johnson v. M'Intosh* and its progeny, making it easy for the Supreme Court to trim Native rights at will and dismiss or trivialize tribal interests that modern international human rights law deems *inherent* and inalienable human rights. Rather than base Native American rights upon those dark notions of race, colonialism, and unjust legal fictions, the *Declaration* asserts that indigenous rights are more properly based upon the principles of equality, non-discrimination, justice, democracy, and good faith; and it subscribes to the notion that indigenous rights are inherent rights that spring from indigenous institutions and cultures and self-determination. These new precepts of a post-colonial world can strongly supplement the *Worcester* foundation for Indian rights in the United States on the "good" side of federal Indian law, if they are incorporated into federal Indian law during the implementation of the *Declaration*; and they can replace the nefarious principles of dispossession and race currently embedded in that body of law, which have long weakened Indian rights in our nation.

From the above survey, it becomes clear that the potential impact of the *Declaration* on the future of federal Indian law is two-fold. First, it can supplement and strengthen the very best of our legal culture in its finest hour, as seen in the ten best Indian cases ever decided, and make those rules of law more dependable and more reliable. At the same time, the principles of the *Declaration* operate to trim away the dark side of federal Indian law, including much of the harm done to Native American rights by the Rehnquist and Roberts Courts in recent decades, making it a more just body of law, better-suited for the post-colonial world of the 21st century. These beneficial impacts are enormous, and they can be realized by implementing the *Declaration* into the legal system.

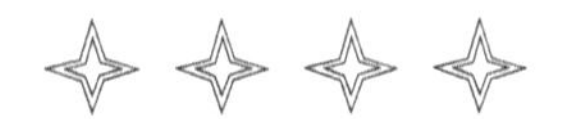

CHAPTER EIGHT
Does United States Law and Policy Meet UN Standards?

This chapter compares the human rights standards in the *Declaration* with federal law and policy to identify areas that need improvement. When President Obama announced United States endorsement of the *Declaration*, the State Department issued an accompanying "white paper" that suggests federal agencies are "already doing" almost everything demanded in the *Declaration*.[1] It contends that the "United States has made great strides in improving its relationship with Native Americans and indigenous peoples around the world," but acknowledges that "much remains to be done."[2] The following comparative analysis shows that US law falls short of the UN human rights standards in several areas.

A side-by-side comparison will bring a blueprint for reform into focus. Our goal here is not to provide an in-depth treatment of the extensive body of federal Indian law, but to highlight or underscore substantive areas that do not meet the UN standards. By highlighting deficiencies, we can pinpoint needed reforms and encourage further scholarship in those areas of the law. It is hoped that discourse and scholarship will produce a thoroughgoing, comparative legal analysis that rivals in ambition the sea-changing national examinations of Indian policy, legal developments, and conditions of life done by the *Meriam Report* (1928) and the *American Indian Policy Review Commission Final Report* (1977), which became important catalysts for change.[3]

The following analysis takes the same thematic approach for examining the *Declaration* followed in Chapter Three (which should be consulted for more information about the contents of the *Declaration*).

1. The Self-Determination Principle

The Supreme Court has suggested that the Indian tribes' interest in self-determination is not a "fundamental right" and in other cases has ruled that Congress may abolish tribal government outright under the plenary power doctrine.[4] However, as indicated in Chapter Three, self-determination is a universal human right. In all likelihood, it is a peremptory norm, which may not be abridged by any nation. In the unique indigenous context, the right supports the notion that tribal communities should be in control of their own destinies. That idea is the foundational principle and framework of the *Declaration* (See Chapter Three). This approach is compatible with the Indian Self-Determination Policy followed by every branch of the federal government since at least 1970.[5]

The United States' obligation to protect the inherent sovereignty of Indian nations as distinct and self-governing political communities within the American political system is recognized by the judicial branch in the *Worcester* line of cases as a foundational principle of federal Indian law. Since 1960, the executive branch has consistently followed that policy, with official support by every American president to the present day.[6] In 1970, President Nixon announced the "Indian Self-Determination Policy" in an historic message to Congress to end years of government termination and paternalism in favor of an enlightened commitment to self-determination that promotes and fosters tribal self-government and Indian control over the lives of Indian people, which is virtually identical to the UN principle described in the *Declaration*.[7] The rationale given by President Nixon rests on the same concerns that motivated the *Declaration*.[8] The policy recognizes that excessive federal dominance over Indian tribes retards their progress and denies tribal people an effective voice in their affairs and relationships; and it seeks to expand tribal control "premised on the principle that Indian tribes are, in the final analysis, the primary or basic governmental unit of Indian policy."[9] The federal responsibility to promote meaningful self-determination is implemented through many acts of Congress affecting Indian life, property, governance, and policy, such as laws granting increased tribal control over programs and services to Indians,[10] Indian children,[11] education,[12] law enforcement and the administration of justice,[13] housing,[14] health,[15] and natural resource management.[16] The Supreme Court has also confirmed the self-government powers of Indian tribes derived from *Worcester* and its progeny, with decisions in the modern era that recognize tribal powers to tax, regulate persons and activities in Indian country, adjudicate disputes that arise on Indian reservations, and punish Indians who violate tribal law.[17] Native Americans have made striking advances under the Indian Self-Determination Policy during the modern era.

The Indian Self-Determination Policy is generally consistent with the self-determination principle of the *Declaration*, except in one critical respect: the *Declaration* recognizes self-determination as an inherent human right. By their nature, inherent rights are not subject to defeasance by the state. By contrast, federal law subjects the Indian right to modification, limitation, or termination by Congress, as recognized in the *Kagama*, *Lone Wolf*, and *Martinez* line of cases. That power arises from an extra-constitutional source: the plenary power doctrine allows Congress to treat Indian tribes as it sees fit pursuant to its guardianship powers. Thus, self-determination has been subject to wild pendulum swings in federal policy: from inherent tribal sovereignty recognized by the Marshall Court (c. 1831–1883), to plenary federal control over Indian tribes under the assimilation, Christianization, civilization, and tutelage guardianship policies (c. 1883–1934), to promoting tribal self-government under Indian Reorganization Act policies (c. 1934–1950), to the Termination and Assimilation Policy (1950–1960), and returning to the Indian Self-Determination Policy (c. 1960–present). It is intolerable for human rights to rest upon shifting sand, to zigzag between prevailing prejudices of the day, or to depend upon ever-changing political winds. Similar to the States' Rights Principle that limits unwarranted federal encroachment upon the states, the *Declaration* would stabilize indigenous self-determination in the American setting by limiting similar encroachment on Indian tribes through unilateral federal power to terminate or place limitations upon the indigenous right to self-determination. After all, when viewed as a human right, the Supreme Court, Congress, or federal agencies could not abridge that indigenous right any more than they can violate other human rights, such as freedom from systematic discrimination, torture, genocide, slavery, or piracy. The failure of federal law to recognize this limitation on federal power needs to be corrected to meet the standards set forth in the *Declaration*. Indian tribes cannot at the same time self-determine their destiny and be subject to the unfettered will of a conqueror, for the two political conditions are mutually exclusive. Doctrines that sanction absolute power and the divestiture of self-determination without indigenous participation and the free, prior, and informed consent of Native Americans are not in keeping with the way democracies act in the post-colonial age. Arcane habits die hard. But the result intended by the UN's self-determination principle is a stronger, more harmonious nation, when states guarantee tribal peoples control over their destiny. That norm simply requires the United States to become a real protectorate, as described in *Worcester*, in which the United States protects the integrity of self-governing Indian nations but cannot oppress them. As the protector-nation, the United States simply acts in their best interests. The will and unfettered power of a conqueror have no place in the self-determination framework of the *Declaration*, or in the closely analogous *Worcester* setting.

As such, it is time to discard *Lone Wolf*. There are many reasons why the infamous case should be overturned by the Supreme Court.[18] Indeed, modern cases have trimmed away parts of the *Lone Wolf* doctrine.[19] A clear limit must be firmly placed upon the power of Congress in Indian Affairs. That begins by recognizing that the power of Congress is not "plenary," but more properly a "protectorate" power described in *Worcester*, which may only be exerted in that protective framework to safeguard the integrity of Indian nations as self-governing communities in the American setting, and never to harm, destroy, or prey upon them.[20] That is a limitation upon the power of the federal government, to be sure, but it is not unlike the constitutional limitations placed upon the central govern, which safeguard the political rights of the states from unwarranted intrusion by Congress. Consistent with *Worcester's* framework, the *Declaration* supports the need to curtail Congress' power to infringe upon the indefeasible human right to self-determination.

2. Equality and Non-Discrimination

Where the mindset of racial, religious, or cultural discrimination exists, indigenous rights cannot be fully realized until the universal values of equality and non-discrimination are extended to indigenous peoples. The *Declaration* condemns all forms of discrimination as "racist, scientifically false, legally invalid, and socially unjust," and the equality principle underpins the human rights standards. This principle theoretically resonates with core values, constitutional principles, statutory protections, and cases like *Brown v. Board of Education* (1954), which rest on the belief that "All men are created equal." Though the United States has not always lived up to this value during the growth of the democracy, this self-evident truth has always impelled the nation to self-correct whenever it strayed from the path. The *Declaration* insists on extending this principle to Native Americans.

We must begin by rooting out the vestiges of racism found in the law. As will be seen, many 19th century notions of racism are embedded in the "dark side" of federal Indian law. Numerous adverse Supreme Court decisions turn upon, or were heavily influenced by, "racism" as defined by *Webster's* dictionary; and those cases are still relied upon today by our courts to decide Native American issues.[21] Racism is a hard-edged word that should never be used lightly. For purposes of this discussion we shall follow *Webster's* definition of racism as "a belief that race is the primary determinant of human traits and capacities" and "racial differences produce an inherent superiority of a particular race."[22] Scholars tell us that racial discrimination springs from doctrines, actions, or programs that assume that one race is inherently superior over others. In *Race and Races: Cases and Resources for a Diverse America* (2007), Juan Perea provides an in-depth definition and discussion of racism.[23] According to Perea, *racism* is marked by antipathy toward people branded as "inferior" due to their biological nature, and that hostility is characterized by bigotry, hatred, and prejudicial treatment.[24] *Racism* is seen in the racist acts, attitudes, language, and behavior of individuals. On a larger scale, a population manifests racism through widely shared racist beliefs, attitudes, and stereotypes expressed in many forms and institutions throughout society.[25] Because it is a distinctly human, man-made institution, common racism harbored by prejudiced laymen can sometimes find its way into the law, as seen in the *Dred Scott*, *Plessy*, and *Korematsu* decisions, including adverse American Indian cases that turned on prevailing prejudices.[26] Some of our leading jurists have feet of clay when it comes to that dark sentiment that lurks in every human breast—no one is immune, even though they may wear black robes and sit in prominent chambers.

In point of fact, the many pejorative racial descriptions and stereotypes of American Indians found in court opinions are classic statements of prejudice that fall squarely within the dictionary definition of *racism*, and the use of these racist invectives when deciding cases and formulating legal doctrines amounts to legal racism. As will be seen, many Supreme Court cases that adversely affect vital tribal interests routinely describe Indians as "racially inferior," "ignorant," "savages," "heathens," or "uncivilized," often in the same paragraph where the court decides the issue and shapes indigenous rights. For example, *Johnson v. M'Intosh* (1823) sees Indians as "heathens" and "fierce savages" with an inferior "character and religion" that "afforded an apology for considering them as a people over whom the superior genius of Europe might claim an ascendency."[27] The *Johnson* Court thus treated American Indians as a brutish race of people that lacks normal attributes of human beings when it destroyed their land ownership rights through the doctrines of discovery and conquest, and the supposed inferiority of the Indian race was used by the Court to justify its manifestly unjust decision. That judicial attitude ushers us directly into the realm of racism, a dark place where prejudice and hatred presides. Just like blacks were "a subordinate and inferior class of beings" in *Dred Scott,* Indian "heathens" are an "inferior race of people" in *Johnson*—the only difference between the two cases is *Dred Scott* has been repudiated as a racist decision that is no longer good law, whereas *Johnson* is still used as legal precedent by the Supreme Court to decide Indian cases to this day.[28] This judicial attitude continued throughout the nineteenth century.

The Marshall court resorted to bare racial stereotypes to support the holding in *Cherokee Nation v. Georgia* (1823), that the Cherokee Nation is not a foreign nation with full sovereignty. Chief Justice Marshall wrote that the founders did not intend to allow Indian tribes to sue in federal court as foreign nations, considering the "habits and usages" of Indians, and, furthermore, the use of courts did not enter "the mind of an Indian" because "[t]heir appeal was to the tomahawk."[29] Justice Johnson heartily agreed with Marshall's pejorative racial stereotypes. His concurring opinion drips with open racism, as described by *Webster's,* and antipathy against Indian tribes that are, in his eyes, "so low in the grade of organized society" as a vile "race of hunters connected in society by scarcely a semblance of organic government" and composed of a "restless, warlike, and signally cruel" people, with "inveterate habits and deep-seated enmity."[30] The racist justice asked, how could "any nation on earth treat them [as] a member of the community of nations?"[31] With deep-seated enmity of his own, Justice Johnson denigrated Cherokee land claims. He wrote their territory is "allotted to them as a boon, from a master or conqueror."[32] He scoffed at Cherokee nationhood ("the law of nations would regard [them] as nothing more than wandering hordes, held together only by ties of blood and habit, and having neither laws or government, beyond what is required in a savage state").[33] Slamming the courthouse doors closed to Indians, *Johnson* chided the savages for going to court in much the same way that the justices in the *Dred Scott* case could not tolerate lawsuits brought by slaves in the federal courts. He wrote that Indians should not "appeal to any arbiter but the sword."[34] This racist tirade was joined by Justice Baldwin, who warned that, if we allow Cherokees into the courthouse, "countless tribes will rush to the federal courts in endless controversies, growing out of the laws of the states or of congress."[35] Unlike *Dred Scott* which has been repudiated as a racist decision, *Cherokee Nation* is hailed as a foundational case in federal Indian law, along with *Johnson.*

Racist jurisprudence continued in the twentieth century. In *Lone Wolf v. Hitchcock* (1903), the Supreme Court announced the plenary power doctrine to clothe Congress with absolute power over the "ignorant and dependent race" of American Indians, unfettered by any constitutional limitations or judicial review.[36] Described as the "Indians' *Dred Scott* decision," *Lone Wolf* explains that the sole check on this absolute power is a bare moral obligation "to act in good faith" by a superior race of people over an inferior race not "fully emancipated from the control and protection of the United States":

> It is to be presumed that in this matter the United States would be governed by such considerations of justice as would control a Christian people in their treatment of an ignorant and dependent race.[37]

The Supreme Court saw Indians with racist eyes when it dismissed the nationhood of Indian tribes in *Montoya v. United States* (1901). It said "uncivilized Indians" possess "the natural infirmities of the Indian character, their fiery tempers, impatience of restraint, their mutual jealousies and animosities, their nomadic habits, and lack of mental training."[38] Indians are held in utter contempt in *United States v. Sandoval* (1913), which describes them with undisguised racism. In upholding federal hegemony over Pueblo Indians, the determinative fact was that Indians are an "inferior people adhering to primitive modes of life, largely influenced by superstition and fetishism, and governed chiefly according to crude customs inherited from their ancestors."[39] The opinion sees Indians as an "intellectually and morally inferior people" who are "victims to evils and debasing influence of intoxicants." It also roundly condemns Pueblo religious ceremonies as a "ribald system of debauchery" attended by "great evils" that must be given up as pagan customs, and it criticizes Pueblo governments as authoritarian, cruel, and inhuman institutions. Such a vile race needed federal guardianship in the view of the *Sandoval* Court.

The legacy of undisguised racism surfaced in *Tee-Hit-Ton Indians v. United States* (1955), which describes Indians as "savage tribes" conquered by the United States.[40] *Tee-Hit-Ton* held that aboriginal land can be confiscated by the government without compensating Indians, because, "after the coming of the white man," original Indian land title became "permission from the whites to occupy" the land, and nothing more.[41] The opinion assumes that all Indian tribes are savage and all tribes in the United States were conquered. Based upon those incorrect legal fictions (i.e., Indians are savages, and all tribes were conquered), the Court granted tribes grossly unequal land rights:

> After conquest they were permitted to occupy portions of territory over which they had previously exercised 'sovereignty,' as we use that term. This is not a property right but amounts to a right of occupancy which the sovereign grants but which may be terminated and such lands fully disposed of by the sovereign itself without any legally enforceable obligation to compensate the Indians.[42]

It shocks the conscience that the unsavory racist jurisprudence laid down in the above decisions remains good law that is still in full force and effect. Their racist descriptions, repugnant judicial attitudes, and nefarious legal doctrines *have never been repudiated or reversed* by the Supreme Court. While the Roberts Court does not use racist language today when trimming Indian rights in its adverse decisions, it routinely cites the tainted cases as legal precedent. For example, *Johnson* was most recently cited with approval in *City of Sherrill v. Oneida Indian Nation* (2005) to crush tribal efforts to obtain former lands and exercise sovereignty over them; and *United States v. Jicarilla Apache Nation* (2011) dredged up *Lone*

Wolf, *Sandoval*, and *Cherokee Nation* to support a ruling that announces (after all these years) that the federal government is not a "real" trustee that must share legal information with its Indian beneficiaries—like all other trustees must do—thereby diluting the Indian trust doctrine.[43] The outright racism prevalent in federal Indian law is closely linked to doctrines of colonialism, conquest, guardianship, and plenary power used to dispossess and subjugate Native Americans; and that same legal racism underpins the heavy use of unjust legal fictions by jurists as a tool to reach unjust results in Indian cases.[44] The non-discrimination and equality principles of the *Declaration* flatly reject racism in the law. That should send a wake-up call to the Supreme Court: the Marble Chamber is the last place to harbor racism against America's Native peoples, long after it has been discarded by the rest of society, and that is anathema to human rights. The high priests who preside in that temple should fundamentally reexamine their tainted principles of racial superiority and bring the judicial branch in line with the equality and non-discrimination principles of the *Declaration*. Otherwise, take down the sign, "Equal Justice Under Law," above the front doors so hypocrisy does not add insult to the injuries inflicted by the discriminatory doctrines that abide there.

3. Survival Rights: Life, Integrity, and Security

The *Declaration* is vitally concerned with the paramount problem facing indigenous peoples in the 21st century: *Will we survive?* In settler states, violence often stalks small groups of indigenous peoples who live in remote places. In the United States, it is estimated that over 50,000 Native Americans were killed during the Indian Wars (1790–1890) as the result of military and civilian violence.[45] The United States is probably the most violent nation on earth, given its military history and soaring domestic crime rate; and Indian reservations are the most violent places in America, according to Justice Department statistics. To protect the security of vulnerable indigenous communities, the *Declaration* prohibits the destruction of indigenous peoples and affirms their right to live in peace and security, free from genocide and any acts of violence.

In *Oliphant v. Suquamish Indian Tribe* (1978), the Supreme Court held that Indian tribes do not have the inherent governmental power to prosecute non-Indians who commit crimes on the reservation.[46] The decision is troubling in three respects. First, it opened the door to reservation violence by non-Indians. Second, until *Oliphant,* it was settled that only Congress could trim the sovereign powers of Indian tribes.[47] Yet, *Oliphant* put the Supreme Court into the business of trimming tribal sovereignty in violation of the long-standing rule that Indian tribes retain all sovereign powers not expressly abrogated by Congress; and the Supreme Court exercised its new-found power to divest the tribes of criminal jurisdiction by projecting its own policy and normative views about the proper scope of tribal government authority—that is, it opined that such power was lost by the tribes "by implication" upon their incorporation into the United States, because the power to try and punish white people is "inconsistent with their status."[48] Third, the judicial divestiture of tribal sovereignty by implication in *Oliphant* puts tribal, state, and federal governments into a terrible fix. Tribes become the only governments in the United States without complete jurisdiction over all persons who come within their jurisdiction, and this strips tribal law enforcement and public safety capabilities to protect tribal members from violence committed by non-Indians in tribal communities. Today, reservation crime rates have skyrocketed: American Indians are almost twice as likely to be victimized by violent crime as any other ethnic group, with above average rates of rape, sexual assault, robbery, and aggravated assault—and sixty-six percent of the Indian victims report that their attacker was a non-Indian.[49] One commenter summarizes the impact of *Oliphant* upon the problem of violence in Indian communities as follows:

> *Oliphant's* jurisdictional scheme for Indian country puts tribes, states, and the federal government in a difficult position. On one hand, tribes cannot adequately maintain sovereign authority over their territory in light of *Oliphant's* jurisdictional preclusions. On the other, federal and state authorities are not often willing or unable to adequately police Indian country, and are often met with cultural resistance from Indians when they do investigate. Outsourcing criminal jurisdiction to state and federal authorities strips tribal governments of their ability to serve their people and runs counter to Congress' stated goal of supporting tribal sovereignty. When an unaccountable, often indifferent foreign sovereign places itself in charge of ensuring reservation safety,

> the authority of the tribal government—the body with the largest stake in protecting Indian tribes—is naturally diminished.[50]

Congress recognized the obligation of the United States to "provide for the public safety of Indian country" when it enacted the Tribal Law and Order Act of 2010, and it found that (1) domestic and sexual violence against Native American women has reached "epidemic proportions," (2) 34 percent of Native American women will be raped in their lifetime, (3) 39 percent of Native women will be subject to domestic violence, and (4) Indian tribes face significant increases in violent crime as a direct result of increased methamphetamine use on Indian reservations. The act increases the powers of tribal governments to deal with the violence crisis, but it does not overturn the *Oliphant* loophole that forbids tribal prosecution of non-Indian criminals.

Until such time as federal law closes that loophole, which opens the door to violence in indigenous communities, and until federal criminal justice policies and programs actually bring down the rate of violent crime in Indian country, US law and policy fail to protect Native Americans from acts of violence as required by Article 7 of the *Declaration*. The *Oliphant* rule undercuts the indigenous right to be free from violence. It infringes upon the self-determination principle of the *Declaration,* because it strips tribes of an essential government function to protect tribal members from violence and to provide for the public safety. Furthermore, the loophole offends the equality and non-discrimination principle, because of its discriminatory impact: it leaves tribal governments as the *only* governments in America without jurisdiction over all persons, including criminals, who come into their territory. No one would suggest that when the states voluntarily entered the union, they were divested of such important criminal justice powers. In contrast to the Marshall Court, which held, in the *Worcester* protectorate framework, that Indian tribes voluntarily came into the union through treaties, with their inherent tribal self-government powers intact, *Oliphant* brings tribes into the political system on an unequal footing through the framework of conquest, divests them of basic governmental powers, and renders them vulnerable to violent crime. Because it is guided by the framework of conquest, the Supreme Court is not the proper institution to trim tribal sovereignty, and it continues to harbor patently racist legal doctrines that necessarily color the Court's assault on tribal sovereignty. The delineation of sovereignty more properly falls to political branches—they are free from discriminatory legal precedent and able to define political relationships in a non-discriminatory manner, subject to the limitations imposed by the human rights provisions of the *Declaration*. The limited role of the Supreme Court is to protect, not destroy, tribal sovereignty and leave any adjustments to Congress.

4. Cultural Rights

The *Declaration* requires effective measures to counteract the massive assault on indigenous culture seen in nations around the world. (See discussion in Chapter Three.) It affirms many sweeping human rights associated with protecting the cultural survival and actualizing cultural self-determination for indigenous peoples on a grand scale, much like the Marshall Plan sought to rebuild war-torn Europe following World War II. Together, these cultural rights and duties are the Magna Carta for protecting indigenous cultures.

The right to culture has many attributes. Indigenous peoples have the rights to: (1) practice and revitalize their cultures, including the manifestations of culture, such as artifacts, designs, ceremonies, arts, literature, technologies, and sites (Art. 11); (2) practice religious ceremonies, including religious and cultural sites (Arts. 12, 25); (3) languages, histories, oral traditions, to be realized through effective measures by the state (Art. 13); and (4) establish and control their own culturally appropriate educational systems in their own languages through effective measures by the state (Art. 14). In Articles 11 and 12, the state is required to provide redress for the taking of cultural, intellectual, religious, and spiritual property, as well as human remains and ceremonial objects, from indigenous peoples without their free, prior, and informed consent, or in violation of their laws and customs, through mechanisms developed in consultation with indigenous peoples. Furthermore, Article 31 recognizes the right of indigenous peoples to control and protect the intellectual property rights over their cultural heritage, and it requires states to take effective measures, in conjunction with indigenous peoples, to recognize and protect the exercise of such rights.

The United States should review its laws and policies in consultation with Native Americans to identify barriers to rebuilding and protecting their cultures and create a national program for fully and effectively realizing all cultural rights affirmed by the *Declaration*. Pending that comprehensive study and plan of action, it is possible to highlight some areas of US law and policy that fail to meet UN standards and require immediate attention.

a) Protection of Religious Places

Federal law that allows the destruction of Native American holy places and interference with tribal worship at those sites does not pass muster under Article 12. The United States lacks a statute, constitutional principle, or policy sufficient to protect these attributes of tribal worship, as made clear by the courts; and Congress has not corrected this long-standing problem. The *Lyng* doctrine fails to meet international standards in three respects: First, *Lyng* suggests that government use of federal land does not violate the free exercise of religion, as a matter of law, which is at odds with Congress' view that land use does impact the free exercise of religion and the *Declaration's* view that indigenous religion requires worship at holy places.[51] Second, *Lyng* protects religious liberty only when the government punishes a person for practicing religion or forces one to violate his or her religion. That crabbed duty violates US treaty obligations, as explained by Special Rapporteur Anaya:

> Under relevant sources of international law, the United States has a duty to respect and protect Native American religion, a duty that goes beyond not coercing or penalizing Native American religious practitioners.[52]

Third, the idea in *Lyng* that the government can destroy an entire tribal religion without burdening anyone's religious practices is sophistry—it is one of many unjust legal fictions found in federal Indian law.

By contrast, the *Declaration* recognizes a meaningful Native American religious right to "maintain, protect, and have access in privacy to their religious and cultural sites" (Art. 12) and a right to "maintain and strengthen their distinctive spiritual relationship with their traditionally owned or otherwise occupied and used lands, territories . . . and to uphold their responsibilities to future generations in this regard" (Art. 25). In short, international law places a duty upon the United States to protect Native American religion "that goes beyond not coercing or penalizing Native American religious practitioners," and the *Declaration* requires "protection of and access to sites of particular religious and cultural significance."[53] This standard is met by the *Comanche Nation* case, discussed earlier as one of the best Indian cases ever decided, but not by *Lyng* and its progeny.

b) Intellectual Property Rights

Intellectual property is a term covering "a collection of intangible rights and causes of action developed by Western nation states at various times to protect particular aspects of artistic and industrial output," according to a scholarly work written by Dr. Jane Anderson, *Law, Knowledge, Culture: The Production of Indigenous Knowledge in Intellectual Property Law* (2009). It includes "copyright, designs, patents, trade secrets, passing off, aspects of competition land and trade marks."[54] It deals with knowledge and that which comes from the mind—intangible, but valuable, property described by one Western jurist in 1769 as follows:

> But the property claimed here is all ideal; a set of ideas which have no bounds or marks whatever, nothing that is capable of a visible possession, nothing that can sustain any one of the qualities or incidents of property. Their whole existence is in the mind alone; incapable of any other modes of acquisition or enjoyment, than by mental possession or apprehension; safe and invulnerable, from their own immateriality; no trespass can reach them; no tort affect them; no fraud or violence diminish or damage them. Yet these are the phantoms which the Author would grasp and confine to himself; and these are what the defendant is charged with having robbed the plaintiff of. [55]

Like all other property owned by human beings, indigenous property is not confined to tangible property, but it also incorporates intangible property. Unfortunately, the body of law for protecting intellectual property developed during the prolonged period of colonization, in which indigenous property rights were stripped away, appropriated, and marginalized; and indigenous interests in intangible property were not recognized or taken into account when the copyright, patent, and trademark laws were being developed. At long last, the paramount challenge of modern intellectual property rights law is to recognize the valuable cultural knowledge produced by indigenous peoples as property, and make space to protect their interests in their intangible property. It is urgent that the law make that space available, because society now places great value upon indigenous art, cultural knowledge, and other intangible property belonging to Native Americans.

The rights to own, control, protect, and develop intangible cultural property are vital to protecting indigenous culture.[56] Article 31 requires effective measures to protect those property rights:

> 1. Indigenous peoples have the right to maintain, control, protect and develop their cultural heritage, traditional knowledge and traditional cultural expressions, as well as the manifestations of their sciences, technologies and cultures, including human and genetic resources, seeds, medicines, knowledge of the properties of fauna and flora, oral traditions, literature, designs, sports and traditional games and visual and performing arts. They also have the right to maintain, control, protect and develop their intellectual property over such cultural heritage, traditional knowledge, and traditional cultural expressions.
> 2. In conjunction with indigenous peoples, States shall take effective measures to recognize and protect the exercise of these rights.

The *heritage* of indigenous peoples is "everything that belongs to the distinct identity of a people and which is theirs to share, if they wish, with others," according to UN Special Rapporteur Erica-Irene Daes; and at the core of every heritage is intangible cultural and intellectual property.[57] Article 31 recognizes that without ownership and control over that intangible property—that is, the ceremonies, songs, stories, music, dance, language, names, ideas, traditions, expressions, traditional knowledge about the world (i.e., flora, fauna, medicines, ceremonial and spiritual matters), artwork, symbols, images, technologies, and science—the cultural heritage of indigenous peoples cannot be protected, transmitted, or shared with dignity. As stated by Daes:

> In summary, then, each indigenous community must retain permanent control over all elements of its own heritage. It may share the right to enjoy and use certain elements of its heritage, under its own laws and procedures, but always reserves a perpetual right to determine how shared knowledge is used. This continuing collective right to manage heritage is critical to the identity, survival and development of each indigenous society.[58]

Without legal protection, indigenous heritage has been appropriated, pirated, and misused. The theft of culture is part of the one-way transfer of property from indigenous to non-indigenous hands seen in colonies and settler states around the world—it includes not only the taking of land, natural resources, personal property, but even the heritage of indigenous peoples and their very identities, plucking them as clean as a Safeway chicken. Daes found that existing laws in those nations are inadequate to protect indigenous cultural and intellectual property rights:

> Above all, it is clear that existing forms of legal protection of cultural and intellectual property, such as copyright and patent, are not only inadequate for the protection of indigenous peoples' heritage but inherently unsuitable. Existing legal measures provide protection of limited duration, and are designed to promote the dissemination and use of ideas through licensing or sale. Subjecting indigenous peoples to such a legal scheme would have the same effect on their identities, as the individualization of land ownership, in many countries, has had on their territories—that is, fragmentation into pieces, and the sale of the pieces, until nothing remains.[59]

She sees indigenous peoples as "the true owners of their works, arts, [and] ideas" and recommends that "no alienation of those elements of their heritage should be recognized by national or international law, unless made in conformity with indigenous peoples' own traditional laws and customs with the approval of their own local institutions."[60]

US intellectual property rights law does not protect intangible Native American property rights over their cultural heritage.[61] Given the failure of *Johnson* and *Tee-Hit-Ton* to recognize Native American land rights, it is not surprising that treatment of their intangible property rights follows the same trajectory. *Cohen's* confirms a "lack of legal protections" for Native American's "intangible cultural resources when tribal interests do not fit into established categories of intellectual property."[62] Westerners and Native Americans view intellectual property differently, and tribes often have different interests at stake. Though some Native American interests are protectable by existing copyright, patent, and trademark laws when they fit into protected categories, the law does not protect the different kinds of unique tribal interests (such as religious interests, or other interests that require keeping information secret, interests in preventing commercial exploitation of certain resources or in giving them special significance or treatment). Nor does it account for the unique forms of tribal property, such as communal property or tribal property held in trust by the tribe, group, or a traditional caretaker; and the law is unresponsive to tribal rules governing the use and alienation of intangible cultural property, such as songs, stories, or ceremonies.[63] The *Declaration* alerts the law to this problem in coverage and the need to identify, classify, and protect indigenous property rights.

Currently, intellectual property law serves other kinds of interests entirely. It is not designed to help indigenous cultures survive and develop. The copyright, patent, and trademark laws are based on an individualistic ideology, and they tie knowledge to economics by focusing on financial incentives and protections for individual owners of intellectual property (i.e., inventors, scientists, artists, and entrepreneurs) to encourage them to share their intellectual property with the public. The laws seek to advance the economy, science, and technology by granting exclusive ownership and control over the products of mental labor for a specified period. Unique collective tribal interests in the production, ownership, and control of communal cultural knowledge and other intangible property are "ignored or granted scant protection"; and tribes are rightfully frustrated from the lack of legal protection when their interests "do not fit into established categories of intellectual property."[64] Communally owned and collectively developed intellectual property, traditional ethnobiological knowledge about nature, and group knowledge embodied in oral traditions are not covered and cannot be protected by existing laws; and remedies to recover tribal knowledge that is appropriated without the free, prior, and informed consent of indigenous peoples or in violation of their laws or customs are non-existent.[65]

How can the law identify these forms of property, grant them status, and address these unprotected interests? Many commentators believe the necessary first step in protecting intangible cultural resources begins with tribal law. It can define and regulate cultural property and control unauthorized alienation in the first instance, and effective mechanisms might be developed in the larger legal system to help enforce tribal law. Many believe a new federal law must be developed to specifically protect intangible cultural property of Native Americans, one that abandons the individualistic orientation, embraces communal rights, and effectively addresses tribal interests. Several ideas and proposals have been developed in the United States and other nations, but the bottom line is that workable laws and effective measures are needed to protect the intangible core of Native American culture, and to restore a stolen heritage. The *Declaration* provides a foundation for making the law accountable to unprotected indigenous interests, and it insists upon "effective measures to recognize and enforce those rights."

c) The Right to Language

For most of its history, the United States has sought to stamp out Native languages. By contrast, the *Declaration* protects the right to language. It requires effective measures by the United States to protect the language rights of indigenous peoples: (1) to use, develop, and transmit their languages (Art. 13); (2) to education systems and institutions in their own languages (Art. 14); and (3) to their own media in their own languages (Art. 16). The Supreme Court has recognized the importance of language in the education setting. The denial of linguistically appropriate education can effectively deprive equal education opportunity, when children speak a minority tongue and only have limited proficiency in English.[66] In such instance, they are entitled to education in their own language. The Native American Language Act of 1990 is compatible with these UN standards. It acknowledges a duty to ensure the survival of Native American languages and finds that a lack of clear federal policy "has often resulted in acts of suppression and extermination of Native American languages and cultures."[67] Section 2903 declares a policy to "preserve, protect, and promote the rights and freedom of Native Americans to use, practice, and develop Native American languages," including using them as a medium of instruction, as a subject taught in the same manner as foreign languages, and to conduct business of Indian tribes. Section 2904 protects the Native Americans' right to speak in their languages in any public proceeding, free from restriction.

However, the Act stops short of providing an effective right to language, because many Native American languages are teetering on the brink of extinction due to past policies. Only about 200 tribal languages of 300 spoken by Native Americans before the coming of the white man survive today, and of those, only about 20 are still being learned by children in the traditional way.[68] As such, the UN standards are meaningless and cannot be met until such time as each indigenous language is fully restored to its former proficiency among every tribe that wishes to preserve and transmit its language. This can only be accomplished with effective federal assistance. To date, the United States has not mounted a sustained national campaign to save and revitalize these endangered languages, nor has it supplied Indian tribes with anywhere near the level of funding or technical assistance needed to meet the crisis. Thus, Native Americans lack the tools to fully realize the right to language without substantial and effective remedial assistance from the United States. That aid should be rendered on an emergency basis, because it is intolerable to destroy Native languages through centuries of suppression, then sit around and do nothing while watching them die out and vanish from the face of the earth. In short, US law and policy is theoretically consistent with the *Declaration*, but it fails to provide an *effective* right to language. The *Declaration* mandates effective measures to fully realize this important right, not empty lip service.

d) The Right to Culturally Appropriate Education

Article 14.3 requires the United States to provide Native American students, both on and off the reservation, with access to "an education in their own culture and provided in their own language." US law and policy appears to favor bicultural Indian education for tribally controlled schools and colleges; however, the government fails to provide sufficient funding for those schools and colleges, and it has not required other public school systems that receive federal funding to provide Native American students with a culturally appropriate education.

Despite great strides in Indian education over the past few decades, significant challenges remain. As a result of congressional policy to transfer control over Indian education to Indian tribes, there are 34 tribal colleges on Indian reservations and about one-half of the 185 BIA elementary and secondary schools are tribally controlled.[69] Unfortunately, educators observe that many of these facilities and programs "remain poorly funded, often in crumbling temporary buildings."[70] In addition, it is "business as usual" in most public schools, with devastating results for Native American students. They follow the same assimilation policies and stereotypic portrayals of Native Americans as in the past, which have proven destructive to the cultural identity and equal education opportunity of Native American students. This is seen in the astounding 36 percent high school drop-out rate of Native American students (which is the highest in the nation) and in their low academic achievement rates.[71] Like the empty right to language, the right to a culturally appropriate education is not an *effective* right until the United States takes effective measures to (1) provide sufficient funding for tribally controlled schools and colleges; and (2) require public schools that receive federal funding to provide a rigorous, culturally appropriate education for Native American children.

e) The Right to Transmit Culture

Article 13 affirms to indigenous peoples "the right to revitalize, use, develop and transmit to future generations their histories, languages, oral traditions, philosophies, writing systems and literatures"; and it requires states to take effective measures to ensure that this right is protected. Article 39 requires financial and technical assistance from the states for the enjoyment of these rights. After all, libraries, archives, museums, and culture centers play a vital role in the transmission of culture in tribal communities, just like these institutions transmit culture in larger society.[72] These institutions are more than static repositories; as home to the treasures of a nation and the history of a people and a place, they play important roles in shaping the cultural life and preserving the collective memory of a community or nation. As indigenous institutions, they serve to undo the cultural damage done to indigenous communities by prolonged colonization and ensure that their cultures are transmitted to future generations.

The United States has only taken baby steps to rebuild Indian culture and to provide tribal communities with tools, technical assistance, and resources needed to transmit their cultures. Of 500 federally recognized Indian tribes, only about 150 have tribal museums and only 200 have tribal libraries. The absence of those vibrant institutions in most tribal communities is testimony to the lack of measures taken by the United States to make the right to transmit culture meaningful and effective.

f) The Right to Indigenous Habitat

Indigenous peoples have land-based cultures. The Inter-American Commission on Human Rights aptly notes that their cultural survival depends upon a profound relationship to place:

> This special relationship is fundamental both for the material subsistence and for the cultural integrity of indigenous and tribal peoples. The [Inter-American Court of Human Rights] has emphatically explained, in this line, that "land, for the indigenous population is structured on the basis of its profound relationship with the land," and that "the recovery, recognition, demarcation, and registration of the lands represents essential rights for cultural survival and for maintaining the community's integrity." Likewise, the Inter-American Court has pointed out that "for indigenous communities, relations to the land are not merely a matter of possession and production but a material and spiritual element which they must fully enjoy, even to preserve their cultural legacy and transmit it to future generations"; that "the culture of the members of the indigenous communities directly relates to a specific way of being, seeing, and acting in the world, developed on the basis of their close relationship with their traditional territories and the resources therein, not only because they are their main means of subsistence, but also because they are part of their worldview, their [religiousness], and therefore, of their cultural identity"; and that "to guarantee the right of indigenous peoples to communal property, it is necessary to take into account that the land is closely linked to their

> oral expressions and traditions, their customs and languages, their arts and rituals, their knowledge and practices in connection with nature, culinary art, customary law, dress, philosophy, and values. In connection with their milieu, their integration with nature and their history, the members of the indigenous communities transmit this nonmaterial cultural heritage from one generation to the next, and it is constantly recreated by the members of the indigenous groups and communities.[73]

Accordingly, the *Declaration* recognizes the rights of indigenous peoples in the natural world—that is, their distinctive spiritual relationship with their traditional lands, territories, and waters, including the historical, cultural, and religious places and the traditional medicines, plants, animals, seeds, and minerals that abide in aboriginal habitats, as well as their traditional knowledge about the natural world and their traditional means of subsistence (Arts. 11, 12, 20, 24–28, 31, and 32). As noted in Chapter Seven (discussions of *Kandra* and *Tee-Hit-Ton Indians*), US law and policy do not provide adequate legal protection, except in rare instances. In that untenable situation, the legal system fails to meet the minimum standards of the UN. Until reliable protections and effective remedies are provided, the fate of Native American cultures hangs in the balance.

5. Education and Public Media

Dominated entirely by non-indigenous voices, the mainstream public media is a powerful force that permeates society. It can fundamentally shape and influence society by promoting tolerance or intolerance, conditions for equality or discrimination; it can disseminate accurate information concerning indigenous peoples, cultures, and issues, or distort that information and trivialize, demonize, and create injurious myths about them; or the media can ignore indigenous peoples altogether. In short, media shapes the way that we view indigenous peoples and their issues, and it tells us how we should comport ourselves to the tribal peoples in our midst.

Article 15 seeks to make public media, in all of its formats (TV, movies, newspapers, schoolbooks, and so on, accountable to indigenous peoples and to the principles of cultural pluralism and equality. It states,

"Indigenous peoples have the right to dignity and diversity of their cultures, histories, and aspirations which shall be appropriately reflected in education and public information." Article 16 integrates the media. It affirms the right of indigenous peoples to establish their own media in their own languages, and it recognizes their right to access to all forms of non-indigenous media, without discrimination. Importantly, Articles 15 and 16 call for "effective measures" to achieve these ends.

Does US law and policy make media accountable to Native Americans by ensuring that media promotes tolerance and combats prejudice against them, and do the regulatory agencies require media to adequately reflect Native American cultural diversity? That is a tall order! As will be seen, public media does *none* of these things. On the contrary, from the inception, the indigenous voice has been effectively silenced by newspapers, movie studios, and television networks. These institutions have not provided indigenous peoples with an effective voice, because they are owned and operated entirely by non-indigenous peoples who produce information or entertainment for white audiences. Instead of being accountable to Native America, the industry historically had an anti-indigenous function during Manifest Destiny. More often than not, the public media has disserved indigenous interests. This is seen in the inflammatory coverage of the Indian Wars and the settlement of the West during the nineteenth century; and throughout the twentieth century derogatory racial stereotypes predominated coverage into the present day, when the public media ignores Native American issues altogether.[74] This shoddy treatment is allowed by federal agencies that regulate public media, even though they have a trust responsibility to Indian tribes.

Why is TV so white? We never see real Indians on TV, even though television shapes the way society views Native Americans. The lack of diversity in TV Land has long been a problem. Black Americans manage to have a few sitcoms involving family life, and they even get to see a token black forecast the weather on national TV from time to time; the Latinos have *George Lopez* and *Ugly Betty*; Asians have Kung Fu movies made in Hong Kong, but they can forget about any family representation or news about Asian families on the small screen—it focuses on ordinary whites. But we never see a real Indian on TV in any capacity, ever. Hollywood Indians are normally portrayed by white actors. We never see *Amos n' Andy* on the TV reruns, but there are "no holds barred" on the endless parade of racially stereotyped Indians. They hold sway on the western channels in old reruns, as whooping savages with beast-like mannerisms, as noble savages in cigar-store Indian costumes, or as non-Indian actors play the Lone Ranger's "loyal Indian companion." The stereotypes, which are continually drilled into the viewers' minds, abhor authentic American Indian images.

The Hollywood Indian deplores accurate reporting of real Indian issues by the mainstream press. In 1958, Edward R. Murrow, the leading newsman of the day, observed:

> If Hollywood were to run out of Indians, the program schedules would be mangled beyond all recognition. Then some courageous soul with a small budget might be able to do a documentary telling what, in fact, we have done—and are still doing—to the Indians in this country.[75]

Whether on TV or in newspapers or national magazines, Native Americans are ignored (unless we turn to the sports page to see the "Redskins" or other Indian mascots getting "massacred" or "scalped"). Coverage addresses real life issues only intermittently, when they intersect with white society. On these rare occasions, the story is written by and for white society and the indigenous voice remains silent. Thus, while the Hollywood Indian overpopulates TV screens, real Indians are "invisible" to the press. The press studiously ignores real life American Indian issues as unimportant. This is not surprising. Uniformed non-Indian reporters with mainstream attitudes are hampered in representing American Indians as real people with legitimate issues. Their dilemma is described by Professor C. Richard King in *Media Images and Representations* (2006):

> Many reporters either are uninformed about central [Native American] issues, such as sovereignty, identity, history, culture, diversity, and worldview, or worse, have been misinformed by popular culture and the superficial lessons imparted by well-meaning teachers and biased textbooks. As a consequence, news reporting regularly wrongly communicates situations and their significance to all who have a stake in them, and in the process do a disservice to their audience, reinforcing

> the systematic miseducation of the public. In some cases, journalism perpetuates damaging stereotypes about indigenous peoples. Although these tend to avoid demonizing Native Americans as evil or subhuman, they do invoke clichéd conceptions that limit their humanity.[76]

In these circumstances, Native Americans can hardly expect accurate coverage, much less treatment in the media that meets the UN standards.

How does this situation affect human rights? The single most important problem facing Native Americans in protecting their human, political, property, and cultural rights as indigenous peoples in the United States is the paucity of accurate information available to the American public about real Indians, their history, and their issues. The root cause of this lack of information is unaccountability in the media. Americans spend most of their time watching a skewed version of life on television. They learn about the world, and what is important, from TV. All they see about Native Americans on TV are injurious racial stereotypes, and nothing more. The lack of responsible journalistic coverage allows the Hollywood Indian to rule the American mindset. It is no wonder that we treat Native Americans in the real world just like cowboys treat Indians in TV westerns. If we take that distorted imagery seriously, we could never logically extend human rights to whooping savages, with murder and destruction in their hearts. Until indigenous peoples are given a voice by the public media, their humanity, issues, and aspirations will remain a mystery. At best, human rights are seen as unimportant and are easily dismissed or trivialized when "invisible" peoples with marginal interests are concerned. After all, Indians are thought to be "extinct" by many media consumers—but they have been sorely misinformed. Despite our national preoccupation with mass media and everyone's constant interaction with hand-held communication devices, Americans are sadly uniformed about the Native peoples in their very midst.

The time to make public media accountable to the UN standards is long overdue. With a few notable exceptions, the doors to mainstream media have been closed to Native America. In Indian Country, there is a vigorous American Indian press, a growing number of professional broadcasters, tribal radio stations, and a treasure trove of vibrant indigenous cinema, starring a talented cadre of Native actors. This indigenous media fills a void for tribal people and provides communication in Indian Country, and it stimulated the cultural renaissance sweeping Native America in recent decades.[77] However, Professor King notes that Native America does not control media consumed by most Americans:

> In the late 1990s, there were 11,577 radio stations, 1,518 television stations, 11,385 cable stations, and 1,450 low-power television operations in the United States. Of these, American Indians owned twenty-five radio stations and a half dozen low-power television operations. These numbers speak volumes about the limitations of indigenous access, authority, and influence in contemporary radio and television. At the same time, much like the standard histories of mainstream media they conceal the vibrancy of indigenous media. Native Americans have actively participated in mainstream media, and more importantly have struggled for more than 150 years to establish alternative media—rooted in Native traditions and tribal communities—that would more accurately and authentically render their experience, and challenge inequalities and misunderstandings, while also reclaiming heritage and identity.[78]

As the Chairman of the newly formed Native Arts and Cultures Foundation[79], I was astounded by the powerful films made in Native America and profiled at the American Indian Film Festival, held each year in San Francisco.[80] The films are testament to "the emergence of a vibrant, culturally literate, and politically engaged American Indian cinema," in the words of professor King.[81] It is too bad that indigenous movies, actors, journalists, and broadcasters have not crossed over into mainstream public media, because they possess vital information about Native America that is much needed by the public sector, and *especially* by the mainstream media organizations who own and operate Hollywood studios, television networks and stations, radio programs, newspapers, and magazines. Blinded by stereotypes of their own making, these institutions fail to recognize indigenous talent (which rivals the best that America has to offer) and cannot see the valuable information that Native America brings to the American public. So long as these barriers remain and the American public remains uniformed about indigenous life and issues in our own country, public media in the United States does not meet the standards set forth by the UN in Articles 15 and 16 of the *Declaration*.

The US agencies responsible for regulating public media and discharging the government's trust duty to Indian tribes should consult with Native Americans to develop a plan for making the media accountable to Native America. Congress has power to regulate public broadcasting in the public domain as a matter of the national interest; and it has passed numerous laws regulating television and radio, beginning with the Communications Act of 1934, which created the Federal Communications Commission (FCC) as the principal agency responsible for regulating the industry, including the content and diversity of public media, as supplemented in the modern era with the Telecommunications Act of 1996 and other laws that keep abreast of new communications technologies.[82] In carrying out its duties, the FCC must be unaware of its duties under the federal trust obligation owed to Indian tribes by the United States, because it simply lumps American Indians in with all other minorities, insofar as diversity mandates are concerned—to the point that Indians vanished into a black hole. The FCC is criticized by all minority groups for decreasing diversity in media staffing and programming, but American Indians were never in the mix to begin with, and they have all but disappeared from the public media. Congressional oversight hearings might be a starting place for making the FCC and the public media accountable, and for developing a plan to implement Articles 15 and 16 in consultation with Native peoples.

6. Participation in Decision-Making; Free, Prior, and Informed Consent

In a colonized land, settler states make decisions affecting indigenous peoples with little or no input from them. Paternalism and unfettered government power over indigenous peoples supplant self-determination, and this destroys their ability to participate in government decisions that affect them. To forestall the "tyranny of the majority" that occurs when the decision-making power over indigenous peoples is absolute, or when the government runs rough-shod over tribal people under its feet, the *Declaration* affirms a right of participation in all decisions that affect indigenous rights and interests (See discussion in Chapter Three).

Article 19 requires states to "consult and cooperate in good faith with the indigenous peoples concerned through their own representative institutions in order to obtain their free, prior and informed consent before adopting and implementing legislative or administrative measures that may affect them." US law does not comport with this minimum standard for two reasons.

First, *Lone Wolf* and its progeny grant Congress "plenary" power over Indian tribes, tribal members, and tribal property. Under the plenary power doctrine, the Court has suggested that Indian tribes do not have a fundamental interest in self-government and Congress may modify, limit, or terminate tribal government as it sees fit; furthermore, in other cases, the Court itself has limited the exercise of tribal sovereignty under the judge-made "implicit divestiture" doctrine. That line of authority purports to create *absolute* legislative and judicial power over tribal governments, people, and property that can be exercised unilaterally, without the "free, prior, and informed consent" of affected Native Americans. That kind of power does not comport with articles in the *Declaration* that require government consultation with indigenous peoples and their free, prior, and informed consent before it can take measures that affect their human rights. The supposed existence of unfettered power stems from notions of colonialism and conquest. It is important to remember that *Lone Wolf's* notion of "plenary" power over Indian tribes is not derived from the constitution, but from the Supreme Court's notion of guardianship in the harsh setting of colonialism.[83] That kind of raw power over indigenous peoples exceeds the limits of state power that is placed upon free and democratic nations by human rights. The power of Congress over Indian tribes is more properly viewed as a "protectorate power" in the *Worcester* framework, where a constitutional grounding exists. Protectorate power can be exercised by the stronger nation only to protect the well-being and integrity of Indian tribes; and in this framework, the consultation and free, prior, and informed consent requirements of the *Declaration* are fully compatible with the exercise of protectorate powers. The *Declaration* calls upon the United States to discard the *Lone Wolf* mentality and restore Chief Justice John Marshall's original vision of Indian tribes in a *bona fide* protectorate relationship established in the *Worcester* framework. Furthermore, this right of participation envisioned by the *Declaration* is tantamount to a declaration of independence from plenary power. It gives Native America a right to participate in decisions that affect them by positing a simple human rights axiom: the United States cannot continue to make unilateral decisions that affect Native American human rights; instead, it must provide Native America with a seat at the table.

Second, US statutes and executive orders in the modern era firmly recognize the need for federal government consultation with Indian tribes in matters affecting tribal trust property, self-government, treaty rights, and other tribal interests; and this duty to consult applies to federal undertakings as well as to policy, regulatory, and legislative proposals.[84] However, the "meaningful consultation" standard does not protect important tribal interests, because it simply calls for a bare level of consultation that agencies may freely disregard once they jump through a procedural hoop. That form over substance approach falls short of the more rigorous "free, prior, and informed consent" standard, which arises under the self-determination principle, because it gives Native Americans more substantive input and control over government action that affects them. This consent-based framework does not create a veto power over federal decisions in every circumstance, but it does require stronger consultation requirements and greater negotiation with indigenous peoples before the government can take action affecting their interests.[85] A policy shift toward the *Declaration's* consent-based framework is especially appropriate when government action may affect core Native American interests.

7. Economic and Social Rights

As indicated in Chapter Three, the *Declaration* recognizes that the legacy of prolonged colonialism has left indigenous peoples as the poorest, most disadvantaged people in the world; and it seeks to reverse their deplorable socio-economic conditions through a human rights framework, by specifying human rights associated with labor (Art. 17), traditional economies (Art. 20), development of land and resources possessed by indigenous peoples (Art. 26), improvement of socio-economic conditions, with special attention paid to the needs of children, women, elderly, and the disabled (Arts. 21, 22, 24), health (Art. 24), and a right to determine, develop, prioritize, and administer socio-economic programs affecting indigenous peoples (Art. 24). Importantly, the *Declaration* calls for effective measures by the states to effectuate these human rights.

The UN goal to uplift socio-economic conditions of indigenous peoples is compatible with the "American Dream." That vision has attracted the world's poor and disadvantaged immigrants to our land of opportunity, where their lot in life can be improved. The fervent daily pursuit of wealth, economic security, employment, health, and housing is at the core of American life; and *nothing* can be allowed to stand in the way of the right to prosperity. Yet, prosperity for Native Americans is illusive, and, worse yet, to many, the idea of prosperous Indians seems oddly out-of-place in the American Dream. We see Indians as poor, and blame them for most of it. We are used to Indian poverty, and in a strange way, we are more comfortable with that status than we are in envisioning a higher, moderate standard of living on Indian reservations. The picture of American Indians driving good cars, living life in good health, in nice homes, with good jobs, and as much education as anyone else brings discomfort; and we *recoil* at the thought of *rich Indians*—that idea is somehow *un-American*. However, the equality principle asks: Why Not?

While earlier federal policies inhibited economic growth on Indian reservations, during the modern era federal and tribal governments have worked hard to alleviate poverty and improve socio-economic conditions under policies that see Indian economic development and self-sufficiency as crucial to self-determination. As stated in *Cohen's*:

> With the emergence of self-determination and its attendant emphasis on tribal control, sustained economic development for Native American nations has begun to take hold once again. This linkage between self-determination and economic development echoes recent thinking on development generally, which recognizes the importance of developing sovereigns directing their own development.[86]

In this period, Congress has passed many laws to promote business development on Indian reservations, create jobs and infrastructure, make grants to improve tribal finance, provide programs to promote economic development, and encourage tribal mineral development.[87] Tribal governments also work to stimulate reservation economies through tax incentives and by enacting commercial laws, providing infrastructure for economic development, and engaging directly in tribal business enterprises. Deborah Welch observes in *Economic Issues and Development* (2006) that the tribal gaming industry "has proven to be the single most successful enterprise Indian tribes have undertaken to gain sufficient revenues and preserve the sanctity of reservation life."[88]

Despite these efforts, the need to improve the depressed socio-economic conditions in Indian Country remains urgent. In 1990, 27 percent of Native American families lived below the poverty line, compared to 10 percent of the population nationwide.[89] In 2006, *Cohen's* observed that those dire conditions remain a sad fact of life:

> Indian nations continue to confront serious issues of poverty and its social consequences. In 1999, according to the Bureau of Indian Affairs (BIA), the unemployment rate among all Indians on or near reservations was 43 percent and still remained as high as 85 percent on the poorest reservations. In 2000, 37 percent of Indians living in reservation areas without gaming and 27 percent of those in reservation areas with gaming lived below the poverty line, and per capita income for reservation Indians was $8816 and $8466 respectively. Health and social welfare indicators are equally troubling. Development thus remains an important priority for tribes and their members.[90]

Effective social and economic rights for Native Americans cannot be fully realized until real and measurable improvement is actually seen in the standard of living on Indian reservations and Native American communities. There are five barriers to achieving the UN standards.

First, while one-in-three reservation Indians live in poverty,[91] significant legal barriers prevent the development of traditional economies based upon hunting, fishing, and gathering in indigenous habitats, as discussed earlier. That habitat is rapidly being degraded under US law and policies, and tribal use of aboriginal habitat to support traditional economies is not legally protected in most places outside of Alaska.

Second, tribal income generated from indigenous arts made in tribal communities has not been optimized, due to the utter lack of federal and philanthropic support for endangered Native American arts and cultures. In comparison to the tons of resources that pour into the support of art and culture, the National Endowment for the Arts (NEA) and our wealthy philanthropy community contribute almost nothing to support indigenous arts and cultures, or the cultural institutions, such as libraries, archives, museums, and culture centers on Indian reservations, which can help support traditional economies and tourism.

Third, in many ways, the biggest socio-economic problem in Native America is in the area of healthcare, as seen in the heart-breaking statistics. The life expectancy rate for Native men and women is considerably lower than for all other races.[92] The astounding gap in health care, in which the average American secures 60 percent more healthcare annually than Native Americans, is widening despite the ongoing trust responsibility of the United States to provide healthcare.[93] Life is cheap in Indian Country, and getting cheaper. Stemming from chronic poverty, lack of access to medical care, and many other causes, researchers reveal hair-raising health disparities:

> Alarmingly, health disparities among Native people are reflected in an array of mortality and morbidity statistics, including diabetes. For example, data from 1994 to 1996 indicate the following causes of age-adjusted death rates for Native Americans which are greater than for all U.S. races: 1) alcoholism–627 percent greater; 2) tuberculosis–533 percent greater; 3) diabetes mellitus–249 percent greater; 4) accidents–204 percent greater; 5) suicide–72 percent higher; 6) pneumonia and influenza–71 percent greater; 7) homicide–63 percent greater.[94]

The healthcare needs of Native Americans overwhelm the overcrowded, underfunded, and understaffed Indian Health Service facilities on Indian reservations ; and the equal health mandate of Article 24.2 ("Indigenous individuals have an equal right to the enjoyment of the highest attainable standard of physical and mental health") is completely out of reach by the hapless, but hard-working, agency and its medical professionals.

Fourth, despite laudable efforts by Congress to pass Indian economic development laws, big challenges remain to close the growing socio-economic gap between indigenous and non-indigenous peoples. It is ironic that our nation was able to rebuild war-torn Europe in fairly short order through a determined national effort, but it seems unable to do the same for economically depressed Indian reservations at home. The *Declaration* urges America to stay the course until the economic and social rights of Native Americans are fully realized. Renewed national commitment is the order of the day, not continued neglect.

Fifth, many tribes have been able to reacquire former lands to be used for economic development purposes, but the Supreme Court and the BIA place roadblocks toward putting that land into tribal trust status. Congress needs to remove those barriers, and the BIA should explain its constant foot-dragging to place land into trust, since it has ample legal authority to do so.

8. Land, Territory, and Resources

The *Declaration* seeks to halt and reverse the trend toward dispossession of indigenous land, territory, and resources, historically seen in colonies and settler states around the world. Articles 10, 25–30, and 32 recognize broad land rights; and state duty-bearers must recognize and protect those rights, provide impartial tribunals to adjudicate indigenous land rights, provide redress for property taken without the free, prior, and informed consent of indigenous peoples or in violation of their laws and customs, and conduct conservation programs to conserve and protect the productive capacity and environmental integrity of indigenous lands, territories, and resources.

The *Declaration* alerts our legal system to the need for reforming and strengthening existing Native American land rights. Indeed, the rights and duties prescribed in the international human rights instrument are a wake-up call for the Supreme Court. At last, it must reverse its discriminatory legal doctrines of dispossession in *Johnson* and its progeny, because they do not comport with the UN standards; and Congress or the courts must find an effective way to preserve and protect indigenous habitat that is not owned or controlled by Native Americans as well as a way to protect their traditional uses of that habitat and its natural resources. If the Supreme Court is not up to the task, perhaps Congress should work with indigenous peoples to establish a bilateral judicial tribunal that meets the requirements of Article 27 to adjudicate Native American land rights in a non-discriminatory manner. Article 27 states:

> States shall establish and implement, in conjunction with indigenous peoples concerned, a fair, independent, impartial, open and transparent process, giving due recognition to indigenous peoples' laws, traditions, customs and land tenure systems, to recognize and adjudicate the rights of indigenous peoples pertaining to their lands, territories and resources, including those which were traditionally owned or otherwise occupied or used. Indigenous peoples shall have the right to participate in the process.

In developing the *Declaration,* the General Assembly and the 150 member nations that endorsed it knew that old habits die hard. However, the about-face in US law and policy that is needed to meet the land rights standards dovetails with other urgent needs in the United States. First, the standards are linked to the development of a sound American land ethic, as previously discussed, which is necessary if we hope to protect the last vestiges of the natural world, which have been nearly destroyed by our unrelenting conquest of nature. No land ethic can be developed until indigenous cosmologies, traditional ecological knowledge, and rights in the natural world are recognized and taken into account. Second, it is linked to human survival. If we hope to safeguard human survival, which has been placed into grave jeopardy by global warming and the mass extinction of animal and plant life brought about by the colonization of the New World, we must forge a kinder, more gentle, and just stance towards the natural world and the tribal people who inhabit it.

9. Treaties and Agreements

Article 37 requires states to recognize, observe, and enforce treaties and agreements with indigenous peoples. By contrast, *Lone Wolf* does not. Little more need be said. It is true that the Supreme Court has acted in several cases during the modern era, such as *Fishing Vessel*, to recognize and enforce Indian treaties, so the concept urged by Article 37 is not utterly foreign to our legal system. During the same period, however, the Court has narrowly construed other Indian treaties by manipulating canons of construction—judicial juggling allows the Court to ignore promises made by the nation. We need Article 37 to prevent judicial juggling.

The comparative analysis shows that US law and policy do not meet the UN standards in many important respects. Our legal system may come close to meeting many standards, more than many regimes that affect significant indigenous populations, and we can thank our core values for that accomplishment. Those same values impel us to finish the task by uplifting our law and social policy so that indigenous human rights are fully recognized and protected.

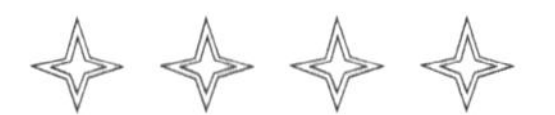

by Bunky Echo-Hawk (Yakama-Pawnee artist)

"Lucy the Litigator"

PART THREE
Implementing the Declaration

Let us put our minds together and see what life we can make for our children.

—Sitting Bull (Hunkpapa Sioux)

CHAPTER NINE
March Toward Justice

The UN Special Rapporteur was seated on the dais, along with his staff, as I made my way to the witness table. James Anaya was conducting an official visit to the United States in 2012. He sought to consult with tribal leaders about human rights problems related to the *Declaration*. A large crowd of tribal leaders from across Oklahoma gathered at the Tulsa University College of Law to present their statements to the United Nations official. The thirty-nine Indian nations had been removed from their homelands by the United States in the nineteenth century and relocated to the Indian Territory in present-day Oklahoma. They assembled that day for a rare opportunity—to tell their story to the world.

Settling into my chair, I began my testimony. As Chief Justice of the Supreme Court of the Kickapoo Tribe of Oklahoma and Associate Justice of the Pawnee Nation, I spoke into the microphone: "Good morning, Special Rapporteur Anaya, I am pleased to be part of this judicial panel and to provide this testimony as a jurist for these two great Indian nations." Throughout the morning, tribal leaders spoke to the United Nations.[1] As they told their stories, the legacy of conquest unfolded. It became increasingly clear: our nation must march toward justice in the coming years. An enormous undertaking is at hand.

The task ahead is immense, even though US law and policies are compatible in many respects with the *Declaration's* framework and principles. The difficulty in closing the gaps and realizing effective human rights lies inside the Washington Beltway: it is inhabited by the most powerful people in the history of the world. At the center sits the stately Supreme Court building, where black-robed lawgivers preside in marble chambers built like an imperial Roman edifice. Nations are naturally resistant to change, especially when it requires the government stop doing things it has always done and entails new programs that may conflict with the interests of strong lobbying constituencies. Where does one start? How can we educate the public about the need to push for change? Who will lead, and what will it take? Will we find friends along the way? The Great Spirit has brought our people to an important juncture. He often acts in mysterious ways.

As we chart the course for the future, we must set our sights on an approach that can make steady gains and avoid costly mistakes. We can search for power within—to the deep spiritual well of the Native American peoples—and without—to the times when the American nation was impelled to make significant social, political, and legal changes to bring justice to oppressed groups. We can also look abroad to see how other nations uplift indigenous rights in the post-*Declaration* era, benefit from their experience, avoid their mistakes, and sidestep pitfalls along the way.

This chapter presents an illuminating case study: black America's rise from slavery and its epic struggle for equality that overturned racial discrimination in *Brown v. Board of Education* (1954).[2] In many ways, that struggle parallels our own. *Brown* addressed widespread human rights problems that plagued black America. They are comparable in scope to the legacy of conquest facing Native America that the *Declaration* seeks to rectify. As will be seen, black America mounted an enormous undertaking. It was conducted on many fronts, over a lengthy period, by an entire race to produce change in the legal culture and social fabric. As black America took its rightful place in our society, the fruits of that campaign are seen everywhere. What lessons can be learned? It is likely that the same kinds of courage, dedication, skill, and resources must be mustered before Native America can take its seat at the table.

What roadmap must be followed before Native America can take its place in a society that recognizes, respects, and safeguards indigenous rights? Drawing from the black struggle that led to *Brown* and lessons learned in the tribal sovereignty movement, this chapter will also identify some organizational and other ingredients for a social campaign, so Native America can begin its march toward justice. The art of social change demands strategy much like that which guides a military campaign.[3] Planning and strategy precede the battle, because the outcome is not always determined by force or the size of one's army. Instead, well-laid plans help a small force overcome one more powerful, and the soldiers must be organized and fall into place before the march begins.

Case Study: How Black America Overturned the Law of Racial Segregation

The Supreme Court has incredible power. Its decisions shape society. We depend on the judicial branch to protect justice for all, but fallible justices can become enmeshed in prevailing prejudices. When that occurs and they implant injustice into the law, it is hard to get rid of it. Arrogance in high places cannot admit that it has feet of clay. It took fifty-eight years of racial torment before the Supreme Court overturned the "separate but equal" doctrine of *Plessy v. Ferguson* (1896) in the landmark *Brown* decision.[4] The long journey to *Brown* should be highly instructive for Native American reformers tasked with overturning *Johnson, Lyng,* and a long-list of adverse Supreme Court decisions that compose the "dark side" of federal Indian law, before the seeds of change can be planted and the fruits of the *Declaration* seen. As we stand at the foot of the mountain, let us go to the year 1896 and examine the *Plessy* decision, which was handed down by the same court that decided *Lone Wolf* a few years later.

In a 7–1 decision, the *Plessy* Court upheld a Louisiana law requiring racial separation of railway passengers. Applying a "reasonableness" test, the Court held that *de jure* segregation does not violate the Thirteenth or Fourteenth Amendments. The lax test let an openly racist state enact "the established usages, customs, and traditions of the people" into law. In a disingenuous opinion, the majority pretended that racial segregation does not place a "stamp of inferiority" upon blacks. It reasoned that if blacks felt inferior by reason of a law compelling their separation, it was their own fault: "If this be so, it is not by reason of anything found in the act, but solely because the colored race chooses to put that construction on it."[5] In their view, the legal system cannot provide racial equality between the white and black races, because laws cannot eradicate prejudice in the minds of men and it is impossible for the Constitution to place a socially inferior race on "the same plane" as whites.[6] As such, *de jure* racial segregation is permissible, so long as "separate but equal" accommodations are provided for white and colored persons.

Justice John Marshall Harlan's dissenting opinion pointed out the "apparent injustice" of the Louisiana law and its invidious purpose to discriminate against blacks "under the guise of giving equal accommodation for whites and blacks."[7] He railed against the majority's sophistry in one of the most eloquent dissents ever written:

> The white race deems itself to be the dominant race in this country. But in view of the constitution, in the eye of the law, there is in this

> country no superior, dominant, ruling class of citizens. In my opinion, the judgment this day rendered will, in time, prove to be quite as pernicious as the decision made by this tribunal in the Dred Scott case. What can more certainly arouse race hate, what more certainly create and perpetuate a feeling of distrust between these races, than state enactments which, in fact, proceed on the ground that colored citizens are so inferior and degraded that they cannot be allowed to sit in public coaches occupied by white citizens? That, as all will admit, is the real meaning of such legislation as was enacted in Louisiana State enactments regulating the enjoyment of civil rights upon the basis of race, and cunningly devised to defeat legitimate results of the [Civil War], under the pretense of recognizing equality of rights, can have no other result than to render permanent peace impossible, and keep alive a conflict of races. This question is not met by the suggestion that social equality cannot exist between the white and black races in this country. That argument, if it can be properly regarded as one, is scarcely worthy of consideration.
>
> The arbitrary separation of races, on the basis of race, is a badge of servitude wholly inconsistent with the civil freedom and the equality before the law established by the constitution. It cannot be justified upon any legal grounds. If evils will result from the commingling of the two races, they will be infinitely less than those that will surely come from state legislation regulating the enjoyment of civil rights upon the basis of race. We boast of the freedom enjoyed by our people above all other peoples. But it is difficult to reconcile that boast with a state of the law that, practically, puts the brand of servitude and degradation upon a large class of our fellow citizens, our equals before the law. This thin disguise of "equal" accommodations will not mislead anyone, nor atone for the wrong done this day.[8]

The far-reaching reverberations of *Plessy* were immediately felt. The decision ratified white supremacy in the South and facilitated the spread of Jim Crow laws over the next fifty years, as lawmakers around the country mandated racial discrimination in all walks of life. As Thurgood Marshall noted in 1969:

> The states took their cue from *Plessy*. Separation of the races soon became firmly entrenched in the South, and elsewhere for that matter. "Jim Crow" pervaded every aspect of life—even homes for the blind were segregated. Challenges were few and sporadic; and when they succeeded, the states reenacted the same scheme in different forms. Their ingenuity was certainly not taxed. The situation was such that in the 1940's one commentator said: "There is no power in the world—not even in all the mechanized armies of the earth which could not force the Southern white people to the abandonment of the principle of social segregation."[9]

The trend fueled by *Plessy* was finally brought to a halt after the "separate but equal" doctrine was struck down in 1954, when *Brown* declared that separate schools for black and white children are "inherently unequal."[10] That history is well-described in Richard Kluger' book, *Simple Justice: The History of Brown v. Board of Education and Black America's Struggle for Equality*, as summarized below.[11]

The American institution of slavery was severe and as demeaning as any in recorded history. The slaves had no legal rights, no access to the courts, no freedom except that allowed by their owners, and no property except the clothes on their backs. Utter human bondage was reflected in the highly controlled lives of slaves marked by hard labor, performed under the control, conditions, and curfews set by harsh masters, complete in every respect with all of the trappings of human slavery. It was illegal to teach enslaved blacks, and Kluger notes that "[w]hile the demands upon their bodies were excessive, the minds of slaves were left frankly to atrophy."[12] Nothing departed so dramatically from the high values said to animate the American nation than the institution of human slavery.

Blood was shed in the Civil War to end slavery. Afterwards, the re-United States sought to achieve equality for the "freedmen" during the Reconstruction Period (1865–1877) through the adoption of the Thirteenth, Fourteenth, and Fifteenth Amendments, along with enactment of the Civil Rights Act of 1875. Despite the determined national effort to provide federal protection, pronounced racism prevailed, especially in the South where legal protections for blacks were begrudged as "special treatment." Against these entrenched forces, the Supreme Court quickly wilted. A series of Supreme Court decisions, which culminated in *Plessy*, steadily eroded the civil rights of the former slaves.[13] By the close of the century, the Supreme Court "had nullified nearly every vestige of the federal protection" conferred on the freedmen since their release from bondage.[14] In the waning years of the nineteenth century, 3,000 blacks were lynched, the Jim Crow laws spread unabated throughout the South, along with the burning cross of the Ku Klux Clan, and tougher times lay ahead.[15] *Plessy* freed American racism from the bounds placed upon it by the law, and from any other inhibitions. Fueled by scientific racism, the decision unleashed a torrent of racial hatred and black degradation. In the ensuing decades, the outpouring of discrimination was based on the firm conviction that *blackness* denoted inferiority.[16] To put it bluntly, whites despised, ridiculed, and tormented the black race as never before, even in slavery. As prejudice engulfed the nation, the National Association for the Advancement of Colored People (NAACP) was founded in 1910. The fledgling group bravely organized to stem the tide, amid early support from diverse figures like Clarence Darrow, Franz Boaz, and William Du Bois.

The Challenges Facing NAACP Were Immense

From the beginning, NAACP placed its trust in the courts. It looked upon them as "the great equalizers" because race is not supposed to matter in the courtroom, where all litigants stand as equals and justice is color-blind. As Supreme Court Justice Thurgood Marshall noted in 1981, our system of government is grounded upon judicial neutrality and judicial protection of vulnerable minorities from majority oppression:

> [J]udges are required in our system to be as neutral as they possibly can, to stand above the political questions in which the other branches of government are necessarily entangled. The Constitution established a legislative branch to make the laws and an executive branch to enforce them. Both branches are elected and are designed to respond to ever changing public concerns and problems. Indeed the failure of either branch to respond to the will of the majority can quickly be remedied at the polls.
>
> But the Framers of the Constitution recognized that responsiveness to the will of the majority may, if unchecked, become a tyranny of

> the majority. They therefore created a third branch—the judiciary—to check the actions of the legislature and the executive. In order to fulfill this function, the judiciary was intentionally isolated from the political process and purposely spared the task of dealing with changing public concerns and problems. Article III judges are guaranteed life tenure. Similarly, their compensation cannot be decreased during their term in office—a provision, as we have recently seen has its tangible benefits. Finally, the constitutional task we are assigned as judges is a very narrow one. We cannot make the laws, and it is not our duty to see that they are enforced. We merely interpret them, through the painstaking process of adjudicating actual "cases or controversies" that come before us.
>
> We have seen what happens when the courts have permitted themselves to be moved by prevailing political pressures, and have deferred to the mob rather than interpret the Constitution. *Dred Scott, Plessy, Korematsu* and the trial proceedings in *Moore v. Dempsey* come readily to mind as unfortunate examples. They are decisions of which the entire judicial community, even after all these years, should be ashamed. There have also been times when the courts have stood proudly as a bulwark against what was politically expedient but also unconstitutional. One need only recall the school desegregation cases to understand why this ability to stand above the fray is so important.[17]

In choosing its ground, NAACP's goal was to provide legal relief for the black race through the courts, taking the only viable path to equality. However, with so many grievances, the hurdles for mounting an effective legal operation for the entire race were mindboggling. On the one hand, the need for legal assistance was great, because the immense problem was severe. Jim Crow laws oppressed life in nearly every place where black Americans lived, and the complaints of ten million people were many, but their access to justice was sorely hampered. Second, not just any lawyers would do. NAACP determined early on that, "If the Negro was ever to achieve equal justice under the law, he would have to act as his own claimant. No white attorney would give his life to the effort—and that is what it would cost."[18] Yet in 1910 black lawyers were practically unheard of, as there was no more than a few hundred in the entire nation.

Most law schools were segregated, and Howard Law School was the only school where black students could get legal training, but that "shoestring operation" did not get full accreditation until 1931.[19] Nonetheless, in the early decades, NAACP saw the need to create an adequate law school as a boot camp training ground for legal warriors:

> It might take years, decades, even generations to build a law school—to enlist a competent faculty, to assemble a big enough library, to attract promising students, to develop the courses and traditions and intellectual rigor. By the 1930s, there were nearly 12 million African Americans and no more than 1,100 of them were lawyers. Of those, fewer than 100 had been trained at ranking law schools. The black man could not continue to depend on the charity of white attorneys to obtain justice. A few whites had served nobly and out of a sense of humanitarian duty, but there was work to be done. The initiative had to be taken on the legal front.[20]

In addition, NAACP had no battle plan, even though it is axiomatic that "a general who wins a battle makes many calculations in his temple ere the battle is fought."[21] NAACP strategists had to lay plans for the coming campaign. But where would funding for planning the strategy come from? Finally, the Law of Racial Segregation was firmly entrenched. NAACP was confronted by a daunting task: reforming the White Man's law and bending it into a more just, accountable legal regime. *Plessy* must be overturned, but would the Supreme Court security guards let blacks into the building? Against these problems, only the brave dare go. NAACP girded itself for great difficulties along the way.

Charles Houston (1895–1950) is one of the NAACP greats. He rose to the challenge. As a 1923 Harvard Law School graduate *cum laude*, he played a significant role in the struggle to kill Jim Crow. In 1929, less than one hundred black lawyers had degrees from ranking law schools. In that year, Houston became Dean of Howard Law School (1929–1935). He transformed the tumble-down brick building into a first-class law school devoted to securing civil rights for the black race. As a civil rights command center and the national database for black culture, the law school soon began to produce black lawyers, a talented cadre instilled with the desire for equality. A new breed emerged as foot soldiers in the legal campaign. Kluger writes:

> Charlie Houston had worked a small revolution. The law school had a whole new curriculum, mostly new and young faculty people, and a small but spirited student body that was thriving on the intellectual demands made of it. By 1931, just two years after Houston's arrival, the school had won full accreditation for the American Bar Association. They had their pedigree now. The next step was settling on a battle plan.[22]

As such, Howard became a "living laboratory," where civil rights law was literally "invented" through teamwork.[23]

The main front would be the courtroom, but the legal campaign presented several questions. What legal principles would guide the fight? Where would the cases be filed, and what were the goals of the campaign? The NAACP's battle plan was drawn up in 1931 by Nathan Ross Margold, a Harvard lawyer experienced in representing Pueblo Indian tribes in New Mexico. Financed by the Garland Fund, he produced a book-length plan of action. Known today as the "Margold Plan," it envisioned a dramatic, large-scale legal campaign. An earlier plan proposed filing seven lawsuits against segregated schools in the Deep South. Rather than change or challenge the law of segregation, it was a helter-skelter strategy calculated to hasten the demise of segregated school systems by: (1) making dual school systems prohibitively expensive, and (2) focusing public attention on flagrant discrimination.

By contrast, the Margold Plan would launch cases for a different purpose: to boldly challenge the constitutionality of existing segregation practices. The goal was **not** to overturn *Plessy*, but to live with it and *enforce* the "separate but equal" doctrine's requirement that black schools be *truly equal* to white schools in every respect. Under this approach, the worst school systems were the most vulnerable targets: their deplorable conditions were habitually unequal in racist places, and there was no intent to equalize them, ever. They would fall prey to the strategy and be declared unconstitutional under *Plessy*. Furthermore, the legal theory forced the issue on the least risky terrain. To minimize the risk of backfire, it did not put the Supreme Court's back against the wall and force a reluctant court to change existing law. Instead, it only asked the Court to enforce *Plessy.* NAACP would simply say, "You bought the ticket, now take the ride" (as Louis L'Amour puts it). Thus, the battle plan targeted segregation *as currently practiced.* It was conceived to end-run a conservative Supreme Court, but still improve black education and put so much financial pressure on the South "that in time it would be forced to abandon the far more costly dual system and integrate the schools."[24]

> So here was a two-pronged weapon with which to attack and eliminate separate-and-*un*equal schools. One prong, in theory, would void segregation laws in seven states that had not safeguarded the African American from unequal school expenditures. The other prong, in theory, would outlaw the practice of segregation in states where inequality was habitual and therefore discriminatory and therefore in violation of equal protection. No doubt suits pursuing such strategy, Margold recognized, would stir "intense opposition, ill-will and strife." But after all, he was not proposing an attack on segregation "under any and all circumstances."[25]

School officials who ran inferior black schools would be given a Hobson's choice: equalize your school or close it and integrate the black students into white schools.[26] The Margold Plan opened new possibilities under existing law. Its author became chief counsel for NAACP.

The litigators turned their eyes to the worst places in America. The attack began where the foe was most vulnerable, and aggressive litigation was the order of the day. Early cases "demonstrated the high competence and cool courage of black counsel arguing freely in Southern courtrooms."[27] In 1935, Houston replaced Margold. He became the first black attorney to argue and win a Supreme Court case, involving all-white juries in Sapulpa, Oklahoma. By then, over one-hundred school segregation lawsuits had been filed in twenty-nine states, with mixed results. But the battle against an endless number of segregated schools had just begun, and the best that Houston could hope for was true enforcement of the "separate but equal" doctrine under the Margold plan.[28]

Houston guided the legal offensive until 1938, when a young man named Thurgood Marshall (1910–1993) took the helm. During the Marshall era (1938–1954), the pace quickened in the march toward *Brown,* and the civil rights lawyers found their leader: "Thurgood Marshall argued or masterminded almost every major lawsuit for black rights throughout the country during the next twenty-five years."[29]

The Marshall Era (1938–1954) Brought the Final Assault on Segregation

Marshall was the grandson of a slave, with family lines extending to the Congo. As a student, he was denied admission to a racially segregated state law school, but graduated first in the Howard class of 1933. He was twenty-eight years old, just five years out of Howard, when he assumed command of the litigation campaign. During a remarkable legal career, Marshall argued more cases before the Supreme Court than anyone in history, winning twenty-nine of the thirty-two cases he argued. In time, the formidable lawyer would become the first African-American Associate Justice on the Supreme Court (1967–1991) and receive the Presidential Medal of Freedom posthumously in 1993.

One the one hand, Marshall was a courageous warrior able to surmount battle fatigue and coax hostile courts into making a full evidentiary record, necessary for a successful appeal; but on the other, he suffered the same degradation and disabilities as his clients when traveling in the South. "I ride in the for-colored-only cabs and in the back of the streetcars—quiet as a mouse," he once told interviewers. "I eat in Negro cafés and don't use white washrooms. I don't challenge the customs personally because I figure I'm down South representing a client—the NAACP—and not myself."[30] But his effectiveness in court could not be denied:

> The job was not so much in winning his cases as getting a fair hearing on the record as the basis for subsequent appeal to higher and, he hoped, friendlier courts. More often than not, he would lose at the local level, but more often than not he would come away with half a loaf in places where the last black attorney to show his face in court had been tarred and feathered afterward. Hostile judges might have cut his presentations and sustained every objection of local white lawyers opposing him, but few did. His low-key lawyering won him respect He handled every kind of case in every kind of place in the years when there were still too few black lawyers with enough talent and courage to stand up to racism and call it what it was. He would

> fight for equal teachers' salaries in angry Little Rock or defend three Negroes charged with murder in a Klan-infested county in Florida or argue against South Carolina's truculent denial to blacks of court-ordered voting rights, and he would not weigh the personal risks. "He was a very courageous figure," says NAACP labor affairs director Herbert Hill, not a sentimental man. "He would travel to the courthouses of the South, and folks would come for miles, some of them on mule-back or horseback, to see 'the nigger lawyer' who stood up in white men's courtrooms." The risks were real enough, though, and they were almost always present because he was almost always showing up in trouble spots.[31]

In 1939, the NAACP Legal Defense and Educational Fund ("the Fund") was founded as a separate entity, with Marshall at the head. Starting with him and a secretary, the Fund built an impressive network of *ad hoc* advisors over the next fifteen years. They were a small army of law professors from Harvard, Yale, and Columbia, who furnished brain-power to supplement the litigation. By 1950, *only five full-time lawyers* worked at the Fund—a small cadre with a remarkable *esprit de corps* that litigated in tandem with the Brain Trust and cooperating local counsel around the country. The pace accelerated during the World War II era. Black servicemen went to war, and grateful presidents issued executive orders integrating the armed services. Gunnar Myrdal's *An American Dilemma* (1944) documented continuing mistreatment at home, denounced it, and called for a more vigorous assault on Jim Crow. The emboldened campaign began taking harder aim at *Plessy,* with strong *amicus* support from the Justice Department and some of the nation's top legal scholars. The battlefront shifted from state courts (which were useful forums for dramatizing the issues and rallying local black support) to the federal court system to speed the campaign by litigation aimed at state-wide relief. The show-down was drawing near.

In 1950, a major strategy shift occurred. It came in the wake of sweeping victories in a trilogy of cases handed down on the same day: *Sweatt v. Painter* (1950), *McLaurin v. Oklahoma* (1950), and *Henderson v. United States* (1950).[32] In these cases, the United States argued for the first time that *Plessy* must be overturned. All three unanimous opinions ruled in favor of the black plaintiffs. They proclaimed: *Equality must be real, or racial separation is unconstitutional.* At long last, Margold's strategy prevailed. But the successful drive for equalization now left the NAACP standing at the crossroads. *Where do we go from here?* It could litigate endlessly on the road ahead, challenging the constitutionality of every unequal facility or discriminatory practice one-by-one. That would be like emptying the ocean, one cup at a time. Or the reformers could strike directly at the heart of *Plessy* itself and attempt to bring down the Law of Segregation altogether. NAACP heeded sage advice from an ancient warrior: "If the enemy leaves the door open, you must rush in."[33] From then on, the goal was to destroy *Plessy* itself through an all-out frontal assault.

In the final push, Marshall needed "overwhelming evidence of the inequalities inherent in segregation in the particular areas involved [to] demonstrate that an extension of the principles of the *Sweat* and *McLaurin* cases is timely."[34] NAACP turned to social science. By 1950, the field was beginning to question the validity of scientific racism. Clinical studies on the psychological impacts of racial segregation upon black children produced heart-breaking findings: *The children hated themselves.* Doll tests revealed that they were plunged into shame by segregation, so deeply that they rejected their own self-images. The studies pinpointed severe trauma seen in soul-killing feelings of inferiority in vulnerable children, and left no doubt about the psychological damage caused by racism. That psychological evidence strongly dispelled the judicial myth, planted by *Plessy*, that segregation is harmless and stamps no badge of inferiority upon the black race. Armed with that powerful evidence, the litigators searched for the right cases and the best judges. Their opportunity came in four cases that worked their way to the Supreme Court in 1952. Crucial findings about the inequities of racial segregation were made in those cases by federal judges based upon NAACP's evidence.

The important role of federal judges in the NAACP campaign must be noted. Judges who preside over controversial trials are indispensable to the capacity of federal courts to be the great equalizers. They are charged in the first instance with the difficult task of impartially protecting vulnerable minorities in legitimate cases from the tyranny of the majority. When unpopular causes are concerned, judicial bravery requires them to withstand the tide of prejudice in a racially charged atmosphere. This was often the case during the *Plessy* era, when the South fought with all of its might to preserve its privileged way of life. Sometimes that courage came at great personal cost.

Judge Julius Waties Waring was one of those judges. He heard several egregious segregation cases in South Carolina that chilled the nation in the pre-*Brown* years.[35] These experiences slowly caused the Southern judge to convert his thinking, integrate his own courtroom, and hand-down courageous decisions that jolted his own community. Kluger notes that furious whites hissed at the Judge and his family, sent hate mail, made obscene phone calls, and youngsters taunted his wife while grown-ups blocked her passage as she walked down the street. In the later years, racists threw bricks through their window and planted a flaming cross in front of the Warings' home, but despite these travails, "the majesty of the federal Judiciary was not going to be spurned" as far as the valiant judge was concerned.[36] In 1950, he sat on a three-judge panel in Charleston when a long black line marched into the courthouse to hear Thurgood Marshall argue that segregation is illegal. Marshall told the judges that it is your responsibility "to end this injustice now."[37] A majority of two judges ruled against NAACP in *Briggs v. Elliot*, but Judge Waring issued a twenty-page dissent declaring that *Segregation is per se inequality.*[38] The Supreme Court would soon vindicate him, but the courageous judge moved from the South soon after writing those important words. He died in exile in 1968 but was buried at Magnolia Cemetery outside of Charleston. Fewer than a dozen whites attended, but more than 200 grateful blacks were on hand to pay tribute and bid farewell to the unsung hero. One black farmer said, "He's dead but living in the minds of the people here still."[39]

In time, four lawsuits raising the legality of segregation made their way to the Supreme Court from South Carolina, Kansas, Virginia, and Delaware. They were consolidated for oral argument on December 9, 1952. On that day, Thurgood Marshall rose to the occasion and would **not** be denied. In that courtroom, the attorneys arrayed against him were on his terrain. As the hammer came down, the formidable civil rights advocate marched into history. It is probably true that most lawyers do not go to heaven. But on the day that Jim Crow died, Thurgood Marshall surly made a special place for civil rights lawyers: they stood up to hate, racism, and intolerance with passion, conviction, courage, and clarity of purpose as they litigated in the face of constant threats and retaliation in the pursuit of justice.

On May 17, 1954, the unanimous decision was handed down.[40] The Supreme Court laid *Plessy* to rest in the most important decision of the twentieth century. Rather than pretend that segregation, solely on the basis of race, is benign, *Brown* found that it "generates a feeling of inferiority" in black students "that may affect their hearts and minds in a way unlikely ever to be undone." It declared separate educational facilities to be "inherently unequal." The ruling changed the face of America, even though it took the rest of the century to implement *Brown.* The focus of NAACP's work then shifted from the courtroom to the political arena, as the civil rights movement took to the streets to integrate the nation, build alliances to pass civil rights legislation, and change the way that society views black America.

Reflecting on the impact of *Brown* over one decade later, Thurgood Marshall wrote:

> I had the privilege of arguing [*Brown*] in the Supreme Court. Because of my participation, I might perhaps overestimate *Brown's* importance, though I doubt it.
>
> My friend Loren Miller prefaces the chapter on the *Brown* case in his recent book with an excerpt from a spiritual:
>
> There's a better day a' comin'
> Fare thee well, fare thee well,
> In that great gettin' up morning
> Fare thee well, fare thee will.
>
> and refers to May 17, 1954—opinion day in *Brown*—as "That Great Gettin' Up Morning." Similarly, Dean Pollack of Yale Law School has said that the decision was, with the exception of the wars, "the single most important government act of any kind since the Emancipation Proclamation." In holding segregated public education unconstitutional, the Court eliminated one of the two primary pillars of the caste

> system (the other being disenfranchisement). The decision was not an easy one to reach, nor did it prove easy to enforce. Several states and many communities were quite recalcitrant and are only now coming to accept the decision.
>
> And the social reform inherent in the decision was achieved by the efforts of men, largely lawyers, who believed that through the rule of law change could indeed be wrought. The Negro who was once enslaved by the law became emancipated by it, and is achieving equality through it. To be sure law is often a response to social change; but as I think *Brown v. Board of Education* demonstrates, it also can change social patterns. Provided it is adequately enforced, law can change things for the better; moreover, it can change the hearts of men, for law has an educational function also.[41]

The legal principle announced in *Brown* revolutionized public education. It planted seeds of change in the housing and employment sectors; brought conditions of equality to public accommodations; opened the doors to the entertainment, sports, and music worlds; opened-up the political process through the right to vote; and it improved the criminal justice system and access to the courts, as well. The entire economy was affected, because every institution and sector was infected by the Law of Segregation. Today, we rarely hear folks like Clarence Thomas, Michael Jordan, and LeBron James speak-up for human rights. But like the rest of America, they owe much to those who paved the way for the conditions of equality. That includes the Black Panthers, Jackie Robinson, Joe Louis, Jesse Owens, Jesse Jackson, Martin Luther King, Jr., and their attorneys, like Thurgood Marshall, the grandson of a slave.

Lessons Learned from the Campaign to Overturn *Plessy*

There are intriguing parallels between the black and red movements. They provide lessons for mounting a campaign to implement the *Declaration*. On the one hand, NAACP's campaign for equality under the law (1910–1954) was conducted in the courts, since legislative relief was unavailable from Jim Crow legislatures in the absence of political clout. In the first phase, segregation cases sought to nullify Jim Crow laws by enforcing existing law (i.e., the equalization component of the "separate but equal" doctrine). Legal strategists were able to find new vistas by looking carefully at the existing law with a fresh eye to find a new compass to steer by. It took forty-four years to overturn *Plessy* itself. For most of that period, NAACP's legal strategy lived with the "separate but equal" doctrine and tried to make the best of it. It was not until 1950 that the strategy changed to a frontal assault upon the law of segregation, once the stars were properly aligned. At that pivotal stage, *Brown* shattered the law of segregation, improved the legal framework, and paved the way for black equality under the law.

On the other hand, the tribal sovereignty movement began in the 1960s. It gained momentum from the Indian Self-Determination Policy inaugurated by President Nixon in 1970. The movement's goal was *self-determination*, broadly defined to include self-government, indigenous institutions, cultural rights, land rights, and related indigenous rights, which are listed today in the *Declaration*, and those indigenous aspirations include the non-discrimination and equality principles as well. To pursue the broad goals of self-determination, the movement used the existing legal framework provided by federal Indian law, as currently described in *Cohen's Handbook of Federal Indian Law* (2005 ed.). The battle took place in all three branches of the federal government, as the movement employed litigation, legislative lobbying, and administrative advocacy—all aimed at strengthening the tribes' political and trust relationship with the United States and make it accountable to the goals of self-determination.[42] Interestingly, the cases filed by Indian tribes during the sovereignty movement were not aimed at assaulting federal Indian law or overturning the Supreme Court cases that defined the legal landscape. They focused instead upon coaxing the federal courts to apply the foundational principles of federal Indian law that were fashioned in the nineteenth century in a modern day context, and the litigators looked carefully inside the existing framework to find and exploit the most protective features. This approach is similar to NAACP's initial strategy, because it uses the White Man's Law against him in his own courtrooms. The legal prong of the Native American movement did not seek to overturn any of the landmark Indian cases on the "dark side" of the law that are tainted with racism, unfettered colonialism, and unjust legal fictions. Instead, over the past forty-two years, lawyers have emphasized the protective side of the law, lived with the internal tension between self-determination and colonialism, and tried to make the best of the existing legal framework, just like NAACP used the best that could be found in the *Plessy* doctrine to advance its goals.

Importantly, there came a time when NAACP changed its legal strategy into a frontal assault upon the legal framework for segregation. That came in 1950, after the Fund achieved the equalization goal set in the Margold Plan and had the winds of change at its back from a wave of dramatic legal victories and a groundswell of support from the Executive Branch, Justice Department, and mainstream legal academia. That momentum brought the campaign to a crossroads. The Fund saw both the opportunity and need to fundamentally change the legal framework, a task that remained before black equality under the law could be actualized.

Indian Country stands at the same crossroads today. Since 1970, great nation-building strides toward self-determination have been made by Indian nations, but the tribal sovereignty movement has fallen short at the doorstep, hampered by a legal framework heavily influenced by (1) the "dark side" of federal Indian law, where the law of colonialism still exists, with its mindset of conquest and racism; (2) unjust Supreme Court decisions that rank alongside of *Plessy*—such as *Johnson, Lone Wolf, Tee-Hit-Ton, Lyng, Smith, Oliphant,* and *Hicks*; and (3) a hostile Supreme Court bent on making matters worse. The time has come to change the legal strategy from living with those factors to an all-out assault upon them.

The stars are aligned by many factors.[43] The intangible ones include the bravery, skill, and experience generated by the tribal sovereignty movement; and Indian Country has the wind at its back, not only from gains at home, but it also has momentum from new vistas opened by the international indigenous human rights movement, as seen in the *Declaration.* Rather than stall-out at the very doorstep of self-determination, as broadly defined by the *Declaration*, and huddle against a judicial assault by the Supreme Court, Indian Country is poised for a final push. It must attack barriers to self-determination head-on. After all, Indian Country is better positioned than NAACP was when it began a legal campaign over one hundred years ago with nothing at its disposal. In

1910, it was confronted by a daunting task. The law of segregation was deeply entrenched, in the same way that the "dark side" of federal Indian law is controlling law today. There were no black attorneys, and a law school literally had to be built before scholars could "invent" civil rights law; and the unfriendly Supreme Court stood against black America like a formidable 500-pound gorilla. By contrast, today more than 2,000 Native American attorneys have degrees from ranking law schools, where indigenous law professors teach federal Indian law and provide brilliant scholarship. Only five full-time staff attorneys worked at NAACP Fund headquarters in 1950, when it mounted the final push; whereas, the Native American Rights Fund (NARF) alone has twice that number, with experience in over 90 Supreme Court cases, and Indian nations have "lawyered-up" all around the country. However, the NAACP model teaches that lawyers cannot meet the challenge at hand by standing-pat on the shoulders of their forbears; law professors must find new vistas and look beyond the existing legal framework; and Native America needs its own Thurgood Marshall—a culturally grounded "lawyers' lawyer," with the Great Spirit at his or her side, to muster a brain trust devoted to improving the legal framework, to command a committed legal cadre, and to work closely with tribal leaders to guide a legal campaign into the human rights realm, where the fruits of self-determination can be found.

Even though the goals between the NAACP campaign and tribal sovereignty movement differ, social and political scientists can identify many important parallels and principles from the NAACP campaign that can be applied in a Native American campaign to implement the *Declaration*. Some of those principles are identified below.

1. Law reform Is Key to a March to Justice and Can Be the Goal Itself

An appropriate legal framework is needed to define human rights and provide justice for oppressed groups. Where that framework is oppressive or bars human rights, it must be changed. Just as the Supreme Court's "separate but equal" doctrine unleashed oppression and had to be changed, aspects of federal Indian law have an anti-justice function and hamper effective self-determination rights. Accordingly, legal principles and strategies must be developed to strengthen that framework before Native American aspirations can be fully realized and effectively protected. Reformers can look inside the existing framework to pull out and emphasize the best and most protective features, as done in the modern era (c. 1970–2010). In addition, many existing doctrines, statutes, and policies, and much case law, can be strengthened in the post-*Declaration* era by re-interpretation through a human rights lens against standards provided by the *Declaration*. For examples, when read with a fresh eye against the framework of the *Declaration*, the Indian Reorganization Act of 1934 (IRA) might provide new vistas; nefarious doctrines of colonialism, conquest, and racism can be seen as unjust and given proper effect; and unjust Indian cases that smack of *Plessy* become the targets for law reform.

2. Lawyers of a Certain Kind Are Vital

In law-oriented justice campaigns, a trained cadre of public interest lawyers led the NAACP campaign, working in tandem with legal scholars and cooperating local counsel. All lawyers have a role, but public interest lawyers with *esprit de corps* are especially important. By definition, they are mission-driven and highly motivated by justice. They perform legal work for non-profit organizations that bear costs and expenses. Private law firms operate on a profit basis and cannot reasonably be expected to maintain such campaigns on a sustained basis, unless the legal work is paid for by clients. The private sector plays a vital back-up role by contributing *pro bono* work, *amicus* support, or even taking the lead in local cases from time-to-time. But the bulk of the sustained work and coordination often comes from the public interest sector, and it deserves tribal and philanthropy support so that it can fulfill that role. In addition, while NAACP sought leadership from black attorneys who were able to devote their life's work to the campaign, Native American attorneys in the tribal sovereignty movement worked closely with non-Indian colleagues—a synergy existed, as each learned from the other. However, leadership from Native American attorneys proved vital during the tribal sovereignty movement.

3. The Role of Legal Scholars

At every important juncture in the NAACP campaign, law professors and scholars played a vital role. They built a law school and transformed it into a civil rights command center; they provided brainpower for inventing civil rights law; litigators relied on the Brain Bank when developing objectives and strategies for the campaign and its guiding legal principles; they provided *amicus* support along the way, lending academic credibility to effort; and they trained a new breed of black attorneys. The same kind of proactive involvement from Native American law professors and legal scholars is needed today to (1) train the next generation of public interest lawyers, (2) impact development of the law through published scholarly works, and (3) assist in developing strategy, goals, and guiding legal principles for a campaign to implement the *Declaration.* It is not enough to teach holdings in Indian cases, without seeing beyond the current legal framework.

4. The Need for a Command Center

The campaign to overturn *Plessy* involved three core entities—Howard Law School, the NAACP, and the NAACP Legal Defense and Educational Fund—and branched out from that nucleus. In 1910, NAACP had to create an infrastructure from ground zero by (1) building a law school, which became the laboratory for inventing civil rights law and a national data base for the movement; and (2) create a legal arm of the campaign, the Fund. Indian Country already has infrastructure (i.e., law schools with Indian law programs, political organizations, and an experienced public interest law sector), but it has not organized those sectors for a sustained campaign to implement the *Declaration.* Where will the command center be located, and how will it be funded?

5. The Need for Seed Money

Every campaign needs resources to organize its infrastructure, develop the strategy, and formulate the guiding legal principles. The Garland Fund provided the seed money to NAACP at the critical moment during the formative years so that the campaign could get organized and advance forward in a planned strategy. The Ford Foundation provided vitally important resources to Indian Country at critical junctures during the formative stages of the tribal sovereignty movement and has a knack for putting its finger on critical social needs in a timely fashion. In addition, the Indian nations themselves have the discretionary wealth from gaming and other economic ventures to provide seed money for a campaign to implement the *Declaration*. Finally, in contrast to NAACP's campaign, the US government must fund and provide technical assistance to assist Native American implementation efforts under the *Declaration*.

6. The Need for Strategy and Guiding Legal Principles

It is true that a small force with a battle plan can overcome a bigger, more powerful foe, as seen in the NAACP campaign. That axiom is also seen in the successful legislative and litigation campaigns in the tribal sovereignty movement. In the march to *Brown*, the strategy and guiding legal principles for the litigation campaign were essential in the assault on a landmark Supreme Court decision and the engrained law of segregation, and in bringing equality under the law to an historically oppressed peoples. These daunting and seemingly impossible goals were accomplished by a small cadre against all odds. The same is true for many successful campaigns mounted by the tribal sovereignty movement to address national problems through a strategic approach, such as the well-known legislative movements leading to the Indian Child Welfare Act of 1978 (ICWA), the Native American Grave Protection and Repatriation Act of 1990 (NAGPRA), and the American Indian Religious Freedom Act Amendments of 1994, or the national litigation campaign conducted by NARF to press for the rights of American Indian inmates (c. 1973–1980).[44]

By the same token, to implement the *Declaration* and overturn a daunting line of adverse Supreme Court decisions that bar full realization of the right of self-determination, the "Mother of all campaigns" must be mounted. A workable set of legal, legislative, and social strategies are needed to guide work on many fronts; and it is essential that appropriate legal principles guide the legal offensive. This book has broadly suggested that many principles in federal Indian law are compatible with the self-determination and human rights framework of the *Declaration*, such as the inherent tribal sovereignty doctrine and the *Worcester* protectorate framework. But how can they be meshed into a seamless body of law and policy, so that one framework can supplement the other, creating synergy to move federal Indian law into a human rights realm where Native American rights can be situated and find stronger protection?

That question can only be answered by the development of strategy, setting goals, and laying plans to accomplish them.

As a point of departure, *In the Courts of the Conqueror* (2010) lays out a reconnaissance-level blueprint for reforming and strengthening federal Indian law in the 21st century. The blueprint presented two objectives: (1) steer federal courts back to *Worcester*, and (2) uplift federal Indian law and policy so they comport with the *Declaration*;[45] and it identifies eight steps for strengthening the law that can be taken in tandem with implementing the *Declaration*:

1. Create a theoretical framework for law reform;
2. Overturn *Johnson v. M'Intosh;*
3. Make courts perform their bulwark function;
4. Overturn *Oliphant* and end violence in Native America;
5. Reform trusteeship and the "dark side" of guardianship;
6. Reform the plenary power doctrine and overturn *Lone Wolf*;
7. Overturn *Lyng* and strengthen cultural sovereignty; and
8. Find effective ways to protect indigenous habitat.

Leading scholars have compiled a sound body of literature in recent years that demonstrates the dark side and structural weaknesses of federal Indian law, but it stops short of providing strategy and guiding legal principles for the reform of those problems.[46] We must now turn to that task at the inception of a campaign to implement the *Declaration.*

7. The Need to Mobilize Indian Country and Build Alliances

The NAACP mobilized the black race in the march toward equality under the law, and it built critical alliances in the legal push to overturn *Plessy* with the Office of the President, the Justice Department, and a small army of leading legal scholars who supported the cases leading to the *Brown* decision. In the ensuing decades, a broad-based political alliance supported the black civil rights movement in the struggle to implement *Brown,* desegregate schools, and to enact and enforce civil rights laws. Those successes could not have been achieved by the black race alone. The importance of mobilization and alliances is seen in the efforts of other nations to uplift indigenous rights and implement the

Declaration. For example, Peru and Paraguay are two Latin American countries that have endorsed the *Declaration*, but have taken different approaches to implementing the standards.

Peru has a large indigenous population that comprises 45 of the nation's population, but most occupy largely inaccessible mountainous regions or the Amazon forests. Mestizos make up 37 percent, and whites comprise only 15 percent. Peru has ratified many international human rights instruments, such as the Charter of the Organization of American States, the American Declaration of the Rights and Duties of Man, the American Convention on Human Rights, and the United Nations' ICCPR, CERD, ICESCR, as well as ILO Convention 169 on Indigenous and Tribal Peoples, and the *Declaration*. But despite these measures, the large indigenous population, and deep world interest in Peru's indigenous past, Peru's indigenous peoples are relegated to life on the margins, as the poorest of the poor and the most neglected people in the nation.[47] Their land and consultation rights are scarcely recognized, as seen in the Peruvian Amazon where more than 70 percent of the territory is allocated to oil companies and where hydroelectric dams threaten to displace tribal peoples.[48] Indigenous protests in 2009 led to police violence in which thirty-three people died and eighty-two were injured.[49] This prompted the enactment of the Law of the Right to Prior Consultation with Indigenous or Tribal Peoples in 2011, the effects of which remain to be seen in Peru.[50] The laws that do exist go largely unenforced. The problem in Peru has been in the mobilization of its indigenous peoples. They live in remote areas, do not speak Spanish or understand Purvian law, and simply want to be left alone; while those who have stood up to the government have been massacred. By contrast, Native Americans in the United States comprise smaller numbers, but are able to mobilize.

Paraguay, on the other hand, has a small indigenous population. It has signed the international human rights instruments but has few laws on the books that implement them, and the bureaucracy is able to block access to those legal protections because they require indigenous peoples to prove their status before the government will recognize their rights. The indigenous peoples attempted to make up for their small numbers by filing lawsuits in international tribunals. They have obtained several rulings that recognize their human rights, which have sent a strong message to Paraguay and the international community, but Paraguay has still not brought its laws into compliance. That strategy has brought pressure on Paraguay to change, but lacks enforcement power that could be brought to bear by domestic courts if they provide suitable access. The choice of the battleground remains important in any strategy to implement the *Declaration*; and the tribal sovereignty movement is versed in all three branches of the federal government, but has not fully complemented those forums by the pursuit of indigenous justice in international tribunals. That avenue might be a useful supplementary avenue, especially when the challenge at hand involves dynamic interplay at the nexus of domestic and international rights law.

Developing a Native American Campaign to Implement the *Declaration*

Over the past year, Indian Country studied the *Declaration* and discussed its implications at various conferences, meetings, and hearings. Two things are certain: First, the *Declaration* holds enormous potential for advancing and improving Native American life in the United States. Second, the *Declaration* is not a self-executing treaty and its provisions are not legally binding, except indirectly, to the extent that they reflect existing treaty obligations or customary international law. It is true that the US government is obligated to cooperate with Native Americans in taking measures to implement the *Declaration* under the preamble and Articles 38–40, and that includes providing "financial and technical assistance" (Art. 39). The wide-ranging obligations placed upon the United States by the *Declaration* implicate every branch of government and require an ambitious nation-building program conducted systematically by the government and Native America in a spirit of cooperation.[51] However, none of these benefits will happen of their own accord, unless pressed for by Native America. Human rights are never freely given. They must be demanded, wrested away, and then vigilantly protected. That is the essence of freedom. Kenneth Deer (Mohawk) states:

> You do not ask for rights, you assert them. When rights are asserted, they grow. Indigenous peoples must assert and exercise our inherent rights. Exercising our rights is what makes us who we are.[52]

We must put the machinery in place to implement the *Declaration*. Even though it places distinct duties on the United States, Native America must set the government's wheels into motion. At the very outset, the Native American campaign must create an implementation framework, setting ground rules and protocols for working with the government, and control that process. It must inform the substantive content of remedial measures and carefully guide the adoption of those measures by courts, Congress, and agencies. Without proactive strategic action, *nothing* will be forthcoming from the government. Worse yet, we will be plagued by setbacks, missteps, false starts, backlash, and bad legal precedent in the mine field that lies ahead. By boldly rising to these challenges in a timely fashion, our window of opportunity will not be squandered, and tribal leaders can bring Native America through the door opened by the *Declaration*.

Planners will be confronted by several problems early on and must identify the components for a successful march to justice:

1. *Who will provide the necessary tribal leadership to mobilize and guide a long-term national campaign?* Tribal leadership is needed to educate Native America about the *Declaration* and encourage legal scholars to (a) research and publish writings to educate the bar, (b) identify areas of the law that do not met UN standards, (c) research the potential impact of those standards on the law, and (4) identify the issues, barriers, challenges, and opportunities entailed in a campaign to realize the standards, and make them binding. In addition, tribal leaders can raise consciousness and rally endorsement from tribal governments, Alaska Native tribes, and Native Hawaiian communities; and they are needed to oversee the development and vetting of political and legal theories, principles, priorities, and strategies for implementing the *Declaration*. Finally, they are spokespersons as the campaign enters the mainstream.
2. *Who will assist tribal leaders in carrying out the above work?* Attorneys, legal scholars, public relations experts, organizers and coordinators, and technical support staff are needed to staff the campaign. How will they be identified and mobilized to assist tribal leaders, and at what command center will they be housed?

3. *What will it cost to organize, plan, and carry out the campaign,; and how will it be funded?*

A strong public education prong can educate society about the *Declaration* and stimulate a constructive climate for a national discourse about the nature and content of human rights for the Native American peoples. Policy analysts involved in implementing the *Declaration* in Canada provide sound advice:

> [T]he development of human rights learning and education programs will be vital for ensuring that the *Declaration* is widely understood, accepted, and applied. The ad hoc coalition in Canada is continuing its educational work on several levels, developing materials, distributing the *Declaration* to academic institutions, and delivering presentations to a wide variety of audiences, from law conferences to community centres. This information-sharing is increasing grassroots awareness and engagement.[53]

Strategists have a big chore in all of this. They must identify short-term work, which might include building alliances, and evaluate what can be accomplished in the short-term through executive orders, Beltway briefings, and congressional field hearings. The brain trust must set goals and develop a legislative and litigation agenda, together with appropriate legal principles, to guide these prongs of the movement toward their targets. In addition, the campaign should have an international component that (1) coordinates with the international indigenous movement at the UN and OAS; (2) keeps abreast of, monitors, and provides strategic support for indigenous efforts to implement the *Declaration* worldwide; (3) makes optimal use of international tribunals; and (4) helps develop favorable international law. Domestic federal Indian law can no longer be viewed in a vacuum. It is inextricably linked to international law in the post-*Declaration* era.

Why should we march? In every age, place, and society, human experience tells us: life is intolerable under unjust conditions. Historically, the redress of injustice is by itself a value that birthed every great American social movement. The instinctual drive toward justice applies to the legacy of conquest—with the manifestly unjust dark side of federal Indian law and the deplorable socio-economic conditions of traumatized Native America communities. The cultural survival of Native America depends on a march to justice, and so does America's evolution from a settler state to a more just society. Even before we march, tribal attorneys can effectively use the *Declaration* by citing it as a persuasive legal standard in appropriate circumstances in day-to-day work. Courts can rely upon the *Declaration* when interpreting federal Indian law. We can ask agencies to look to the *Declaration* when interpreting policy and developing new policy. Lobbyists can ask Congress to consider the *Declaration* when legislating. And we can ask law schools and colleges to train the next generation in the values and principles of the *Declaration*. Finally, as we await the emergence of our champions, let us embrace the words of one lawyer, activist, and social engineer:

> Joy lies in the fight, in the attempt, in the suffering involved, not in the victory itself.
>
> —Mahatma Gandhi, India.[54]

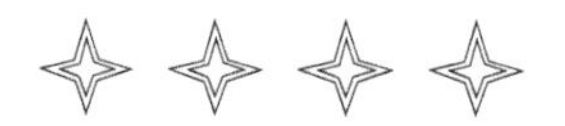

CHAPTER TEN
In the Light of Justice

Is there an obligation to repair harm caused by historical wrongs and heal a painful past? To find the answer to this question, we shall journey into the realm of human compassion and learn how the power that springs from our wisdom traditions can heal even the most grievous injury inflicted by humans upon other humans. Once there, we can see that whenever an egregious collective injury occurs during the growth of a nation, it can produce traumatic human suffering that calls for reconciliation. This book addresses one such situation: the deleterious impacts of the legacy of conquest.

We cannot turn back the hands of time, but the *Declaration* shows how we can heal historical injuries inherited from the misdeeds of Manifest Destiny—the missteps of our ancestors that have engendered harm lasting to this very day. We have long been baffled about what to do about that painful past. As of 2012, the United States has not taken any steps specifically designed to to implement the *Declaration* or even held a meeting with Native American leaders to discuss a national plan of action. The general public, including tribal leaders, has not demanded action or laid plans to push for change. On the fifth anniversary of the *Declaration*, the time draws nigh to confront our inaction, see what it is all about, and overcome the forces of inertia. We must join the rest of the world in implementing the *Declaration* so that restorative justice can heal lingering inequities that stalk Native America.[1]

This chapter pursues three goals. First, it confronts and examines the reasons for complacency, inaction, and inattention by the government, general public, and Native America itself. Much of the inertia can be attributed to a simple lack of information about the *Declaration*. Most people have never heard about the *Declaration*, evaluated its implications, or engaged in informed discourse about the need to embrace it in our treatment of Native Americans. Instead, knee-jerk hostility by uninformed journalists stifles serious discourse. For example, after I gave a recent speech about the *Declaration*, an editorial featured in *The Oklahoman* screamed that the *Declaration* is an "unnecessary and useless waste of time" that would "uproot" happy Oklahoma Indians and set them upon "a reverse Trail of Tears" back to "the land of their ancestors."[2] To that, we can add the usual governmental paralysis. Beltway gridlock grinds government to a stop in election years, when politicians scurry for cover and bureaucrats run swiftly from the work of the nation. Not a soul in the Capital can be found to prod the government. The general public is inattentive, because most folks think Indians are "extinct." The few who know better avert their eyes from the painful legacy of conquest. And many brave souls willing to face that legacy know little about the complexities and realities of Indian affairs, and their confusion hampers meaningful discourse about the nature of human rights for Native Americans. The powerful forces that stymie attention must be overcome before the public can open its eyes to the *Declaration*, see its import, and understand why we should support the rise of human rights in Native America.

Second, this chapter presents a framework for healing historical wrongs. Our forebears developed traditions long ago to address a universal problem: acute human suffering. They provide principles, models, and techniques to heal societal trauma. Once brought into focus, they impel positive acts to unify people divided by historical misdeeds. To be sure, the collective wrongs committed by the United States against its Native peoples were appalling, and they color life today. However, misdeeds are common in world history. Misfortune stalks every walk of life. Acute trauma has gripped untold millions, as humans spread across the planet. Faced by the painful side of history, our ancestors developed principles for healing human misery of the sort inflicted by man's inhumanity to man. Healing unresolved grief is painfully difficult, but it is not rocket science. As will be seen, our teachings contain a framework for healing injuries of the kind inflicted upon Native Americans by the forces of conquest and colonialism. They impel us to actualize the remedial provisions of the *Declaration* that alleviate those injuries, and we do not have to remake the wheel to heal the wounds of the past. This chapter applies that wisdom to measure our progress in redressing the legacy of conquest and chart the steps that lay ahead.

Third, along the way, we shall attempt to better understand the remedial nature of restorative justice in a legal system. At its core, the essence of justice flows from the righting of wrongs. Gandhi, the lawyer, once said the goal of the law is to "unite parties who have been riven asunder."[3] This concept bears heavily upon the question before us: *What is justice*? We think we know it when we see it. But relief from historical wrongs committed against Native Americans has proven difficult for our legal system to achieve, if not altogether elusive. How do we situate Native American claims and grasp the distinctive notions of reparative justice that are placed before us by the *Declaration*? We can agree in abstract principle that a grave historical injury always creates a need to heal wounds of the past. In such an instance, national unity *demands* a cathartic process, which is necessary to purge the wrong, cleanse damage, and then release everyone concerned from the angst of societal trauma. Restorative justice allows those who have been driven apart to come together with dignity, as a reunified whole. Can this critical transformative task elude our system of justice? In addition, our history agrees time and again that the redress of injustice is, by itself, a value justifying the development of social movements. Is that value defeated by the unique circumstances of indigenous peoples? Does indigenous justice *by definition* overtax our notions of justice? As we stand paralyzed by the legacy of conquest, we cannot simply throw up our hands, like the hapless *Plessy* Court or the rambling judicial discourse found in the law of conquest, and say: "It is impossible to provide indigenous justice in America." International human rights law invites us to break the chains of paralysis. The human rights approach of the *Declaration* condemns an amoral framework for defining indigenous rights in the absence of justice. It insists that we make room for indigenous justice; and that is the challenge put forward in this essay.

Are Complacency, Inaction, and Inattention Warranted?

Many readers wonder: *Why should I help implement the Declaration?* It is easy to assemble reasons for inaction, especially when the work promises to be difficult. The reasons can be persuasive at first blush. However, inaction in Native America makes First Americans look soft and complacent, and inattention by the general public makes America look implacable and uncaring. However, these descriptions are incorrect and do not explain our inaction. When we drill deeper to examine the arguments for refusing to heal the past, we find they are made of straw. Because none have merit when held up against the light, social action is warranted, especially when we consider (1) principles of atonement; (2) every nation's need to heal societal trauma in its midst, regardless of cause; and (3) the historical commitment to core values that has animated the United States from its inception.

Native America hardly needs a new social cause. It is hard-pressed on many fronts by everyday needs. Tribal government meets daily challenges in the framework created by the tribal sovereignty movement, federal Indian law, and the United States' Indian Self-Determination Policy. Since 1970, striking advances were made, but lasting solutions for many hard-to-solve social ills seem beyond reach. Progress has stalled-out at the very doorsteps of *self-determination*, as broadly defined in the *Declaration*. The Supreme Court bars entry through the doorway. The Roberts Court is intent upon eroding, not maintaining or strengthening, tribal rights. It will not rethink its unjust legal precedent and nefarious legal doctrines anytime soon; meanwhile, none of the other branches prod for changes necessary to heal the legacy of conquest. To its credit, Native America has made the best of those doctrines since 1970—just as the NAACP sought to enforce and make the best of *Plessy's* law of segregation prior to 1950. However, people can only advance so far under an unjust legal regime, and any gains remain subject to divestment at the discretion of the government. It is therefore timely for tribal leaders, lawyers, and scholars to step-back from the press of daily affairs and examine the larger picture. Root structural problems must be clearly seen and targeted, and Native youth cannot take victories of the past for granted, passively tolerate injustice, or live complacently with social ills produced by intergenerational trauma. Together, all must march into a new self-determination framework founded upon justice and human rights to meet and resolve the challenges of the hour.

Above all, we must see that the social ills described in this book are endemic to an outmoded settler culture that defines the indigenous station in the absence of human rights through the lens of conquest, colonialism, and race. This legacy has produced unsolved problems, which have lingered for more than a century, and they threaten to become permanent. To name a few:

1. Congress can curtail self-determination and self-government at will.
2. The Supreme Court can trim tribal sovereignty at will.

3. Equality and non-discrimination in the law are beyond reach so long as notions of conquest, colonialism, and racism flourish in the law.
4. Survival, life, and security are jeopardized in tribal communities where life is cheap in the most violent places in America, yet the law prevents tribal governments from protecting their citizens from violence at the hands of non-Indians.
5. Tribal culture is under assault due to a failure to effectively protect indigenous holy places and intellectual property, as well as rights to language, culturally appropriate education, indigenous habitat, and to effectively transmit culture.
6. Hard-to-solve social ills blossom in a just nation simply because public education, information, and media are unaccountable to Native America.
7. The political relationship falls short of the protectorate intended by *Worcester*, because indigenous participation in government decision-making fails to meet UN standards.
8. Deplorable Native American socio-economic conditions, shocking gaps in physical and mental healthcare, and other indicators of societal trauma remain permanent fixtures until the United States takes duties prescribed by the *Declaration* to heart.
9. Native America is plagued by second-class land rights and no indigenous habitat rights until UN standards are fully realized.

These problems bar the door to self-determination.[4] They are end-products of the current legal regime. Native America must take one step beyond the existing legal framework and enter the human rights realm to see whether these barriers can be eliminated at last. To its credit, the tribal sovereignty movement has taken us far, but now Native America must enter into the light of justice.

Why should Native America act? Time has proven that it cannot rely upon the inherent tribal sovereignty and protectorate principles alone, as they now stand in the current legal framework. Without a stronger and more just human rights foundation, our dignity, survival, and well-being as indigenous peoples remain at stake. At this juncture, we must inform ourselves to see the vision provided by modern international human rights law, overcome inertia to reach for justice, and set aside resources to implement the *Declaration,* not unlike that pivotal time when our forebears girded themselves during the nadir of Indian Country in the 1950s to halt destructive government policies and push for self-determination.[5] Our task is to take up the mantle of self-determination and stride toward indigenous human rights in the post-*Declaration* era.

The reasons to act are much less apparent to the general public. It is always difficult to motivate the non-Indian public to support Native American issues. Even though Americans are a freedom-loving and fair-minded people who pride themselves on the core values of equality, justice, and human rights, there has never been a national program of reparation for Native Americans.[6] Some folks are implacable. They know a wrong has been committed, but do not care. Others care, but would rather be haunted by the legacy of conquest[7] and gross inadequacies[8] than do anything about appalling collective wrongs committed against Native Americans—wrongs that would constitute, by today's standards, serious violations of international human rights. This mindset is especially strong among those who prosper from past abuses. In addition, many people of goodwill wonder, "Why is the *Declaration* needed here?" They are swayed by several arguments against *reparations*, as that term is used in this essay,[9] but upon close examination, none are convincing.

The first argument is: "we are not responsible for the sins of our fathers." It claims we have no obligation to heal the past. In fact, it is patently *unfair* to ask innocent people, who personally committed no wrong, to repair harm done to Native Americans when they had no part in committing the harm, and it is *unfair* to apply today's standards to past conduct, because modern standards are not retroactive. However, present generations are responsible for the past, because it shapes the present. When harm from past wrongs is still seen and felt today, our complicity in perpetuating the lasting injury cannot be ignored, and there is no issue of non-retroactivity at all. Furthermore, we cannot absolve responsibility for collective misconduct simply by changing governments, just like a corporation cannot escape liability by changing management. Many historical abuses of Native Americans were illegal or immoral at the time they were committed, violated existing norms, or were committed at a time when equality and fundamental human rights were the order of the day for non-indigenous peoples. In such instances, savage treatment, appalling misconduct, and manifest injustice, meted out to Native Americans, fairly call out for justice. The non-retroactive argument never applies to gross violations of human rights (such as mass murder, genocide, ethnocide, widespread discrimination, or the theft of a nation) to shelter egregious conduct from scrutiny. Historical abuses committed by settler states during colonialism fall squarely into the kinds of wrongs that fairly call out for reparations. Indeed, nations around the world are being asked to account for such wrongs and make things right.[10] One international law expert points out that reparation for wrongs of the past in colonized lands is not unusual at all:

> [T]he memory and legacy of past injustice haunts contemporary international law. Striving for truth and justice, which includes reparation, is part of a system based on the rule of law and on the equal dignity of all human beings. Indigenous peoples are unquestionably entitled to remind us of the past atrocities that colonizers and foreign conquerors visited upon them in the name of empire and racial superiority. They are surly entitled to demand reparation for the deprivations and suffering they endured in that not so distant past. Yet, the memory of past injustice has also a dark side: the feeding of a sense of enmity and the lingering on old resentment which may hinder reconciliations and solidarity in the society of the present time. Ensuring that the memory of past injustices does not manifest itself in present and persistent rancour is probably the most important function of reparation for past injustices.[11]

Nor is the lapse of time an equitable defense that bars restorative justice when: (1) victims were unable to secure redress in settler courts, (2) wrongdoers unjustly enriched themselves through privilege gained by suppression or other abuses at Native American expense, or (3) past abuses created socio-economic disparities still seen today. In these instances, unjust enrichment cannot be ignored. The notion that the passage of time bars reparations like a "statute of limitations" in a court of law is misguided. As a matter of fact, the passage of time has not barred reparation in other nations. While that legalistic argument may bar relief in legal proceedings, it is not a legal barrier in social, political, or legislative settings, where remedial relief and restorative justice can be granted.

In sum, the equitable argument is unpersuasive. It is not unfair to ask descendants to atone for the wrongs of their ancestors. What is *actually* unfair is to turn a blind eye to unjust enrichment, manifest injustice, or human suffering in Native American communities, when fairness and good conscience demand reparation and appropriate legal safeguards to protect against the repetition or continuation of that harm. Thus, for most Americans, the fairness contention that we should not have to pay for the sins of our fathers is unavailing.

The political argument against repairing injuries of the past is two-fold: (1) reparations unfairly create "special rights" for Native Americans and that is illegal, because special rights violate equal protection principles; and (2) "if we acknowledge historical wrongs committed against Native Americans and provide relief to repair damage done to them, we must provide reparations for every other aggrieved group and we do not have the resources to do that."

As previously indicated, the political argument is legally incorrect.[12] Neither the Supreme Court nor the *Declaration* sees indigenous rights as "special rights" or Native Americans as a "privileged group." In *Washington v. Washington State Commercial Passenger Fishing Vessel* (1979), the Supreme Court reaffirmed the well-settled rule: recognition of federally protected treaty and other Indian rights does not violate the Equal Protection Clause of the Fourteenth Amendment.[13] This rule also applies to federal legislation pertaining to Indians due to their unique constitutional status.[14] Otherwise, the entire body of federal Indian law would be null and void, including hundreds of statutes in Title 25 of the United States Code, several clauses in the United States Constitution, over three hundred treaties, and nearly two hundred years of federal jurisprudence. The same rule applies in the international sphere. CERD makes it clear that special measures for indigenous peoples are permissible under international law, when taken to protect human rights and fundamental freedoms of vulnerable groups.[15] On the international level, widespread agreement and worldwide practices treat indigenous peoples as "vulnerable groups worthy of the law's heightened concern," according to Siegfried Wiessner.[16] Experts do not interpret the *Declaration* as creating "privileged" citizens with "special rights." Rather, its purposes fall within the equality principle, according to Special Rapporteur Anaya.[17]

As such, the International Law Association emphasizes that the *Declaration* does not create special rights apart from fundamental human rights of universal application. It simply "elaborates upon these fundamental rights in the specific cultural, historical, social and economic circumstances of indigenous peoples."[18]

The second political argument cannot be taken seriously. We cannot withhold remedial justice from one injured group, simply because another may demand reparations in the future. That would destroy our legal system, because remedies would be prevented altogether if relief cannot be granted for an injured party on the ground that another injured party might seek relief in the future. The result would be an ineffectual system of justice without teeth. That is unthinkable, because the principle function of every legal system is to ensure adequate relief for every wrong done.[19] It is axiomatic that every wrong must be redressed. That is the essence of every system of justice. At bottom, the real cost of full reparations for Native Americans to repair damage caused by the legacy of conquest and restore their human rights is not dollars. It is a loss of unwarranted power and social or economic advantages, enjoyed by the privileged, from the legacy of conquest that may be undermined by restructuring the rights, relationships, and responsibilities among indigenous and non-indigenous peoples on a more just basis.

Admittedly, it is difficult for our political and legal systems to come to grips with collective claims for widespread historical wrongs, as suggested by the political argument. This is especially true when the legal system normally provides remedies for individual claims. However, collective relief is frequently granted by the courts in class actions and *parens patriae* litigation brought by governments on behalf of their citizens or by Congress in statutes that provide remedial relief for widespread social ills. The real problem in according collective relief for collective wrongs committed against Native Americans is not a legal one, but the deep psychological barrier described in Chapter One. It arises because we cannot confront our inner demons from the legacy of conquest and bring ourselves to face the collective wrongs committed against Native Americans, because their claims implicate the legitimacy of a nation built upon the taking of tribal land, undermining of sovereignty, and the historical mistreatment inflicted upon American Indians, Alaska Natives, and

Native Hawaiians during the growth of the republic. This painful legacy impugns our inflated self-image as the most fair, just, morally pure, and exceptional people in the world.[20] Instead of being stymied by a psychological barrier that requires us to ignore the need to heal wounds of the past, the best course is to admit that we have feet of clay and normalize our self-image. That frees us to repair harm through the restorative justice measures provided by the *Declaration*, so that trauma is healed and unity restored in a nation-building process. National soul-searching through discourse can alleviate the psychological barrier and open the doors to collective remedies for collective historical wrongs committed against Native Americans, just like those doors were opened to make space for African-American claims and account for the legacy of slavery in the wake of the landmark decision in *Brown v. Board of Education*.

We can set aside reasons for inaction. Once that is done, we must find a suitable framework to make reparations for collective wrongs committed by a young nation during a painful past, not unlike other millions in innumerable times past who sought to heal societal trauma of their day, or the many other nations around the world that are now working to restore indigenous justice pursuant to the *Declaration*. Thankfully, we possess sound principles inherited from our wisdom traditions that address human misfortune in a positive way, which are old as the human race itself. We turn to them now.

The Wisdom Traditions Teach Us How to Heal Historical Injuries

Traumatic injury, calamity, atrocity, and other cataclysmic events produce great human suffering that has plagued people through the ages. Indeed, a large slice of history can be viewed through the lens of societal trauma, as discussed in Chapter Five. The painful side of life raises a universal question: How do we respond to human suffering, especially that which we have inflicted? It often seems impossible to heal grievous hurt brought to traumatized communities by the onslaught of traumatic events. In the face of grief over a tragic loss, acute human suffering, or the shocking aftereffects of successive traumatic events, it is hard to find words to express heartfelt sympathy. "I am sorry" is sometimes not enough. What does one do? For help, I recently read an insightful collection of essays written by prominent thinkers and compiled by author Phil

Cousineau in his recent book, *Beyond Forgiveness: Reflections on Atonement* (2011).[21] The essays discuss our accumulated wisdom traditions on this subject, which have been gleaned by the human race over millennia. That wisdom produces axioms that help answer the age-old question before us. In them we can find time-tested methods for healing collective historical wounds and readily understand why it is necessary, *for all concerned*, that a cathartic process takes place in hard-hit communities.

Historically, we respond to human suffering in several ways. We can respond to an injury (1) by harboring anger and seeking revenge, (2) by coping or living life with unresolved grief, or (3) by healing injury through restorative justice and reconciliation. Revenge is certainly a low road. It drives people apart, increases hatred, and overtakes the lives of both perpetrator and victim—filling them with ill will, hostility, distrust, and anger. These are unwanted and self-destructive traits of the kind seen in the protracted Palestinian and Israeli dispute. Because revenge perpetuates historical wrongs, it is not commended as it only makes matters worse. By the same token, we cannot heal human suffering by forcing victims to cope indefinitely or live permanently with unresolved grief created by historical wounds. Unborn generations inherit a life scarred by intergenerational trauma,and the perpetrator community remains mired in guilt and locked in injustice.[22] This coping strategy is the *de facto* result of inattention, and it is observed in the United States and other settler states that have not come to grips with historical wrongs committed during the conquest and colonization of indigenous peoples. Coping with injustice is not a solution. Living with injustice never heals historical wounds, and it is hard for victims to bear over time. It leaves dirty little pockets of injustice that sorely contradict our ideals.

By contrast, the wisdom traditions counsel the high road to peace and reconciliation. Restorative justice is the best way to respond to human suffering resulting from a historical wrong. Though it is often painful, this path *actually heals* wounds. Through reparations it brings peace to both parties, rebuilds friendship, and forges unity. South Africa took this path. In the aftermath of apartheid rule, the peace and reconciliation work of the Truth and Reconciliation Commission took precedence over revenge and unresolved grief in rebuilding that nation from the rubbles of racism. Another example is the rebuilding of Rwanda: death squad killers apologized to the families of their victims and performed acts of atonement designed to heal the tragic wounds of genocide. As seen time and again over our long human experience, the high road repairs the past by making amends. It restores balance in the world around us and is consonant with the finest principles that animate human behavior. We need not look far to find the amazing key for seemingly miraculous solutions for hard-to-solve social ills, including the stubborn "Indian problem" in the United States that has baffled the government ever since it embarked upon the painful process of colonizing the continent.

Taking the High Road: Apology, Acceptance, and Acts of Atonement

There is a five-step process to heal human suffering caused by an historical wrong: (1) a serious injury has occurred and human suffering results, (2) an apology is sincerely and truthfully offered, (3) acceptance of the apology is genuinely made and the wrongdoer is forgiven, (4) concrete acts of atonement make things right, and finally (5) unresolved grief and open wounds are actually healed, with a cleansing reconciliation for all concerned. The ethical foundation for this cathartic process comes from the world religions. All point to the High Road, and they remind us that man does not live by brutish instincts or selfish behavior alone. Some experts trace modern forgiveness practices derived from our religious scruples to our earliest ancestors who were more likely to survive if they responded with compassion to a friend in need or helped, and not hurt, a stranger suffering in pain.[23]

Regardless of origin, the widespread religious tenants regarding mercy, compassion, absolution, amnesty, clemency, restitution, and restorative justice abound in every religion. They universally exhort us to practice truth-telling and forgiveness, act selflessly, and live cooperatively in peace; and they enjoin the brutish opposites of these high ideals. For example, Jewish tradition teaches that when you have offended someone, you must go to the injured person, seek forgiveness, and then atone.[24] In the face of egregious injury, it is seemingly impossible to "turn the other cheek" and forgive those who have trespassed against us, but Christ said, "Forgive them, for they know not what they do." Forgiveness is an all-powerful healing force, and it is cruel not to forgive someone who genuinely seeks forgiveness on bended knee. However, it is important that we forgive trespassers *for our own good.* Anger is bad for your health, even though it is hard to let resentment go. The Buddha said, "Anger will never disappear so long as thoughts of resentment are cherished in the mind. Anger will disappear just as soon as thoughts of resentment are gone."[25] Buddhism regards hatred and ill will as self-destructive karma, with dire consequences, in the law of karma, and it urges that forgiveness be cultivated to prevent harmful thoughts from destroying our mental well-being. Similarly, asking for forgiveness is a central practice in Hinduism; and, likewise, the Koran commands, "Hold to forgiveness, commend what is right." In the Indigenous World, the healing of wounds, forgiveness, peacemaking, and reconciliation are found in tribal ceremonies aimed at restoring balance in the world, including the Pawnee Pipe Dance, Navajo Blessing Way, Iroquois atonement practices, and Siouan wiping the tears ceremonies, to name a few in Native North America.[26] These noble forces mustered by our ancestors not only freed them from human suffering and the grip of brutish instinct, but bound them close together as clans, tribes, communities, and nations. Cousineau concludes:

> Over time the understanding and practice of atonement has evolved from its theological underpinnings to more generally refer to *an act that rights a wrong, makes amends, repairs harm, offers restitution, attempts compensation, clears the conscience of the offender, relieves the anger of the victim, and serves justice with a sacrifice commensurate with the harm that has been done.*
>
> If performed willingly and honestly, atoning acknowledges the harm and grief of the victim that, if not dealt with, often leads to a wider cycle of revenge in communities. Anger and shame are open wounds that can fester for decades.[27]

These are powerful healing practices of the highest spiritual order. They extend far beyond forgiveness to concrete acts of atonement. They are effective and humane justice practices that *make you believe in the highest values* that animate human behavior, and they are nothing less than time-tested axioms that have the "uncanny power to restore balance and justice."[28]

It stands to reason that modern political and religious leaders resort to these practices time and again. Like a medicinal salve, they *always* solidify torn relationships; they *never fail* to bind troubled communities together; whereas anger, resentment, and violence *always* drive us apart and perpetuate the injuries we have suffered, or caused. As sure as the rain must fall, these are axioms in the long human experience. We see them at work everywhere, even in the toughest situations. Once a man spat on Martin Luther King, Jr. Instead of responding with anger, Dr. King pulled out his handkerchief, wiped off the offending fluid, folded the hankie, and handed it back to the man, saying: "I think this belongs to you." Instead of retribution after apartheid South Africa was overthrown, President Mandela and Archbishop Tutu focused on peacemaking and reconciliation. They stunned the world by offering their former oppressors "amnesty in exchange for truth" and "healing in place of retribution."[29] Tutu explained, "This kind of justice seeks to rehabilitate both the victim and the perpetrator, who should be given the opportunity to be integrated into the community he or she has injured by his or her offense."[30] Restorative justice carries remarkable power. It allows *an entire country* to regain its dignity after an unjust and painful past. As a member of the Truth and Reconciliation Commission, Archbishop Tutu understood how forgiveness makes us healthy:

> Unless you deal with the past in a creative and positive manner, then you run the terrible risk of having no future worth speaking of. The past can be a baleful or beneficial impact on the future. South Africa will be seriously undermined if those who benefitted from the obnoxious apartheid system, perceived as the oppressors, will not ask forgiveness for the awful things done under apartheid and if the victims, the oppressed, do not offer forgiveness.[31]

At home in another time, the same notions stirred Abraham Lincoln's rebuilding effort after the Civil War. He exhorted the nation: "With malice toward none, with charity for all, let us strive on to finish the work we are in . . . to do all which may achieve and cherish a just and lasting peace among ourselves and with all nations." And on the eve of the government's forcible removal of his people from their ancestral lands, Chief Keokuk of the Sauk Nation tapped that same spiritual well. He made a famous speech forgiving America. With seemingly impossible words of forgiveness, very similar to those uttered by Jesus when he lay mortally wounded upon the cross, Chief Keokuk stated:

> The many moons and sunny days we have lived here will long be remembered by us. The Great Spirit has smiled upon us and made us glad. But we have agreed to go. We go to a country we know little of. Our home will be beyond a great river on the way to the setting sun. We will build our wigwams there in another land. In peace we bid you goodbye. If you come to see us, we will gladly welcome you.[32]

Out of the darkest hour, the best in human behavior can sometimes emerge. This is almost always seen in our splendid forgiveness traditions. They elevate the human spirit, because they aim to bring reconciliation for people torn apart by acts of inhumanity. In the next section, we examine the ingredients that make each step work, even in the most difficult cases.

1. An Injury Has Occurred

The acts of man are fallible and necessarily imperfect. Not one of us is free from human weakness. The painful side of history is generated by dark behavior. The kind of egregious "injuries" it brings knows no bounds, but the historical injuries that require healing most definitely include raw conquest and its nasty little brother, colonialism. The theft of a nation, systematic appropriation of lands belonging to others, and outright subjugation simply cannot be done without inflicting, and maintaining, grave historical abuses. That is why the law of war prohibits conquest or warfare, except for just causes, and that is why the United Nations sternly condemned colonialism in the strongest possible terms. This book concerns the lingering injuries inflicted by conquest and colonialism. They are powerful forces that taint the law with inequities; perpetrate intergenerational trauma over an extended span of time upon hard-hit tribal communities again and again, with each new generation; and this legacy can exist only at great cost, by the persistent denial of protection for indigenous human rights, as readily seen in the serious discrepancies between existing federal Indian law and policy and the minimum human rights standards put forth by the *Declaration*. Such historical wrongs scar both the victim and perpetrator communities, shaping the lives, mindset, well-being, and institutions of all concerned, like a festering wound that will not heal without conscious and determined good faith efforts.

2. A real "Apology" Is Sincerely Made

The first step in healing injury that we have inflicted, and making things right, is a heartfelt apology. We must go to the injured party and genuinely say, "I am sorry," and then humbly ask for forgiveness. This is a straightforward gesture. It seems simple enough, but is often very difficult to do, and it is surrounded by complexities that warrant further discussion. *Why do we apologize when this is so painful and difficult to do?* Aside from basic good manners, the purposes of this painful step are two-fold. First, an apology helps relieve the injured party from anger, resentment, and shame; and it restores lost dignity. Without wiping away anger, reducing pain, and alleviating resentment, true forgiveness is impossible. Second, it relieves the burden of shame, guilt, and remorse for harming another. The need to apologize arises from the remorse that we experience for committing a terrible wrong, even though it may take decades to muster an apology. Unless we actually feel remorse, any changes in conduct that we are willing to undertake to make things right will not go deep enough to make a difference in the pain that we have caused. Thus, real and honest remorse allows us to atone and gird ourselves to take whatever steps are necessary to actually make things right. The working ingredients of an apology are discussed below.

An apology cannot be made without first recognizing, accepting, and admitting to our shortcomings, imperfections, and flaws that created the injury in the first place, however difficult or painful that humbling experience may be. For that reason, false pride, arrogance, and our inflated egos resist apology-making. These are strong character traits. They are adamantly opposed to any humbling experience and cannot be subordinated in many people, even for a moment. Unless reined in, we cannot humble ourselves to offer a sincere apology of the type needed to heal historical wrongs. Those who fall victim to these character flaws must continue to bear a heavy burden of unrelieved guilt over a wrong that they, or their forebears, have inflicted upon others, instead of facing up to the music. That places them upon the coward's path, one frequently taken to protest apologies as "a sign of weakness." However, an apology is a sign of strength, because it requires a difficult act of bravery. Arrogance in high places can effectively forestall healing, even in the most compelling circumstances, but that implacable stance comes at a great price: the forces that prevent apology would rather live with shame and guilt over a terrible wrong that has been done than rectify it, and people are driven apart into a divisive world when we choose not to heal wounds that we have caused. The best that can be done under this approach is to cover-up our misdeeds as much as possible and ignore festering injustice. Once we become implacable and forsake apologizing, atonement is not possible and the high road is beyond reach. Given these unsatisfactory choices, it becomes important to overcome the forces that prevent an apology when one is due.

Nor can an apology be meaningfully offered without truth-telling about the injustice inflicted upon the victim and honestly acknowledging the pain that we have caused. At its heart, no apology is effective unless true *regret* is actually extended to the injured party. Thus, *honesty* and *truth-telling* must undergird a sincere apology, and that is hard to achieve when guilt and denial make us avert our eyes from historical wrongs and close our eyes to the harm inflicted on other people, whether by us or our ancestors. Yet we must open our eyes, see the damage, and apologize for what has been done as a matter of fact. This element of any apology is truly painful, and that is why it frequently takes many years to muster the courage to confront historical misdeeds. For these reasons, the politics of apology are among the most complex in the nation's capital. When confronted by a proposal to apologize, upheaval quickly occurs and panic sets in. Government lawyers scramble to their battle stations to research potential liability; OMB bean-counters rush into their silos to calculate the costs; politicians weigh the political risks in being Big Enough to say, "I am sorry"; while everyone else swiftly runs for cover. The words "I am sorry" not only bring panic to politicians, but are among the hardest in our vocabulary. Though it is difficult, a simple apology is a bridge that all must cross to heal the wounds of a painful past.

Nor is it enough to simply say, "I am sorry," because one must also ask the injured party for forgiveness, and that is what makes the healing process so painfully difficult. We often resent the victims of our crimes, wish them ill, hold them up to ridicule, or torment them with forms of racism and discrimination. That mental analogue is absolutely essential in every conquered or colonized land to justify injustice and rationalize misdeeds when settlers are faced with the dirty business of dispossessing indigenous peoples and trammeling their right of self-determination against their will, especially when those deeds contradict mainstream ideals, core values, and traditions that otherwise guide our behavior. After a prolonged period of holding injured people in contempt, it is unthinkably difficult to go to them, prostrate ourselves before them, apologize, and then ask them to forgive us, especially when it is much easier to resent them for causing our guilt and ignore their plight. However, the wisdom traditions do not promise that penance, contrition, and forgiveness are easy tasks. Instead, in the nature of things, it is a difficult cross for trespassers, perpetrators, aggressors, and wrongdoers to bear. It is equally difficult to forgive. Victims in traumatized communities are often *unable to forgive* the perpetrator society.[33] That is a natural response to trauma and a characteristic that marks traumatized populations, and we therefore turn to the problem of forgiveness next.

However, we cannot leave the apology discussion without underscoring one final point regarding the procedure and protocols that must be followed to proffer an effective apology: It must be done in a proper way. That is, the wrongdoer must go to the victim—not the other way around—to make the apology. The apology must emanate from the perpetrator, be honestly made, and done in the proper time, place, and manner that is appropriate and suitable for such an occasion, depending upon the parties involved, the gravity and extent of the injury, and other pertinent circumstances. Sometimes, the way in which an apology is made can be important as the words themselves.

3. Accepting the Apology and Forgiving the Wrongdoer

Once a real apology is offered, the burden shifts to the injured party to carry the healing process forward. That is done by accepting the apology and forgiving both the perpetrators and those who perpetuated the injury. This is a heavy burden. Some victims are unable to forgive. That inability is often found in communities characterized by historical trauma.[34] *Can we genuinely forgive those who have trespassed against us—even those who destroyed our lives or murdered relatives?* On a secular level, victims can decide whether to forgive or not. Sometimes that right is the *only right* they have, but it is the power to heal harm, from even the most heinous crime. On a spiritual plane, most religions exhort, if not enjoin us, to forgive; and every person has the capacity to forgive, though it may be hard for some to muster.

There is much truth to the saying, "To err is human; to forgive, divine." The wisdom traditions provide strength to forgive. Every religion focuses on forgiveness from God, from each other, and some require us to ask forgiveness from other creatures, as well.[35] We cannot survey these teachings without seeing that forgiveness may be the highest spiritual virtue on earth. Forgiveness traditions are practiced in every age, place, culture, and religious tradition. The axiom that emerges from this pattern is "forgiveness is better than revenge," and we actually do ourselves a favor by releasing our anger, even though it is hard to let it go. Some think it is "unmanly" to forgive. That belief is mistaken. It is dispelled by the many courageous figures that have practiced forgiveness on every continent throughout history. To name a few, Jesus, Mahatma Gandhi, Martin Luther King, Jr., Nelson Mandela, and Archbishop Tutu were not wimps.

Real forgiveness is *indispensable* to healing collective historical wrongs inflicted by humans upon each other. When perpetrators offer a real apology for their transgression, seek forgiveness, and receive amnesty, the path is cleared for the cathartic process. Forgiveness not only lifts our anger and resentment. It also grants the great gifts of pardon, reprieve, and amnesty. This has immediate effects on both parties: First, guilt, remorse, anger, and resentment over the injury dissipate, and the hard feelings that once drove them apart are lifted away. Second, once cleansed of these inner demons, our eyes are opened to compassion and to rebuilding the relationship between the forgiver and the forgiven. At this stage, the parties are ready to proceed to the next steps in the venerated process that our ancestors trod many times before: namely, to undertake acts of atonement that make things right, repair the situation, and enter into a stronger relationship so that the parties can stride toward healing, achieve reconciliation, and advance into the future as a more unified whole.

In short, peace is achieved after forgiveness is granted. Nevertheless, more work remains to heal the wound. Damage must be repaired by wiping away the consequences of the wrong and restoring the situation ante, as much as possible. In many circumstances, unconditional forgiveness can be granted gratuitously by the forgiver, without any expectation of restorative justice, punishment, or restitution. This is done simply as a matter of grace. However, without acts of atonement to repair damage or amend harmful conduct, the healing process envisioned by the wisdom traditions is incomplete, and the haunting specter of injustice still sits before us.

4. Acts of Atonement: The Process of Making Things Right

Once forgiveness is obtained, the offender must undertake concrete actions to make things right. This we do out of compassion because we are truly sorry, and because we *want* to make amends, heal wounds, and enter into reconciliation with the injured community. Without amends, our apology is an empty and meaningless gesture that is likely to bring insult and greater pain. We cannot simply say "I am sorry," then walk away without cleaning up the mess. Instead, we must enter into the realm of restorative justice.

As indicated, Cousineau defines "atonement" as an act that "rights a wrong, makes amends, repairs harm, offers restitution, attempts compensation, clears the conscience of the offender, relieves the anger of the victim, and serves justice with a sacrifice commensurate with the harm that has been done."[36] This is the very essence of "restorative justice" or "reparations," as those remedial concepts are discussed earlier in this book.[37] As used here, *reparation* is not so much monetary damages or compensation alone, but any "act of making amends" for a wrong that has been committed, and it includes any "measure aimed at restoring a person and/or a community of a loss, harm or damage suffered consequent to an action or omission."[38] Thus, reparation and atonement are used interchangeably. Both concepts act to repair damage, heal injury, and allow all concerned to go forward in good faith once justice has been restored and the injurious consequences of the wrong have been repaired.

This axiom applies to the damage caused by colonialism. Just nations do have a responsibility to repair damage done by colonialism through appropriate reparations. As Lenzerini described in Chapter One, reparations in this instance are "measures aimed at *restoring justice* through *wiping out all the consequences* of the harm suffered by the individuals and/or concerned as a result of the wrong, and at *re-establishing the situation which would have existed if the wrong had not been produced*."[39]

In step four, the burden is upon the offending party to carry the healing process forward. At this stage, the offender must provide restorative justice, and he is responsible to see that appropriate acts of atonement lead to healing and open the possibility for reconciliation. Acts of atonement are selfless acts we all must pay for, as part of being members of the human family and as the price for selfish behavior. Protocol for this step is important. The efficacy of the healing process demands that appropriate acts of atonement be done *voluntarily* and out of compassion—without prodding, complaint, or wheedling. If our apology is sincere, atonement shows the depth of our desire to be forgiven, repair harm, and stride toward reconciliation. Atonement is done as much for ourselves as for the injured party, for, as Cousineau notes, our inner being *needs to prove* we are truly sorry for committing a terrible deed and demonstrate our words are not empty.[40] As such, the injured party should not be made to beg for, lobby on bended knee, or demand reparative acts. Instead, the dignity of all concerned requires that restorative justice be freely granted, not meted out reluctantly or begrudgingly; and this should be done without supplication, prompting, or cajoling, *simply because we want to*. After all, we are upon a cathartic path seeking to restore balance, as the goal of the wisdom traditions, and the *manner* in which we amend our conduct can be important as the reparative relief itself. Though we are dealing with distinctly human errors and misdeeds, we are also upon a spiritual path set before us by our wisdom traditions, and the protocol followed really matters. As we navigate the human and spiritual planes throughout the healing process, remember, the guiding axiom is "to err is human; to forgive, divine."

5. Healing and Reconciliation

By following the best traditions of our ancestors in the above steps and protocols, we have done all that humans can do to mend human suffering caused by collective historical wrongs and injuries. There is nothing more that we can do to make things right, and we cannot turn back the hands of time.

But we are healed in three ways. First, the victim community regains its dignity; and ill feelings of hatred, resentment, and suspicion dissolve. Further, the chain placed by intergenerational trauma is broken. Second, burdens of remorse, guilt, and shame have been lifted from the perpetrator society, relieved by apology, forgiveness, and atonement. It has accepted responsibility for wrongs committed, proven it is sorry, assuaged pain caused, and has been redeemed. Guilt is purged and shame dissolved through difficult acts of apology and repair. Third, the cleansing process of compassion has restored the torn relationship: friendship is reborn, and instead of being divided by a painful past, the communities are reunited. As Gandhi stated, that is the real point of the law, to reunite opposing sides. Upon reconciliation, we sit at the core of human compassion, having stripped away the forces that bar entry into that realm by following a path paved by the highest values conceived by our race. From there, we can honestly say, "I am you, you are me, and we are one."

In these splendid acts of repair and reconciliation, we see the essence of nation-building, difficult steps that all must take after the missteps of history. When we or our ancestors have taken torturous detours that frequently plague humanity, people of goodwill are impelled to correct the misdeeds of man by following the best traditions that we have; and we can do no more.

The Wisdom Traditions Are an Antidote for the Legacy of Conquest

We have a workable framework to address the legacy of conquest. It can solve social ills from the most heinous injury and restore dignity to entire nations. Our antidote is inherited from our ancestors. It beckons us to heal ourselves, by following the best available advice gleaned by the human race over millennia, and step through a time-tested process. But where do we begin? We must situate the nation's progress in addressing the legacy of conquest along the five-step continuum. Once we have taken quick stock of that progress, we can see what work lies ahead. Accordingly, before we end this essay on the *Declaration*, we will identify a starting place in the five-step healing process for nurturing the rise of human rights in Native America.

1. An Injury Has Occurred

We are confronted by a historical injury in the United States that must be rectified through a cathartic nation-building process. Like many nations around the world, the United States is heir to a heritage of colonialism. That legacy brought injustice to Native Americans. This form of traumatization still lingers in our legal system, institutions, and mindset. It is strongly seen and felt in tribal communities. They are heirs to historical trauma, handed down as a dark gift from the legacy of conquest and colonialism; and this has been with us so long that it is seen as "normal." Despite this problem, ours is a just nation. It has continually strived to live up to its core values and been willing to self-correct at every painful detour, but it has been unable to come to grips with the "Indian problem." At the same time, Native America has tried hard to make the best of the existing legal framework for many years but is still plagued by legal inequities and hard-to-solve social ills inherited from the legacy of conquest and colonialism. In short, an injury has occurred, and we are confronted with the unwanted consequences.

2. A Real "Apology" Is Sincerely Made and Forgiveness Requested

As seen from the above discussion, apologizing is really a fine art that demands our best skills, thoughtfulness, and sincere compassion. With varying degrees of regret, the United States Congress has apologized for historical misdeeds committed by the nation against Japanese-Americans, Native Hawaiians, and Native Americans. While all three branches of the federal government have taken steps to rectify the legacy of slavery and systematic discrimination against black Americans, no national apology has been made for slavery or our complicity in its lingering effects. Even though both houses of Congress resolved to celebrate the end of slavery, several states have issued actual apologies.[41] Let us examine the apologies to see whether they comport with our wisdom traditions and are sufficient to set wheels in motion for healing the past.

Due to a miscarriage of justice by the Supreme Court in the *Korematsu* and *Hirabayashi* cases, the United States Government destroyed the liberty of over 120,000 Japanese-Americans when the authorities rounded-up that entire race of people on the West Coast and summarily interred them solely on the basis of race during the World War II era from 1942 to 1946. The innocent internees were finally released with nowhere to go.[42] Many decades later, Congress recognized this grave injustice and enacted a law extending a national apology to the interred Japanese-Americans and monetary reparations of $20,000 to each of the surviving victims were made.[43] The law found that "a grave injustice was done," which was "motivated largely by racial prejudice, wartime hysteria, and a failure of political leadership," and it "resulted in significant human suffering."

The statute went beyond an apology to provide several concrete forms of restitution and atonement. It provided the following relief: (1) an official acknowledgment of "the fundamental injustice of the evacuation, relocation and internment of citizens"; (2) a formal apology "on behalf of the people of the United States" for those acts; (3) a "public education fund" was established to inform the public "about the internment so as to prevent the recurrence of any similar event"; (4) it made actual monetary "restitution to those individuals of Japanese ancestry who were interned"; and (5) it proclaimed that these restorative measures were taken out of American compassion for human rights violations worldwide to vividly demonstrate our concern and resolve, so as to "make more credible and sincere any declaration of concern by the United States over violations of human rights committed by other nations."

When he signed the bill into law, President Ronald Reagan apologized to Japanese Americans at an official signing ceremony. He told them:

> [N]o payment can make up for those lost years. So what is most important in this bill has less to do with property than with honor, for here we admit to a wrong, here we reaffirm our commitment to equal justice under the law.[44]

The first reparation payments were made timely, publically, and in person by the President of the United State in 1992 at a second White House ceremony. Each subsequent reparation check was sent by mail, but accompanied by a letter of apology from President Clinton, stating:

> Over fifty years ago, the United States Government unjustly interned, evacuated, or relocated you and many other Japanese Americans.

> Today, on behalf of your fellow Americans, I offer a sincere apology to you for the actions that unfairly denied Japanese Americans and their families fundamental liberties during World War II.
>
> In passing the Civil Liberties Act of 1988, we acknowledged the wrong of the past and offered redress to those who endured such grave injustice. In retrospect, we understand that the nation's actions were rooted deeply in racial prejudice, wartime hysteria, and a lack of political leadership. We must learn from the past and dedicate ourselves as a nation to renewing the spirit of equality and our love of freedom. Together, we can guarantee a future with liberty and justice for all. You and your family have my best wishes for the future.[45]

Over the next ten years, more than 1.6 billion dollars were paid to 82,250 Japanese American claimants before the reparations program ended its work to make amends to those victims of a historical wrong.[46] As seen from the statute and language of two presidents, a sincere apology stood at the center of this national effort to ease the pain of the injured community and restore balance. Even though the apology statute did not ask for forgiveness, it was accompanied by a robust program of reparations.

We turn next to the nation's apologies to its indigenous peoples. In 1993, Congress enacted an Apology Resolution extending a national apology to Native Hawaiians for the illegal overthrow of the Kingdom of Hawaii, a historical wrong committed by the United States one hundred years earlier.[47] In thirty-seven whereas clauses, the Apology Resolution recounts the Government's complicity in the overthrow and how it opened the way for devastating impacts upon the Hawaiian people who are "determined to preserve, develop and transmit to future generations their ancestral territory, and their cultural identity in accordance with their own spiritual and traditional beliefs, customs, practices, language and social institutions"; and therefore Congress saw the need to "express deep regret to the Native Hawaiian people" and "support reconciliation efforts of the State of Hawaii and the United Church of Christ with Native Hawaiians." The operative language of the joint resolution is found in section 1, which reads as follows:

The Congress

1. on the occasion of the 100th anniversary of the illegal overthrow of the Kingdom of Hawaii on January 17, 1893, acknowledges the historical significance of this event which resulted in the suppression of the inherent sovereignty of the Native Hawaiian people;
2. recognizes and commends efforts of reconciliation initiated by the State of Hawaii and the United Church of Christ with Native Hawaiians;
3. apologizes to Native Hawaiians on behalf of the people of the United States for the overthrow of the Kingdom of Hawaii on January 17, 1893, with the participation of agents and citizens of the United States, and the deprivation of the rights of Native Hawaiians to self-determination;
4. expresses its commitment to acknowledge the ramifications of the overthrow of the Kingdom of Hawaii in order to provide a proper foundation for reconciliation efforts between the United States and the Native Hawaiian people; and
5. urges the President of the United States to also acknowledge the ramifications of the overthrow of the Kingdom of Hawaii and to support reconciliation efforts between the United States and the Native Hawaiian people.

The Apology Resolution recognized Native Hawaiian grievances for a historical wrong and took a step in laying the foundation for the healing process. One goal of an apology is to open dialogue, as a first step for healing in a long and difficult five-step process. However, when we compare the words expressed in the joint resolution to the working ingredients of a real apology, the healing effectiveness of this apology is open to question. Whether it actually conveyed the *sincere regrets* of the nation remains to be seen, because the operative language contains no expression of regret, does not ask forgiveness, and, on the political level, the resolution was a quickie legislative measure, deftly passed, but done with almost no discourse or debate, and signed by the president on the same day. Though it vaguely encouraged federal support for local reconciliation efforts, almost twenty years later no concrete measures to move the healing process forward have been forthcoming from the United States.

Native Hawaiians are still waiting on Congress to follow-up on the apology, with an act of atonement for suppressing the inherent sovereignty and depriving the self-determination rights of the Native Hawaiian people, by enacting restorative legislation to recognize and confirm some measure of their indigenous right to self-determination.

To be sure, legislative proposals were introduced, beginning in 2000. But the so-called Akaka Bill, the "Native Hawaiian Government Reorganization Act" (NHGR), still has not passed.[48] While the healing process is not entirely stalled, it twists slowly in the wind, causing this writer to doubt the efficacy of the Apology Resolution. Even though it was no doubt advanced in perfectly good faith, perhaps the measure was not a real expression of true regret. After all, it did not seek forgiveness, whereas real apology-making requires that we prostrate ourselves and ask forgiveness; and that is the next logical step in making the congressional apology complete. The failure to accord restorative justice is explained by the absence of the forgiveness element in the apology-making process. Once forgiveness is *actually* requested and *freely given*, a political climate for restorative justice is generated; and legislative reparations may come easier in that climate as a concrete act of atonement. Thus, when examined against our wisdom traditions, the Apology Resolution is not a complete apology. It is an honest first step toward an apology but incomplete until forgiveness is requested.

In 2009, Congress enacted a national apology to the Native Peoples of the United States, but we are unsure whether the nation ever extended the apology to Native America. As will be seen, it turned out to be a puzzling exercise in apology-making, despite the best intentions of legislation's sponsors, Senators Sam Brownback (R-KS), Byron Dorgan (D-ND), and Daniel K. Inouye (D-HI). The apology is buried deeply in the 161 page Defense Department Appropriations Act of 2010, as an obscure amendment.[49] Here is what it says:

Apology to Native Peoples of the United States

Sec. 8113(a) Acknowledgment and Apology-the United States, acting through Congress—

1. recognizes the special and legal relationship Indian tribes have with the United States and the solemn covenant with the land we share;

2. commends and honors Native Peoples for the thousands of years that they stewarded and protected this land;
3. recognizes that there have been years of official depredations, ill-conceived policies, and the breaking of covenants by the Federal Government, regarding Indian tribes;
4. apologizes on behalf of the people of the United States to all Native Peoples for the many instances of violence, maltreatment, and neglect inflicted on Native Peoples by citizens of the United States;
5. expresses its regret for the ramifications of former wrongs and its commitment to build on the positive relationships of the past and present to move toward a brighter future where all the people of this land live reconciled as brothers and sisters, and harmoniously steward and protect this land together;
6. urges the President to acknowledge the wrongs of the United States against Indian tribes in the history of the United States in order to bring healing to the land; and
7. commends the State governments that have begun reconciliation efforts with recognized Indian tribes located in their boundaries and encourages all State governments similarly to work toward reconciling relationships with Indian tribes within their boundaries.
    a. Disclaimer-Nothing in this section—
        1. authorizes or supports any claim against the United States; or
        2. serves as a settlement of any claim against the United States.

These are appropriate words of regret, and they are a long time in coming, but oddly enough, there is no evidence that the president went to Native America to offer the apology and ask forgiveness. Inexplicably, President Obama signed the Appropriations Act, but did not heed paragraph (6) in section 8113(a), which urged him to acknowledge the misdeeds and to bring about a healing. (Perhaps it was buried too deeply in the act for him to notice and escaped his attention.) In any event, he signed the Appropriations Act in private, never issued a press release regarding the apology, held no ceremony of acknowledgment, and took no steps to notify anyone. It remains the world's quietest apology.

The president has kept the apology under wraps. He never uttered a word of apology, passing up several opportunities to do so in face-to-face meetings with tribal leaders. His confounding failure to provide a verbal apology may stem from political calculations about potential fall-out, but his refusal to apologize stands in marked contrast to public statements of apology and regret made by Senator Brownback (who suffered no backlash and is now the Governor of Kansas), as well as the dignified apologies made by the heads of state in Canada and Australia, who publically apologized to their indigenous peoples in special sessions before parliament and indigenous leaders.

The most that can be said for our strange situation is: President Obama made oblique reference to the apology one year later on December 16, 2010, when he announced United States endorsement of the *Declaration* at a White House meeting with tribal leaders; however, his reference (to a "resolution passed by both parties in Congress, finally recognizing the sad and painful chapters in our shared history") omitted any word of apology, and he simply told the assembled tribal leaders: "No statement can undo the damage that was done."[50] This oblique remark falls short of the example provided by Kevin Gover, Assistant Secretary-Indian Affairs, Department of the Interior, during the Bush Administration. In 2000, upon the 175th anniversary of the establishment of the Bureau of Indian Affairs (BIA), the Assistant Secretary issued a formal apology to Indian people for the historical conduct of the BIA. Gover's elegant words provide an exemplary model. The president should study those words and the manner in which they were rendered.[51]

In short, the United States' obscure apology is stillborn. It was made, but never offered. Most Americans know nothing about it; and those that do are puzzled, if not put off in anger. In point of fact, the congressional apology is almost impossible to find, as it is an obscure provision buried deeply inside the mammoth Defense Department Appropriations Act. One perplexed tribal attorney wondered, "What kind of an apology is it when they don't tell the people they are apologizing to?"[52] To breathe life into the well-meant congressional apology and set a national healing process into motion, the wisdom traditions counsel the president to do three things. On behalf of the American people, the president should: (1) go to Indian Country, (2) publically deliver the national apology to the Native Peoples of the United States, with appropriate words of regret and apology, and (3) request them to forgive the nation for the misdeeds that are listed in the apology. Once those painful tasks are done and the apology is properly issued, the burden of carrying the healing process forward shifts to Native America. At that stage, the wisdom traditions will ask Native Americans to accept the apology and forgive the United States for the misdeeds, to advance the process, or refuse and live with the consequences of that decision. The above analysis concludes: the United States has initiated an apology process, but has not completed this step, and that is where we stand today.

3. Accepting the Apology; and Forgiving the Wrongdoer

For the reasons discussed above, the United States has not yet reached the acceptance and forgiveness stage in the healing process. Once the apology process produces a national apology that is properly offered to the Native Peoples of the United States, together with an appropriate forgiveness request, the working ingredients for the cathartic process can be set in motion and the burden will shift to Native America. At that stage, indigenous peoples must decide whether to accept the apology and render forgiveness to advance the healing process.

As indicated, forgiveness is a high spiritual virtue with immense healing power. Though it is a difficult gift to give, the wisdom traditions, dialogue, and a desire to heal the past can produce genuine forgiveness among the strong. "The weak can never forgive, forgiveness is the attribute of the strong," according to Gandhi; and the Native American peoples are among the strong. Their willingness to forgive has been demonstrated time and again by uniformed American Indian warriors in our nation's armed forces, as just one example.[53] These men and woman selflessly serve the nation at a higher rate than any other group. Their record tells a story of heroism on behalf of the nation, including payment of the ultimate sacrifice many times over; and this is voluntarily done without waiting for an apology or act of atonement. In Operation Desert Storm, American Indians went to war, while the Supreme Court stripped their religious liberty at home in the *Smith* decision, something an unforgiving people would never do.[54]

4. Acts of Atonement: The Process of Making Things Right

Step four stands towering before us. But it is well-mapped by the *Declaration*. The landmark human rights instrument was conceived for the very purpose of righting the historical wrongs of conquest and colonialism inherited by we who are living today. It plants the seeds for transformative change. The United States embarked upon the process of strengthening Native American rights many years ago in the tribal sovereignty movement, during the modern era of federal Indian law. Our nation's resolve is abundantly seen in President Nixon's Indian Self-Determination Policy, the many splendid acts of Congress, the elegant words and actions of our presidents, and in the stirring decisions of our courts rendered in their finest hour. In this, we do not have to look far to find the compassion of the American people or the vitality of our democratic institutions. The *Declaration* aids our march toward restorative justice by pinpointing the work that remains and providing standards for completing the task, so that all might stand in the light of justice.

5. Healing and Reconciliation

This can be a historic time in the growth of the nation. We have been given a rare opportunity to make things right. We can seize the chance for redemption that was beyond reach by our forbears, if we heed the wisdom from our ancestors and take the transformative steps that lead to reconciliation. That is the invitation offered by the *Declaration*. It affirms that "indigenous peoples are equal to all others, while recognizing the right of all peoples to be different, to consider themselves different, and to be respected as such," and "all peoples contribute to the diversity and richness of civilizations and cultures, which constitute the common heritage of humankind." The addition of these self-evident truths to our core values is a long-overdue amendment. It promises to bind indigenous and non-indigenous peoples into a more just union that completes a remarkable revolution in a unique land. To be sure, reconciliation between the conqueror and the conquered is one of the most difficult to achieve. But whenever we witness the rise of human rights among our peoples, the power of restorative justice found in the law of man is invariably at work with a higher power, human compassion. The amazing synergy produces the unforgettable moment that we experience, when justice is at hand.

Appendix
United Nations Declaration on the Rights of Indigenous Peoples

Resolution adopted by the General Assembly

[without reference to a Main Committee (A/61/L.67 and Add.1)]

61/295. United Nations Declaration on the Rights of Indigenous Peoples

The General Assembly,

Taking note of the recommendation of the Human Rights Council contained in its resolution 1/2 of 29 June 2006,* by which the Council adopted the text of the United Nations Declaration on the Rights of Indigenous Peoples,

Recalling its resolution 61/178 of 20 December 2006, by which it decided to defer consideration of and action on the Declaration to allow time for further consultations thereon, and also decided to conclude its consideration before the end of the sixty-first session of the General Assembly,

Adopts the United Nations Declaration on the Rights of Indigenous Peoples as contained in the annex to the present resolution.

107th plenary meeting
13 September 2007

Annex

United Nations Declaration on the Rights of Indigenous Peoples

The General Assembly,

Guided by the purposes and principles of the Charter of the United Nations,

---

* *See Official Records of the General Assembly, Sixty-first Session, Supplement No. 53* (A/61/53), part one, chap. II, sect. A.

and good faith in the fulfilment of the obligations assumed by States in accordance with the Charter,

Affirming that indigenous peoples are equal to all other peoples, while recognizing the right of all peoples to be different, to consider themselves different, and to be respected as such,

Affirming also that all peoples contribute to the diversity and richness of civilizations and cultures, which constitute the common heritage of humankind,

Affirming further that all doctrines, policies and practices based on or advocating superiority of peoples or individuals on the basis of national origin or racial, religious, ethnic or cultural differences are racist, scientifically false, legally invalid, morally condemnable and socially unjust,

Reaffirming that indigenous peoples, in the exercise of their rights, should be free from discrimination of any kind,

Concerned that indigenous peoples have suffered from historic injustices as a result of, inter alia, their colonization and dispossession of their lands, territories and resources, thus preventing them from exercising, in particular, their right to development in accordance with their own needs and interests,

Recognizing the urgent need to respect and promote the inherent rights of indigenous peoples which derive from their political, economic and social structures and from their cultures, spiritual traditions, histories and philosophies, especially their rights to their lands, territories and resources,

Recognizing also the urgent need to respect and promote the rights of indigenous peoples affirmed in treaties, agreements and other constructive arrangements with States,

Welcoming the fact that indigenous peoples are organizing themselves for political, economic, social and cultural enhancement and in order to bring to an end all forms of discrimination and oppression wherever they occur,

Convinced that control by indigenous peoples over developments affecting them and their lands, territories and resources will enable them to maintain and strengthen their institutions, cultures and traditions, and to promote their development in accordance with their aspirations and needs,

Recognizing that respect for indigenous knowledge, cultures and traditional practices contributes to sustainable and equitable development and proper management of the environment,

Emphasizing the contribution of the demilitarization of the lands and territories of indigenous peoples to peace, economic and social progress and development, understanding and friendly relations among nations and peoples of the world,

Recognizing in particular the right of indigenous families and communities to retain shared responsibility for the upbringing, training, education and well-being of their children, consistent with the rights of the child,

Considering that the rights affirmed in treaties, agreements and other constructive arrangements between States and indigenous peoples are, in some situations, matters of international concern, interest, responsibility and character,

Considering also that treaties, agreements and other constructive arrangements, and the relationship they represent, are the basis for a strengthened partnership between indigenous peoples and States,

Acknowledging that the Charter of the United Nations, the International Covenant on Economic, Social and Cultural Rights[*] and the International Covenant on Civil and Political Rights,[†] as well as the Vienna Declaration and Programme of Action,[‡] affirm the fundamental importance of the right to self-determination of all peoples, by virtue of which they freely determine their political status and freely pursue their economic, social and cultural development,

---

* See resolution 2200 A (XXI), annex.

† *Id.*

‡ A/CONF.157/24 (Part I), chap. III.

Bearing in mind that nothing in this Declaration may be used to deny any peoples their right to self-determination, exercised in conformity with international law,

Convinced that the recognition of the rights of indigenous peoples in this Declaration will enhance harmonious and cooperative relations between the State and indigenous peoples, based on principles of justice, democracy, respect for human rights, non-discrimination and good faith,

Encouraging States to comply with and effectively implement all their obligations as they apply to indigenous peoples under international instruments, in particular those related to human rights, in consultation and cooperation with the peoples concerned,

Emphasizing that the United Nations has an important and continuing role to play in promoting and protecting the rights of indigenous peoples,

Believing that this Declaration is a further important step forward for the recognition, promotion and protection of the rights and freedoms of indigenous peoples and in the development of relevant activities of the United Nations system in this field,

Recognizing and reaffirming that indigenous individuals are entitled without discrimination to all human rights recognized in international law, and that indigenous peoples possess collective rights which are indispensable for their existence, well-being and integral development as peoples,

Recognizing that the situation of indigenous peoples varies from region to region and from country to country and that the significance of national and regional particularities and various historical and cultural backgrounds should be taken into consideration,

Solemnly proclaims the following United Nations Declaration on the Rights of Indigenous Peoples as a standard of achievement to be pursued in a spirit of partnership and mutual respect:

Article 1

Indigenous peoples have the right to the full enjoyment, as a collective or as individuals, of all human rights and fundamental freedoms as recognized in the Charter of the United Nations, the Universal Declaration of Human Rights* and international human rights law.

Article 2

Indigenous peoples and individuals are free and equal to all other peoples and individuals and have the right to be free from any kind of discrimination, in the exercise of their rights, in particular that based on their indigenous origin or identity.

Article 3

Indigenous peoples have the right to self-determination. By virtue of that right they freely determine their political status and freely pursue their economic, social and cultural development.

Article 4

Indigenous peoples, in exercising their right to self-determination, have the right to autonomy or self-government in matters relating to their internal and local affairs, as well as ways and means for financing their autonomous functions.

Article 5

Indigenous peoples have the right to maintain and strengthen their distinct political, legal, economic, social and cultural institutions, while retaining their right to participate fully, if they so choose, in the political, economic, social and cultural life of the State.

Article 6

Every indigenous individual has the right to a nationality.

Article 7

1. Indigenous individuals have the rights to life, physical and mental integrity, liberty and security of person.

---

* Resolution 217 A (III).

2. Indigenous peoples have the collective right to live in freedom, peace and security as distinct peoples and shall not be subjected to any act of genocide or any other act of violence, including forcibly removing children of the group to another group.

Article 8

1. Indigenous peoples and individuals have the right not to be subjected to forced assimilation or destruction of their culture.

2. States shall provide effective mechanisms for prevention of, and redress for:

> *(a)* Any action which has the aim or effect of depriving them of their integrity as distinct peoples, or of their cultural values or ethnic identities;
>
> *(b)* Any action which has the aim or effect of dispossessing them of their lands, territories or resources;
>
> *(c)* Any form of forced population transfer which has the aim or effect of violating or undermining any of their rights;
>
> *(d)* Any form of forced assimilation or integration;
>
> *(e)* Any form of propaganda designed to promote or incite racial or ethnic discrimination directed against them.

Article 9

Indigenous peoples and individuals have the right to belong to an indigenous community or nation, in accordance with the traditions and customs of the community or nation concerned. No discrimination of any kind may arise from the exercise of such a right.

Article 10

Indigenous peoples shall not be forcibly removed from their lands or territories. No relocation shall take place without the free, prior and informed consent of the indigenous peoples concerned and after agreement on just and fair compensation and, where possible, with the option of return.

Article 11

1. Indigenous peoples have the right to practise and revitalize their cultural traditions and customs. This includes the right to maintain, protect and develop the past, present and future manifestations of their cultures, such as archaeological and historical sites, artefacts, designs, ceremonies, technologies and visual and performing arts and literature.

2. States shall provide redress through effective mechanisms, which may include restitution, developed in conjunction with indigenous peoples, with respect to their cultural, intellectual, religious and spiritual property taken without their free, prior and informed consent or in violation of their laws, traditions and customs.

Article 12

1. Indigenous peoples have the right to manifest, practise, develop and teach their spiritual and religious traditions, customs and ceremonies; the right to maintain, protect, and have access in privacy to their religious and cultural sites; the right to the use and control of their ceremonial objects; and the right to the repatriation of their human remains.

2. States shall seek to enable the access and/or repatriation of ceremonial objects and human remains in their possession through fair, transparent and effective mechanisms developed in conjunction with indigenous peoples concerned.

Article 13

1. Indigenous peoples have the right to revitalize, use, develop and transmit to future generations their histories, languages, oral traditions, philosophies, writing systems and literatures, and to designate and retain their own names for communities, places and persons.

2. States shall take effective measures to ensure that this right is protected and also to ensure that indigenous peoples can understand and be understood in political, legal and administrative proceedings, where necessary through the provision of interpretation or by other appropriate means.

Article 14

1. Indigenous peoples have the right to establish and control their educational

systems and institutions providing education in their own languages, in a manner appropriate to their cultural methods of teaching and learning.

2. Indigenous individuals, particularly children, have the right to all levels and forms of education of the State without discrimination.

3. States shall, in conjunction with indigenous peoples, take effective measures, in order for indigenous individuals, particularly children, including those living outside their communities, to have access, when possible, to an education in their own culture and provided in their own language.

Article 15

1. Indigenous peoples have the right to the dignity and diversity of their cultures, traditions, histories and aspirations which shall be appropriately reflected in education and public information.

2. States shall take effective measures, in consultation and cooperation with the indigenous peoples concerned, to combat prejudice and eliminate discrimination and to promote tolerance, understanding and good relations among indigenous peoples and all other segments of society.

Article 16

1. Indigenous peoples have the right to establish their own media in their own languages and to have access to all forms of non-indigenous media without discrimination.

2. States shall take effective measures to ensure that State-owned media duly reflect indigenous cultural diversity. States, without prejudice to ensuring full freedom of expression, should encourage privately owned media to adequately reflect indigenous cultural diversity.

Article 17

1. Indigenous individuals and peoples have the right to enjoy fully all rights established under applicable international and domestic labour law.

2. States shall in consultation and cooperation with indigenous peoples take

specific measures to protect indigenous children from economic exploitation and from performing any work that is likely to be hazardous or to interfere with the child's education, or to be harmful to the child's health or physical, mental, spiritual, moral or social development, taking into account their special vulnerability and the importance of education for their empowerment.

3. Indigenous individuals have the right not to be subjected to any discriminatory conditions of labour and, inter alia, employment or salary.

Article 18
Indigenous peoples have the right to participate in decision-making in matters which would affect their rights, through representatives chosen by themselves in accordance with their own procedures, as well as to maintain and develop their own indigenous decision-making institutions.

Article 19
States shall consult and cooperate in good faith with the indigenous peoples concerned through their own representative institutions in order to obtain their free, prior and informed consent before adopting and implementing legislative or administrative measures that may affect them.

Article 20
1. Indigenous peoples have the right to maintain and develop their political, economic and social systems or institutions, to be secure in the enjoyment of their own means of subsistence and development, and to engage freely in all their traditional and other economic activities.

2. Indigenous peoples deprived of their means of subsistence and development are entitled to just and fair redress.

Article 21
1. Indigenous peoples have the right, without discrimination, to the improvement of their economic and social conditions, including, inter alia, in the areas of education, employment, vocational training and retraining, housing, sanitation, health and social security.

2. States shall take effective measures and, where appropriate, special measures to ensure continuing improvement of their economic and social conditions. Particular attention shall be paid to the rights and special needs of indigenous elders, women, youth, children and persons with disabilities.

Article 22

1. Particular attention shall be paid to the rights and special needs of indigenous elders, women, youth, children and persons with disabilities in the implementation of this Declaration.

2. States shall take measures, in conjunction with indigenous peoples, to ensure that indigenous women and children enjoy the full protection and guarantees against all forms of violence and discrimination.

Article 23

Indigenous peoples have the right to determine and develop priorities and strategies for exercising their right to development. In particular, indigenous peoples have the right to be actively involved in developing and determining health, housing and other economic and social programmes affecting them and, as far as possible, to administer such programmes through their own institutions.

Article 24

1. Indigenous peoples have the right to their traditional medicines and to maintain their health practices, including the conservation of their vital medicinal plants, animals and minerals. Indigenous individuals also have the right to access, without any discrimination, to all social and health services.

2. Indigenous individuals have an equal right to the enjoyment of the highest attainable standard of physical and mental health. States shall take the necessary steps with a view to achieving progressively the full realization of this right.

Article 25

Indigenous peoples have the right to maintain and strengthen their distinctive spiritual relationship with their traditionally owned or otherwise occupied and used lands, territories, waters and coastal seas and other resources and to uphold their responsibilities to future generations in this regard.

Article 26

1. Indigenous peoples have the right to the lands, territories and resources which they have traditionally owned, occupied or otherwise used or acquired.

2. Indigenous peoples have the right to own, use, develop and control the lands, territories and resources that they possess by reason of traditional ownership or other traditional occupation or use, as well as those which they have otherwise acquired.

3. States shall give legal recognition and protection to these lands, territories and resources. Such recognition shall be conducted with due respect to the customs, traditions and land tenure systems of the indigenous peoples concerned.

Article 27

States shall establish and implement, in conjunction with indigenous peoples concerned, a fair, independent, impartial, open and transparent process, giving due recognition to indigenous peoples' laws, traditions, customs and land tenure systems, to recognize and adjudicate the rights of indigenous peoples pertaining to their lands, territories and resources, including those which were traditionally owned or otherwise occupied or used. Indigenous peoples shall have the right to participate in this process.

Article 28

1. Indigenous peoples have the right to redress, by means that can include restitution or, when this is not possible, just, fair and equitable compensation, for the lands, territories and resources which they have traditionally owned or otherwise occupied or used, and which have been confiscated, taken, occupied, used or damaged without their free, prior and informed consent.

2. Unless otherwise freely agreed upon by the peoples concerned, compensation shall take the form of lands, territories and resources equal in quality, size and legal status or of monetary compensation or other appropriate redress.

Article 29

1. Indigenous peoples have the right to the conservation and protection of the environment and the productive capacity of their lands or territories and resources. States shall establish and implement assistance programmes for

indigenous peoples for such conservation and protection, without discrimination.

2. States shall take effective measures to ensure that no storage or disposal of hazardous materials shall take place in the lands or territories of indigenous peoples without their free, prior and informed consent.

3. States shall also take effective measures to ensure, as needed, that programmes for monitoring, maintaining and restoring the health of indigenous peoples, as developed and implemented by the peoples affected by such materials, are duly implemented.

Article 30

1. Military activities shall not take place in the lands or territories of indigenous peoples, unless justified by a relevant public interest or otherwise freely agreed with or requested by the indigenous peoples concerned.

2. States shall undertake effective consultations with the indigenous peoples concerned, through appropriate procedures and in particular through their representative institutions, prior to using their lands or territories for military activities.

Article 31

1. Indigenous peoples have the right to maintain, control, protect and develop their cultural heritage, traditional knowledge and traditional cultural expressions, as well as the manifestations of their sciences, technologies and cultures, including human and genetic resources, seeds, medicines, knowledge of the properties of fauna and flora, oral traditions, literatures, designs, sports and traditional games and visual and performing arts. They also have the right to maintain, control, protect and develop their intellectual property over such cultural heritage, traditional knowledge, and traditional cultural expressions.

2. In conjunction with indigenous peoples, States shall take effective measures to recognize and protect the exercise of these rights.

Article 32

1. Indigenous peoples have the right to determine and develop priorities and strategies for the development or use of their lands or territories and other resources.

2. States shall consult and cooperate in good faith with the indigenous peoples concerned through their own representative institutions in order to obtain their free and informed consent prior to the approval of any project affecting their lands or territories and other resources, particularly in connection with the development, utilization or exploitation of mineral, water or other resources.

3. States shall provide effective mechanisms for just and fair redress for any such activities, and appropriate measures shall be taken to mitigate adverse environmental, economic, social, cultural or spiritual impact.

Article 33

1. Indigenous peoples have the right to determine their own identity or membership in accordance with their customs and traditions. This does not impair the right of indigenous individuals to obtain citizenship of the States in which they live.

2. Indigenous peoples have the right to determine the structures and to select the membership of their institutions in accordance with their own procedures.

Article 34

Indigenous peoples have the right to promote, develop and maintain their institutional structures and their distinctive customs, spirituality, traditions, procedures, practices and, in the cases where they exist, juridical systems or customs, in accordance with international human rights standards.

Article 35

Indigenous peoples have the right to determine the responsibilities of individuals to their communities.

Article 36

1. Indigenous peoples, in particular those divided by international borders, have the right to maintain and develop contacts, relations and cooperation, including activities for spiritual, cultural, political, economic and social purposes, with their own members as well as other peoples across borders.

2. States, in consultation and cooperation with indigenous peoples, shall take

effective measures to facilitate the exercise and ensure the implementation of this right.

Article 37

1. Indigenous peoples have the right to the recognition, observance and enforcement of treaties, agreements and other constructive arrangements concluded with States or their successors and to have States honour and respect such treaties, agreements and other constructive arrangements.

2. Nothing in this Declaration may be interpreted as diminishing or eliminating the rights of indigenous peoples contained in treaties, agreements and other constructive arrangements.

Article 38

States, in consultation and cooperation with indigenous peoples, shall take the appropriate measures, including legislative measures, to achieve the ends of this Declaration.

Article 39

Indigenous peoples have the right to have access to financial and technical assistance from States and through international cooperation, for the enjoyment of the rights contained in this Declaration.

Article 40

Indigenous peoples have the right to access to and prompt decision through just and fair procedures for the resolution of conflicts and disputes with States or other parties, as well as to effective remedies for all infringements of their individual and collective rights. Such a decision shall give due consideration to the customs, traditions, rules and legal systems of the indigenous peoples concerned and international human rights.

Article 41

The organs and specialized agencies of the United Nations system and other intergovernmental organizations shall contribute to the full realization of the provisions of this Declaration through the mobilization, inter alia, of financial cooperation and technical assistance. Ways and means of ensuring participation of indigenous peoples on issues affecting them shall be established.

Article 42
The United Nations, its bodies, including the Permanent Forum on Indigenous Issues, and specialized agencies, including at the country level, and States shall promote respect for and full application of the provisions of this Declaration and follow up the effectiveness of this Declaration.

Article 43
The rights recognized herein constitute the minimum standards for the survival, dignity and well-being of the indigenous peoples of the world.

Article 44
All the rights and freedoms recognized herein are equally guaranteed to male and female indigenous individuals.

Article 45
Nothing in this Declaration may be construed as diminishing or extinguishing the rights indigenous peoples have now or may acquire in the future.

Article 46
1. Nothing in this Declaration may be interpreted as implying for any State, people, group or person any right to engage in any activity or to perform any act contrary to the Charter of the United Nations or construed as authorizing or encouraging any action which would dismember or impair, totally or in part, the territorial integrity or political unity of sovereign and independent States.

2. In the exercise of the rights enunciated in the present Declaration, human rights and fundamental freedoms of all shall be respected. The exercise of the rights set forth in this Declaration shall be subject only to such limitations as are determined by law and in accordance with international human rights obligations. Any such limitations shall be non-discriminatory and strictly necessary solely for the purpose of securing due recognition and respect for the rights and freedoms of others and for meeting the just and most compelling requirements of a democratic society.

3. The provisions set forth in this Declaration shall be interpreted in accordance with the principles of justice, democracy, respect for human rights, equality, non-discrimination, good governance and good faith.

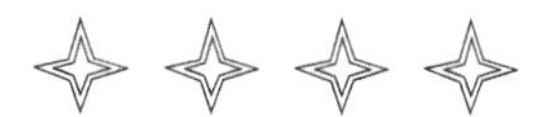

ENDNOTES

CHAPTER ONE: THE SEEDS OF CHANGE

1. Kirkpatrick Sale, *The Conquest of Paradise* (New York: Alfred A. Knopf 1990) at 3 (quoting words used by historian Francisco Lopez de Gómara in 1552 to describe the discovery of America).
2. *Brown v. Board of Education,* 347 U.S. 483 (1954).
3. General Assembly "Resolution 63/295: Declaration of the Rights of Indigenous Peoples" UN Doc A/61/67, Annex (13 September 2007).
4. See, Luis Rodriguez-Piñero Roya, "Where Appropriate': Monitoring/Implementing of Indigenous Peoples' Rights Under the Declaration," in Claire Charters and Rodolfo Stavenhagen (eds.), *Making the Declaration Work: The United Nations Declaration on the Rights of Indigenous Peoples* (International Work Group For Indigenous Affairs: Copenhagen 2009) at 320–372 (comparing the provisions of the *Declaration* with existing UN human rights treaties). This Spanish researcher concluded at 319: Analysis of these UN human rights standards and the jurisprudence of their monitoring bodies with regard to indigenous peoples clearly shows a significant synergy between general state human rights obligations and the rights affirmed in the Declaration.
5. Testimony of James Anaya before the Senate Committee on Indian Affairs, Oversight Hearing on Setting the Standard: Domestic Policy Implications of the UN Declaration on the Rights of Indigenous Peoples (June 9, 2011). The UN Special Rapporteur is also a professor of law who is widely considered a foremost specialist on the rights of indigenous peoples in international law. His groundbreaking treatise, *Indigenous Peoples In International Law* (New York, Oxford: Oxford University Press, 1996), remains the classic text on the subject.
6. For an authoritative analysis of the *Declaration's* legal status, *See,* S. James Anaya, *International Human Rights and Indigenous Peoples* (New York, NY: Aspen Publishers, 2009) at 65, 79–105. Chapter Four discusses the legal status of the *Declaration.*
7. Neil Jessup Newton (editor-in-chief), *Cohen's Handbook of Federal Indian Law* (2005 ed.), §5.07[1] at 457. *See also,* § 5.0[2](b) at 460–461 (on other non-binding UN resolutions), §5.07[3](b) at 480-481 (Draft UN Declaration on the Rights of Indigenous Peoples is not a legally binding convention or treaty). Even treaties or conventions that are not "self-executing" require implementing legislation to be enforceable in United States courts. *Id.* §5.07[4](a) at 490. Julian Burger agrees that the Declaration "is not binding on states" but points out that the basic principles espoused in the instrument are legally binding on states through other UN treaties and, at minimum, provide guidance to those treaty monitoring bodies in interpreting those treaties and conventions; and he urges that the rights contained in the Declaration be implemented in national laws, used in domestic courts, and given practical meaning through administrative changes. *See,* Julian Burger, "The UN Declaration on the Rights of Indigenous Peoples: From Advocacy to Implementation," in Stephen Allen & Alexandra Xanthaki (eds.) *Reflections on the UN Declaration on the Rights of Indigenous Peoples* (Oxford and Portland, OR: Hart Publishing, 2011) at 55.
8. Charters & Stavenhagen (2009) at 315 (United Kingdom's position).
9. *Id.* at 317.
10. *Cal et al v. Attorney General of Belize,* (Supreme Court of Belize, Claim No. 171, 2007), para 131.
11. *Cohen's Handbook of Federal Indian Law, supra,* §5.07[1] at 457–458. International customary law is a major source of binding international law that originates in international custom. The content of the norm is determined by the widespread practices of nations; and a customary law norm binds a nation unless it openly dissents from an international law standard while it is being developed. *Id.* at 458. In the United States, it is well established that rules of customary international law form part of the federal common law. *Id.* As such, it is applicable law in United States courts to the same extent as any other aspect of federal common law. *Id.* §5.07[4](a)[ii] at 491. *See also,* Erica-Irene Daes, "The UN Declaration on the Rights of Indigenous Peoples: Background and Appraisal," in Allen & Xanthaki (eds.) (2011) at 38; Anaya (2009) at 65 (the inclusion of human rights standards in a declaration are not binding on states unless they reflect customary international law).

12. *See,* note 12, *supra.*
13. *Cal et al v. Attorney General of Belize,* (Supreme Court of Belize, Claim Nos. 170 and 171, 2007) (incorporating the Declaration into Belize's domestic law); *Saramaka People v. Suriname* (Series C No. 172) Inter-American Court of Human Rights (IACHR) (Nov. 28, 2007), para. 131 (applying the Declaration's free, prior, and informed consent standards for the use of Native land). In addition, the Columbian Constitutional Court drew heavily upon the free, prior, and informed consent provisions of the then-Draft Declaration to decide cases in 2003 and 2006 regarding land demarcation and exploitation of natural resources. *See,* Constitutional Court of Columbia, Judgment SU.383/03 and Judgment T-880/2006, cited by Clive Baldwin and Cynthia Morel, "Using the United Nations Declaration on the Rights of Indigenous Peoples in Litigation," in Allen & Xanthaki (eds.) (2009) at 125, n. 12-13. Bolivia incorporated the Declaration into its domestic law through legislation in National Law 3760 enacted on November 7, 2007. The African Commission on Human and Peoples Rights also drew heavily from the Declaration to decide indigenous land rights in 2010. *Id.* at 125. Together, these developments comprise an emerging judicial trend toward establishing customary international law through incorporating the provisions of the Declaration into the domestic law of a growing number of affected nations and into international law applied by international courts around the world.
14. *Mabo v. Queensland,* 174 FLR 1, 58 (Australia High Court, 1992) (rejecting the doctrine of *Terra Nullius* and other unjust legal fictions embedded in aboriginal land rights law of Australia).
15. *Black's Law Dictionary* (Abridged 9th Ed. 2010) defines "human rights" as: The freedoms, immunities, and benefits that, according to modern values (esp. at an international level), all human beings should be able to claim as a matter of right in the society in which they live.
16. The words of Alexander Hamilton, quoted in Jordan J. Paust, "On Human Rights: The Use of Human Rights Precepts In U.S. History And The Right To An Effective Remedy In Domestic Courts," 10 Mich. J. Intl. L. 543 (1989).
17. *Id.* at. 543.
18. *Id.* at 552-553.
19. *Id.* at 546-570.
20. *See,* Newt Gingrich, *A Nation Like No Other: Why American Exceptionalism Matters* (Regnery Publishing Co., 2010).
21. *See,* Jack F. Trope and Walter Echo-Hawk, "The Native American Graves Protection and Repatriation Act: Background and Legislative History," 24 Az. S. L. J. 35, 57–58 (1992).
22. Paust (1987) at 572-611.
23. *Fletcher v. Peck,* 10 U.S. 87, 133 (1810), quoted in Paust (1987) at 574.
24. Paust (1987) at 650.
25. *Blacks Law Dictionary* (2010) at 1107.
26. *Oxford English Dictionary,* online version: http://dictionary.oed.com.
27. Quoted by Federico Lenzerini, "Reparations for Indigenous Peoples in International and Comparative Law: An Introduction," in Federico Lenzerini (ed.), *Reparations for Indigenous Peoples: International & Comparative Perspectives* (Oxford Univ. Press, 2008) at 3.
28. *Id.* at 8.
29. Dinah Shelton, "Reparations for Indigenous Peoples: The Present Value of Past Wrongs," in Lenzerini (ed.) (2008) at 64–69.
30. Lenzerini (2008) at 13.
31. Claire Charters, "Reparations for Indigenous Peoples: Global and International Instruments and Institutions," in Lenzerini (2008) at 163–195.
32. Patricia N. Limerick, *The Legacy of Conquest: The Unbroken Past of the American West* (New York: W.W. Norton & Co., 1987) at 17–18.
33. *Johnson v. M'Intosh,* 21 U.S. 543, 572, 588 (1823).
34. *Id.* at 588–593.
35. *Cherokee Nation v. Georgia,* 30 U.S. 1, 20–21 (1831) (J.J., concurring).
36. *Id.* at 21, 23–24.
37. *Lone Wolf v. Hitchcock,* 187 U.S. 553, 565–66 (1903) (quoting *Beecher v. Wetherby,* 95 U.S. 525).
38. *Tee-Hit-Ton Indians v. United States,* 348 U.S. 272, 281 (1955) (italics supplied).
39. *Id.* at 289–91.
40. *Employment Division v. Smith,* 494 U.S. 872 (1990).

41. *See,* discussion in Walter Echo-Hawk, *In The Courts of the Conqueror: The 10 Worst Indian Law Cases Ever Decided* (Golden: Fulcrum Publishing, 2010) at 273–322.
42. John Delaney, "Police Power Absolutism and Nullifying the Free Exercise Clause: A Critique of *Oregon v. Smith*," 25 Ind. L. Rev. 71, 126 (1991).
43. *Id.* at 132–134 (footnotes omitted).
44. *Cohen's Handbook of Federal Indian Law* (1982 ed.) at 144–145, 205. *See also,* Echo-Hawk (2010) at 429.
45. *Oliphant v. Suquamish Indian Tribe,* 435 U.S. 191 (1978). *See also, Duro v. Reina,* 495 U.S. 676 (1990). *See, generally,* Curtis G. Berkey, "International Law and Domestic Courts: Enhancing Self-Determination for Indigenous Peoples," 5 HARV. HUM. RTS. J. 65 (1992) at 70–75.
46. *State v. Foreman,* 16 Tenn. 256, 266 (1835).
47. Gingrich (2011).
48. Theodore Roosevelt, *The Winning of the West, Vol. I* (New York: G.P. Putnam's Sons, 1895) at 90.
49. *State v. Foreman,* 16 Tenn. 256, 1835 WL 945, *12 (Tenn.).
50. David C. Williams, "In Praise of Guilt: How the Yearning for Moral Purity Blocks Reparations for Native Americans," in Lenzerini (2008) at 229–249.
51. *Id.* at 248.
52. *Id.*
53. *Id.* at 249.
54. *Id.* at 249.
55. Nicholas A. Robinson, "'Minimum Standards:' The UN Declaration on the Rights of Indigenous Peoples," PACE ENVRN'L L. R. 346, 348 (2010)
56. *See, e.g.,* Robert A. Williams, Jr., *Like a Loaded Weapon: The Rehnquist Court, Indian Rights, and the Legal History of Racism in America* (Minneapolis: Univ. of Minnesota Press, 2005); Robert J. Miller, "The Discovery Doctrine in American Indian Law," 42 Idaho L. Rev. 2 (No. 1, 2005); David H. Getches, "Beyond Indian Law: The Rehnquist Court's Pursuit Of State's Rights, Color-Blind Justice, and Mainstream Values," 86 Minn. L. Rev. 267 (2001); Philip P. Frickey, "A Common Law for Our Age of Colonialism: The Judicial Divestiture of Indian Tribal Authority over Nonmembers," 109 Yale L. Rev. J. 1 (October, 1999); David H. Getches, "Conquering the Cultural Frontier: The New Subjectivism of the Supreme Court in Indian Law," 84 California L. Rev. 1574 (1996); Robert N. Clinton, "Redressing The Legacy of Conquest: A Vision Quest for a Decolonized Federal Indian Law," 46 Arkansas L. Rev. 77 (1993); Robert A. Williams, Jr., *The American Indian in Western Legal Thought: The Discourses of Conquest,* (New York: Oxford Univ. Press, 1990).
57. Matthew L.M. Fletcher, "The Tenth Justice Lost in Indian Country," Legal Studies Research Papers Series, Research Paper No. 07–12 (Michigan State University College of Law) (http://ssrn.com/abstract=xxxxxx); Walter R. Echo-Hawk, *In The Courts of the Conqueror: The 10 Worst Indian Law Cases Ever Decided* (Fulcrum Press, 2010).

CHAPTER TWO: THE MAKING OF THE DECLARATION

1. Chief Wilton Littlechild, "Consistent Advocacy: Treaty Rights and UN Declaration," in Jackie Hartley, Paul Joffe, and Jennifer Preston (eds.), *Realizing the UN Declaration on the Rights of Indigenous Peoples* (Saskatoon: Purich Publishing, Ltd., 2010) at 112.
2. Energy and Water Development Appropriations Act, Pub. Law No. 96–69 (September 28, 1979), quoted in *Sequoyah v. Tennessee Valley Authority,* 620 F.2d 1159, 1161 (6th Cir. 1980).
3. *Sequoyah, supra,* 620 F.2d at 1161.
4. *See, e.g.,* Claire Charters and Rodolfo Stavenhagen (eds.), *Making the Declaration Work: The United Nations Declaration on the Rights of Indigenous Peoples* (Copenhagen: International Work Group for Indigenous Affairs, 2009).
5. S. James Anaya, *Indigenous Peoples In International Law* (New York, Oxford: Oxford Univ. Press, 1996) at 20–21 (There was a "categorical exclusion of indigenous peoples as subjects of international law" and they "had no status or rights in international law.").
6. S. James Anaya, *International Human Rights and Indigenous Peoples* (New York: Aspen Publishers, 2009) at 37–50.
7. Scholars have thoroughly studied the use of early international law to colonize indigenous peoples and analyzed how nefarious doctrines created in medieval times continue to plague Native

Americans today, as unjust vestiges from a bygone era. *See, e.g.,* Walter R. Echo-Hawk, *In The Courts of the Conqueror: The 10 Worst Indian Law Cases Ever Decided* (Golden, Colorado: Fulcrum Publishing, 2010) at 15–22, 43–51; Tim Alan Garrison, *The Legal Ideology of Removal: The Southern Judiciary and the Sovereignty of Native American Nations* (Athens: Univ. of Georgia Press, 2002) at 60–71; Robert N. Clinton, "Redressing the Legacy of Conquest: A Vision Quest for a Decolonized Federal Indian Law," 46 Arkansas L. Rev. 77 (1993); Robert A. Williams, Jr., "Encounters on the Frontiers of International Human Rights Law: Redefining the Terms of Indigenous Peoples' Survival in the World," 1990 Duke L. J. 660 (1990); Robert A. Williams, Jr., *The American Indian in Western Legal Thought: The Discourses of Conquest* (New York: Oxford Univ. Press, 1990); Robert A. Williams, Jr., "The Algebra of Federal Indian Law: The Hard Trial of Decolonizing and Americanizing the Whiteman's Indian Jurisprudence," 1986 Wisconsin L. Rev. 219 (1986).

8. Anaya (2009) at 37.
9. UN General Assembly Declaration on the Granting of Independence to Colonial Countries, G.A. Res. 1514 (Dec. 14, 1960).
10. *Id.,* 2, 5.
11. Siegfried Wiessner, "Indigenous Sovereignty: A Reassessment in Light of the UN Declaration on the Rights of Indigenous Peoples," 41 Vand. J. Transnational L. 1141, 1150–1151 (2008) (footnotes omitted).
12. Erica-Irene Daes, "The UN Declaration on the Rights of Indigenous Peoples: Background and Appraisal," in Allen & Xanthaki (2011) at 11.
13. Cobo's 1984 report, "The Problem of Discrimination against Indigenous Populations," UN Doc E/CN.4/Sub. 2/1986/7/Add.4.
14. Quoted by Valerie Taliman, "A Voice for the Unheard," in Indian Country Today (Vol. 1, Issue 17, May 18, 2011) at 26.
15. The *Universal Declaration of Human Rights* (1948) presented a comprehensive human rights vision for all of humanity. Its provisions are codified in over a dozen core treaties and conventions ratified by a majority of the world's nations. Together, they form an imposing body of modern international human rights law. The codifying treaties and conventions include the *International Convention on the Elimination of All Forms of Racial Discrimination* (1965) (CERD); *International Bill of Human Rights* (1966, 1976); *International Covenant on Civil and Political Rights* (1966) (ICCPR); *International Covenant on Economic, Social, and Cultural Rights* (1966) (ICESCR); *Convention on the Elimination of All Forms of Discrimination against Woman* (1979); and *Convention against Torture* (1984) (CAT). The United States ratified the *Universal Declaration of Human Rights.* But it has ratified only a few codifying treaties, such as, the ICCPR (ratified 1992), CERD (ratified 1994), and the CAT (ratified 1994). Each ratification states that the treaty is not self-executing in the United States.
16. *ILO Convention No. 169* (1989), ¶4. This is a legally binding international instrument, which has been ratified by twenty nations (not including the United States). It deals specifically with the rights of indigenous and tribal peoples. Once ratified, a country has one year to align its laws and policies to the Convention and, under the terms of the Convention, ratifying countries are subject to monitoring and supervision in implementing the instrument. *See,* ILO summary of Convention No. 169 (available at: *http*://www.ilo.org/indigenous/Conventions/no169/lang--en/index.htm)
17. S. James Anaya, Report of the Special Rapporteur on the Human Rights and Fundamental Freedoms of Indigenous Peoples (Human Rights Council), UN Doc. A/HRC/9/9, (Aug. 11, 2008), 18–33. (Available at: http://papers.ssrn.com/sol3/papers.cfm?abstract_id=1242451) (hereinafter referred to as "Report of the Special Rapporteur (2008)").
18. Andrea Carmen, "International Indian Treaty Council Report From The Battle Field—The Struggle For The Declaration," in Charters and Stavenhagen (2009) at 86.
19. Kenneth Deer, "Reflections on the Development, Adoption, and Implementation of the UN Declaration on the Rights of Indigenous Peoples," in Hartley, Joffe, and Preston (eds.) (2010) at 18.
20. United Nations Declaration on the Rights of Indigenous Peoples, with an introduction by Robert T. Coulter, Executive Director of the Indian Law Resource Center (Indian Law Resource Center, Dec. 16, 2010) at 1.

21. Testimony of Robert T. Coulter before the Senate Committee on Indian Affairs, Hearing on "Setting The Standard: Domestic Implications of the UN Declaration On The Rights Of Indigenous Peoples" (June 9, 2011) at 1.
22. Anaya (1996). The second edition of this important treatise was published in 2004.
23. Anaya (2009) at 12, 14.
24. Report of the Special Rapporteur (2008), 18–43.
25. *See, .e.g.* Robert A. Williams, Jr., *Like A Loaded Weapon: The Rehnquist Court, Indian Rights, and The Legal History of Racism in America* (Minneapolis: University of Minnesota, 2006); "Encounters on the Frontiers of International Human Rights Law: Redefining the Terms of Indigenous Peoples' Survival in the World," 1990 Duke L. J. 660; "The Algebra of Federal Indian Law: The Hard Trial of Decolonizing and Americanizing the White Man's Jurisprudence," 1986 Wis. L. Rev. 210.
26. Except for the U.S. statement and New Zealand statement (http://www.parliament.nz/en-NZ/PB/Debates/Debates/6/5/a/49HansD_20100420_00000071-Ministerial-Statements-UN-Declaration-on.htm), these statements are taken from Hartley, Joffe, and Preston (eds.) (2010) at 209–217.

CHAPTER THREE: MOUNTING THE BIG HORSE

1. Story told to the author by his grandfather, the late Charles (Babe) Shunatona. Though I am an enrolled member of the Pawnee Nation, I am also a descendent of the Otoe-Missouri Tribe through my grandmother, Lucille (Shunatona) Echo-Hawk.
2. Art. 43, United Nations Declaration on the Rights of Indigenous Peoples (hereinafter cited in these endnotes as "UNDRIP').
3. S. James Anaya, Report of the Special Rapporteur on the Human Rights and Fundamental Freedoms of Indigenous Peoples (Human Rights Council), UN Doc. A/HRC/9/9, (Aug. 11, 2008) (hereinafter referred to as "Report of the Special Rapporteur (2008)") 40. (available at: http://papers.ssrn.com/sol3/papers.cfm?abstract_id=1242451).
4. UN Permanent Forum on Indigenous Issues, Frequently Asked Questions: Declaration on the Rights of Indigenous Peoples (http://www.un.org/esa/socdev/unpfii/en/declaration.html). The legal status of the Declaration as a binding instrument is examined *infra*. Though not binding in the same way that treaties are, nations are not expected to disregard the Declaration, because its provisions are related to (1) existing human rights obligations, (2) general principles of international law, and (3) the normative behavior of a growing number of states. As a result, some scholars, courts, and international bodies have determined that at least some provisions reflect existing customary international law.
5. *See,* cases cited in Chapter One, n. 12, *supra.*
6. Brenda Gunn, *Understanding and Implementing the UN Declaration on the Rights of Indigenous Peoples: An Introductory Handbook* (Winnipeg: Indigenous Bar Association, 2011) at 8 (citing Jackie Hartley, Paul Joffe and Jennifer Preston, "From Development to Implementation: An Ongoing Journey" in Hartley, Joffe, and Preston (eds.), *Realizing the UN Declaration on the Rights of Indigenous Peoples: Triumph, Hope and Action* (Saskatoon: Purich Publishing Ltd. 2010) at 12.
7. 6, UNDRIP.
8. 7–8, UNDRIP.
9. 2, UNDRIP.
10. 3, 5, UNDRIP.
11. 4, UNDRIP.
12. *Worcester v. Georgia,* 31 U.S. 515 (1832).
13. 18, UNDRIP.
14. 11, UNDRIP.
15. *See, e.g.,* Walter Echo-Hawk, "Under Native American Skies," 26 The George Wright Forum No. 3 (2009) at 58–79.
16. 15, 19, UNDRIP.
17. S. James Anaya, *Indigenous Peoples In International Law* (New York, Oxford: Oxford Univ. Press, 1996) at 75.
18. S. James Anaya, "The Right of Indigenous Peoples to Self-Determination in the Post-Declaration

Era," in Claire Charters and Rodolfo Stavenhagen (eds.), *Making the Declaration Work: The United Nations Declaration on the Rights of Indigenous Peoples* (Copenhagen: International Work Group for Indigenous Affairs, 2009) at 187.

19. The UN conventions and multilateral treaties include Art.1, *United Nations Charter* (UN purpose is to develop friendly relations among nations based on principles of equality and "self-determination of peoples"); Art. 1, *Covenant on Economic, Social and Cultural Rights* ("All peoples have the right of self-determination. By virtue of that right they freely determine their political status and freely pursue their economic, social and cultural development."); Art. 1, *Covenant on Civil and Political Rights* (all peoples have a right to self-determination, including the right to freely determine their political status and pursue their economic, social and cultural goals).
20. Article 3 is linked to Articles 4 and 5, and many others as well, including Articles 18–20, 27, 34–36, and 46 are linked to the self-determination principle. *See*, International Law Association (2010), *supra* n. 26, at 9–16.
21. Art. 46(1), UNDRIP.
22. Anaya (2009), *supra* n. 19, at 189.
23. Federico Lenzerini, "Sovereignty Revisited: International Law and Parallel Sovereignty of Indigenous Peoples," 42 TEX. INT'L L.J. 155, 189 (2006). *See also*, Siegfried Wiessner, "Indigenous Sovereignty: A Reassessment in Light of the UN Declaration on the Rights of Indigenous Peoples," 41 VAND. J. TRANS'L L. 1141, 1166–1170 (2008).
24. International Law Association (2010) at 10–16.
25. Vine Deloria, Jr., "Self-Determination and the Concept of Sovereignty," in John R. Wunder (ed.), *Native American Sovereignty* (1996) at 123 (quoted in Wiessner (2008) at 1171).
26. This pervasive problem in studied in Walter Echo-Hawk, *In The Courts of the Conqueror: The 10 Worst Indian Law Cases Ever Decided* (Golden: Fulcrum Publishers, 2010)
27. Eugene Linden, "Lost Tribes, Lost Knowledge," *Time* (Sept. 23, 1991), pp. 46–56.
28. These provisions correspond to well-established standards of customary international law. *See*, International Law Association (2010) at 16–17.
29. International Law Association (2010) at 19.
30. Articles 1 and 4, UNESCO *Universal Declaration on Cultural Diversity* (2001), available at: –http://portal.unesco.org/en/ev.php-URL_ID=13179&URL_DO=DO_TOPIC&URL_SECTION=201.html
31. International Law Association (2010) at 16.
32. *Id.* at 16–20.
33. Anaya (2009), *supra* n. 5, at 100.
34. International Law Association (2010) at 27.
35. *Id.* at 27–28, notes 149–164.
36. Andrea Carmen, "The Right to Free, Prior, and Informed Consent: A Framework for Harmonious Relations, and New Processes for Redress," in Jackie Hartley, Paul Joffe, and Jennifer Preston (eds.), *Realizing the UN Declaration on the Rights of Indigenous Peoples: Triumph, Hope, and Action* (Saskatoon: Purich Publishing, 2010) at 124–145.
37. Helen Quane, "New Directions for Self-Determination and Participatory Rights?," in Allen & Xanthaki (2011) at 278–279.
38. Scholars are already coming to grips with this problem and providing recommendations. *See, e.g.*, Akilah Jenga Kinnison, "Indigenous Consent: Rethinking U.S. Consultation Policies in Light of the U.N. Declaration on the Rights of Indigenous Peoples," 53 Ariz. L. Rev. 1301 (2011).
39. International Law Association (2010) at 28.
40. 8, UNDRIP.
41. 15, UNDRIP.
42. 24, UNDRIP.
43. Report of the Special Rapporteur (2008), 46.
44. *See*, The Republic of Bolivia, National Law No. 3760, as amended by National Law No. 3897 (Rights of Native Peoples), 26 June, 2008 (cited in International Law Association (2011) at 29, n. 115).
45. Joint Statement of Indigenous World Association, et al. to Expert Mechanism on the Rights of Indigenous Peoples, Fourth Session, Geneva, 11–15 July 2011, Agenda Item 5: Implementation

of the UN Declaration on the Rights of Indigenous Peoples (cited in International Law Association (2011) at 29, n. 113).
46. Anaya (2009), *supra* n. 5, at 114.

CHAPTER FOUR: LEGAL STATUS OF THE DECLARATION

1. *Cohen's Handbook of Federal Indian Law* (2005 ed.), § 5.07 at 456.
2. *Johnson v. M'Intosh*, 21 U.S. 543 (1823).
3. *Cherokee Nation v. Georgia*, 30 U.S. 1 (1831).
4. *Worcester v. Georgia*, 31 U.S. 515 (1832).
5. *Cohen's, supra*, n. 1.
6. *See, Filartiga v. Pena-Irala*, 630 F. 2d 876, 881 (2nd Cir., 1980).
7. *See, Mabo v. Queensland*, 174 FLR 1, 42 (Australia High Court, 1992).
8. Curtis A. Bradley and Jack L. Goldsmith, "Customary International Law As Federal Common Law: A Critique Of The Modern Position," 10 Harv. L. Rev. 816, 822 (No. 4, 1997); *Cohen's*, § 5.07[4][a].
9. *See, e.g.*, International Law Association, Interim Report, "Rights of Indigenous Peoples," The Hague Conference (2010) at 43 ("Although by its nature UNDRIP, just like any other declaration of principles, cannot be considered as a binding legal instrument, the question arises as to whether and to what extent the text of the Declaration corresponds to established general international law as a whole some of its key provisions can reasonably be considered as corresponding to established principles of general international law, therefore implying the existence of equivalent and parallel international obligations to which States are bound to comply with."); Julian Burger, "The UN Declaration on the Rights of Indigenous Peoples: From Advocacy to Implementation," in Stephen Allen & Alexandra Xanthaki, (eds.), *Reflections on the UN Declaration on the Rights of Indigenous Peoples* (Oxford: Hart Publishing, 2011) at 55 (The Declaration is "not binding on states" but the basic principles are binding on states through other international instruments); *Cohen's*, §5.07[1] at 457 ("a declaration is generally considered an aspirational statement that is not legally binding and not directly enforceable in United States courts"), § 5.07 [3}(b) at 480–481 (The Draft UN Declaration on the Rights of Indigenous Peoples is 'not a legally binding convention or treaty."); Robert T. Coulter, "The U.N. Declaration on the Rights of Indigenous Peoples: A Historic Change in International Law," 45 Idaho L. Rev. 539, 546 (2009) ("The Declaration is a non-binding instrument, meaning that countries are not, strictly speaking, legally bound to recognize the rights in the Declaration."); S. James Anaya, *International Human Rights and Indigenous Peoples* (Aspen Publishers 2009) at 65, 79 (UN declarations are not legally binding, but they do carry some measure of authority when invoked; and some provisions of the UN Declaration on the Rights of Indigenous Peoples might be enforceable to the extent that they relate to international norms and treaty obligations found elsewhere in international human rights law); Stefania Errico, "The Draft UN Declaration on the Rights of Indigenous Peoples: An Overview," 7 Hum. Rts. L. Rev. 741, 745–746 (2007) (reprinted in Anaya (2009) at 65) (The standards in the Declaration "are not legally binding on States, unless they reflect customary international law.")
10. *See*, n. 9, *supra*. *See also*, 21, 24 and Arts. 38–40, 42–43, United Nations Declaration on the Rights of Indigenous Peoples (hereinafter, "*Declaration*").
11. Luis Rodriquez-Pinero Royo, "Where Appropriate: Monitoring/Implementing of Indigenous Peoples' Rights Under the Declaration," in Claire Charters and Rodolfo Stavenhagen (eds.), *Making the Declaration Work: The United Nations Declaration on the Rights of Indigenous Peoples* (Copenhagen: International Work Group For Indigenous Affairs, 2009) at 319.
12. A "state" in the international context refers to a "nation" (such as the United States) and not its political subdivisions. The terms are interchangeable.
13. International Law Association (2010) at 51–52. *See also*, Siegfried Wiessner, "Indigenous Sovereignty: A Reassessment in Light of the UN Declaration on the Rights of Indigenous Peoples," 41 Vand. J. Transnational L. 1141, 1157 n. 105 (2008) (citing Siegfried Wiessner, "Rights and Status of Indigenous Peoples: A Global Comparative and International Legal Analysis," 12 HARV. HUM. RTS. J. 57, 127 (1999).
14. Wiessner (2008) at 1147 (footnotes omitted).

15. *See*, n. 10, *supra*.
16. Report of the Special Rapporteur on the Situation of human rights and fundamental freedoms of indigenous peoples, S. James Anaya, "The Human Rights of Indigenous Peoples in Light of the New Declaration, and the Challenge of Making them Operative," Human Rights Council (Aug. 5, 2008), 45–46 (footnotes omitted).
17. *Id.*, 45–59.
18. *Id.*, 59.
19. Testimony of James Anaya, UN Special Rapporteur on the Rights of Indigenous Peoples, before Committee on Indian Affairs, Oversight Hearing on Setting the Standard: Domestic Policy Implications of the UN Declaration on the Rights of Indigenous Peoples (June 9, 2011); Anaya (2009) at 79.
20. Quoted in *Sosa v. Alvarez-Machain,* 542 U.S. 692, 714 (2004).
21. *Id.* at 714–715.
22. J. L. Brierly, *The Law of Nations* (New York and Oxford: Oxford University Press, 1963) at 1.
23. *Id.* at vii–viii. *See also,* discussion in chapter two.
24. *Black's Law Dictionary* (9th ed., 2010). *Black's* definition of modern "international law" comports with the definition in RESTATEMENT (THIRD) OF THE FOREIGN RELATIONS LAW OF THE UNITED STATES (1987), §101 (hereinafter, "RESTATMENT (THIRD)"): "rules and regulations of general application dealing with the conduct of states and international organizations and with their relations inter se, as well as with some of their relations with persons, whether natural or judicial."
25. *Filartiga v. Pena-Irala,* 630 F.2d at 885.
26. *Id.* at 881. *See also, UN Charter,* Art. 55–56; and *Declaration,* 1, 14, 16.
27. Wiessner, (2008) at 1148–1149 (2008) (footnotes omitted).
28. Bradley & Goldsmith (1997) at 818, 831.
29. *Kiobel v. Royal Dutch Petroleum Co.,* 621 F.3d 111, 118 (2nd Cir. 2010).
30. Siegfried Wiessner, "Rights and Status of Indigenous Peoples: A Global Comparative and International Legal Analysis," 12 HARV. HUM RTS. J. 57, 125–126. (1999).
31. *Id.* (footnotes omitted). *See, also,* Jordan J. Paust, "On Human Rights: The Use Of Human Rights Precepts In U.S. History And The Right To An Effective Remedy In Domestic Courts," 10 Mich. J. Int'l. L. 543, 628 (1989).
32. Bradley & Goldsmith (1997) at 838.
33. *Cohen's,* 5.07[1] at 457–458; Bradley and Goldsmith (1997) at 817 ("[T]here are two principal sources of international law: treaties and [customary international law]. Treaties are express agreements among nations. [Customary international law] by contrast, is the law of the international community that 'results from a general and consistent practice of states followed by them from a sense of legal obligation.'") (footnotes omitted).
34. *Cohen's,* §5.07[4][a][i] at 489 (footnotes omitted).
35. *The Paquete Habana,* 175 U.S. 677 (1900); *Tel-Oren v. Libyan Arab Republic,* 726 F.2d 774, 797 (D.C. Cir. 1984).
36. *Filartiga v. Pena-Irala,* 630 F.2d at 880 (citing *U.S. v. Smith,* 153, 160–161 (1820).
37. *Fernandez v. Wilkinson,* 505 F. Supp. 787, 798 (D. Kan. 1980), *aff'd on other grds.,* 654 F.2d 1382 (10th Cir. 1981).
38. *Cohen's,* § 5.07[1] at 457.
39. *Id. See also,* U.S. Const., Art. VI, §2.
40. *Cohen's,* 5.07[4][a] at 490–491.
41. *Id.* at 490.
42. *Foster and Elam v. Neilson,* 27 U.S. 253 (1829). *See also,* Wiessner (1999) at 125 n. 44.
43. *Santovincenzo v. Egan,* 284 U.S. 30, 40 (1931); *Asakura v. City of Seattle,* 255 U.S. 332, 341 (1924) (A valid treaty "operates of itself without the aid of any legislation, state or national; and it will be applied and given effect by the courts."); *Foster v. Neilson,* 27 U.S. 253, 314 (1829) (A self-executing treaty is "equivalent to an act of the legislature, whenever it operates of itself without aid of any legislative provision," whereas legislation is needed to give effect to a non-self-executing treaty.); *Spiess v. Itoh & Co.,* 643 F.2d 353, 356 (5th Cir. 1981). *See also,* Bradley and Goldsmith (1997) at 858 n. 276 and accompanying text (citing RESTATEMENT (THIRD), III(3)).

44. *Frolova v. USSR*, 761 F.2d 370, 373-374 (7th Cir. 1985) (The factors include: the language and purposes of the treaty, circumstances surrounding its execution, the nature of the obligations imposed, the implications of permitting a private cause of action, and the availability and feasibility of alternative enforcement mechanisms.).
45. *Cohen's*, §5.07[4][a] at 491–492. *See also*, RESTATEMENT (THIRD), §III ("In general, agreements that can be readily given effect by executive or judicial bodies, federal or state, without further legislation, are deemed self-executing, unless a contrary intent is manifest.").
46. *Id.* at 490 ("A non-self-executing treaty requires implementing legislation to make it operative within the United States.") (citing *Foster v. Neilson, supra*). *See also*, notes 30–31.
47. *Medellin v. Texas*, 552 U.S. 491, 504–505 (2008).
48. *Id.* at 525-526. However, the President may comply with treaty obligations "by some other means, so long as they are consistent with the Constitution" (*id.* at 529), presumable by executive branch orders, regulations, policies, and practices.
49. *Cohen's*, 5.07[4][a] at 491.
50. *Id*, 5.07[1] at 457.
51. Brenda Gunn, "Understanding and Implementing the UN Declaration on the Rights of Indigenous Peoples: An Introductory Handbook," (Indigenous Bar Association: University of Manitoba, Faculty of Law, 2011) at 7 (quoting the United Nations Permanent Forum on Indigenous Issues, Frequently Asked Questions of the United Nations Declaration of the Rights of Indigenous Peoples].
52. *Filartiga v. Pena-Irala*, 630 F.2d at 882–884 (The Universal Declaration of Human Rights evidences universal agreement among nations that the prohibition against torture has become part of customary international law).
53. *Cohen's*, §5.07[3][b] at 480–481 (Draft UN Declaration on the Rights of Indigenous Peoples is not a legally binding convention or treaty.). *See also*, n. 9, *supra*.
54. *Declaration*, 21, 24.
55. *Cohen's*, §5.07[2][at 459–472. *See also*, Discussion in Chapter Three.
56. *Filartiga v. Pena-Irala*, 630 F.2d at 882–884 (The Universal Declaration of Human Rights evidences universal agreement among nations that the prohibition against torture has become part of customary international law).
57. 1, 16 and Arts. 1, 46, *Declaration*.
58. *Universal Declaration of Human Rights*, G.A. Res. 217A, U.N. GAOR, 3rd Sess., 67th plen. mtg., U.N. Doc. A/810 (III) (1948).
59. *International Convention on the Elimination of All Forms of Racial Discrimination*, 660 U.N.T.S. 171, *reprinted in* Basic Documents in International Law 311 (Ian Brownlie, ed., 4th ed., Clarendon Press, 1995) (CERD).
60. *International Covenant on Civil and Political Rights*, 999 U.N.T.S. 171, *reprinted in* Basic Documents in International Law 311 (Ian Brownlie, ed., 4th ed., Clarendon Press, 1995) (ICCPR).
61. *See*, Office of the United Nations High Commissioner for Human Rights, "The United Nations Human Rights Treaty System: An Introduction to the core human rights treaties and the treaty bodies" (Fact Sheet No. 30).
62. For a summary of selected UN human rights treaties and their status in the United States, see: http://academic.udayton.edu/race/06hrights/unitednations/USStatus.htm (last checked January 30, 2012). *See also*, Bradley and Goldsmith (1997) at 869–870.
63. Bradley & Goldsmith (1997) at 870.
64. *Id.*
65. Wiessner (1999) at 125 n. 253 ("the U.S. Government has seen fit to declare" UN treaties "non-self-executing in the process of ratification, thereby blocking a private cause of action in U.S. courts arising out of an alleged treaty violation. This practice has attracted domestic and international criticism.").
66. *Kiobel v. Royal Dutch Petroleum*, 621 F.3d at 137 (citing *Flores v. S. Peru Copper Corp.* 414 F.3d 233, 256 (2nd Cir. 2003)).
67. *Cohen's*. § 5.07 [2][a] at 459 n. 488 and accompanying text. For example, in *Frolova v. USSR, supra*, the court held that the UN Charter is not a self-executing treaty (761 F.2d at 373-375) and does not supply the basis for a lawsuit in American courts to vindicate rights created by its articles. *See also*, *Filartiga v. Pena-Irala*, 630 F.2d at 881-882 (UN Charter mandates are not

"wholly self-executing"); *Spiess v. Itoh Co.*, 643 F.2d at 363 (UN Charter is not a self-executing international obligation of the United States); *Manybeads v. U.S.*, 730 F. Supp. 1515, 1521 (D. Az. 1989) (accord).

68. *Cohen's* 5.07[2][b] at 459–460.
69. *Id.* at 460 n. 492. *See also, Kiobel v. Royal Dutch Petroleum,* 621 F.3d at 131 n. 34 and accompanying text. *Kiobel* notes that declarations that are merely aspirational, such as the Universal Declaration of Human Rights, are not "authoritative sources" of customary international law in and of themselves and they are also of "little utility" in discerning norms in customary international law, in comparison to the role of binding treaties creating customary international law and providing evidence of its content.
70. *Id.*, 5.07[2][c] at 462.
71. *Id.* at 462–463.
72. *Id.* at 462–465. *See also,* Bradley & Goldsmith at 869–870.
73. *Id.* 5.07[2][d] at 466. *See also,* Walter Echo-Hawk, *In the Courts of the Conqueror: The Ten Worst Indian Law Cases Ever Decided* (Golden: Fulcrum Publishing Co., 2010) (Examining the racially discriminatory legal fictions and doctrines found in federal Indian law).
74. Anaya (2004) at 130.
75. *Id.* at 131.
76. *Cohen's* at 466.
77. Bradley & Goldsmith (1997) at 832.
78. RESTATEMENT (THIRD) 115 states: Since international customary law and an international agreement have equal authority in international law, and both are law of the United States, arguably later customary international law should be given effect as law of the United States, even in the face of an earlier law or agreement, just as a later international agreement of the United States is given effect in the face of an earlier law or agreement.
79. Bradley & Goldsmith (1997) at 817.
80. *Cohen's.* 5.07[1] at 458 (footnotes omitted).
81. Anaya (2009) at 80.
82. RESTATEMENT (THIRD), 102 (comment k); Bradley & Goldsmith (1997) at 840. *See, also, Committee of U.S. Citizens v. Reagan,* 859 F.2d 929, 935 (D.C. Cir. 1988) (peremptory norms enjoy the highest status in international law and prevail over treaties and customary international law).
83. *See, e.g.,* Anaya (2009) at 80–82, 99–101; *Cohen's,* 5.07[1] at 458 n. 481 (citing RESTATEMENT (THIRD) 102); 458 n. 459 (citing federal case law); *Kiobel v. Royal Dutch Petroleum Co.* 621 F.3d 111, 131–145 (2nd Cir. 2010).
84. *Kiobel v. Royal Dutch Petroleum Co.* 621 F.3d at 131 (citing *Flores v. S. Peru Copper Corp.* 414 F.3d at 248).
85. *See, e.g., id.*, 621 F.3d at 131.
86. Anaya (2009) at 99.
87. *Banco Nacional de Cuba v. Sabbatino,* 376 U.S. 398, 428 (1964) ('the greater the degree of codification or consensus concerning a particular area of international law, the more appropriate it is for the judiciary to render decisions regarding it."); *Filartiga v. Pena-Irala,* 630 F.2d at 881, 884 (55 constitutions outlawed torture); *Tel-Oren v. Libyan Arab Republic,* 726 F.2d at 792.
88. *Sosa v. Alvarez-Machain,* 542 U.S. at 725, 732; *Banco Nacional de Cuba v. Sabbatino,* 376 U.S. 398, 428 (1964); *Kiobel v. Royal Dutch Petroleum Co.* 621 F.3d at 131.
89. *Cohen's,* 5.07[1] at 458 ("[I]t is well-established that the rules of international customary law form part of the federal common law applicable in certain actions in United States courts.") (footnote omitted); RESTATEMENT (THIRD) 102 cmt. i. *See also, Sosa v. Alvarez-Machain, supra*; *The Paquete Habana,* 175 U.S. 677, 700 (1900); *United States v. Buck,* 690 F. Supp. 1291, 1297 (S.D.N.Y. 1988); *Ishtyaq v. Nelson,* 627 F. Supp. 13, 27 (E.D.N.Y. 1983).
90. Bradley & Goldsmith (1997) at 818.
91. *The Paquete Habana,* 175 U.S. 677, 700 (1900).
92. *Cohen's,* §5.07[4][a][ii] at 491.
93. Wiessner (1999) at 125-126.
94. Jordan J. Paust, *International Law as Law of the United States* (1996) at 6 (cited in Wiessner (1996) at 126 n. 445). The RESTATEMENT (THIRD) reiterates this settled principle: Matters

arising under customary international law also arise under 'the laws of the United States' since international is "part of our law" and is federal law. Quoted in Wiessner (1996) at 126 n. 445). Even critics agree with this rule. *See, e.g.*, Bradley & Goldsmith (1997) at 816–817: During the last twenty years, almost every court that has considered the position has endorsed it. Indeed several courts have referred to it as "settled." The position also has the overwhelming approval of the academy. *See also, Banco Nacional de Cuba v. Sabbatino*, 376 U.S. at 423 ("United States courts apply international law as part of our own in appropriate circumstances."); *Filartiga v. Pena-Irala*, 630 F.2d at 884; *United States v. Buck*, 690 F. Supp. 1291, 1299–1300 (S.D.N.Y. 1988); *Ishtyaq v. Nelson*, 627 F. Supp. at 27 (Customary international law "is part of the laws that federal courts are bound to ascertain and enforce in appropriate cases.").

95. *Filartiga v. Pena-Irala*, 630 F.2d at 885.
96. *Sosa v. Alvarez-Machain*, 542 U.S. at 725–731. Justice Scalia disfavors independent judicial recognition of actionable international norms in the absence of congressional action recognizing those norms. *Id.* at 739–752 (J. Scalia, minority op.).
97. *Filartiga v. Pena-Irala*, 630 F.2d at 880–881.
98. Bradley & Goldsmith (1997) at 840.
99. *Id. at 841* (footnotes omitted).
100. In addition, it follows that established norms in customary international law can also influence the judge-made doctrines in federal Indian law, because they too are part of federal common law.
101. International Law Association, Interim Report, The Hague Conference (2010), *Rights of Indigenous Peoples* (hereinafter, "International Law Association (2010)") at 44.
102. *See, generally,* Inter-American Commission on Human Rights (Organization of American States), *Indigenous And Tribal Peoples' Rights Over Their Ancestral Lands And Natural Resources: Norms and Jurisprudence of the Inter-American Human Rights System* (OEA/Ser.L/V/II. Doc. 56/09, December 30, 2009) (Examining how modern international law, treaties, declarations—including the *United Nations Declaration on the Rights of Indigenous Peoples*—customary norms, and jurisprudence of the Inter-American Human Rights System protect indigenous land rights and other human rights in the post-*Declaration* era of the 21st century.); S. James Anaya, *International Human Rights and Indigenous Peoples* (Aspen Publishers, 2009) at 99–103 (reviewing the status and development of indigenous human rights norms in customary international law from 1999–2009); S. James Anaya, *Indigenous Peoples in International Law* (2nd ed.) (Oxford Univ. Press, 2004) at 69–70, 72 (This treatise evaluates the normative status of indigenous rights in customary international law in the pre-*Declaration* era as of 2004.)
103. Here are nine surveys of indigenous rights norms in customary international law done by various treaties, reports, and law review articles that span the period from 1992 to 2011: (1) International Law Association (2010) at 43–52 (A survey and summary of indigenous human rights that have become norms in the post-*Declaration* era as of 2011, done by 30 leading international law scholars and practitioners); Inter-American Commission on Human Rights (2009) (focusing on customary international law norms on indigenous land rights recognized in the jurisprudence of the Inter-American Human Rights System); (3) Anaya (2009) at 99–103 (this textbook summarizes various surveys from 1999, 2001, and 2004); (4) *Cohen's* §§ 5.07[3][b]-[c] at 473–88 (this leading federal Indian law treatise examines emerging norms of indigenous self-determination and land rights); (5) Anaya (2nd ed., 2004) at 69–70, 72, 97–128, 185–216 (This leading treatise on indigenous rights in international law updates the first edition's 1996 survey of indigenous rights norms in customary international law with relevant developments in the field between 1997–2004); (6) S. James Anaya & Robert A. Williams, Jr., "The Protection of Indigenous Rights over Lands and Natural Resources Under the Inter-American Human Rights System," 14 HARV. HUM. RTS. J. 33 (2001) (These prominent scholars focus on indigenous land and natural resource rights); (7) Wiessner (1999) (An extensive survey of domestic laws and practices around the world concerning indigenous peoples that draws conclusions about indigenous rights norms in customary international law in the pre-*Declaration* era as of 1999); (8) Anaya (1996 ed.) at 75–125 (A 1996 survey on indigenous rights in customary international law in a leading treatise); (9) Curtis G. Berkey, "International Law and Domestic Courts: Enhancing Self-Determination for Indigenous Peoples," 5 HARV. HUM. RTS. J. 65 (1992) (An early legal analysis by a prominent federal Indian law practitioner focusing on the extant normative status of the indigenous right of self-determination in customary international law in 1992).

104. Berkey (1992).
105. *Id.* at 75–78.
106. *Id.* at 78–81.
107. *Id.* at 81.
108. *Id.* at 91.
109. Anaya (1996 ed.) at 75–125.
110. *Id.* at 97–125.
111. *Id.* at 98.
112. *Id.* at 110.
113. *Id.* at 112.
114. *Id.* at 104.
115. *Id.* at 107.
116. *Id.* at 109.
117. Wiessner (2009).
118. *Id.* at 116–120.
119. *Id.* at 109.
120. *Id.* at 110 (citation omitted).
121. Anaya (2004) at 129–184.
122. *Id.* at 69–70.
123. *Id.* at 72.
124. *Cohen's* (2005) at §§5.07[3][a]–[c] -at 472–488.
125. *Id.* at 474, 477.
126. *Id.* at 481.
127. *Id.* at 478.
128. *Id.* at 485.
129. *Id.* §5.97[3][c][ii]at 485.
130. Anaya (2009) at 100, 103–104.
131. *Id.* at 100–104.
132. Inter-American Commission on Human Rights (2009), 6 at 3. This survey of human rights norms and jurisprudence covers the specific content of recognized indigenous rights to land (55–152 at 20–63), including territories (77–152 at 31–63), natural resources (179–272 at 73–103), participation over decisions affecting indigenous property (273–334 at 103–121), and to state protection of such rights (335–394 at 122–140).
133. International Law Association (2010) at 6.
134. *Id.* at 43.
135. *Id.* at 49.
136. *Id.* at 49–50.
137. *Id.* at 51–52.
138. *Cohen's,* §5.08[4][a][iii] at 492 n. 710 (citing *Macleod v. U.S.,* 229 U.S. 416, 434 (1913); *Murray v. The Schooner Charming Betsy,* 6 U.S. 64, 118 (1804)).

CHAPTER FIVE: THE LEGACY OF CONQUEST

1. The remedial purpose of the *Declaration* is expressed in paragraphs 6-7 of the preamble: *Concerned* that indigenous peoples have suffered historic injustices as a result of, inter alia, their colonization and dispossession of their lands, territories and resources, thus preventing them from exercising, in particular, their right to development in accordance with their own needs and interests, *Recognizing* the urgent need to respect and promote the inherent rights of indigenous peoples which derive from their political, economic and social structures and from their cultures, spiritual traditions, histories and philosophies, especially their rights to their lands, territories and resources.
2. Russell Thornton, *American Indian Holocaust and Survival: A Population History Since 1492* (Norman: University of Oklahoma, 1987) at 42–49.
3. J.M. Roberts, *The Penguin History of the World* (Oxford University Press, 1990) at 483–484.
4. Philip Gourevitch, *We Wish To Inform You That Tomorrow We Will Be Killed With Our Families: Stories From Rwanda* (Pacador 1999).

5. Thornton (1987).
6. *See, e.g.,* Thomas Ball, "Prevalence Rates Of Full And Partial PTSD And Lifetime Trauma In A Sample Of Adult Members Of An American Indian Tribe," A Dissertation presented to University of Oregon Graduate School, Dept. of Special Education and Community Resources (Dec. 1998). Maria Yellow Horse Brave Heart, PH.D., "The Return To The Sacred Path: Healing The Historical Trauma And Historical Unresolved Grief Response Among The Lakota Through A Psychoeducational Group Intervention," *Smith College Studies in Social Work,* 68(3) (June 1998) 288–305.
7. Ball (1998) at 62; Brave Heart (1998) at 288.
8. The history documented by Thornton (1987) leads to a troubling debate among scholars whether our misdeeds have amounted to acts of genocide, as currently defined by the *UN Convention on the Prevention and Punishment of the Crime of Genocide.* Article 2 defines "genocide" as "any of the following acts committed with intent to destroy, in whole or part, a national, ethnical, racial or religious group, such as:(a) Killing members of the group; (b) Causing serious bodily or mental harm to members of the group; (c) Deliberately inflicting on the group conditions of life calculated to bring about its physical destruction in whole or part; (d) Imposing measures intended to prevent births within the group; (e) Forcibly transferring children of the group to another group."

   This research and its implications are analyzed in my book, *In The Courts of the Conqueror: The 10 Worst Indian Law Cases Ever Decided* (Golden: Fulcrum Publishing, 2010), especially at 399–420 where I analyzed Thornton's six causes of the American Indian population decline and found that the courts sanctioned misdeeds that could qualify as genocidal under the *Convention.*
9. *State v. Foreman,* 16 Tenn. 256, 1835 WL 945 (Tenn.) at *8–9.
10. *See,* http://thinkexist.com/quotes/william_glasser
11. For this discussion, I am indebted to research and analysis performed my brother, Lance G. Echo-Hawk, a behavioral health therapist who has studied trauma, as it relates to addictions and mental health disorders. Much of his research can be found at http://www.ehcounseling.com (hereinafter, "Echo-Hawk website") (last visited 5/6/12)
12. *Id.* (citing http://www.noanxiety.com/psychology-psychotherapy-glossary/terms-with-letter-s.html)
13. Echo-Hawk website.
14. *Id.*
15. *Id.*
16. *Id.*
17. The incredible healing power of restorative justice will be explored in Chapter Ten.
18. *Merriam-Webster's Collegiate Dictionary* (11th ed., 2005).
19. *Johnson v. M'Intosh,* 21 U.S. 543, 589 (1823).
20. *Id.* at 591.
21. *Id.* at 588.
22. *Id.* at 588–589.
23. David H. Getches, "Conquering the Cultural Frontier: The New Subjectivism of the Supreme Court in Indian Law," 84 Cal. L. Rev. 1573, 1578 (1996).
24. Philip J. Prygoski, "War as the Prevailing Metaphor in Federal Indian Law Jurisprudence: An Exercise in Judicial Activism," 14 T.M. Cooley L. Rev. 491 (1997).
25. *Cherokee Nation v. Georgia,* 30 U.S. 1, 22–23, 29 (Johnson J., concurring).
26. *Id.* at 24, 29.
27. *State v. Foreman,* 16 Tenn. 256, 1835 WL 945 (Tenn.); *Caldwell v. State,* 1 Stew. & P. 327 (Ala. 1832), 1832 SL 545 (Ala.); *Georgia v. Tassels,* 1 Georgia Reports, Annotated 478 (Hall Superior Court, 1830) (Charlottesville, VA: The Michie Co., 1903).
28. Historian Tim Alan Garrison studies the jurisprudence of conquest evident in these disturbing cases in *The Legal Ideology of Removal: The Southern Judiciary and the Sovereignty of Native American Nations* (Athens: Univ. of Georgia Press, 2002). *See also,* Echo-Hawk (2010) at 87–120.
29. *Caldwell v. State,* 1832 WL at *45.
30. *Id.* at *53.
31. *State v. Foreman,* 1835 WL at *8–9.
32. *Tee-Hit-Ton Indians v. United States,* 348 U.S. 272, 322 (1955).
33. Stuart Banner, *How the Indians Lost Their Land: Law and Power on the Frontier* (Cambridge: Belknap Press of Harvard Univ., 2005); Robert J. Miller, *Native America, Discovered and Conquered: Thomas Jefferson, Lewis & Clark, and Manifest Destiny* (Westport: Praeger Publishers,

2006) at 57 (It is "a proven fact that the vast majority of Indian lands in America were purchased with tribal assent at treaty sessions and were not taken by military conquest."); Felix S. Cohen, ""Original Land Title," 32 Minn. L. Rev. 28, 34–43 (1947). Only in isolated instances was Indian law appropriated in war. *Cohen's Handbook of Federal Indian Law* (2005 ed.) at 44, 72. Far more acres were obtained by treaty cession (two billion acres), Indian removal, and allotment policies (50 million acres). *Id.* at 8, 16–17, 45, 79.

34. *Worcester v. Georgia,* 31 U.S. 515, 544–545, 555–556, 561 (1832).
35. *See,* discussion in Chapter One.
36. *Declaration,* 18.
37. Scholars have studied the roots of early international law as it pertains to indigenous peoples of the New World. *See, e.g.,* the work of Robert A. Williams, Jr. in *The American Indian in Western Legal Thought: The Discourses of Conquest* (New York: Oxford Univ. Press, 1990); "Encounters on the Frontiers of International Human Rights Law: Redefining the Terms of Indigenous Peoples' Survival in the World," 1990 Duke L. J. 660 (1990); "The Algebra of Federal Indian Law: The Hard Trial of Decolonizing and Americanizing the Whiteman's Indian Jurisprudence," 1986 Wisconsin L. Rev. 219 (1986). *See also,* Echo-Hawk (2010) at 15–22; Garrison (2010) at 60–71; Robert N. Clinton, "Redressing the Legacy of Conquest: A Vision Quest for a Decolonized Federal Indian Law," 46 Arkansas L. Rev. 77 (1993).
38. Robert J. Miller, "The International Law of Colonialism: A Comparative Analysis," 15 Lewis & Clark L. Rev. 847(2011). *See also,* Robert J. Miller and Jacinta Ruru, "An Indigenous Lens into Comparative Law: The Doctrine of Discovery in the United States and New Zealand," 111 W.VA L. Rev. 849 (2009); Robert J. Miller, "The Doctrine of Discovery in American Indian Law," 42 Idaho L. Rev.1 (2005).
39. Robert J. Miller, Lisa Lesage & Sebastián López Escarcena,'The International Law of Discovery, Indigenous Peoples, and Chile," 89 Neb. L. Rev. 819, 820 (2011).
40. Franciscus de Victoria, *De Indis et de Belli Reflectiones* (Washington D.C. The Carnegie Institute of Washington, 1917) (J.B. Scott and E. Nys., eds., J. Bate, trans. 1917) at 155.
41. *Cherokee Nation v. Georgia,* 30 U.S. at 17.
42. *United States v. Kagama,* 118 U.S. 375, 384 (1886).
43. Echo-Hawk (2010) at 189–214.
44. *Felix S. Cohen's Handbook of Federal Indian Law* (Albuquerque: UNM Press, 1948) at 175. *See, also,* Echo-Hawk (2010) at 189–214.
45. *United States v. Clapox,* 35 F. 575, 577 (D. Ore., 1888).
46. *In re Can-ah couqua,* 29 F. 687, 688 (D. Alaska, 1887).
47. *United States v. Sandoval,* 231 U.S. 28, 39 (1913).
48. S. James Anaya, *Indigenous Peoples in International Law* (New York: Oxford Univ. Press, 2004) (2nd ed.) at 31. As explained in a 1919 State Department study, colonizing nations have a "positive duty" under international law and the practice of nations "to undertake directly the education and training of the aborigines in the arts and sciences of civilization and in the political principles on which all civilized societies is based." *See,* Alpheus H. Snow, *The Question of Aborigines in the Law and Practice of Nations* (Washington: Government Printing Office, 1919), reprinted in *The Inquiry Handbook,* V. 20 (London Scholarly Resources, Inc., 1974) at 12 (quoting an 1837 British House of Commons report). Continuing at 34, the study laid out the accepted basis for the governance of colonized peoples: [D]omination of distant communities by a Republic [is] permissible when needful and to the extent needful, but only provided the State recognized and fulfilled the positive and imperative duty of helping these dominated communities to help themselves by teaching and training them for civilization, as the wards and pupils of the nation and of the society of nations. [C]ivilized States have recognized that guardianship of aboriginal tribes implies not merely protection, not merely a benevolence toward private missionary, charitable, and educational effort, but a positive duty of direct legislative, executive, and judicial domination of aborigines as a minor wards of the nation and of equally direct legislative, executive, and judicial tutorship of them for civilization, so that they may become in the shortest possible time civil and political adults participating on an equality in their own government under democratic and republican institutions.
49. *Lone Wolf v. Hitchcock,* 187 U.S. 553, 565 (1903).
50. *See, discussion* in Echo-Hawk (2010) at 161–186.

51. *Carino v. Insular Government of the Philippine Islands,* 212 U.S. 449, 458 (1908).
52. *Id.*
53. *Id.*
54. *Tee-Hit-Ton Indians v. United States,* 348 U.S. at 284–285.
55. The problem of adaptation to the land is explored in Chapter Six.
56. The law of colonialism continues to erode tribal sovereignty and self-government, most recently in federal common law decisions that divest tribal police power over all persons who come within their territory under the Supreme Court's "implicit divestiture" theory, which sees Indian tribes existing in a regime where self-government exists only at the pleasure of Congress. *See, e.g., Nevada v. Hicks,* 533 U.S. 353 (2001); *Duro v. Reina,* 495 U.S. 676 (1990); *Montana v. United States,* 450 U.S. 544 (1981); *Oliphant v. Suquamish Indian Tribe,* 435 U.S. 181 (1978).
57. Echo-Hawk (2010) at 43–48.
58. *See, The Law of Trusts and Trustees,* §471 ("The constructive trust may be defined as a device used by equity to compel one who unfairly holds a property interest to convey that interest to another to whom it justly belongs. The individual, the defendant, may have obtained the property interest by unjust, unconscionable, or unlawful means. Equity will then vest title in the wronged party.")
59. Jen Camden and Kathryn E. Fort, "Channeling Thought: The Legacy of Legal Fictions from 1823," 33 AM. INDIAN L. REV. 77, 79 (2008–2009).
60. *Mabo and Others v. Queensland (No. 2),* 13 CLR 1 (1992).
61. *State v. Foreman,* 16 Tenn. 256, 266 (1835).
62. *Cohen's Handbook of Federal Indian Law* (2005 ed.), §§4.01 and 4.02 at 204–237.
63. *Worcester v. Georgia,* 31 U.S. 515 (1832).
64. *Cohen's* (2005 ed.), §§4.01-.02 at 204–237. The "implicit divestiture theory" is discussed in §4.02[3][a] at 224–226.
65. *Cohen's* (2005 ed.), §4.01[1][a] at 205–206.
66. *Worcester,* 31 U.S. at 542–543.
67. *Id.* at 557.
68. *Id.* at 559.
69. *Id.* at 562.
70. *Id.* at 555.
71. *Black's Law Dictionary* (9th ed. 2009), protectorate.
72. *Worcester,* at 554.
73. *Id.* at 560–561.
74. *Id.,* at 556.
75. *Id.*
76. *See,* Charles Wilkinson, *Blood Struggle: The Rise of Modern Indian Nations* (New York, London: W.W. Norton & Co., 2005).
77. *See, Cohen's* (2005 ed.), §5.07[4][a][iii] at 492 (International law as an Interpretative Guide).
78. Duane Champagne, "Rethinking Native Relations with Contemporary Nation-States," in Duane Champagne, Karen Jo Torjesen, and Susan Steiner (eds.), *Indigenous Peoples and the Modern State* (AltaMira Press, 2005) at 3–23.
79. *Id.*
80. S. James Anaya, *International Human Rights and Indigenous Peoples* (New York: Aspen Publishers, 2009) at 61.
81. *Id.* (citing Erica-Irene A. Daes, "Some Considerations on the Right of Indigenous Peoples to Self-Determination," 3 Transn'l L. & Contemp. Probs. 1, 9 (1993).)
82. Champagne (2005) at 18.
83. *Id.* at 18–19.
84. *Id.* at 19.
85. *Id.* at 20.
86. *See, Washington v. Washington State Commercial Passenger Fishing Vessel,* 443 U.S. 658, 672–673 n. 20 (1979) (recognizing treaty and other rights for Indians does not violate the equal protection clause of the Fourteenth Amendment, even if non-Indians do not possess such rights); *Cohen's* (2005 ed.), §14.03 (federal legislation dealing specifically with Indians does not constitute impermissible racial discrimination, because Indians have a distinct constitutional status). *See also,* S. James Anaya, *International Human Rights and Indigenous Rights* (New York: Aspen Publishers

2009) at 64 (The *Declaration* does not create a category of "privileged" citizens benefitting from "special" rights, because its purposes are "fully in accordance with the principle of equality. Article 1(4) of the International Convention on the Elimination of All Forms of Discrimination 1966... provides that special measures are permitted when they are taken for the purpose of "securing" adequate advancement of certain racial or ethnic groups or individuals requiring such protection in order to ensure such groups or individuals equal enjoyment of human rights and fundamental freedoms."). Indeed, there is widespread agreement and practice in both international and domestic law that "indigenous peoples are vulnerable groups worthy of the law's heightened concern." Siegfried Wiessner, "Rights and Status of Indigenous Peoples: A Global Comparative and International Legal Analysis," 12 HARV. HUM RTS J. 57, 109 (1999).

87. 19, *Declaration.*

CHAPTER SIX: TOWARD AN AMERICAN LAND ETHIC

1. This chapter draws heavily from two previous writings authored by Walter R. Echo-Hawk: (1) "Under Native American Skies" published in *Ethnography in the National Park Service*, 26 GEORGE WRIGHT FORUM (No. 2) (2009) at 58–79; and (2) it also draws on environmental, cosmological, and religious thinking discussed by *In the Courts of the Conqueror: The 10 Worst Indian Law Cases Ever Decided* (Golden: Fulcrum 2010). They are used by the author to draw attention to the environmental reasons for implementing the *Declaration,* in spite of the unavoidable overlap.
2. Aldo Leopold, *A Sand County Almanac* (New York, Oxford: Oxford University Press (1949) 1989) at 203.
3. Scott Sonner (Associated Press Writer), "Palin Appeals to Nevadans to Help Swing Election," San Jose Mercury News (Nov. 4, 2008) (http://www.mercurynews.com/news/ci_10893972)
4. In *Lyng v. Northwest Indian Cemetery Protective Association,* 485 U.S. 439 (1988), the United States Forest Service decided to clear-cut a critical tribal holy place, even though it would destroy the religions of three Indian tribes and endanger their cultural survival. Congress later intervened and placed the area into a protected wilderness status before it could be despoiled by the agency. In *Navajo Nation et al. v. U.S. Forest Service*, 535 F.3d 1059 (9th Cir., 2008) (*en banc*), the agency desecrated the most important tribal holy place in the American Southwest by pouring fecal matter on it to make artificial snow with treated sewer water in order to support a local ski resort business. There is a long line of cases allowing federal agencies to trammel Native American holy places located on public lands in ways that would never be tolerated if Judeo-Christian holy places were at stake. They include *United States v. Means,* 858 F.2d 404 (8th Cir. 1988) (Black Hills); *Wilson v. Block,* 708 F. 2d 735 (D.D. Cir. 1983) (San Francisco Peaks); *Inupiat Community of the Arctic Slope v. United States,* 746 F.2d 570 (9th Cir. 1984) (Arctic coastal area); *Badoni v. Higginson,* 638 F.2d 172 (10th Cir. 1980); *Sequoyah v. TVA,* 620 F.2d 1159 (6th Cir. 1980) (Cherokee homeland and burial ground); *Crow v. Gullet,* 706 F.2d 856 (8th Cir. 1983) (Bear Butte).
5. *Cohen's* (2005 ed.), §15.01 at 965.
6. Executive Order 13007 (Indian Sacred Sites), 61 *Federal Register* 26771 (May 24, 1996).
7. Jerry Rogers, "The National Park Service Centennial Essay Series," in *Ethnography in a National Park Service Second Century,* 26 GEORGE WRIGHT FORUM (No. 3) (2009) at 9–10 (quoting from Jerry Rogers, *et al.* "A Different Past In A Different Future: The Report of the Cultural Resource and Historic Preservation Committee of the National Parks Second Century Commission," July 6, 2009).
8. *See, e.g.,* David Ruppert, "Rethinking Ethnography in the National Park Service," in *Ethnography in the National Park Service* (2009), *supra,* at 51–57.
9. Gregory Cajete, *Native Science: Natural Laws of Interdependence* (Santa Fe: Clear Light Publishers, 2000).
10. *See,* Jim Mason, *An Unnatural Order: The Roots of Our Destruction of Nature* (New York: Lantern Books, 2005).
11. *Id.*
12. Luther Standing Bear, *Land of the Spotted Eagle* (Lincoln: University of Nebraska Press, 1970) at 248.

13. Melvin R. Gilmore, *Uses of Plants by the Indians of the Missouri River Region* (Lincoln and London: University of Nebraska Press (1914) 1977) at 1–2.
14. Mason (2005).
15. Cajete (2000).
16. Cited by Charles Patterson, *Eternal Treblinka: Our Treatment of Animals and the Holocaust* (New York: Lantern Books, 2002) at 2 (quoting Sigmund Freud, "A Difficulty in the Path of Psycho-Analysis," (1917) in *The Standard Edition of the Complete Psychological Works of Sigmund Freud* (London: Hogarth Press, 1955), Vol. XVII, 130 (James Strachey, transl.)).
17. *Id.* (quoting Sigmund Freud, "Fixation to Traumas—The Unconscious" in Introductory Lectures on Psychoanalysis—Part III (1916–1917), Lecture XVIII, *Complete Works,* Vol. XVI, 285).
18. Genesis (9:2).
19. *See,* Allison M. Dussias, "Ghost Dance and Holy Ghost: The Echoes of Nineteenth-Century Christianization Policy in Twentieth-Century Native American Free Exercise Cases," 49 Stan. L. Rev. 773 (1997); Walter R. Echo-Hawk, "Native American Religious Liberty: Five Hundred Years After Columbus," Am. Ind. Culture & Research J. 17:33 (1993).
20. The holy places form a rich tapestry where humans experience direct communication with God, in places like Mount Sinai, Bethlehem, the Wailing Wall, Mecca, the summit of Gologotha (where Adam was created and buried), Jerusalem (where Jesus was crucified and sects await his return), the revered Ganges River (a pathway to salvation in India), and the Bhodi Tree (where Siddhartha attained nirvana and became the Buddha). In other parts of the world, sacred mountains, waterfalls, pools, caves, and lakes that dot the Philippines, Indonesia, Hawaii, Australia, Canada, and South America are holy places where indigenous people pray. As Huston Smith notes, "Many historical religions are attached to places," but no historical religion "is embedded in place to the extent that tribal religions are." Huston Smith, *The World's Religions: Our Great Wisdom Traditions* (Harper San Francisco, 1991) at 371. *See also,* Walter Echo-Hawk, *In The Courts of the Conqueror: The 10 Worst Indian Cases Ever Decided* (Golden: Fulcrum Publishing 2010) at 325-356, for a more detailed discussion about the nature of Native American holy places and their role in world religion.
21. Daniel K. Inouye, "Discrimination and Native American Religious Rights," 23 UWLA L. Rev. 3, 12–13 (1992).
22. Smith (1991).
23. *Id.* at 366.
24. Quoted in Paul Goble, *All Our Relations: Traditional Native American Thoughts About Nature* (Bloomington: World Wisdom, Inc., 2005) (citing Joseph Epes Brown, *The Sacred Pipe* (University of Oklahoma Press, 1953).
25. Smith (1991).
26. *Id.* at 384–385.
27. *Id.* at 386.
28. *See.* Vine Deloria, Jr., "Secularism, Civil Religion, and the Religious Freedom of American Indians," Am. Ind. Culture and Research J., Vol. 16, No. 2 (1992): 9; "A Simple Question of Humanity: The Moral Dimensions of the Reburial Issue," NARF L. Rev., Vol. 14, No. 4 (Fall 1989).
29. Deloria (1992) at 10.
30. *Id.* at 15.
31. Huston Smith, *Why Religion Matters: The Fate Of The Human Spirit In An Age Of Disbelief* (Harper San Francisco, 2001).
32. *Id.*
33. Quoted in Smith (2001) at 72.
34. Kirkpatrick Sale, *The Conquest of Paradise: Christopher Columbus and the Columbian Legacy* (New York: Alfred E. Knopf, 1990).
35. *Johnson v. M'Intosh, supra,* 21 U.S. at 590–91.
36. Russell Thornton, *American Indian Holocaust and Survival: A Population History Since 1492* (Norman: University of Oklahoma Press, 1987); Walter R. Echo-Hawk, "Genocide and Ethnocide in Native North America," in John Hartwell Moore (ed.), *Encyclopedia of Race and Racism, V. 2, g-r* (Thompson Gale, 2007), p. 48.
37. Quoted in Goble (2005).
38. Quoted in Huston Smith and Phil Cousineau (eds.), *A Seat at the Table: Huston Smith In Con-*

versation With Native Americans on Religious Freedom (Berkley, Los Angeles, London: University of California Press, 2006) at XIII.

39. Quoted in Frances Densmore, *Teton Sioux Music* (Washington, D.C.: Smithsonian Institution, Bureau of American Ethnology, Bulletin 16, 1918) at 184.
40. Luther Standing Bear, *My Indian Boyhood* (Boston: Houghton Mifflin, 1931) at 13.
41. Quoted in Richard Erdoes, *Lame Deer* (London: Davis Poynter, 1973) at 136.
42. Quoted in John G. Neihart, *Black Elk Speaks* (New York: William Morrow, 1983)) at 58.
43. James Dorsey, *A Study of Siouan Cults* (Smithsonian Institution BAE 11th Report, 1894) at 435.
44. Jay C. Fikes (ed.) *Reuben Snake: Your Humble Serpent—Indian Visionary and Activist* (Santa Fe: Clear Light Publishers, 1996) at 8.

CHAPTER SEVEN: HOW DOES THE *DECLARATION* AFFECT THE FUTURE OF INDIAN LAW?

1. *Worcester v. Georgia,* 31 U.S. 515 (1832).
2. *Williams v. Lee,* 358 U.S. 217 (1959).
3. *See, e.g., Oliphant v. Suquamish Indian Tribe,* 435 U.S. 181 (1978) (tribes have no power to prosecute crimes committed by non-Indians on the reservation) and its progeny: *Nevada v. Hicks,* 533 U.S. 353 (2001) (tribes have no power to adjudicate torts committed by state police against tribal members in their reservation homes); *Strate v. A-1 Contractors,* 520 U.S. 438 (1997) (tribes have no jurisdiction over accidents caused by non-Indian motorists on reservation roads); *Duro v. Reina,* 495 U.S. 676 (1990) (tribes have no power to prosecute crimes committed by nonmember Indians on the reservation); *Montana v. United States,* 450 U.S. 544 (1981) (tribes have no civil jurisdiction over non-Indian activities on fee lands within the reservation except in limited instances).
4. *See,* Lindsay G. Robertson, *Conquest by Law* (Oxford Univ. Press, 2005) at 138–142 for a discussion of *Martin v. Lessee of Waddell,* 41 U.S. 367 (1842); *Mitchell v. United States,* 49 U.S. 52 (1841); *Clark v. Smith,* 38 U.S. 195 (1839); *United States v. Fernandez,* 34 U.S. 303 (1836); *Mitchel v. United States,* 34 U.S. 711 (1835).
5. *United States v. Kagama,* 118 U.S. 375 (1886).
6. *Cohen's* (2005 ed.), §4.92[3] [a] at 223–225.
7. *Id.*, §4.02[3] [b] at 227.
8. *Nevada v. Hicks,* 533 U.S. at 361 (citing *White Mountain Apache Tribe v. Bracker,* 448 U.S. 136, 141 (1980)).
9. *United States ex rel. Standing Bear v. Crook,* 25 Fed. 695 (C.C. D. Neb. 1879) (Case No. 1489).
10. During this period, it was the common practice of the government to confine Indians to the reservation and not allow them to leave without permission of the Indian agent. However, just like Judge Dundy, Felix S. Cohen found no legal authority for that practice: "Although there was never any legal authority for confining Indians on reservations, administrators relied upon the magic solving word "wardship" to justify the assertion of such authority." *Felix S. Cohen's Handbook of Federal Indian Law, supra,* at 177. Military authorities cannot simply arrest and confine Indians without some legal source of authority, even though they are wards of the government. *Ex Parte Bi-A-Lil-Le,* 100 P. 450 (Az. Terr. 1909).
11. Echo-Hawk (2010) at 123–159.
12. *Id.*
13. Mary Kathryn Nagle, "*Standing Bear v. Crook:* The Case for Equality under Waaxe's Law," 45 Creighton L. Rev. (Apr. 2012).
14. *Ex Parte Crow Dog,* 109 U.S. 556 (1883).
15. 109 U.S. at 568.
16. *Cohen's,* §1.04 at 81.
17. *Winters v. United States,* 207 U.S. 564 (1908).
18. *Cohen's,* §15.02 at 966; §19.01 at 1168.
19. *Cohen's,* Ch. 19 at 1167–1226.
20. *Washington v. Washington State Commercial Passenger Fishing Vessel Ass'n,* 380 U.S. 658 (1979).
21. *Id.*, 380 U.S. at 675.
22. *Id.* at 695.
23. *California v. Cabazon Band of Mission Indians,* 480 U.S. 202 (1987).

24. *Id.*, 480 U.S. at 216–222.
25. *Id.* at 219.
26. *Oklahoma Tax Commission v. Sac and Fox Nation*, 508 U.S. 114, 125 (1993).
27. *Brendale v. Confederated Tribes and Bands of Yakima Indians*, 492 U.S. 408 (1989).
28. *People v. Woody*, 394 P. 2d 813 (CA. 1964).
29. *See, e.g., Cohen's*, §14.03[2] [c] (Protection of Religious Liberty) at 936–949.
30. *People v. Woody*, 394 P. 2d at 821.
31. *Id.* at 821–822.
32. *Employment Division v. Smith*, 492 U.S. 872 (1990).
33. Echo-Hawk (2010) at 273–322.
34. *Kandra v. United States*, 145 F. Supp. 2d 1192, (D. Or. 2001).
35. *Declaration*, Arts. 25–30, 32.
36. Recent amendments to some environmental laws treat Indian tribes as states for purposes of protecting the environmental integrity of land and resources within the borders of Indian reservations, *See, e.g.*, Clean Water Act, 33 U.S.C. §1377(e)(2) (2006); Clean Air Act, 42 U.S.C. § 7601(d)(2) (2006). However, tribal environmental protection standards can not be enforced outside of Indian Country, except in rare instances when non-compliance for waterway standards directly and adversely impact Indian reservations. *See, City of Albuquerque v. Browner*, 97 F.3d. 415 (10th Cir. 1996). By contrast, the *Declaration* calls for protection for off-reservation indigenous habitat.
37. *Tennessee Valley Authority v. Hill*, 437 U.S. 154, 180 (1978).
38. *Employment Division v. Smith, supra* (no protection for the peyote religion); *Washington v. Washington State Commercial Passenger Fishing Vessel Ass'n*, 443 U.S. at 665 ("Religious rites were intended to insure the continual return of the salmon and trout."); *Lyng v. Northwest Indian Cemetery Protective Association*, 485 U.S. 439 (1988) (protection and use of sacred site is not protected by the First Amendment); *Anderson v. Evans*, 2002 WL 31856697, *4, *6 (9th Cir. 2002) (cultural and religious use of whales); *Rupert v. Director, USFWS*, 957 F.2d 32 (1st Cir. 1992) (religious use of eagles); *Peyote Way Church of God v. Thornburgh*, 922 F.2d 1210, 1216 (5th Cir. 1991) (religious use of peyote cactus plant); *Kandra v. United States*, 145 F. Supp.2nd at 1201 ("Many customs and traditions revolve around the fish harvest, which is now reduced, or in the case of the suckers, non-existent."); *United States v. Billie*, 667 F. Supp.1485 (S.D. 1987) (religious use of panthers); *Frank v. State*, 604 P.2d 1068 (Alaska, 1978); *People v. Woody, supra* (religious use of peyote plant is protected by the First Amendment). This widespread judicial recognition of the spiritual relationship between Native Americans and the natural world rarely leads to any legal protection by the courts under the Bill of Rights, or other laws. The executive and legislative branches are also aware of these indigenous spiritual and cultural connections to the natural world as seen in a wide-variety of treaties, conservation laws and policies.
39. *Tennessee Valley Authority v. Hill*, 437 U.S. at 168–169 ('Whether a dam is 50% or 90% completed is irrelevant in calculating the social and scientific costs attributable to the disappearance of a unique form of life. Courts are ill-equipped to calculate how many dollars must be invested before the value of a dam exceeds that of the endangered species."). In passing the ESA, "Congress viewed the value of endangered species as 'incalculable.'" *Id.* at 187–188. *See also, Kandra*, 145 F. Supp.2d at 1201 ("Threats to the continued existence of endangered and threatened species constitute ultimate harm."); *Bensman v. USFS*, 984 F. Supp. 1242, 1250 (W.D. Mo., 1997) ("[D]eath is an irreparable harm and the extinction of a species is 'incalculable.' While those individual timber companies will regrettably lose a few contracts, this harm is negligible in light of continuing decline of the Indiana bat. The public interest lies on the side of protecting the endangered species.")
40. Shucks, Native Americans could have told the courts that the value of life cannot be measured by money. *State of Ohio v. U.S. Dept. of the Interior*, 880 F.2d 432 (D.C. Cir. 1989) ("From the bald eagle to the blue whale and snail darter, natural resources have values that are not fully captured by the market system."); *Rivers v. U.S. Army Corps of Engineers*, 2003 WL 21638223, *26 (D.D.C., 2003) ("Defendants have presented primarily economic injuries that would result but the Court finds that loss of the least tern, piping plover, and pallid sturgeon cannot be translated into such simple economic terms, because as the Supreme Court has noted, the 'value of this genetic heritage is, quite literally, incalculable.'"); *GDF Realty Investments, Ltd. v. Norton*,

169 F. Supp.2d 648, 662 (S.D. Tex., 2001) ("Quite obviously, it would be difficult for a court to balance the loss of a sum certain—even $100 million—against a congressionally declared 'incalculable value.")

41. *United States v. Bramble,* 103 F.3d 1475, 1482 (9th Cir. 1996) ("with each species we eliminate, we reduce the [genetic] pool available for use by man in future years. Since each living species and subspecies has developed in a unique way to adapt its to the difficulty of living in the world's environment, as a species is lost, its distinctive gene material, which may subsequently prove invaluable to mankind in improving domestic animals or increasing resistance to disease of environmental contaminants, is also irretrievably lost.' S. Rept. No. 526, 91st Cong., 1st Sess. (1969), *reprinted in* 1969 U.S.C.A.N. 1413, 1415, *and quoted in Roman,* 929 F. Supp. at 508. The Supreme Court has also recognized Congress' concern 'about the unknown uses that endangered species might have and about the unforeseeable place such creatures may have in the chain of life on this planet.' *TVA v. Hill,* 437 U.S. at 178–179"). *See also,* H.R. Rep. No. 412, 93rd Cong., 1st Sess., at 4–5 (1973) ("[T]he value of [endangered species'] genetic heritage is, quite literally, incalculable. From the most narrow point of view, it is in the best interests of mankind to minimize the losses of genetic variations. The reason is simple: they are potential resources. They are keys to puzzles which we cannot solve, and may provide answers to questions which we have not yet learned to ask.").
42. *Rio Grande Silvery Minnow v. Keys,* 333 F.3d 1109, 1138 (10th Cir. 2003) (Endangered species are more important than projects that threaten their continued existence or critical habitats, because "loss of species is irreversible and irretrievable" and this injury has an "enduring and permanent nature."); *Biodiversity Legal Foundation v. Badgley,* 309 F.3d 1166, 1177 (9th Cir. 2002) ("In Congress' view, projects which threaten the continued existence of endangered species' threatened incalculable harm; accordingly, it decided that the balance of hardships and the public interest tip heavily in favor of endangered species. We may not use equity's scales to strike a different balance."); *Sierra Club v. Marsh,* 816 F.2d 1376, 1383–1384 (9th Cir. 1987) ("Congress has spoken in the plainest of words, making it abundantly clear that the balance has been struck in favor of affording endangered species the highest of priorities"); *Kandra,* 145 F. Supp.2d at 1201 ("Threats to the continued existence of endangered and threatened species constitute ultimate harm."); *Palila v. Hawaii Dept. of Land and Natural Resources,* 471 F. Supp. 985, 994–995 (9th Cir. 1979) (Congress "determined that protection of any endangered species anywhere is of the utmost importance to mankind."). The survival of endangered species have been given priority over the "primary mission" of federal agencies, and several courts have ruled that the rights of project irrigators in Bureau of Reclamation projects do not override concerns protected by the Endangered Species Act. *See, Rio Grande Silvery Minnow v. Keys, supra,* 333 F.3d at 1114; *Carson-Truckee Water Cons. Dist. v. Clark,* 741 F.2d 257, 262 (9th Cir. 1984); *Kentucky Heartwood,* 20 F. Supp.2d at 1083–1084; *Kandra, supra,* 1200-1201; *Pacific Coast Federation of Fishermen's Ass'n. v. United States,* 138 F. Supp.2d 1128, 1239 (N.D. Ca., 2001); *Carson-Truckee Water Cons. Dist. v. Watt,* 549 F. Supp. 704 (D. Nev. 1980).
43. *Cappaert v. United States,* 440 U.S. 128, 134 (1976) (insufficient water level "reduce[s] the ability of fish to spawn in sufficient numbers to prevent extinction"); *Pyramid Lake Paiute Tribe v. Navy,* 898 F.2d 1410, 1413 n. 5 (9th Cir. 1990) (higher water levels are necessary to restore self-sustaining fish population); *Carson- Truckee Water Cons. Dist. v. Clark, supra,* 741 F.2d at 262-263 ("Fish cannot reproduce in water that warm such a temperature renders it too hot for fish to reproduce successfully."); *Carson-Truckee Water Cons. Dist. v. Watt,* 549 F. Supp. 704, 707 (D. Nev. 1982) (low water causes extinction of a species); *Pyramid Lake Tribe v. Morton,* 354 F. Supp. 252, 255 (D.D.C. 1973) (decreased lake level threatens extinction and "the continued utility of the lake as a useful body of water is at hazard.").
44. *Kandra v. United States,* 145 F.Supp.2d at 1196–1197.
45. Id. at 1201.
46. Id. at 1204.
47. Matthew G. McHenry, "The Worst of Times: A Tale of Two Fishes In The Klamath Basin," 333 Envtl. L. 1019, 1020 (Fall 2003).
48. *See,* Harold Shepherd, "Conflict Comes To Roost! The Bureau of Reclamation And The Indian Trust Responsibility," 31 Envtl. L. 901, 937–938 (2001).
49. *Cohen's,* §5.05[4][a] at 438–441.

50. *Nevada v. United States,* 463 U.S. 110, 128 (1983).
51. *Comanche Nation v. United States,* No. CIV-08-849-D, 2008 WL 4426621 (W.D. Okla., Sept. 23, 2008).
52. *Lyng v. Northwest Indian Cemetery Protective Association,* 485 U.S. 439 (1988); *Navajo Nation v. U.S. Forest Service,* 535 F.3d 1059 (9th Cir. 2008) (rehearing en banc). *See also,* Echo-Hawk (2010) at 325–420 (analyzing the *Lyng* doctrine).
53. *Santa Clara Pueblo v. Martinez,* 436 U.S. 49 (1978).
54. *Id.* at 56.
55. *Id.* at 62–63.
56. *Id.* at 58.
57. *Id.* at 59–60.
58. *Id.* at 56.
59. *Johnson v. M'Intosh,* 21 U.S. 543 (1823).
60. *Id.* at 588–591.
61. 4, *Declaration.*
62. *See,* Lindsay G. Robertson, *Conquest by Law* (Oxford University Press, 2005); Echo-Hawk (2010) at 62–74.
63. *Cherokee Nation v. Georgia,* 30 U.S. 1 (1831); *Tassels v. Georgia,* 1 Georgia Reports Anno. 478 (Hall Superior Court, 1830) (Charlottesville, VA: The Michie Co., 1903); *Caldwell v. State,* 1 Stew. & P. 327 (Ala. 1832), 1832 WL 545 (Ala.); *State v. Foreman,* 16 Tenn. 256, 1835 WL 945 (Tenn.). *See also,* Echo-Hawk (2010) at 87–120.
64. Connors v. United States and Cheyenne Indians, 33 C. Cl. 317 (1898). See also, Echo-Hawk 123–159.
65. Echo-Hawk (2010) at 189–214.
66. Id. at 217–271.
67. Id. at 217–232.
68. *Id.* at 237–271.
69. Employment Division v. Smith, 494 U.S. 872 (1990); Lyng v. Northwest Indian Cemetery Association, 485 U.S. 439 (1988). See, Echo-Hawk (2010) at 273–356.

CHAPTER EIGHT: DOES UNITED STATES LAW AND POLICY MEET UN STANDARDS?

1. Department of State, Announcement of U.S. Support for the United Nations Declaration on the Rights of Indigenous Peoples: Initiatives to Promote the Government-to-Government Relationship & Improve the Lives of Indigenous Peoples (Jan.2010) at 2. Available at: http://www.state.gov/documents/organization/153223.pdf
2. Id. at 15.
3. Cohen's (1982 ed.) at 144–145, 205.
4. Washington v. Confederated Bands and Tribes of the Yakima Indian Nation, 439 U.S. 463, 500–501 (1978) ("The tribes' interest in self-government is not a "fundamental right"); Santa Clara Pueblo v. Martinez, 436 U.S. 49, 57 (1978) ("Congress has plenary power to limit, modify, or eliminate the powers of local self-government which the Tribes otherwise possess.").
5. Cohen's (2005 ed.), §1.07 at 97–113.
6. Id. at 98.
7. Nixon Special Message to Congress, 213 Pub. Papers of the President of the United States: Richard Nixon 564 (July 8, 1970), pp. 564–567.
8. President Nixon told Congress: The first Americans—the Indians—are the most deprived and most isolated minority in our country. On virtually every scale of measurement—employment, income, education, health—the condition of Indian people ranks at the bottom. This condition is the heritage of centuries of injustice. From the time of their first contact with European settlers, the American Indians have been oppressed and brutalized, deprived of their ancestral lands and denied the opportunity to control their own destiny.

   It is long past time that the Indian policies of the Federal government began to recognize and build upon the capacities and insights of the Indian people. Both as a matter of justice and as a matter of enlightened social policy, we must begin to act on the basis of what the Indians themselves have long been telling us. The time has come to break decisively with the past and to create the conditions for a new era in which the Indian future is determined by Indian acts and Indian decisions. Self-determination among the Indian people can and must be encouraged without the threat of eventual termination. In my view, in fact, that is the only way that self-determination can effectively be fostered. This, then, must be the goal of any new national policy toward the Indian people to strengthen the Indian's sense of autonomy without threatening his sense of community. We must assure the Indian that he can assume control of his own life with being separated involuntarily from the tribal group. And we must make it clear that Indians can become independent of Federal control without being cut off from Federal concern and support. In place of policies which oscillate between the deadly extremes of forced termination and constant paternalism, we suggest a policy in which the Federal government and the Indian community play complimentary roles.

9. *Cohen's*, §1.07 at 98.
10. Indian Self-Determination and Education Assistance Act, 25 U.S.C. §§ 450 *et seq.*
11. Indian Child Welfare Act, 26 U.S.C. §§ 2801 *et seq.;* Indian Tribal Justice Act, 25 U.S.C. §§3201 *et seq.*
12. Improving America's Schools, 20 U.S.C. §§ 7801 *et seq.*; Indian Self-Determination and Education Assistance Act, *supra.*
13. Indian Law Enforcement Reform Act, 25 U.S.C. §§ 28011 *et seq.*; Indian Tribal Justice Act, 25 U.S.C. §§ 3601 *et seq.*
14. Native American Housing Assistance and Self-Determination Act, 25 U.S.C. §§ 4101 *et seq.*
15. Indian Health Care Improvement Act, 25 U.S.C. §§1601 *et seq.*
16. American Indian Agricultural Resource Management Act, 25 U.S.C. §§ 3701 *et seq.*; National Indian Forest Resource Management Act, 25 U.S.C. §§ 3101 *et seq.*
17. A short list of decisions that support the self-determination policy includes: *United States v. Lara,* 541 U.S. 193 (2004) (upholding the power of Congress to bolster the inherent power of Indian tribes to punish Indians of other tribes for violations of tribal law); *California v. Cabazon Band of Mission Indians, supra* (no state power to regulate gaming by an Indian tribe on its reservation); *Santa Clara Pueblo v. Martinez, supra* (recognizing tribal self-government powers and sovereign immunity); *New Mexico v. Mescalero Apache Tribe,* 462 U.S. 324 (1983) (tribal regulation of hunting and fishing by non-Indians on the reservations upheld); *Merrion v. Jicarilla Apache Tribe,* 455 U.S. 130 (1982) (power to tax resource development on the reservation by non-Indians). *See, generally, Cohen's,* Ch. 4 (Indian Tribal Governments) at 201–364.
18. Echo-Hawk (2010) at 180–184, 445–452.
19. *Id.* at 184.
20. *Id.* at 432–436, 445–452
21. *See, generally,* Echo-Hawk (2010) at 41–51; Robert A. Williams, Jr., *Like a Loaded Gun: The Rehnquist Court, Indian Rights, and the Legal History of Racism in America* (Minneapolis: Univ. of Minnesota Press, 2005).
22. *Merriam-Webster's Collegiate Dictionary* (11th ed. 2005), "racism." Racism includes "racial prejudice or discrimination"; and "discrimination" means "prejudiced or prejudicial outlook, action, or treatment." *Id.*
23. Juan F. Perea, *et al., Race and Races: Cases and Resources for a Diverse America, 2nd Ed.* (Thompson/West, 2007), pp. 5–72.
24. *Id.* at 35.
25. *Id.* at 37.
26. Echo-Hawk (2010) at 35–51.
27. *Johnson v. M'Intosh,* 21 U.S. 543, 572, 577, 590 (1823).
28. *Dred Scott,* 60 U.S. at 405; *Johnson,* 21 U.S. at 577, 690–670.
29. *Cherokee Nation v. Georgia,* 30 U.S. 1, 18 (1831) (Marshall, C.J., majority opinion).
30. *Id.* at 20–21 (Johnson, J., concurring).
31. *Id.* at 23.
32. *Id.* at 24.
33. *Id.* at 27–28.
34. *Id.* at 29.
35. *Id.* at 32 (Baldwin, J., concurring).
36. *Lone Wolf v. Hitchcock,* 187 U.S. 553, 564–565 (1903).

37. *Id.* 565–566 (quoting *Beecher v. Wetherby,* 95 U.S. 525).
38. *Montoya v. United States,* 180 U.S. 261, 265,266 (1901).
39. *United States v. Sandoval,* 231 U.S. 28, 39 (1913).
40. *Tee-Hit-Ton Indians v. United States,* 348 U.S. 272, 289–290 (1955).
41. *Id.* at 279.
42. *Id.*
43. *United States v. Jicarilla Apache Nation,* 131 S. Ct. 2313, 2323-2325 (2011).
44. For a summary of the outlandish legal fictions used by courts to dispossess and subjugate indigenous peoples in the United States and other settler states, *See,* Echo-Hawk (2010) at 43–51.
45. Echo-Hawk (2010) at 123–159.
46. *Oliphant v. Suquamish Indian Tribe,* 435 U.S. 191 (1978). *See, also, Cohen's* (2005 ed.), §4.02[3][b] at 226–228.
47. *Cohen's* (2005 ed.), §2.01[1] (Congress dominates Indian affairs over other branches; and judicial deference to the paramount authority of Congress concerning Indian policy is a central principle in federal Indian law); Phillip P. Frickey, "A Common Law For Our Age Of Colonialism: The Judicial Divestiture Of Indian Tribal Authority Over Nonmembers," 109 Yale L. J. 1, 13 (1999). *See also, Merrion v. Jicarilla Apache Tribe,* 544 U.S. 130, 139 (1982).
48. *Oliphant,* at 208; *Cohen's* (2005 ed.), §4.02[3][b] at 227.
49. Samuel E. Ennis, "Reaffirming Indian Tribal Court Criminal Jurisdiction Over Non-Indians: An Argument For A Statutory Abrogation of *Oliphant,*" 57 UCLA L. Rev. 553 (2009) (citing Justice Department statistics).
50. *Id.* at 571–572 (citations omitted).
51. Congress does not share that odd view expressed in *Lyng* that government land use cannot by its nature violate religious freedom as a matter of law. Congress passed the Religious Land Use and Institutionalized Persons Act, 42 U.S.C. §§ 2000cc *et seq.* (RULIPA) to prevent government land use from interfering with religious practices at religious properties unless the burden placed upon worship by the government passes muster under the "compelling state interest" test. Unfortunately, by its own terms, RULIPA does not protect tribal holy places on federal land, because it requires that the plaintiff own a property interest in the religious property before the act applies.
52. *See,* James Anaya," UN Human Rights Council (A/HRC/18/35/Add.1) (Aug. 22, 2011), 16. That bare "tolerance standard" utilized by the Supreme Court in *Lyng* for Native American religious freedom does not comport with the core values of the American people nor religious rights recognized in international human rights treaties and customary international law. In examining that legal standard as applied in *Navajo Nation,* James Anaya, the UN Special Rapporteur on the Rights of Indigenous Peoples, explains that a ruling that "only protects against government action that actively coerces Native American practitioners into violating their religious beliefs or that penalizes them for their religious activity with loss or threat of loss of government benefits" does not pass muster. *Id.,* 16-20. First, the Forest Service decision does not meet the free, prior, and informed consent standards of Article 19 of the *Declaration,* or existing United States treaty obligations set forth in Articles 1 and 27 of the *International Covenant on Civil and Political Rights,* and General Recommendation 23 of the Committee on the Elimination of Racial Discrimination (CERD), to which the United States is a party. *Id.* ¶17. Second, the crabbed legal standard does not meet the religious freedom provisions of Article 18, *International Covenant on Civil and Political Rights,* Article 5, *International Convention on the Elimination of All Forms of Racial Discrimination* as interpreted by CERD General Recommendation 23 and 32, or Articles 12 and 25 of the *Declaration. Id.* 17–19. *T*he Special Rapporteur points out in 20 that:

    The international law duty of States to ensure the exercise by indigenous peoples of their religious traditions extends to safeguarding against any meaningful limitations to that exercise, not just limitations that entail coercion to act against one's religious beliefs or penalties for doing so. Under Article 18(3) of the Covenant on Civil and Political Rights, "Freedom to manifest one's religion or beliefs may be subject only to such limitations as prescribed by law and are necessary to protect public safety, order, health or morals, or the fundamental rights and freedoms of others." With this standard there is no qualification on the basis of the stated purposes. Under the plain language of Article 18 of the Covenant, *any* clearly observable limitation that makes for a meaningful restriction on the exercise of religion is subject to scrutiny.
53. *Id.,* 16, 19.

54. Jane E. Anderson, *Law, Knowledge, Culture: The Production of Indigenous Knowledge in Intellectual Property Law* (Cheltenham, UK: 2009) at 30.
55. *Id.* Introductory quotations (citing Justice Yates, *Millar v. Taylor* (1769) 98 RE 233).
56. *See,* Erica-Irene Daes, Special Rapporteur of the Sub-Commission on Prevention of Discrimination and Protection of Minorities and Chairperson of the Working Group on Indigenous Populations, "Study on the protection of the cultural and intellectual property of indigenous peoples," Commission on Human Rights (E/CN.4/Sub.2/1993/28 (July 28, 1993).
57. *Id.* 23–24.
58. *Id.* 30.
59. *Id.* 32.
60. *Id.* 171.
61. *Cohen's* (2005 ed.), §20.02[6] at 1266–1276.
62. *Id.,* §20.02[6][a] at 1268.
63. *Id.,* §20.02[6][a] at 1267–1268. *See, also,* Yuqin Jin, "Necessity: Enacting Laws to Protect Indigenous Intellectual Property Rights in the United States," 19 Transnat'l L & Contemp. Problems 950 (2011).
64. *Id.* at 1268.
65. *See, e.g.,* Nancy Kremers, "Speaking With A Forked Tongue In The Global Debate On Traditional Knowledge and Genetic Resources: Are U.S. Intellectual Property Law And Policy Really Aimed At Meaningful Protection For Native American Cultures," 15 Fordham Intell. Prop. Media & Ent. L. J. 1, * 3 (2005) (traditional knowledge, genetic resources, and folklore "have unique attributes not addressed by the standard IP categories"); Stephen D. Osborne, "Protecting Tribal Stories: The Perils of Propertization," 28 Am. Ind. L. Rew. 203, 207, 224; Jin, *supra* at 956–957 (the products and knowledge of nature are not patentable; and the novelty requirement in patent law is an obstacle to patenting indigenous knowledge already in the public domain), 962-965 (laws, ideas, and proposals for protecting indigenous property in other nations), 965–972 (how Articles 1, 10, 19, 28, 31, 40–42 of the *Declaration* provide the basis for an effective law to protect intangible cultural property); Suzanne Milchan, "Whose Rights Are These Anyway?—A Rethinking of Our Society's Intellectual Property Laws In Order To Better Understand Native American Religious Property," 28 Am. Ind. L. Rev. 157.
66. *Lau v. Nichols,* 414 U.S. 563 (1974).
67. Native American Languages Act, 25 U.S.C. §§ 2901 *et seq.* (*See,* findings in §2901 (1), (5)).
68. Gina Cantoni (ed.), *Stabilizing Indigenous Languages* (Northern Arizona University, 1996 & 2007).
69. Jon Allan Reyhner, *Education and Language Restoration* (Philadelphia: Chelsea House Publishers, 2006) at 34, 37. The applicable laws that form the United States Indian education framework are: the No Child Left Behind Act of 2001, Pub. L. No. 107–110, 115 Stat. 1425, §701 (United States will work with education agencies to ensure that programs which serve Indian students are of the "highest quality" and provide "unique and culturally related academic needs of these children."); Tribally Controlled School Grant Act, 25 U.S.C. §2501(b) (there is a trust duty to establish a meaningful Indian self-determination policy for education); Native American Languages Act of 1990, 25 U.S.C. §§2901 *et seq.* (promoting the use of Native American language in the education setting); Tribally Controlled College and University Assistance Act of 1978, 25 U.S.C. § 1801 *et seq.* (grants for operation and improvements of tribally controlled colleges); Indian Self-Determination and Education Assistance Act of 1975, 25 U.S.C. §§ 450 *et seq.* (promoting tribal control of BIA schools); Indian Education Act of 1972, Title IV of Pub. L. 92–319, as amended (funding for Indian school children needs on and off the reservation).
70. Reyhner (2006) at 38.
71. *Id.* at 75.
72. *See, e.g.,* Julie Biando Edwards & Stephan P. Edwards (eds.), *Beyond Article 39: Libraries and Social and Cultural Rights* (Duluth: Library Juice Press, 2010).
73. Inter-American Commission on Human Rights, *Indigenous and Tribal Peoples' Rights Over Their Ancestral Lands and Natural Resources: Norms and Jurisprudence of the Inter-American Human Rights System* (Organization of American States) (OEA/Ser.L/V/II. Doc. 56/09 (Dec. 30, 2009), 56 (citations omitted).
74. *See, generally,* C. Richard King, *Contemporary Native American Issues: Media Images and Representations* (Philadelphia: Chelsea House Publishers, 2006), for a good overview of the historical

treatment of Native Americans by the mainstream media in the United States.

75. *Id.* at 50 [quoting from Jay Rosenstein, "In Whose Honor?, Mascots and the Media," in C. Richard King and Charles F. Springwood (eds.), *Team Spirits: The Native American Mascots Controversy* (Lincoln: University of Nebraska Press, 2001)].
76. C. Richard King, *Contemporary Native American Issues: Media Images and Representations* (Philadelphia: Chelsea House Publishers, 2006), at 43–44.
77. *Id.* at 71–88.
78. *Id.* at 73.
79. *Visit* http://nativeartsandcultures.org for more information.
80. *Visit* http://americanindianfilminstitute.com for more information.
81. *Id.* at 82.
82. Communications Act of 1934, 47 U.S.C. §§ 151 *et. seq.*
83. Echo-Hawk (2010) at 176–180, 445–452.
84. *See,* President Obama's November 5, 2009 Memorandum, 74 Fed. Reg. 57,881 ("Consultation is a critical ingredient of a sound and productive federal-tribal relationship"; and directing the Administration to have "regular and meaningful consultation and collaboration with tribal officials in policy decisions that have tribal implications including, as an initial step, through complete and consistent implementation of Executive Order 13175."); Executive Order 13,175, Consultation and Coordination with Indian Tribal Governments, 65 Fed. Reg. 67,249 (Nov. 6, 2000) (executive departments and agencies must conduct meaningful consultation with tribal officials on a government-to-government basis in the development of federal policy that have tribal implications). *See also,* National Historic Preservation Act, 16 U.S.C. §§ 470 *et seq.* (Section 106 requires consultation with Indian tribes to determine the impact of federal undertakings upon historic properties that have historic, cultural, or religious importance to them); Native American Graves Protection and Repatriation Act, 25 U.S.C. §3001 *et seq.* (consultation required in carrying out the inventory and repatriation provisions of the act).
85. *See, e.g.,* Akilah Jenga Kinnison, "Indigenous Consent: Rethinking U.S. Consultation Policies In Light Of The U.N. Declaration On The Rights Of Indigenous Peoples," 53 Az. L. Rev. 1301 (2011).
86. *Cohen's* (2006 ed.), §21.01 at 1279 (footnotes omitted).
87. *Id.,* Ch. 21 at 1277–1334.
88. Deborah Welch, *Contemporary Native American Issues: Economic Issues and Development* (Philadelphia: Chelsea House Publishers, 2006) at 84. *See also, Cohen's* (2005 ed.), Ch. 12 at 857–892.
89. Welch (2006) at 31 (citing U.S. Census Bureau statistics).
90. *Cohen's* (2006 ed.), §21.01 at 1280 (footnotes omitted).
91. Roe W. Bubar and Irene S. Vernon, *Contemporary Native American Issues: Social Life and Issues* (Philadelphia: Chelsea House Publishers, 2006) at 24.
92. *Id.* at 9.
93. *Id.* at 11.
94. *Id.* at 23.

CHAPTER NINE: MARCH TOWARD JUSTICE

1. The video recording of the hearing is posted on the College of Law website: http://www.utulsa.edu/academics/colleges/college-of-law/About%20the%20College%20of%20Law/News%20Events%20and%20Multimedia/Multimedia/United%20Nations%20Consultation%20on%20the%20Rights%20of%20Indigenous%20Peoples.aspx

   In addition, video recordings of an international law conference held at the law school about the *Declaration* in 2011, *available* at: http://www.utulsa.edu/academics/colleges/college-of-law/About%20the%20College%20of%20Law/News%20Events%20and%20Multimedia/Multimedia/Symposium%20Videos%20-%20International%20Law%20-%20Future%20Impacts%20on%20the%20Tribal-Federal%20Relationship.aspx
2. *Brown v. Board of Education,* 347 U.S. 483 (1954).
3. Sun Tzu, *The Art of War* (New York: Barnes & Nobles Books, 2003) (Dallas Galvin ed., transl. by Lionel Giles).
4. *Plessy v. Ferguson,* 163 U.S. 537 (1896).

5. *Id.* at 551–552.
6. *Id.*
7. *Id.* at 553, 556-557 (Harlan, J., dissenting).
8. *Id.* at 559–562 (Harlan, J., dissenting).
9. Mark V. Tushnet (ed.), *Thurgood Marshall: His Speeches, Writings, Arguments, Opinions, and Reminiscences* (Chicago: Lawrence Hill Books 2001) at 230–231.
10. *Brown,* 347 U.S. at 495.
11. Richard Kluger, *Simple Justice: The History of Brown v. Board of Education and Black America's Struggle for Equality* (New York: Vintage Books 1975, 2004).
12. *Id.* at 26–27.
13. *See e.g.,* cases discussed in *Plessy,* at 544–549; Kluger (1975, 2004) at 63–82.
14. Kluger (1975, 2004) at 83.
15. *Id.* at 67.
16. *Id.* at 305–308.
17. Tushnet (ed.) (2001) at 188–189.
18. Kluger at 106.
19. *Id.* at 131.
20. *Id.* at 125.
21. *Id.* at 9, 20.
22. *Id.* at 131.
23. *Id.* at 128.
24. *Id.* at 136.
25. *Id.* at 135.
26. Kluger (1975, 2004) at 134–135.
27. *Id.* at 158.
28. *Id.* at 169.
29. *Id.* at 157.
30. *Id.* at 324.
31. *Id.* at 222.
32. *Id.* at 276. *See, Henderson v. United States,* 339 U.S. 816 (1950) (railroad that provided black passenger with a separate dining table failed to provide equal service); *Sweatt v. Painter,* 339 U.S. 629 (1950) (Texas law school improperly denied admission to Negro applicant on the basis of race); *McLaurin v. Oklahoma, State Regents,* 339 U.S. 637. (1950) (Black graduate student provided separate but unequal treatment, including a separate table in the dining room).
33. Sun Tzu (2003) at 53.
34. Kluger (1975, 2003) at 339.
35. *Id.* at 295–301.
36. *Id.* at 300.
37. *Id.* at 365.
38. *Id.* at 367.
39. *Id.*
40. The decision was issued only after a grueling three-day re-argument on various issues.
41. Tushnet (ed.) (2001) at 223–225 (quoting an address given by Thurgood Marshall in 1967).
42. *See,* Charles Wilkinson, *Blood Struggle: The Rise of Modern Indian Nations* (New York, London: W.W. Norton & Co. 2005). The legal framework of the tribal sovereignty movement is set forth in *Cohen's* (2005 ed.).
43. Walter R. Echo-Hawk, *In The Courts of the Conqueror: The 10 Worst Indian Law Cases Ever Decided* (Golden: Fulcrum Publishing 2010) at 424–426.
44. *See, e.g., Id.* at 217–322.
45. *Id.* at 423–460.
46. One step in this direction has been taken by the attorneys of the Indian Law Resource Center, which has given thought to possible legal principles that can address some of the infirmities in extant law. See, Indian Law Resource Center, "Native Land Project: Draft General Principles of Law Relating to Native Lands and Natural Resources," (Indian Land Tenure Foundation, Feb. 2010).
47. Milagros Salazar, "Indigenous Peoples, Ignored Even by the Statistics," Inter Press Service News Agency (IPS), (Oct. 10, 2006).

48. "Peru: Bagua, Six Months On," Amnesty International Publications, 12 (Dec. 2, 2009), *available at* http://www.amnesty.org/en/library/info/AMR46/017/2009
49. *Id.*
50. Christina M. Fetterhoff, "Peru Enacts Law of Prior Consultation with Indigenous Peoples," The Human Rights Brief (Oct. 5, 2011), http://hrbrief.org/2011/10/peru-enacts-law-of-prior-consultation-with-indigenous-peoples/
51. S. James Anaya, Report of the Special Rapporteur on the Human Rights and Fundamental Freedoms of Indigenous Peoples (Human Rights Council), UN Doc. A/HRC/9/9 (Aug. 11, 2008), 46, *available* at http://papers.ssrn.com/sol3/papers.cfm?abstract_id=1242451. *See also,* Chapter Three discussion, *supra.*
52. Brenda Gunn, "Understanding and Implementing the UN Declaration on the Rights of Indigenous Peoples: An Introductory Handbook" (Indigenous Bar Association 2011) at 29 (quoting Kenneth Deer, "Reflections on the Development, Adoption, and Implementation of the UN Declaration on the Rights of Indigenous Peoples," in Jackie Hartley, Paul Joffe, and Jennifer Preston (eds.), *Realizing the UN Declaration on the Rights of Indigenous Peoples: Triumph, Hope and Action* (Saskatoon: Purich Publishing Ltd. 2010) at 28.
53. Hartley, Joffe, and Preston (2010) at 193.
54. Richard Attenborough (ed.), *The Words of Gandhi* (New York: Newmarket Press 2000) at 3.

CHAPTER TEN: IN THE LIGHT OF JUSTICE

1. *See,* definitions and discussion of reparations and restorative justice in Chapter One.
2. "U.N. Declaration could have extreme consequences," *The Oklahoman* (6-11-12), available at: http://newsok.com/u.-n.-declaration-could-have-extreme consequences/article/3683245#ixzz1x X0XYAbG
3. Quoted by Michael N. Nagler, "We Can Work It Out: Heart, Mind, and Action in the Struggle for Atonement," in Phil Cousineau (ed.), *Beyond Forgiveness: Reflections on Atonement—Healing the Past, Making Amends, and Restoring Balance in Our Lives and World* (San Francisco: Jossey-Bass 2011) at 42.
4. *See,* discussion in Chapter Eight.
5. *See,* Charles Wilkinson, *Blood Struggle* (New York: W.W. Norton & Company, 2005).
6. Sporadic attempts at righting the wrongs of the past in the United States have been half-hearted, short-lived, and ineffectual—demonstrating ambivalence between wanting the "Indian problem" to go away, but stopping short of effectively redressing the legacy of conquest. This includes the Indian Claims Commission Act of 1946 (60 Stat. 1049) (ICCA), which granted Indian tribes access to the Court of Claims to seek damages for unfair and dishonorable dealings. The ICCA allowed restricted relief in a "one time only" approach. Its limited reparative goals were not met in many cases; and many claims were denied because they were outside the limited jurisdiction conferred by the statute. Indian land claims litigation brought some limited successes, but that avenue toward reparative relief has largely been cut-off by the Supreme Court in *City of Sherrill v. Oneida Indian Nation,* 544 U.S. 197 (2005). *See generally,* Sarah Krakoff and Kristen Carpenter, "Repairing Reparations in the American Indian Nation Context," in Federico Lenzerini, *Reparations for Indigenous Peoples: International & Comparative Perspectives* (Oxford University Press 2008) at 252-269.
7. *See,* Chapter Five.
8. *See,* Chapter Eight.
9. *See,* note 1, *supra.* As discussed in Chapter One, "reparations" is a concept in restorative justice that means "the act of making amends" for a wrong that has been committed. It includes any "measure aimed at restoring a person and/or a community of a loss, harm or damage suffered consequent to action or omission." *See,* Black's Law Dictionary (2010) at 1107; Oxford English Dictionary, online version: http://dictionary.oed.com
10. Dinah Shelton, "Reparations for Indigenous Peoples: The Present Value of Past Wrongs," in Federico Lenzerini (ed.), *Reparations for Indigenous Peoples: International & Comparative Perspectives* (Oxford University Press 2008) at 47–51.
11. Francesco Francioni, "Reparation for Indigenous Peoples: Is International Law Ready to Ensure Redress for Historical Injustices?," in Federico Lenzerini (ed.) (2008) at 45.

12. *See,* discussion on the best approach for incorporating Native Americans into the body politic in Chapter Five.
13. *Washington v. Washington State Commercial Passenger Fishing Vessel Ass'n,* 443 U.S. 658, 672–673 n. 20 (1979).
14. *Cohen's* (2005 ed.), §14.03 (federal legislation dealing specifically with Indians does not constitute impermissible racial discrimination, because Indians have a distinct constitutional status.).
15. CERD, Art.1 (4).
16. Siegfried Wiessner, "Rights and Status of Indigenous Peoples: A Global Comparative and International Legal Analysis," 12 HARV. HUM. RTS. J. 57, 109 (1999).
17. S. James Anaya, *International Human Rights and Indigenous Rights* (New York: Aspen Publishers 2009) at 64.
18. International Law Association, "Rights of Indigenous Peoples," (Sofia Conference 2012) at 2, n.1 (quoting UN Special Rapporteur S. James Anaya, "Report of the Special Rapporteur on the situation of human rights and fundamental freedoms of indigenous peoples," UN Doc. A/HRC/9/9 of 11 August 2008, para. 40).
19. 636 *See,* discussion in Chapter One.
20. *Id.*
21. Cousineau (2011), note 3, *supra.*
22. *See,* discussion on societal trauma in Chapter 5.
23. Cousineau (2011) at xxii.
24. Jacob Needleman, "The Wisdom of Atonement," in Cousineau (2011) at 22.
25. Cousineau (2011) at xxiii.
26. Douglas M. George-Kanentiio, "The Iroquois Great Law of Peace: Atonement among the Haudenosaunee," in Cousineau (2011) at 171–179.
27. Cousineau (2011) at xxviii.
28. *Id.* at xxix.
29. *Id.* at xxix–xxx.
30. *Id.* at xxx.
31. *Id.* at xxxiii.
32. Richard J. Meyer, "The Revival of an Ancient Awareness," in Cousineau (2011) at xxxvii.
33. *See,* discussion of the characteristics of a traumatized population in Chapter Five, *supra.*
34. *Id.*
35. "Forgiveness" in Wikipedia, the free encyclopedia (http://en.widipedia.org/wiki/Forgiveness).
36. Cousineau (2011) at xxviii.
37. *See,* Chapter One (discussion on making amends, the concept of "reparation" and notions of "restorative justice").
38. *See, Black's Law Dictionary* (2010) (reparation); *Oxford English Dictionary,* online version (reparation) (available at: http://dictionary.oed.com).
39. Federicio Lenzerini, "Reparations for Indigenous Peoples in International and Comparative Law: An Introduction," in Federicio Lenzerini (ed.), *Reparations for Indigenous Peoples: International & Comparative Perspectives* (Oxford University Press, 2008) at 13.
40. Cousineau (2011) at xxxiv.
41. *See,* S. Res. 584 (sentiments of the Senate), 110th Cong., 2d. Sess. (2008) (enacted); H. Res. 1237 (sentiments of the House), 110th Cong., 2d. Sess. (2008) (enacted). The resolutions are hortatory expressions that may have symbolic meaning to the enacting chamber, but lack binding legal effect of a law passed by Congress and signed by the President.
42. *Korematsu v. United States,* 323 U.S. 214 (1945); *Hirabayashi v. United States,* 320 U.S. 81 (1943). *See also,* discussion in Walter R. Echo-Hawk, *In The Courts of the Conqueror: The 10 Worst Indian Law Cases Ever Decided* (Golden: Fulcrum Press 2010) at 39–40.
43. Civil Liberties Act of 1988, 50 App. U.S.C.A. § 1989.
44. See, http://www.youtube.com/watch?v=MooPi2Ycuxo (last visited on 7/12/12).
45. Letter from President William Clinton (10-1-93), available at: www.pbs.org/childofcamp/history/clinton.html (last visited on 7/12/12).
46. See, http://www.justice.gov/opa/pr/1999/February/059cr.htm (last visited 2/12/12).
47. Apology Resolution, Pub. Law 103–150 (107 Stat. 510).
48. For more information about the status of the Akaka Bill, *See*: http://akaka.senate.gov/issue-

native-hawaiian-federal-recognition.cfm (last visited 7/13/12).

49. Department of Defense Appropriations Act of 2010, Title VIII, § 8113.
50. "President Obama Acknowledges Need for Native American Apology," Progressive American Liberal (Dec. 20, 2010), available at: http://proamlib.blogspot.com/2010/12/president-obama-acknowledges-need-for.html (lasted visited 7/14/12).
51. Available at: http://www.youtube.com/watch?v=zu52ig696L4 (last visited on 7/14/12).
52. Rob Capriccioso, "Don't Read My Lips: Why an Apology from Obama on 'Geronimo' is Unlikely," Indian Country Today (June 20, 2011), available at: http://indiancountrytodaymedianetwork.com/2011/06/20/don%E2%80%99t-read-my-lips- (last visited 7/14/12).
53. *See, e.g.*, Herman J. Viola, *Warriors In Uniform: The Legacy of American Indian Heroism* (Washington, D.C.: National Geographic).
54. *See*, Huston Smith & Reuben Snake (eds.), *One Nation Under God: The Triumph of the Native American Church* (Santa Fe: Clear Light Publishers (1996).

INDEX

ABOUT THE AUTHOR

Walter R. Echo-Hawk (Pawnee) is of counsel to the Crowe & Dunlevy Law Firm of Oklahoma and adjunct Professor of Law at the University of Tulsa College of Law. As a staff attorney for the Native American Rights Fund for thirty-five years, he represented tribes and Native Americans on significant legal issues during the modern era of federal Indian law. In addition to litigation, he worked on major legislation, such as the Native American Graves Protection and Repatriation Act and federal religious freedom legislation. He is a prolific writer whose books include *In The Courts of the Conqueror: The 10 Worst Indian Law Cases Ever Decided* and the award-winning *Battlefields and Burial Grounds*. Bookings: www.walterechohawk.com